Made For Eternity

MADE FOR ETERNITY

DR. WALKER WALKER

© 2015 Dr. Walker Walker

All rights reserved.

No part of this book may be used or reproduced by any means, graphic, electronic, or mechanical, including photocopying, recording, taping or by any information storage retrieval system without the written consent of the author except in the case of brief quotations embodied in reviews, books, critical articles, and as allowed by the United States of America copyright law.

Optional Dr. Walker-Walker
P. O. Box 618761
Orlando, FL 32861
E-mail: kwaler@yahoo.com

Cover design by Jhameek Walker
(Copyright Reserved)

SMJ Publishing

ISBN: 0692402012
ISBN 13: 9780692402016

Made For Eternity

"….How God uses our faithful participation in worship, mission and eschatological expectations to transform us, aid our growth in Christ, and position us for eternity."

A faith driven discussion and examination of the three components and means of faith that most occupy the Christian's thought, practice, and time— worship, mission, and eschatology

Dedication

DEDICATED TO THE MEMORY OF MY GRANDMOTHER—**MUM!**
The foundation of my spiritual formation, the bedrock of my moral affinity, and the model for my Christian principles

Table Of Contents

Acknowledgements xix
   1. Introduction xxi

   2. The Problem and Basis for the Development
      of this Resource xxv

   3. What You Will Find in this Book xxxi

Chapter One
You Were Made For Eternity 1
   You Were Made For Eternity (Section One). 2
   You Were Made for Eternity (Section Two) 9

Chapter Two
Spiritual Transformation 15
   1. Overview: 16
      What is Spiritual Transformation?. 16

   2. Spiritual Transformation is the Work of the Holy Spirit 17

   3. Six Steps For Understanding Spiritual Transformation. 19
      A. Step One: Recognizing and Knowing God 19

        (i)   *Knowing God by His Divine Qualities and Works (Through Creation, Incarnation and Redemption)* . . . 20
        (ii)   *Knowing God through God's Own Self-Revelation* . . . 23
        (iii)   *Knowing God by Studying His Word* 25
        (iv)   *Knowing God Intellectually* 27
        (v)   *Knowing God Experientially* 32
  B. Step Two: Repentance 40
  C. Step Three: Forgiveness (Section One) 42
        Forgiveness (Section Two) 50
        Forgiveness (Section Three) 57
        Forgiveness (Section Four) 66
  D. Step Four: Justification 71
  E. Step Five: Sanctification 74
  F. Step Six: Moving from Glory to Glory (Section One) . . . 74
     Step Six: Moving from Glory to Glory (Section Two) . . . 78

Chapter Three
Christian Worship 83
  1. Overview 85

  2. What is Worship? 86

  3. Knowledge of God and True Worship 87

  4. Worship: A Divine Initiative and a Human Response
     (Section One) 91
     Worship: A Divine Initiative and a Human Response
     (Section Two) 94

  5. Christian Worship as Communion and Participation
     (Section One) 99
     Christian Worship as Communion and Participation
     (Section Two) 100

      6. Worship as a Dialogue: The Channel of Mediation. 103

      7. Motives for Worship (Section One) 105
          Motives for Worship (Section Two) 107
          Motives for Worship (Section Three). 112

Chapter Four
The Liturgy Of Worship 119
    1. Overview. 120

    2. The Purpose of the Liturgy. 121

    3. Selected Liturgical Components of Worship 124
       A. The Call to Worship: A Reminder and Preparation
          for Worship 124
       B. Preaching (Section One). 126
          Preaching (Section Two). 131
       C. The Sacrament of Holy Baptism. 135
          (i)   Overview *135*
          (ii) *What is Baptism? (Section One)* *136*
                What is Baptism? (Section Two) *139*
          (iii) *Baptism and the Death and Resurrection of Jesus* . . . *144*
          (iv) *The Baptism of Children (Section One)* *145*
                The Baptism of Children (Section Two). *147*
          (v) *Baptism: A Replacement for Circumcision?* *148*
          (vi) *The Holy Spirit and the Effects of Baptism*
                (Section One). *151*
                The Holy Spirit and the Effects of Baptism
                (Section Two) *153*
          (vii) *Baptism: An Opportunity to Grow in Grace*
                (Section One). *157*
                Baptism: An Opportunity to Grow in Grace
                (Section Two) *160*

	(viii) Baptism and Our Restored Personhood 164
D.	The Sacrament of Holy Communion 166
	(i) Overview 166

    (viii) Baptism and Our Restored Personhood 164
D. The Sacrament of Holy Communion 166
    (i)   Overview 166
    (ii)   What is Holy Communion?
           (The Passover at a Glance). 166
    (iii) The Symbolic Value of the Bread and
           the Wine / Grape Juice 169
    (iv) The Holy Spirit at Work in Holy Communion 170
    (v)   Holy Communion as Satisfaction for Our Souls 171
    (vi) The Spiritually Restorative and Transforming
           Effects of Holy Communion 172
    (vii) Holy Communion Redefines Who We
           Are in Christ 173
    (viii) Holy Communion: A Re-presenting of and
           A "Re-membering with" Christ 175
    (ix) Holy Communion and the Forgiveness
           of Our Sins 176
    (x)   Holy Communion as an Opportunity
           for Thanksgiving 178
E. The Doxology 179
    (i)   What Is The Doxology? 179
    (ii)   Living Doxological Lives:
           The Liturgical and Doxological Nature of Christian
           Living (Section One) 182
           The Liturgical and Doxological Nature of Christian
           Living (Section Two) 184
           The Liturgical and Doxological Nature of Christian
           Living (Section Three) 187
           The Liturgical and Doxological Nature of Christian
           Living (Section Four) 190

Chapter Five
Christian Mission 196
    1. Overview 198

    2. What is Christian Mission? 198

    3. The Relations Between Worship and Christian Mission
       (Section One) 200
       The Relations Between Worship and Christian Mission
       (Section Two) 203
       The Relations Between Worship and Christian Mission
       (Section Three) 205

    4. The Coming and Necessity of the Holy Spirit for Mission
       (Section One) 211
       The Coming and Necessity of the Holy Spirit for Mission
       (Section Two) 216

    5. The Holy Spirit as the Gift of Power for
       Christian Mission 219

    6. God Is a Missional God
       Confronted and Sanctified for Mission (Section One) 223
       Confronted and Sanctified for Mission (Section Two) 225
       Confronted and Sanctified for Mission (Section Three) 226

    7. Practicing Christian Mission and the Shaping of the
       Christian Life 230
          A. Christian Mission as Character Building and
              Spiritual Formation 230

    B.   Christian Mission and The Building of Relationships:
The Four Levels of Interrelated
Christian Relationships 233

Chapter Six
Diversity And Christian Mission 238
    1.   What is Diversity? 239

    2.   The Mission of the Church in a Diverse/
Pluralistic Society 240

    3.   Diversity and Pastoral Care. 245

Chapter Seven
Living Eschatologically 252
The Impact of Eschatology on Our Spiritual
Formation and Transformation 252
    1.   Overview. 254

    2.   What Is Eschatology? 255

    3.   Eschatology as a Component of Spiritual Formation and
Transformation (Section One). 259
Eschatology as a Component of Spiritual Formation and
Transformation (Section Two). 261

    4.   Eschatological Living: Making Ourselves Accessible
Through Active Witnessing. 265

    5.   Eschatology Realized, Eschatology Expected
(The Paradox of Time and Eternity) (Section One) 269
Eschatology Realized, Eschatology Expected
(The Paradox of Time and Eternity) (Section Two) 271

      Eschatology Realized, Eschatology Expected
      (The Paradox of Time and Eternity) (Section Three) 276

  6. Eschatology and the Christian Community:
     Our Continuous Working for Christ in the
     World 277

  7. Eschatological Hope As An Alternative to a
     Secular Worldview and Faulty Human Optimism
     The Eschatological Task of the Church (Section One) 280
     Eschatological Hope As An Alternative to a
     Secular Worldview and Faulty Human Optimism
     The Eschatological Task of the Church (Section Two) 283

  8. Rationales for Projecting Christ as the Only Alternative
     and Hope (An Overview) 288
        (i)   *The Evidence of Creation, Faith, and the Activities*
             of God in the World *289*
        (ii)   *The Resurrection of Jesus (Section One)* *294*
             The Resurrection of Jesus (Section Two). *296*
        (iii) *The Promised Return of Jesus* *302*
        (iv) *God Cannot Lie (The Immutability of God)*. *305*
        (v)   *History Is Not Accidental (God Controls Time and*
             History). *307*

  9. What Do We Do While We Wait? 316

Chapter Eight
Motivated And Transformed By Love. 320
  1. Love As The Divine Economy of God. 322

  2. Our Response to the Love of God 324

    3. Practicing Love for God and Neighbor 326

    4. Love as the Evidence that We Have Been Changed 328

Chapter Nine
One Final Question:
Do You Know Jesus? 330
    1. On Knowing Jesus (Section One) 332
        On Knowing Jesus (Section Two) 335

    2. Our Necessary Confession of Jesus 337

    3. Jesus, the Only Way 342

    4. The Significance of the Ascension of Jesus 344

Chapter Ten
Reflections, Implications, And Potential Contributions 351

Appendices 369
    Appendix 1
    Methodologies:
    Development and Implementation of the Study 371

    Appendix 2
    Worship, Mission, and Eschatology Questionnaire
    (WMEQ) 377

    Appendix 3
    Sample Questions for the Interview/
    Discussion Segment of the Study 379

Appendix 4
Final Evaluation 381

Appendix 5
Samples of Calls to Worship 385

Appendix 6
Vision and Mission Statements 389

References 393

Bibliography 396

Acknowledgements

I WISH TO EXPRESS my sincere gratitude to a number of persons, who, in one way or another, have contributed to the successful completion of this book. I especially thank Bishop Dr. Frederic Hilborn Talbot who has been a lifelong inspiration to me. My encounter with Bishop Talbot in February 1976 changed the direction of my life for good. Without him and the early support of his beautiful wife, Dr. Sylvia Ross-Talbot, I would not have acquired the level of education I have today. Bishop Talbot laid the foundations for my early learning and continues to inspire me after changing the direction of my life upon our first meeting in Kingston, Jamaica. Bishop Talbot is Bishop among bishops. I love you Bishop Talbot!

Special thanks to my esteem colleague, Dr. Kennedy Obiri Annor of Ghana for his prayers, faithful friendship, encouragement, and support during our academic pursuit of the doctoral degree and the developmental stages of my study. I owe a depth of gratitude to all the members of the Focus Group in particular, and the Sunday school and Bible Study groups in general, established within the context of the local church (Burns, Des Moines, Iowa). I served there at the time of compiling data, developing, and executing an Informative Teaching Tool for the doctoral course of study, out of which this book is birthed. Their time, constructive criticisms, useful evaluations, and suggestions were very affirming.

I acknowledge and express my gratitude to the following persons: Thanks to Jean Butcher-Lashley, Arlene Mendez, and Sofia Green for their editorial comments, discoveries and suggestions for clarification.

I am forever grateful to Mike Germaine for his intelligent suggestions, keen eyes, patience, invaluable, and thorough editorial skills. Many refinements and clarifications came out of the proofreading and editorial processes and I am grateful to you.

My very profound gratitude goes to my children: Shenette, Remon, and Jhameek. Thank you for believing in and with me. I am also grateful to my daughter Shenette for her assistance in the restructuring and content alignment in the final coming together of this book and the accompanying study outline. To my son Remon, for pushing me and reminding me to stay the course and accomplish my purpose, I say thanks. I am grateful to my daughter Jhameek for creating the cover design of this book. It is a constant reminder of the perspective of innocence, and a projection of the narrow way that leads to that bright City we call Heaven. Thanks for the inspiration and the joy that you have brought into my life. My beloved children, God puts me to bed with you always on my mind and wakes me up every morning inspired by His grace and wonderful thoughts of you. You are my greatest inspirations and I love you!

1. Introduction

CHRISTIANITY IS A relationship with Christ that takes us on a faith journey towards spiritual transformation and ultimately glorification.[1] This book is intended to be an *Information Model* developed as a teaching tool that is aimed at creating a paradigm shift in people's awareness of the means of faith and components of Christianity that engage us the most on our Christian faith journey. These means of faith are worship, Christian mission, and eschatology. This book seeks to demonstrate how God uses our faithful participation in worship, mission and eschatological expectations to transform us, aid our growth in Christ, and position us for eternity. In order to do so, I have set out to examine the relations between the three most prominent components of Christianity and our faith formation that most occupy the Christian's life and practices. These are worship, Christian mission, and eschatology.

These three means of faith are the basic foundational ordinances upon which the process of our spiritual formation and transformation rests. Our participation and engagements in worship, mission and eschatology, are our first steps in a spiritual journey that continues into eternity. It is my intention to help you develop an understanding and appreciation of how the Christian's spiritual life is shaped into holiness as a result of our faithful participation in these means of faith. I also intend to help you understand how we are shaped and empowered by the Holy Spirit to acknowledge and experience God in our daily walk with Christ as we faithfully participate in these means of faith.

These spiritual components or means of faith are participated in and acted upon at different levels of the Christian faith response and journey toward

---

[1] Rom 8:17, 8:30; Phil 3:21; 2 Tim 2:10; Col 3:4; 1 Pet 5:1

God. As such, they should be understood as foundational means of faith and spiritual formation at three levels. Worship is the level of recognition and formation of divine knowledge and faith. Mission is the level of dedication where faith is practiced and developed. It is also the level where Christian character is formed. Eschatology, as a result of the promised manifestation of the greater glory and all that this promised glory entails, is the level of ultimate spiritual transformation. It is here that we not only get a glimpse of glory based on the present operation of the Holy Spirit, but also where we hold fast to the promised glory because of the commendable nature of the lifestyle that is inspired and lived in anticipation of the return of Christ.

Through these foundational means of faith, God imparts Himself to us as a relational God through the Son, and sustains that relationship through the gravitating and transforming presence and work of the Holy Spirit. As we faithfully participate in these means of faith, the design of God is to transform and draw us into His divine life through Christ. That way, on every step of our faith journey we are empowered to live and grow into the standard and dignity that God established for us before the foundations of the earth. The spiritually transforming value of worship, mission, and eschatology should therefore not be taken lightly. Indeed, it is our proximity to these means of faith that positions us to hear from, believe in, experience, and therefore hope in God. As we shall see, participating in these means of faith, along with God aiding us by His grace, keeps us in tune with and connected to Christ in whom and through whom we grow in grace and the maturity of God's eternal love.

A good starting point for clarity on the process of our growth is to understand that the Christian life, like the Church, is caught up in a process of existence that begins with our initial knowledge of God. This initial knowledge of God is based fundamentally on the evidence of creation. Our knowledge is then renewed and elevated by the reorientation of our minds, the regeneration of our human attitude and spirit and our reconciliation with God through faith in the person and finished work of the Lord Jesus. This knowledge is then translated and faithfully manifested and sustained in worship. Our knowledge and worship of God are then put into practice through Christian mission where our faith and Christian character are developed. Ultimately, our knowledge, worship, and mission attain their eternal purpose with our realization of the greater glory, which is the theme of eschatology. Put differently, our Christian life journey, which begins with knowledge of God, is nurtured by grace in worship and life. The Christian life is further strengthened and developed through mission as we are sustained by the Holy Spirit. The Holy Spirit then daily reminds us of the promise of eternity, the theme of eschatology, which is the consummation or realization of the greater glory. This consummation is a sort of end product, so to speak, of God's work in us, whereby the believer is spiritually renovated or made new and eternally transformed and fitted for eternity.

I propose then, that these three components of Christianity (worship, mission, and eschatology) are means of faith and the Pillars of Spiritual Transformation. Through these components of Christianity, the truth of faith is set forth, learned, inspired, practiced, and developed by the Holy Spirit that works in us to change us and bring us into conformity to the will and purpose of God. How God applies the Christian's faithful participation in these three components of Christianity for the spiritual development of the Christian's life and faith sets the tone and establishes the backdrop for the development of this book.

I believe it is safe to say that we cannot faithfully and sincerely participate in the things of God without knowing Him and without being transformed by His Holy Spirit to contemplate and pursue the holiness and righteousness of God. Through these three areas of interrelated components of faith and spiritual transformation, God has provided the Holy Spirit to Christian believers as an empowering presence to train us in spiritual things while all the time, engrafting us into Christ. As the Holy Spirit shapes and develops in us those principles and practices that are reflective of the divine holiness of God the Father, we become more like His begotten Son, Jesus, the Christ. Our becoming like Christ is the ultimate goal of spiritual transformation.

As we participate in these means of faith, the Holy Spirit draws us into our life giving center, God, in whom we live, move and have our being. While living and sharing in the life of God may become the Christian's desire, ultimately, the Holy Spirit is the One who shapes and empowers us to exercise holy tempers (attitudes and behaviors) that are reflective of our walk of faith with God. The Holy Spirit shapes us by giving us a clearer, or even better, a new vision of God, while remolding us so that our moral DNA will match the moral attributes of the One in whose image and likeness we were created. As we obediently respond to the divine patterning of the Holy Spirit on our lives, we are transformed into Christ-likeness. That way, we might appropriately live in and reflect the true nature and divine values that God implanted in us in the first place. The Christian life is therefore not a static life, but rather, a dynamic and visional life that changes or is being transformed for the better, so that it might unfold to reveal the beauty that is Christ within us.

Through worship, mission, and eschatological living, God is constantly shaping and reshaping our lives into the fashion of His own likeness. In worship, the Holy Spirit facilitates and lifts our worship to the Son, who, as our High Priest, mediates our worship to the Father. In mission, the Holy Spirit directs our actions. He also sustains and renews our spirit so that what we do in mission may also bring glory to God. As we live eschatologically, with the expectation of Christ returning, the Holy Spirit stirs us to active worship and service and, through grace, keeps us steadfast as He guides us into the promises of eternity with Christ. By virtue of the present work and operations of the Holy Spirit through whom the grace of God is channeled to us, we are in one sense, living in the realization of Christ, while in another sense, we are being moved or carried toward our completion in Christ. This matter of what we have already realized and are still hoping for will be further developed in our discussion on realized yet expected eschatology in chapter seven.

2. The Problem and Basis for the Development of this Resource

This book emerged from the coming together of several strands of projects done as partial fulfillment of the Doctor of Ministry (D. Min.) program at the University of Dubuque Theological Seminary, Dubuque, Iowa, with an emphasis on congregational renewal.

In my first year project, I developed a curriculum that was aimed at assessing and increasing parishioners' awareness of worship. The desire to pursue that line of inquiry came out of discussions during the first year of residency for the D. Min. course of study which carried over into a weekend academic exercise. As a weekend exercise, students were required to attend a worship service of choice in the area. Based on our observations, we were to write a paper reflecting on any existing indicators in the worship service that may have led to an understanding of the relations between the unity of the Father, Son, and Holy Spirit based on the structure, language, and doctrinal formulations of that church's liturgical content.

The content and liturgical execution of the worship service I attended seemed rather self-directed in focus. Based on the theological language and content of the worship service, there did not appear to be any clear understanding of the God-humanward and the human-Godward movement of grace. Indicators of worshippers' understanding, faithful response, and participation were virtually nonexistent. It was as though worshippers were mere observers of prescribed set in stone routines, whereby clergy and lay worship leaders did their thing, as in the performance of a prescribed theatrical role, rather than as faithful respondents and participants in a meaningful encounter with each other and with God. The worship experience was also made to seem like "something we do," rather than what God, through Christ in the power of the Holy Spirit, does in us, for us, and ultimately for God's glory. The "we" element (the Father, Son, Holy Spirit, and the people) of worship was missing. There were no clear connections between the liturgical affirmations and the human real life experiences that are often brought to bear on the worship encounter in the human search for clarity, affirmation, understanding and hope. The worship service was also void of meaningful theological connections between the work of the Father, Son and Holy Spirit for worship as well as for life. An example of theological disconnection was gathered from the message of the day. The message was based on the Genesis account of creation. Notwithstanding that, no reference was made to "the executive arm of God"— the Holy Spirit of God— who was the creative power that "was hovering over the face of the waters."[2] Also, the message made no connection with the work of God in creation and the place, value, and role of humans in relationship with God and as stewards in the advancement of creation. It was a missed opportunity to reaffirm the theological as well as the relational, existential and custodial value that God in creation placed on humanity.

The worship process also came across as being based on repetitive formulations that left worshippers in a state of "what does that mean?" instead of having a clear understanding of the process aided by the liturgical content. That loss of clarity was highlighted by an apparent disconnect between the worship leader and the rest of the congregation. This disconnect was probably due to the absence of any liturgical understanding between the worship leader and the rest of the congregation. The failure to relate the message to the life experiences of those gathered to hear it may have also contributed to that great divide between the speaker and the hearers of the message. I discovered that without that connection, the message remains a mere cognitive

---

[2] Gen 1:2

feeding without the impetus of passion invoked by the experiential encounters of worshippers with God who kept them throughout the week and brought them to that place of worship for celebration, renewal, and reaffirmation of their dignity and worth. The celebratory aspect of worship was absolutely nonexistent.

I also observed that there was preoccupation with the human performance, which made the worship experience a sort of preconditioned routine rather than an anticipated opportunity to actually experience God. The worship atmosphere and content seemed to imply that this is how "*we* do worship." This is what *our* worship service is like. These are the songs that *we* sing and this is how **we** sing them. As it relates to the channel of worship— from God, to God, by worshippers, through Christ in the power of the Holy Spirit— no clear understanding was established. Any understanding of the Fatherhood of God, the Sonship and Priesthood of Christ, and the facilitating and sanctifying work of the Holy Spirit during the worship service, was at best, an illusive and disconnected one.

In both practice and doctrine, the worship service lacked any focus on the sole priesthood of Christ. The liturgy itself demonstrated no clear indication of the sanctifying power and presence of the Holy Spirit. Not once was the name of Jesus mentioned and at no time was the Holy Spirit mentioned during the worship service. My concern was that not enough was said or done in the worship service to exalt the unity of the Father, Son and Holy Spirit in whom the fullness of Deity dwells. This type of worship setting according to Torrance is "too often non-sacramental, and can engender weariness."[3]

The immediate realization of the existence of an improper understanding, approach and attitude toward the channel of worship in contemporary Christian worship, led me to pursue an examination of worshippers' perceptions and understanding of worship within the context of the local church where I was the appointed pastor. In all honesty, I was also led to reexamine my own liturgical and pastoral/preaching practices. I was moved by the need for theological depth, clarity, shared spiritual understanding of the worship

---

[3] James B. Torrance, <u>Worship, Community and the Triune God of Grace</u> (Downers Grove, IL., InterVarsity Press, 1996), 20

encounter, the concretization of our faith practices, and a mutually shared worship experience by clergy and laity.

In order to gain knowledge of the extent of the overt and/or covert areas of deficiencies among worshippers concerning worship and liturgical practices in the local setting in which I was embedded, using a Worship, Mission and Eschatology Questionnaire (WMEQ),[4] I set out to examine those worshippers' awareness and perceptions. While there was a relatively reasonable understanding of worship as "homage" and reverence to God, "deficiencies" were found to exist in the overall congregational understanding at three levels. At the first level, deficiencies were found in their overall understanding of God, and the place and role of Christ and the Holy Spirit in the worship encounter. At the second level, there were fundamental deficiencies regarding participants' understanding of liturgical practices and the relations between Christian worship, Christian mission, and eschatology. At the third level, significant deficiencies were identified regarding worshippers' understanding of how our participation in worship, mission, and an eschatological lifestyle spiritually impacts and changes our lives.

Concerned with the adverse impact those deficiencies may have on parishioners' faith formation, intentional participation in the worship process, liturgical understanding, and spiritual transformation, my immediate response was to develop a curriculum with the intention to inform and elevate congregational awareness while addressing and correcting those deficiencies. The curriculum was developed on a sort of tri-level thesis. At the first level, the thrust of the thesis was that increased knowledge of God results in increase participation in worship. At the second level, proper knowledge of God leads to proper worship of God. At the third level, the objective was to demonstrate that understanding of liturgical practices leads to intentional participation, passionate worship, and spiritual transformation. Specifically, the curriculum addressed knowledge of God, worshippers' understanding of God, Christian worship, and the Godward-humanward and the humanward-Godward movements of grace and faith response in worship. The curriculum also included the affirmation of Jesus as our sole intercessor in worship, the

---

[4] Appendix 2

Holy Spirit as the facilitator and lifter of our worship, as well as the human response and contribution to worship.

In developing and applying this level of the curriculum, I set out to examine how knowledge of God affects worshippers' understanding and attitude toward worship. The content of the curriculum was also incorporated with sermons that were shared with the entire congregation over a six month period nestled in a teaching paradigm. The objective was to elevate and nurture mutual awareness while developing a common consensus and understanding of the worship and liturgical processes.

Having developed the curriculum, a Focus Group was established within the local ministry setting to be a resource team for the four year duration of the D. Min. program. The Focus Group was made up of adults and teenage members of the Sunday school and Bible study classes. Although the project was set in a didactic paradigm designed to appeal to and elevate participants' cognition, it also included opportunities for experiential sharing, meaningful participation, and open discussions of the subject areas presented. A detailed outline of the implementation (methodology) of the study can be found in Appendix 1.

I was satisfied with the results of the study. The Focus Group's final evaluation of the study also shows significant advancements in their understanding when measured against where they had begun. My satisfaction was further enhanced as I witnessed the intentional participation, sense making, and practical application of the learning processes as manifested through conversations and the ensuing worship experiences. These, altogether, translated into higher levels of passionate worship. The thesis that increased knowledge results in increase participation, that proper knowledge leads to proper worship, and that understanding leads to passionate worship participation, was affirmed.

The second year project focused on Christian mission and the relations between Christian worship and mission. The third year project was a critical content analysis of eschatology and the importance of eschatology for our spiritual formation, transformation, and growth in Christ. The development, advancement, and weaving together of the components of worship, mission, and eschatology came in the final year of D. Min course of study. The original study for the fulfilment of the D. Min. program was about 165 pages. That study has since been vastly expanded to become what is now this book.

My effort was to help worshippers (parishioners) understand, through a teaching format, how the Christian's life is a continuous process of participation that finds expression through knowledge of God, our faithful participation in worship, mission, and an eschatological lifestyle. How that participation impacts Christians' spiritual growth, as the Holy Spirit transforms our lives and engrafts us in Christ, formed the platform for that project and now saturates the content of this book.

3. What You Will Find in this Book

This book is not a self-help book. It is not another step-by-step how to claim it and receive it get-rich formula. This book is about worship, Christian mission, and eschatology. It is a Spirit-driven attempt to glorify God in its content, witness, and experiential affirmations. This resource is expressly designed to direct people toward God through their faith response to Christ and their faithful participation in those means of faith formation (worship, Christian mission, and eschatology), which God uses to develop godly characters and therefore Christ-mindedness in us.

Though this book is grounded in an informative paradigm, it is a practical coming together of information, Christian experience, personal witness, exhortation, and the affirmation of hope. The issues raised and the discussions lifted up in the content of this book are not limited to academic interests and theological discussions or argumentations. They are of relevant and practical spiritual value and significance based on sound biblical applications, testimonies and experiences of God's outworking grace and favor.

This resource is an intentional attempt to concretize our theological understanding by the development of a systematic synthesis of the three components of the Christian faith— worship, mission and eschatology— that are grounded in the human experience. The objective is to give feet to our faith, hands to the gift of grace, and understanding and sense making to our participation in these components of faith that most occupy our time and thinking.

The goal is to remove the myth, the mystical, and the abstract, and bring the process of our faith response to God, our faithful participation in the components of the Christian faith, and the operation of the Holy Spirit into the existential (the realm of human existence). That way, we can see, experience, and understand how God, through Christ, in the presence and power of the Holy Spirit, accompanies Christian believers in all areas of their lives in order that He might spiritually transform, accumulatively nurture, refashion us into His own likeness, and ready us for eternity.

As such, I hope that this resource will help you understand more clearly this process of spiritual transformation. I also hope to help you come to grips with what will eternally become of all the things we participate in as Christians and people of faith.

This book will help you understand through scripture, that you were made for eternity and how intent God is on sharing His eternity with you. You will develop a sense of how intent God is on saving and transforming your life in readiness for eternity with the knowledge that eternity with God has always been a predisposed preference established by God for us, before the foundations of the earth.

This book is built on the premise that knowledge of God, worship, mission, and eschatology are the foundational pillars and means of faith that God uses for our spiritual formation and renewal and our becoming all that we can be in Christ. Worship, mission, and eschatology are therefore not three separate components of Christian practices. They are one continuously interlocking process that engulfs our spiritual transformation.

This book posits that if, indeed, worship is the spiritual encounter, then mission, must necessarily lead to the spiritual formation and development of the Christian life and character through service and self-giving love. Eschatologically, as we continuously share in the Holy Spirit's gift of mission to the world, we are kept diligent because of our expectation of Christ's returning. Worship, liturgical practices, and life experiences are our training models for knowing God. Christian mission in the world is the training ground for the formation of Christian character and the place where the seeds planted in worship grow into fuller blooms of the knowledge of God.

As we shall see later, our eschatological expectations, based on the promises of Christ to return, invoke a lifestyle that orients us toward the future. However, in the present, those eschatological expectations also keep us grounded in holiness and instill within us the desire to faithfully worship God. In turn, this invokes in us an awesome sense of responsibility that leads us to service and the making of disciples for Christ.

It is my goal to use this medium to transform the way we think about worship while inspiring our faithful participation in worship. It is also my intention to help you, the reader, discover information that will help you develop a clearer understanding of God, what worship is, the purposes of liturgical practices, your role as an active and participative worshipper, the Priesthood of Christ, and the role of the Holy Spirit in our worship encounters and missional pursuits.

Throughout the pages of this book, you will receive information that will help you concretize your understanding and experience as they relate to your faithful participation in the worship and mission of Jesus, the Son, to God, the Father. This information will transform the way you think about worship and Christian mission because it will take you beyond yourself and what you do in worship and mission to focus on Christ and what He has already accomplished. You will be empowered to see that worship and mission are not distinct components that separately impact the Christian's life. Rather, they are combined and continuous processes whereby the faith we confess in formal worship becomes the practical manifestation of our faith through mission and our service to God in the world.

This book is therefore designed to assist and nurture your understanding of the relations between the formal Sunday worship and everyday Christian life and mission. You will become inspired by the realization that Christian mission is in fact, a practical living out of the formal worship and a way of presenting and glorifying God in the world.

You will be presented with a fresh look at eschatology that will help you develop an understanding concerning the nearness of God and how that nearness is a daily challenge as well as an opportunity for you to respond to that nearness with faith and obedience. As you live in the anticipated fulfillment of

God's promise of eternity for you, which is the eschatological lifestyle I speak of, you will be challenged to exercise diligence in your worship of God and your service to others inspired by this lifestyle that is lived in readiness for Christ's reappearing.

Guided by biblical and sound theological persuasions, this book promotes the conviction that our encounter with the Lord does not only lead to personal faith renewal and holiness. That encounter also comes with a faith response which leads to an assignment and a responsibility. You shall see then, that in this book, theology and faith talks are not merely theological ramblings. Such discourses are convictions and declarations of faith in the God whom we seek to know, worship, understand, trust, and intentionally serve. The purpose of faith is to connect us with God as well as to nurture belief in God who infinitely loves us. The purpose of faith is also to change one's attitude and inspire a Christian lifestyle that is pleasing and acceptable to God. This lifestyle is the manifestation of our changed lives because of what we know and believe about God and have become in Christ Jesus. Certainly, faith not only encourages belief; faith is also manifested behavior and demonstrative service. This is precisely what James meant when he said, "…Faith by itself, if it does not have works, is dead." [5]

We shall see that while faith encourages belief and finds genuine expression through our intentional participation in the ministry of Christ to God the Father, it is also the impetus for our service to God in the world. An encounter with God is therefore an opportunity as well as a privilege to honor and bow down to worship God. At the same time, as we shall see, our encounter with God is a commission, and therefore a responsibility to go out on assignment to serve God in the world. While some of us may claim to possess great faith, or even a little, as if it were a privilege, faith is not a privilege. Faith is a gift of grace. As such, faith becomes our active response to God through obedience, and our duty to our neighbor through loving service. Our active faith response to God and the good works we exercise on behalf of our neighbor, make faith practical, and keep faith alive and working because faith without works is dead. Faith that transforms is faith that is alive and working

---

[5] Jas 2:17

to give God glory while moving us to use our active faith to change the human condition.

In this book, you will also discover a multitude of easy in-text and footnote scriptural references to inspire and guide you in your reading and daily study.

Also, at the beginning of each chapter, you will find selected and inspiring prayers, suggested scripture readings, and hymns to encourage and guide your devotional lifestyle. My prayer is that the God of grace will be with you in your study, worship and service, to enlighten, transform, strengthen, guide, renew, and empower you.

If such pursuits and understanding are of value for you in your personal search for understanding and spiritual and theological clarity, or for application in your congregational settings, and I suspect that they are, then the content of this book and the Made For Eternity Study Outline that accompanies this resource will be of tremendous value to such pursuits and understanding.

Having issues with forgiveness? There is a section on forgiveness tailor-made for you. Struggling with sin and your growth in Christ? Check out chapter four, section C: "Baptism: An Opportunity to Grow in Grace." Here you will see that it takes time to grow in Christ and that you have His help to do so. Do you have a desire to know Jesus better? Read chapter nine, "One Final Question: Do you know Jesus?" Do you need to understand why God does the things He does for us? Read chapter eight, "Motivated and Transformed by Love."

Come with me! This is going to be a spiritually transforming ride that takes us to new levels of understanding of the means of faith that we participate in as Christians, and the way God uses our faithful participation in these means of faith to transform us and position us for eternity.

Chapter One

You Were Made For Eternity

Prayer:

Dear God, I give my life to You. By faith, I make You the God and Savior of my soul. I believe that Jesus, begotten of You before there was time, died for me. Let Your Holy Spirit take control of my mind, my thoughts, my actions, and all of my ways. Complete me with Your love and grace. Keep me steadfast, intentional, and faithful as I continue to worship and serve You in anticipation of the return of Christ. Ready me for Your eternity by instilling in me the spirit of faith and obedience. I give You the glory and the praise for all that You are, all that You have done, and all that You have promised to do. In the precious name of Jesus I pray, Amen!

Suggested Scripture Readings: Jn 5:24, 6:39, 17:2; 1 Jn 3: 2, 5: 11, 13; Rom 8:18-19, 29-30; Tit 1:2; Jude 21; Gal 5: 22-26; Col 3: 9-10; Heb 10: 1-18

Hymns: "All to Jesus I Surrender"
"Lord Jesus, I Long To Be Perfectly Whole"
"O, They Told Me of A Home"

DR. WALKER WALKER

You Were Made For Eternity
(Section One)

1. You were made for eternity! Yes, you! You were made by God, for God, to express His glory on the earth, and to share in His eternity. Your hope of eternal life was established before the world began by God who cannot lie.[6] Now, you may be wondering and perhaps asking the question "Why on earth would the Creator of the universe be interested in me?" Or, perhaps you may be asking, "Why would someone like God use His time to pursue someone like me?" God is interested in you and is pursuing you because He loves you! God made you to have fellowship with Him. God is after you because you have a part of God in you carrying around. God wants to preserve Himself in you. Inspite of our faults and shortcomings, God loves us too much to let us go. God is so intent on sharing His eternity with us, that while we were still sinners, He sent His only begotten Son, Jesus Christ, to die for us.[7]

2. The truth is, when we are far away from God, God misses us far more than we miss Him. From the beginning, it was never God's intention for any of us to perish but that all of us would, through repentance and true faith in the Lord Jesus, come to Him.[8] God is so intent in having us come to Him that He did not wait for us to make the first move. The Bible says in Romans 5: 8 that, "While we were still sinners Jesus died for us." God would rather have His beloved Son die in our place so that He may reconcile us back to Himself, than to live without you and me.[9] Keep in mind that the blood of Christ was shed so that you and I would not be lost. Through His reconciling blood, and redeeming love and grace, we are drawn back into fellowship with God. That fellowship begins with developing knowledge of God, which moves us to repentance, positions us for forgiveness, develops holy attitudes in us and sanctifies us for worship. Having worshipped, we are then equipped

---

[6] Titus 1:2
[7] Rom 5:8
[8] 2 Pet 3:9 1 Tim. 2:4
[9] Jn 3:16

to serve God through Christian service (mission to the world). In both our worship and service to the world, we are constantly reminded by the Holy Spirit of the promised return of Jesus. That reminder keeps us faithful as we anticipate the return of Christ to usher us into that eternity for which God made us.[10]

3. The Bible further indicates in Ephesians 2: 4-5 that "God is rich in mercy and because of His great love with which He loves us, even when we were dead in trespasses He made us alive together with Christ. By grace you are saved." That is good news and a good reason to rejoice in the Lord. **Hallelujah!** More good news! God never intended for anyone to perish but for all people to come to Him through repentance and share eternity with Him. Let me just say this. Eternity with God has always been part of God's plan for your life and destiny. Hell was not made for you and me. Hell was made for the devil and the devil's angels. Listen to the words of Matthew 25:41: "Then the Lord will say to those on the left (that is, those who intentionally did not come to Him through faith and repentance), depart from Me, you cursed, into the everlasting fire *prepared for the devil and his angels.*"

4. Hell was not prepared for you. Eternity with God has always been your destiny. Choose Him, believe Him and His Christ, Jesus, and eternity with God shall be yours. Those who choose God in time will get to relate to Him in eternity with the gift of eternal life; but those who, in time, choose evil over good, the devil over God, have decided for themselves to relate to the devil in eternal torment and misery.

5. Notwithstanding that however, do not become overly preoccupied with hellfire and brimstone and the massively unending burning lake. Instead, think about heaven and eternity with God. That is you destiny. When writing or speaking of eternity, the writers and preachers of the first century used metaphors that would depict for their readers and listeners what it would be like existing without God for all eternity. It would be like hell because living without God is unfulfilling and miserable. It is to be thirsty and not having a drop of water to quench that thirst. It is to be hungry and not being able to satisfy that hunger. Living apart from God is hell because it would be like

---

[10] See for example 1 Jn 3:2

having excruciating pain and having no relief from that pain. Living apart from God is hell because it is like being lonely and not finding good company. In hell you will have no one to talk with about your pain and sorrow because everyone who did not make a faith choice to believe in God and His Christ and so live eternally with God, will be preoccupied with their own sorrow and pain; with hunger that cannot be satisfied, thirst that cannot be quenched, severe pain that cannot be relieved, and endlessly perplexed by a loneliness that they cannot escape.

6. You were not made for a place like that. You were made for a place where the Bread of Life is always in abundance. You were made for a place where the Fountain of Living Water is always freshly flowing. You were made for a place where there is no more pain and no more loneliness because eternity with God is a state of great and joyful fellowship and communion. I encourage you to become preoccupied with the thought and conviction of eternity with God. Begin that journey to eternity with God by accepting Christ today.

7. Our journey towards God begins with God. God, through Christ, in the power of the Holy Spirit, gives us knowledge of Himself, imparts His pardon, grace, and power to us, and sets us free from the limitations of self and sin by His forgiveness of us. This sets the stage for our liberating journey of faith and renewal in Christ. Having been set free from the constraints or bondage of sin and human limitations by the atonement of Christ, we are empowered by the Holy Spirit to faithfully respond to God who is always seeking communion and fellowship with us.

8. God, as we shall see later, is a communal God who lives in fellowship with Jesus the Son and the Holy Spirit. Through Christ, God seeks to invite and embrace us into that fellowship and communion. God made us to pursue eternity and to have fellowship and communion with Him. From the beginning God has put eternity in our hearts.[11] This is an intimation of the timelessness to which human intuition is persistently caught up in the pursuit of God's divine revelation and promise. Eternity was not placed in our hearts to be merely contemplated. It was put there by God for us to

---

[11] Eccl 3:11

pursue. We were made as creatures of time; but time will never be enough for us because our completion is only found in the timeless God. God placed eternity in our hearts and it has become a sort of built-in satellite that signals us to a grander frontier beyond temporal horizons, to the level of the invisible and eternal. Eternity has been the pursuit of generations. Many before us died with their hearts yearning for it and buried with their faces positioned and ready to greet the arrival of another and more glorious life, which for those who live and die believing in God and His Christ, death cannot hinder. For, indeed, those who lived and died believing in the Lord Jesus, who conquered death by His resurrection, shall also be raised up with Him. We were made for eternity and God placed that desire in us for us to diligently and faithfully pursue.

9. God placed eternity in our hearts so that we would not become satisfied with, and therefore surrender to the mundane and unworthy pursuits which are also prisoners of time. Rather, God placed eternity in our hearts so that we would invest our time and efforts into viewing life and death with the perspective of eternity. God placed eternity in our hearts and minds so that we would know and believe that there is a superior existence and indeed, Someone more desirous and more superior than who we are, where we are, and what we have already attained in space and time. Because God made us and implanted eternity in our hearts, we were made to submit to that superior existence and pursue the Source of divine excellence from whom we emanate in the first place.

10. Eternity with God is therefore a predisposed preference for our pursuit implanted in each of us by God. Now, we may choose to believe that, suppress it,[12] or deny it; but it does not make it any less true. We were predisposed to choose God as much as we were predisposed or predestined to share in God's eternity because God is intent on having eternal fellowship with us.

11. We are creatures of time destined for eternity. Inasmuch as we are creatures of time and living in time, and finite though we are, we have the affinity to yearn for the Creator and infinite God by reason of the God-implanted

---

[12] Rom 1:18

sensor in each and every one of us. This God implanted sense or desire for eternity in our hearts, implies that God in creation constituted us with the potentiality to become offspring of God. If in creation we were so constituted, then in His final consummation, we, having believed in Christ and accepted God's gift of grace in Christ, will realize that potentiality of life eternal with the infinite God.

12. This finite grasping for the infinite is God's blueprint in us that motivates and inspires us to follow His design for our growth and development in Him. We were created to be blessed and our hearts were designed to not settle for less than what God intends for us. That way, when we follow any other design, our hearts are left unfulfilled and still needing to yearn after God. That is why, no matter what we have already experienced, accomplished, or have had a foretaste of in this life, it is never enough. Because eternity is implanted in us, nothing less than that future glory to which we were created to attain, can satisfy us in this temporal life. St. Augustine grasped this essential conviction when he made the point that our hearts are restless until they find rest in God.

13. The Eternal God has, by the act of His own will, created and brought into existence from nothingness, all things that were not but now are. This Infinite Intelligence, God, could not and would not act aimlessly or without divine purpose. God has an objective for His action. God created all things and all peoples with an eternal purpose in mind. God destined His creatures to some purposeful outcome and that purposefulness is God, the beginning and the ending, the Alpha and Omega, the First and the Last. Because nothing exists apart from God, everything therefore has its beginning in Him. If everything has its beginning in God, nothing and no one but God Himself, could be the ending, or better yet, the culmination of all things.

14. Furthermore, if we conclude that human existence encompasses the respective dimensions of the past, present and future, we would be remiss had we not also concluded that it is the coming together of these three dimensions which completes human existence and selfhood. Indeed, we have memory of the past while living in and being committed to the present state of existence. There was a time for example, when the present was the future; and look at

the vast difference time has made in our lives. Certainly, in the present, we are not mentally, emotionally, or physiologically the same as we were in the past. Therefore, a belief in the transforming potentialities of the not yet realized future must continue to be an overarching possibility if we are to become complete or reach our divine potential. Our eschatological potential, indeed our eternity with God, is a possibility that drives us to live with a sense of moral obligation to God and our neighbor in the here and now until we attain eternity with God.

15. Our infinite God puts humans in time, placing temporality (the limitation of space and time) upon us, so that we have the time we need to develop knowledge of God and learn of His will and divine nature. That way, we may grow and expand and express ourselves based on what we know about God, as He, in time, makes us more like Him. This, altogether, is God preparing and positioning us for eternity, which is that future we talk about and where we are made complete in Him. God did not aimlessly create us without a plan and a destiny. He made us to spend eternity with Him. God is a communal God and He made us for His eternal community and communion.

16. God, as the essence of Being, embodies time and eternity. In other words, we live in time but time lives in, by, and through God. God is the Creator and therefore the Master of time. He, who creates time, is working in time, to bring us through time, into eternity. Because God is eternal and because we live, move and have our being in Him, our being is of eternal value and worthy of eternal preservation. Time may not always be good to us but God is always good to us. God being good to us in time is indicative of His preservation of us and His safeguarding of our souls in time, as He positions us for eternity.

17. With the end of time, all things are gathered up in God who has been their Source in the first place. If we believe and therefore affirm that the end of time means all things are gathered up in God, then we are also saying that we, along with all things, will be gathered up for our liberation from time so that we may come into our ultimate completion in the One who began that good work in us. The apostle Paul says it best when he writes in Romans 8:19-22:

"...The creation waits in eager expectation for the children of God to be revealed. For the creation was subjected to frustration, not by its own choice, but by the will of the one who subjected it, in hope that the creation itself will be liberated from its bondage to decay and brought into the freedom and glory of the children of God. We know that the whole creation has been groaning as in the pains of childbirth right up to the present time."

You Were Made for Eternity
(Section Two)

1. Since we were not created to find fulfillment in ourselves, but rather, in God, eternity and the realization of our greater potential, our transformation into the glory of Christ and therefore the perfect holiness of God, must be God's ultimate design for us. If indeed we see an affinity between Christ the Son and God the Father, and, if indeed we believe that the Holy Spirit has and is engrafting us into Christ the Son, then we should not find it difficult to accept that the human selfhood is being moved toward Christhood and if toward Christhood, then toward the glorious image of the One who made us. This is indeed the affirmation of 1 John 3:2: *"Dear friends, now we are children of God, and what we will be has not yet been made known. But we know that when Christ appears, we shall be like Him, for we shall see Him as He is."* Selfhood, indeed the full human potentiality is only realized in accordance to the degree of affinity that the person has developed in his/her relationship with God. We human beings are always becoming, always transforming, always being renewed and transformed to become like the divine Being and essence from which we were created. Our eternal purpose is to become like the only begotten Son of God, Jesus Christ.

2. This Christhood or Christ-likeness, toward which we are progressively being drawn by the Holy Spirit at work in us, is the culmination of God's purpose for those who recognize His nearness in Christ and believe in Him for salvation. Our becoming Christ-like or acquiring Christhood is our coming into the ultimate or greater glory. That is the glory that transcends the glory we now live in and under by reason of the present reign of God and the continuous manifestations of the Holy Spirit who is progressively positioning us for that realization.

3. Through creation, God conferred Himself on us and fit us, in time, with the capacity for a virtuous living that prepares us for eternity. The believer's life that came out of the splendor of creation, where God conferred Himself on us with the capacity to give of ourselves to others as we participate

with divinity in the liberation of the cosmos, is destined to exist in the realm of the eternal. That life, emerging from creation and therefore from the Mind and Spirit of God, having fallen because of the sin of disobedience, has been lifted up by divine grace to start a new life through the conviction of sin, repentance, forgiveness, justification, and sanctification. The subject of repentance, forgiveness, justification and sanctification will be given more attention in the following chapter where we explore the matter of spiritual transformation.

4. For the time being, let us go back to the matter of our being made for eternity. As the Holy Spirit works in us to conform our new life to Christ, He is also stretching our faith, widening our imagination, fitting us with new ways of thinking, and extending our hope to see and understand that we were made with the fiber of the eternal God. If, indeed, we emanate from the eternal God, and we are so persuaded, it follows that we also have the potentiality for eternal duration. Assuredly, it is God that made us; we did not make ourselves.

5. Since all things created come from God, it follows that the moral and divine DNA of God is intertwined in our humanity. That way, the more dominant trait in us, God's moral and divine DNA, and therefore God's divine purpose, ultimately will prevail over the human will or tendencies. Let us bring this closer to our human understanding of inherited DNA. If two parents contribute certain sets of traits in the conception of a child, and one parent has a dominant trait and the other has a recessive trait, the child is probably more likely to acquire the dominant trait rather than the recessive trait. It is that dominantly divine (trait) nature of God in us that continues to override those natural and humanly innate and recessive traits in us that so often make us weak, prone to evil, and driven by conflicting imperatives. That divinely dominant trait, inherited from our Maker, stirs up in us attitudes and behaviors which are fitting for believing sons and daughters of God. God made us to behave like Him in the world. If we were made in the image of God with the similitude of God, and if it is indeed in Him that we live

and move and have our being, as attested by scripture,[13] not only are we His offspring, we are also inheritors of His eternity. We were made for eternity!

6. Notwithstanding our shortcomings and failures, God loves us.[14] So intent is God on having fellowship with us, that while we became messed up and sinful through the inherited traits and disobedience of the first Adam, God sent Christ, the Second Adam, to clean us up, forgive our sins and faults, mend our brokenness, and restore us to a right relationship with Him. God's fixing and mending of us and restoring of our relationship with Him we call reconciliation. This reconciliation and repositioning of us is attained by our faith response to the finished work of Christ as well as by our subsequent demonstrative walk of obedience before God, which is all the time made possible by grace.

7. In Christ we have redemption and forgiveness according to the riches of His grace.[15] Through Christ, then, God made known His will for fellowship with us which He had purposed in Himself from the beginning.[16] Before time began, God had purposed to call us who had fallen into sin, so that He might restore us through forgiveness by grace, through the Lord, Jesus Christ.[17] Even now, we are not all that we can be. But thank God, we are a work in progress. As a work in progress, while it does not yet appear what we shall be, we know that when He appears, we, who have been redeemed by the precious blood of Jesus, shall be like Him and see Him as He is.[18]

8. Because of this anticipation of glory, this promise of eternity with God, inspired by the present manifestation of God's love for us, we are motivated to continuously love, worship, and serve God in time and space. As we worship and serve God in time, He is all the time preparing us for eternity without the restrictions of time and space. This prospect, indeed, this promise of eternity, is also what motivates us on our faith journey to faithfully,

---

[13] Gen 1:26; Acts 17:28; Jas 3:9

[14] Jn 3:16

[15] Eph 1:7

[16] Eph 1:9

[17] 2 Tim 1:9

[18] 1 Jn 3:2

diligently, and actively engage ourselves in Christian mission. Put differently, God's promise of eternal life gives meaning, purpose, and vigor to our present existence and Christian activities. In view of God's promise of eternity, notwithstanding the hardships, letdowns, and tests of this life, we still possess the promise and are therefore driven to live, worship, pray, and serve God confidently and faithfully in the present. We are confident and assured in the present because we believe and have come to know, on the grounds of the resurrection of Jesus, that our life will ultimately culminate in the realization of a greater hope, and a greater glory which is eternity with God.

9. As we have already established, the three components or areas of participation and opportunity for fellowship with God on our faith journey are worship, Christian mission, and an eschatological lifestyle that is inspired by our expectation of Christ's returning. By our faithful response to God and our faithful participation in these areas of our lives, God instills within us the gift of faith to believe and respond to His actions and work of transformation in us. God has also implanted in us and therefore gifted us with the Spirit of obedience and humility, thus making us pliable to the operations of the Holy Spirit who initiates spiritual formation in the process of transforming us into the likeness of Christ. As we obediently conform to the will and purposes of God, the Holy Spirit works in us to engraft us into Christ, thus making us more and more like Christ in terms of our attitudes and behaviors that are reflective of all that Christ is.

10. Through worship, mission, and eschatological living, God is constantly shaping and reshaping our lives into the fashion of His own likeness and holy standards. That is God's way of positioning us for eternity. By our participation in worship, mission, and eschatology, God the Father initiates and sustains a spiritual and life transforming relationship with us. God, through the Holy Spirit, is therefore involved in every aspect of the life and work that He has called us to live and do.

11. Through the Holy Spirit, then, we live in the realization of Christ and yet are being moved or carried toward our completion in Christ through grace. This grace is manifested through Christ and lived through the available means of faith and spiritual transformation— worship, mission, and

eschatology. By virtue of our participation in these spiritual means of faith, the operation of God's grace lovingly invades our lives and experiences to transform us and develop our faith. The development of our faith, coupled with a renewed awareness of God, enables us to grow in grace and divine favor while God progressively imparts His life and dignity to us.

12. It may be useful to point out at this juncture that eternity is not a place. Eternity, though we believe that it will be spent in a place called heaven, is not a place. Eternity is a state of life or existence and clarity of mind that is eternally connected with the eternal will and presence of God. Consequently, eternity is a mode or condition of being or existence in the realm or state of infinite duration. Instead of a place, eternity is characterized by infinite spiritual fellowship that comes from knowing God. As a result, we do not have to wait until we die to have eternal life because it begins with knowing God and being absorbed into His divine life right now. The difference is that right now, from a physical point of view, we are still restricted and still confined to time and its nuances and ills. But when we shall have been caught up to meet Jesus,[19] we shall be changed to attain to that greater glory that we talk about and time will no longer restrict us.

13. According to Jesus in John 17:3, we have eternal life the moment our minds are reoriented to God through knowledge that transforms, and the very moment that we believe in Christ and turn to God through Him in repentance and faith.[20] Eternity therefore begins with knowledge of God. The Bible teaches that God is eternal. As a result of the knowledge we obtain of the eternal God, the Holy Spirit works in us to develop glimpses of eternity in the "here and now." These glimpses of eternity strengthen our hope and keep our expectation of a greater glory at a high peak.[21] When we have knowledge of God we will begin to walk in sync with Him. When we walk in sync with Him, we will begin to live in Him. When we begin to live in Him, we will begin to grow in Him. When we grow in Him, we will begin to become like

---

[19] 1 Thess 4:16-17

[20] Jn 3:16, 18; 5:24; 6:47

[21] This expectation of the greater glory will be a large part of our discussion on eschatology in chapter seven.

Him. Growth in God, through the Lord Jesus Christ, is the mark of a surrendered life. A surrendered life to Christ is, at best, a spiritually transformed life and a preparation for eternity.

Let us now turn our attention to the matter of spiritual transformation and the processes applied and used by God to ready us for eternity.

Chapter Two

Spiritual Transformation

Prayer:

Most holy and eternal God, take hold of us and transform us by the power of Your Holy Spirit so that we may be renewed in our minds. Help us we pray, to reflect the newness we have found in Christ Jesus so that we may walk before You in obedience and faith and by the way that we behave toward others. This we pray in the redeeming name of Jesus. Amen!

Scriptures:

Ps 51:10; Isa 40:31; Rom 12:2; 2 Cor 3:18, 4:16, 5:16-17; Eph 4:23, 5:8-9; Col 3:10; Tit 3:5; 1 Pet 1:14-15

Hymns:

"Breathe On Me Breath Of God"
"This Is The Day Of New Beginnings"
"Spirit Of The Living God"
"Something Beautiful"
"Nothing But The Blood"
"I Know It Was The Blood"

1. Overview:
What is Spiritual Transformation?

What God is seeking to do through the process of spiritual transformation is to infuse His Spirit in us and with our human spirit. That way, He can gracefully and progressively override our human tendencies and develop in us the affinity to become like Him and so reflect Him in the world.

A word about what it means to be spiritual may be helpful in furthering our understanding of this segment of our study as well as the ensuing and prevailing theme that runs throughout the pages of this book. Being spiritual has to do with a mindset that is oriented toward God. That is why any relationship with God and any understanding of the ways of God must necessarily begin with a renewing of the mind. To be spiritual is to be liberated from the limitation of individualism and self-centeredness. Being spiritual implies that our focus is shifted from the natural human inclinations, to embrace the will and purposes of God. To be spiritual is to exercise mastery of self or our natural human tendencies while allowing the Spirit of God to exercise control over us. Being spiritual is therefore a striving toward, a submission to, as well as a connection with a higher power, God! To be spiritual also has to do with the demonstration of faith, obedience, love, justice, mercy, truthfulness, positive thinking, peace, kindness and joy, within the framework of our day-to-day activities. These are outpouring manifestations of the Spirit's presence in the believers' lives as the Spirit of God works in us to transform us.

Now, then, spiritual transformation is the result of change that has taken place in someone's thinking, behavior and attitude. The spiritually transformed person is therefore a person who has been radically changed to respond to God with a renewed mind that is fixed on God, who is essentially our divine center and activity. Spiritual transformation is followed by our willingness to follow the indicative faith statements of the Gospel of Christ, as we intentionally seek to live that Gospel's imperatives in the world for the expressed purpose of glorifying God. Spiritual transformation is a process of renewal in the Christian's attitude and behavior.

Spiritual transformation begins with a renewed mind and therefore a new perspective of one's self in relation to God. Spiritual transformation is the reorientation or the redirection of the believer's mind toward things that pertain to divine values and purpose. The mind that is spiritually renewed is the mind that is turned toward Christ whom we confess and accept as Lord and Savior. The transformed life is the sanctified and liberated life that is lived in Christ and under the authority of the Holy Spirit. To be spiritually transformed is to be renewed and empowered or anointed to live the Christian life through faith that honors and pleases God,[22] having been set free from the limitations of individualism and the bondage of self and sin. By extension, the transformed life is the life that follows the indicative faith statements of the Gospel of Christ. It is also the life that embodies the Gospel's imperatives to walk in faith, obedience, and holiness before God, as well as to serve and do the will of God as we are empowered by the Holy Spirit of grace to do so.

2. Spiritual Transformation is the Work of the Holy Spirit

1. The work of spiritual transformation is the work of the Holy Spirit. It is not our task. We cannot change ourselves without God's holy influence. The Holy Spirit is the One that gives us a new vision of God and draws our attention to the fact of Christ. The Holy Spirit brings about spiritual transformation by His persistent influence and prompting of our minds and spirits for every area of our lives beginning with our confession of Christ and our Baptism.[23] As our confession of Christ is a work of the Holy Spirit, our Baptism is also the Baptism of the Holy Spirit.[24] We, who are transformed by the Holy Spirit, are not only renewed, we are also sealed by Him for the day of redemption.[25] The implication of this

---

[22] Heb 11:6
[23] See chapter four for a discussion on Baptism
[24] 1 Cor 12:13
[25] Eph 4:30; 2 Cor 1:22

is that once God places His stamp of renewal on you, the matter is sealed and settled.

2. As we continue to worship, witness through mission, and live in the eschatological hope of Christ returning, our strength, boldness and hope in the promise of Christ, are renewed in us by the Holy Spirit who indwells us. As a result of the Holy Spirit working in us, the person that is considered spiritual or acting in the Spirit is marked by the characteristics of God. That which is spiritual, or in the Spirit as Wainwright asserts, "appertains to God in the first place and then to humanity in its openness to God."[26]

3. Spiritual transformation is therefore marked by the extent of affinity in the relationship between the Spirit of God and the human spirit. To be spiritually transformed therefore implies that the moral characteristics or qualities by which the Christian life is lived reflect the moral attributes of God. That mirroring of the moral attributes and holiness of God is the direct result of the Holy Spirit persistently molding us into the likeness of God's begotten Son, Jesus Christ. Through the Holy Spirit then, Christ in us becomes not merely the foundation of a religion, but the life giving stream for sustaining and carrying a relationship and a lifestyle that are engrained into the very fiber, indeed, the very DNA of our spirits and souls. Owing to the Christ in us, the life we now live ought to express itself through holiness which is the new identity of the spiritually transformed person. Let us now move our attention to a discussion of the six selected, but not mutually exclusive steps in spiritual transformation.

---

[26] Gregory Wainwright, <u>Doxology: The Praise of God in Worship, Doctrine, and Life</u> NY: Oxford University Press, 1980, 87

3. Six Steps For Understanding Spiritual Transformation

There are six steps in the process of spiritual transformation. These are: (1) Recognizing and knowing God (2) Repentance (3) Forgiveness (4) Justification (5) Sanctification and (6) Moving from glory to glory.

A. Step One: Recognizing and Knowing God

1. The first step in the process of spiritual transformation is to recognize and know God; who God is and what He has done for us in Christ Jesus. As noted above, transformation begins with the Holy Spirit redirecting our minds and attitudes toward God. Enlightening or illuminating the human mind is the first step God uses to draw us to Himself. The renewed mind as Romans 12:2 indicates is the mind which, having been directed toward God by the Holy Spirit, has developed a way of thinking that is in keeping with the ideals of the kingdom purposes of God. By the power of the Holy Spirit, we are drawn into becoming what we know and believe about God. Our becoming more like God is deeply grounded in what we know about God.

2. The greatest gift one can receive is the gift of knowing God because, knowing God as Jesus indicates, is eternal life.[27] Knowing God is a gift because as we shall soon see, such knowledge is a revealed knowledge. Knowledge of God is not restricted to mere information about God. Knowledge of God extends to, and is only spiritually transforming when we have experienced God, and are inspired by that knowledge and experience to develop a personal relationship with God. The term knowledge, where used in the Bible, is more often than not, used in reference to a personal relationship with God as evidenced by behaviors that reflect godliness. The statement of Jesus in John 8:19 and 44 to the teachers of the Jews is therefore a strong indictment to any person that claims to know God but whose life and behaviors replicate

---

[27] John 17: 3

the response of the devil. To claim knowledge of God should therefore be reflected in our attitude and behavior.

3. To better understand this principle of knowing God, the following questions may be useful in guiding our discussion:
- (a) What are the ways by which we may have knowledge of God?
- (b) How can we get to know God relationally and how does that knowledge change us?
- (c) How is knowledge of God the basis for human excellence?

4. The first question for aiding our understanding of the principle of knowing God is "What are the ways by which we may know God?" We can develop knowledge of God in five mutually inclusive ways. These are:
- (i) **Knowing God by His Divine Qualities and Works (Through Creation, Incarnation and Redemption)**
- (ii) **Knowing God through God's own Self-revelation**
- (iii) **Knowing God through studying His Word**
- (iv) **Knowing God intellectually**
- (v) **Knowing God experientially**

Let us examine these separately.

(i) Knowing God by His Divine Qualities and Works (Through Creation, Incarnation and Redemption)

1. The first way by which we know God is by His divine qualities and works as evidenced in history through creation, incarnation, redemption through Christ, and His continuous work of restoration and sanctification through the Holy Spirit. God created the heavens and the earth so that He would not leave Himself without witnesses of His existence. God wants us to know that He exists. Acts 14:15-17 for example, speaks of God as the Living God who made heaven and earth and all created things as witnesses of His existence. We therefore know of God because of the evidences of creation. My own existence and yours are evidences that there is God. Our existence is not a perception. Our existence is

not a figment of our own imagination. Our thoughts and feelings, our understanding and will, are as real as the sun that God "pulls up" in the morning and "pushes down" in the evening. Existence is not a perception; it is a reality that is witnessed by our own presence in the created order and as a direct result of our empirical participation in the life and ministry of the historical Christ. You are not here by chance. God created you because He wanted to. God created you for His own glory and to share in His eternity.

2. The Psalmist is not at all presumptuous when he affirms that only a fool after observing the order and beauty of creation, and after recognizing his/her own existence, can say in the heart that there is no God.[28] Human beings exist because of God. The essence and First Cause of life purposed us to exist in His created world. Romans 1:19-20 affirms that what may be known of God is manifested in creation. By the created and visible world the invisible attributes of God are made visible because, in them, we recognize order and designing excellence which must be the product of a Greater Mind. No one seeing these can have an excuse for not knowing God. Romans 1:22 says that they who seek excuses only profess to be wise in their own eyes but are really fools.

3. Through the incarnation of Christ, God came to us as Redeemer. From the perspective of incarnation, which is God coming to us in the person of Christ in human form, we also believe and know that God is the God and Father of our Lord Jesus Christ through whom and by whom God invaded the world to redeem us.[29] Assuredly, God's invisible presence continues to be manifested by the presence, power, and work of the Holy Spirit in the world, in our lives, and in the church.

4. To illustrate the point about the invisible presence being manifested in the world and the human experience, I recall a story about a woman who worked really hard to send her son through school and later to college. In the early semesters of his college career, the young man would write home asking for prayers and reporting to his mother in his letters to her, about how good

---

[28] Ps 14:1

[29] 2 Cor 5:19

God had been to him. After a while, having become engrossed in the sciences and studies of evolution, he seemed to have lost perspective and would no longer write home talking about God or asking for his mother's prayers. After graduating, he went home to be with his mother. One evening, as they sat at the table for supper, his mother asked: "Son, how come you stopped writing about God in your letters while you were in college?" After pausing for a while, with a subtle indication of discomfort he said, "Mom, I am no longer sure about this God thing." After another brief but uncomfortable silence, he then asked, "Mom, can you touch God like you can touch me?" She said, "No son." Pausing for a moment he asked, "Can you see God like you can see me?" She said, "No son." He then said, "Well, until you can touch God and see God like you can touch me and see me, I do not want to hear about this God thing."

5. Later that night they both went to bed. In the early hours, way before dawn, the mother was awakened by painfully groaning sounds coming from the direction of her son's room. As any caring mother would, she headed to her son's room to see what the matter was. As she got closer to his room the groaning got louder. She knocked on the door that was already ajar and asked, "Are you OK son?" Under the strain of pain, he said, "O mamma, it hurts so bad." "What son?" she asked. Hardly able to speak because of the excruciating pain, he said, "My toothache mamma; it hurts so bad." Just then his mother remembered the conversation they had at supper concerning God and her son's questions as to whether or not she can touch and see God as she can touch and see him. Though driven with concern for the pain her son was experiencing, the condition of his faith convictions concerning God and the eternity of his soul took precedence over a temporal condition and the experience became a teachable moment. Inspired by their earlier conversation, she asked her son: "Son, can you touch that toothache like you can touch me?" He said, "No mamma." She proceeded to ask, "Can you see that toothache like you can see me?" He said, "No mamma." As if inspired to open the boy's eyes to the reality of the invisible God, she asked: "How then do you know that the toothache is there?" He said, "Because I feel it moving up and down my face!" His mother, though obviously concerned for her son's discomfort, said with a voice filled with trembling emotions and conviction, "Son, during supper you

asked me if I can touch God like I can touch you or see God like I can see you. I told you no. I cannot touch or see God like I can touch or see you son. But I know He is there because every now and then I feel Him moving up and down my soul." Her son made sense of the conversation and the experience. From his toothache, he developed new ways of understanding just how the invisible and immaterial God can be manifested in the visible and material world.

6. The God we worship may indeed be a mystery; but He is not a myth nor is He a human construct or a figment of the human imagination. You may not be able to physically touch God, but I guarantee you that every now and then He will touch you and reveal Himself to you. And when He does, He will not leave you unchanged. You will not be left unchanged because God has promised to cause the least to the greatest to know Him as the One who reveals Himself, offering us love and forgiveness from sins that He vows to remember no more.[30]

(ii) Knowing God through God's Own Self-Revelation

1. The second way for getting to know God is by God's own self-revelation. It is not conceivable for finite beings to discover or find the infinite Being. It is not conceivable for humans to come to a full or even partial knowledge of the divine without the help and inspiration of the divine. We do not have the capacity to contain a fraction of God, much less, the fullness of God. If we recall it was not Adam in his error to sin through disobedience that sought after God for forgiveness. It was God, filled with grace and mercy that went to Adam. Adam would not have been able to find the omnipresent God. The omnipresent God can find us everywhere and anywhere we are. God coming to Adam, and to us through the Lord Jesus, is so that we may know that He is there and so that with that knowledge, we would seek after Him in order that He might lead us by the hand to find Him, pour His forgiveness upon us, help us to know Him more deeply, and also that He might draw us into the next dimension of living the transformed Christian life.

---

[30] Jer 31:34

2. The human intellect is incapable of knowing God without God's help. The finite mind can only grasp what the infinite God elects to reveal about Himself. What we know of God is what God has chosen to tell us about Himself. Knowledge of God does not come from human beings but from God Himself. Whether scripturally, intellectually, historically, traditionally, culturally, socially, or experientially, the knowledge we have of God is the result of God's own self-revelation. It is by God's own self-revelation and our taking notice of that revelation which we have come to know God. We are incapable of discovering things about God on our own. However, God does not wait for us to discover Him. Otherwise we never will. God reveals Himself to us, through creation and emphatically through Jesus Christ, because He wants us to know Him and realize that He is there. As we take notice and as we respond in faith to what God has revealed, He reveals more of Himself to us. God feeds us with what we are able to understand and gives us more as we grow and mature in our faith and knowledge of Him.[31] As a result of God's own self-revelation and as we learn more and more about God, we progressively become and reflect what we know about God through our attitudes and behaviors which are manifestations of our transformation.

3. Since knowledge of God comes to us from God's own self-revelation, God is therefore the centrality of revelation and the Source of human wisdom. As a result of God's self-revelation, and as a consequence of the Holy Spirit stirring up within us thoughts or contemplations of God, our lives are transformed by that deeper contemplation of God, His nature, His power, His holiness, and His perfection. This knowledge or new vision of God is a source of spiritual renewal.

4. Indeed, by our intentional faith response to the prompting of the Holy Spirit to contemplate God, we develop new knowledge of ourselves. John Calvin, for example, believed that knowledge of ourselves comes from our knowledge of God. Hence, for Calvin, "without knowledge of God there is no knowledge of self."[32] This must be taken to mean knowledge of the re-

---

[31] Heb 5:12-14

[32] Calvin, John: <u>Institutes of the Christian Religion</u>, ed John T. McNeill, (Philadelphia: Wesminster Press, V.xx., 37

deemed self with a renewed dignity that is now caught up in the blessed life of God. Knowledge of God not only stirs us to seek to intellectually know more about God. That knowledge also "leads us by the hand to find Him,"[33] and develop the desire in us to remain in fellowship with the Father and the Son in the unity of the Holy Spirit.

5. By virtue of God's self-revelation, and as a direct result of the Holy Spirit stirring up within us thoughts of God, we are moved to pursue knowledge of God.[34] Knowledge of who God is, what He has done for us in Christ, as well as our understanding of His purpose for us in this life and for eternity are what change and reorder our lives. Knowledge of God changes us because such knowledge prompts our longing to become what wisdom reveals to us about God. The Bible, the written word of God, is a major source of that wisdom.

(iii) Knowing God by Studying His Word

1. The third way by which we can get to know God is by studying His Word, the Bible. Studying the Bible offers the believer a sense of freedom and empowerment that comes from knowing the truth.[35] The Word of God is a source of enrichment for those who diligently pursue divine truth. One of the best ways for Christians to grow and develop healthy and balanced Christ-centered living is by studying the Word of God. Study here means to pay attention to the detail and discern the truth concerning the Object of the study. To study the Word of God also means to prayerfully contemplate what the Word says about God and us, our relationship with Him, and our relationship with each other. Such approach to our study may help us capture the true spirit of the Word which is life and fellowship and communion through our transformation and continuous renewal.

---

[33] Calvin, *Institutes*, 37
[34] Hos 6: 3; Acts 17:27
[35] Jn 8:32

2. As we are led to capture the true spirit of the Word, what we understand and proceed to teach, becomes a matter of divine influence orchestrated by God through the working of His Holy Spirit.[36] When what we know and understand about God is inspired by the Spirit of God Himself, we are in a better position to accurately understand as well as to share and apply the Word through our teaching of those who are diligently seeking understanding. A commitment to studying the Bible, accompanied by an intentional adherence to sound Bible based teachings, are good indications that we are both seeking and allowing the Holy Spirit of grace and wisdom to direct our minds toward God. It is the obligation of all Christian believers to diligently pursue a study and understanding of the Word of God.[37] It is important to follow the Word of God because it is by God's Word that our understanding and knowledge are directed to the path that leads to righteousness and divine truths. It is also by our understanding of the Word that our behavior is guided. The Word of God is therefore to be read, studied, understood, memorized by those who can, implanted in our hearts, and believed, so that we can faithfully live out the Word in a lifestyle that is reflective of our knowledge and understanding of God.

3. Studying and living by the Word are important to Christian formation and subsequent transformation. If we only read or merely glance over the Word, we are more likely to forget it and therefore not be influenced by its rich content and Spirit. But when we study and make the Word a lifestyle, we are blessed and transformed by its precepts.[38]

4. The Word of God is our sword for Christian witness and warfare.[39] To that extent, the Word of God is a guard against negative and evil forces and influences. When God's Word is believed, studied, and lived, it will accomplish the task of spiritual formation and transformation for which it is intended.[40] God's Word will produce the fruit for which it is intended because

---

[36] 1 Cor 2:13

[37] 2 Tim 2:15

[38] Jas 1:22-25

[39] Eph 6:17; Heb 4:12

[40] Is 55:11

God's Word has God's own life-giving power and inspiration. Life-giving power and inspiration are profitable as well as attainable to those who read and believe it. As we live with and relate to one another, the Word of God also calls us to be accountable because it is good for both our reproof and our correction.[41]

(iv) Knowing God Intellectually

1. The fourth way by which we get to know God is by our intellect. As indicated above, the human intellect is incapable of developing knowledge about God without God's help and self-revelation or self-disclosure. Let me emphasize however, that if spiritual transformation is to take place, the process needs to involve the human mind as well as the human heart and faith in the Lord Jesus Christ. As Charry posits, "Cognitive assent to a set of correct ideas is only a small piece of the knowledge that renews the believer."[42] Regarding intellectual knowledge of God, Paul in Ephesians 3:18-19 writes: "[That you]...may be able to comprehend with all the saints what is the width and length and depth and height— to know the love of God that surpasses knowledge; that you might be filled with all the fullness of God." The implication of this is that Christian sanctity and transformation require intellectual comprehension of God. Also implied is the notion that this understanding should not be void of faith and experiential engagement in the work of God, the redemptive act of Christ, and the sanctifying work of the Holy Spirit of grace. Without experiential engagement with God's act of grace and love, human knowledge and understanding by itself will not be sufficient for bringing about our complete transforming.

2. Christian excellence, transformation, and spiritual maturation are therefore the results of both grace through faith and a rehabilitation of the human mind and way of thinking. Again, Paul affirms in Colossians 3:10:

---

[41] 2 Tim 3:16

[42] Ellen T. Charry, By the Renewing of Your Minds: The Pastoral Function of Christian Doctrine (New York, Oxford University Press, 1997), 115

"...Put on the new man, which is renewed in knowledge after the image of Him that created [you]." Consequently, knowing God, assimilating oneself to God, and believing in His Christ, are central to salvation. Knowing God is the result of God's self-revelation but accepting God and responding to Him by faith are the results of divine prompting as well as an intellectual choice. To that extent, on the one hand, as the fool makes an unintelligent choice to reject God,[43] on the other hand, the wise person makes an intellectual choice to accept God and His Christ.

3. Regarding intellectual knowledge of God and our growth into that knowledge and understanding, Charry observes that two requirements for progress in the Christian life immediately present themselves. The first requirement is sapiential knowledge of the Triune God. Sapiential knowledge has to do with knowledge or understanding that is gained by wisdom, especially the wisdom of God imparted to us by God's own self-disclosure. The immediate presumption is that appropriate enlightenment regarding God assists us in our participation in, and living of, the divine life. The second requirement for progress in the Christian life is the desire to be transformed by this knowledge. Here it is presumed that if what we know about God does not move us to change, such knowledge would be to no avail. In short, inasmuch as the "theology that renders God accessible to believers is essential to spiritual transformation,"[44] the believer must also now make an intelligent choice and a faith response to God in order for change in the direction of the believer's life to take place. Intellectual knowledge of God must therefore be accompanied by, nay, interlocked with our faith and sincere desire to be transformed in order for real change to take place.

4. Intellectual knowledge by itself cannot change us. Changes in a person's behavior and attitudes are the direct results of knowing God intellectually, spiritually, and experientially. Intellectual knowledge makes us aware. It informs us. But we must act upon that awareness and that information in order to become changed persons. Intellectual knowledge of God is of no value for salvation and eternity if we do not come to know, believe, experience, and

---

[43] Ps 14:1
[44] Charry, 103

respond with faith to the God who is made known as Savior through Jesus Christ. A believing heart must be applied to the process of intellectual understanding. God is not satisfied with us just having head knowledge of Him. God wants our hearts and spirits engaged in the process of obtaining knowledge that leads to belief in Him and a saving relationship with Him.

5. When we speak in theological or spiritual discourses of the human heart, we are not speaking of that muscular pulsating organ in the chest cavity that uses rhythmic and contracting forces to pump blood in order to supply and maintain the circulatory system. When we speak in theological or spiritual terms of the heart, we are speaking specifically of the human moral capacity, ethical disposition, and therefore the inclination to believe, feel, care, act rightly, and respond to God with passion and love. The heart is the human moral and spiritual compass. The heart is where God gives revelation and direction for right action, ushers in illumination, invokes compassion, and ignites human sensitivity. When this human moral capacity that we refer to as the heart, is applied to knowledge and faith in God, we are able to care about God and the divine principles about which the intellect makes us aware. Intellectual knowledge makes us aware of God but faith, obedience, and a heart for God, prompt our response to God as well as invoke in us the desire to believe, love, and therefore do the will of God. When our hearts are involved we are more prone to take God seriously. It is the heart, that moral capacity and proclivity toward righteousness that God seeks to influence and change by our initial thought or intellectual contemplation of Him.

6. God is seeking to influence the human heart for three reasons. The first reason is that the human heart, that moral capacity in us, is believed to be the fountainhead and filter of thought, understanding, the human will (inclination, disposition, heart's desire, mind), and all the issues of life. It is there that the Lord and the Holy Spirit dwell to direct and influence change and character building in all those who believe. The second reason is that heart belief makes our understanding and faith personal, relational, real, and applicable to Christian fellowship and service.[45] When our heart connects with our intellectual awareness, faith emerges. That way, our faith response

---

[45] Heb 10:22-25

becomes one that is based on understanding as well as a personal love for God, which is vital to our relationship with God. The third reason God seeks to influence the human heart is because God created us with that inner moral capacity or inclination to believe and act toward Him with passion and a desire for righteousness.[46] God wants His people to have more than an intellectual understanding of the principles of His kingdom; more than mere awareness of His existence. God's desire for mankind is that we enter into a very personal and intimate spiritual relationship with Him. With the head we gather knowledge, but with the heart there is understanding and the motivation to relate to and therefore love God. This is the message of Jeremiah 9:23-24 where the word of God declares that we should not boast in our knowledge and wisdom but rather, in our understanding of who God is. It is in such that God delights. It is not merely the revelation of facts or intellectual truths that God wants us to have. According to Jeremiah 31:33-34, God wants us, above all, to get a personal revelation of Him so that we may develop a personal relationship with Him. For that reason, God gives us a new heart in which to deposit His purpose, establish a covenant relationship with us, and lovingly influence our actions toward Him.

7. Contrary to popular opinion, it is not the human will that influences our faith, heart response, or holy actions toward God. While everything begins in our thoughts through the working of the mind or intellect, if any action is to take place, the mind or thought must necessarily inform the heart; that moral capacity and inclination to act toward God of which we speak. The heart influences the will and the will is moved by the human desire and passion to act. Because of God's creation of the human heart, thus endowing us with the capacity for moral affinity, our response to God is a gift of faith. It is also the action and influence of grace upon the human heart by which we are motivated to move in pursuit of holy and purposeful actions. The human will, left alone, will at best, only pursue selfish and unprofitable things. The human will is such that even when it knows the difference between right and wrong, will still selfishly pursue what is wrong simply because it is pleasing to the human natural desire. Even though it

---

[46] Rom 10:9-10

might be to the detriment of the human soul, the human will naturally inclines us to do it. Without divine direction and influence, the human will does not know any better. If the human thought is not influenced by the Spirit of God who stirs up our hearts to respond, the human will cannot and will not be moved toward holiness. Since we cannot and will not change ourselves by our own power and desire to do so, spiritual transformation is and always will be the work of the Holy Spirit of grace. It is the Holy Spirit alone that moves us by the intellect and influences us by our hearts to act toward God and His Christ.

8. In order to transform us and set us on our way to eternity then, God moves us at four levels. These four levels are: (1) by our thoughts; (2) by our hearts; (3) by our will; and (4) by our actions. Holy pursuits are the results of God's grace acting on our thoughts, informing our hearts, and harnessing our will so that we may pursue actions that are pleasing to God. When our thoughts of God are conceived, by a working of the Holy Spirit, they give birth in us to holiness and godly pursuits. When our thoughts and knowledge of God become mature in us, they give birth to eternal life. This is precisely what Jesus means when He says to know God is eternal life.[47]

9. Intellectual awareness may begin the process but we need to apply our faith and heart so that we may both know and experience God as Creator and Redeemer. By the intellect the human heart is informed; but our heart, that moral capacity to love God, must be applied so that our human knowledge and understanding can be of spiritually transforming value. We become what we know and believe about God not only by the illumination of our minds but also by the conformation and submission of our thoughts, will, and behavior. Also, as we humble ourselves under the authority of the Holy Spirit, He transforms the Christian life and fashions it into the likeness of God. Without awareness of God and illumination of the mind, followed by faith on the Lord Jesus Christ, and the engagement of the heart, which generates our obedience to the divine will of God, and without our experiential knowledge of God, we cannot participate in the divine life of God. Intellectual knowledge of

---

[47] Jn 17:3

God should therefore lead us to an actual experience of God. Knowing God experientially has to do with knowing God in practical terms and by our life experiences of Him.

(v) Knowing God Experientially

1. The fifth way for developing knowledge of God is through our experience of God in our personal lives. This is known as experiential knowledge of God. There are many ways by which we may experience God in our personal lives.

You may have experienced Him as Love because when those who should have loved you turned away from you, you found that God was always there to unconditionally love you in spite of you.

You may know Him as Liberator because you have experienced Him freeing your captive mind from stress and distress. As you look back over your life experiences, some things you went through should have either killed you or driven you crazy. But God kept you sane and has continued to bless you with a right and stable mind.

You may know Him as Healer because you or somebody you know may be able to recall how, when you were sick and the doctors said you would not get well, somebody prayed and God took over and brought healing to your body or mind.

You may have experienced Him as Defender because when the enemy and self-appointed haters around you came upon you to destroy you, God took over the battle, defended your cause, and brought you the victory.

You may know Him as Justice because when you were mistreated, misunderstood, or taken advantage of in your dealings with others, God showed up, vindicated you and justified your cause.

You may have experienced Him as Provider because there might have been a time when you or someone that you know did not know how your bills were going to be paid, and just in the nick of time, God made a way out of no way.

You may know Him as Bread because that time when your cupboards were empty and you did not know where your next meal was coming from for you and your children, God sent someone to put food on your table.

You may have experienced Him as Water, because you experienced His refreshing when your brook dried up.

You might have experienced Him as Hope because there might have been times when life's circumstances left you feeling so discombobulated and overwhelmed with despair that you felt like giving up. But God intervened, gave you a glimpse of something better to get up and live for, and hope was born anew in your life.

You may know Him as Rock because perhaps at one point in your life everything around you seemed like sinking sand that was slowly sucking you under; but God, your sure foundation, held you up and prevented you from going under.

You may have experienced Him as Grace because when sin was messing up your life, God bestowed grace and forgiveness upon you and rescued you from the destructive power of sin.

You may know Him as Peace, because when life's troubles were knocking you about and filling your life with turmoil, God took charge of the circumstances and turmoil and spoke tranquility into your life.

And yes, you ought to, and if you have not, you can experience Him as Redeemer through Christ because He is Author of salvation and the Savior for your soul. **Hallelujah!**

2. Knowing God experientially also has to do with someone having the recognition or the acknowledgment of God accompanied by a demonstrative faith response to God. The notion of knowing God through demonstrative faith in Him is critical; because, as God reveals Himself and acts in our life situations, we come to know and believe Him more. That is accumulative faith. Accumulative faith comes about as a result of our accumulated encounters and experiences of God. The more we experience God and the more He reveals Himself to us and does greater things in our lives, the more our faith in Him grows and we learn to trust Him more.

3. Knowing God experientially and therefore personally, means that God plays a significant part in your life, in your thinking, in your planning, and in the way you conduct yourself. The way we think, behave, or act toward others gives some indication of whether or not we really know God. Hosea 4:1-2 for example, points out that where there is no knowledge of God sin is prevalent. Conversely, where God is known and taken seriously, people are more inclined to do justice, show mercy, demonstrate love and respect to others, live peaceably with others and help the poor and needy.[48] Jesus says in Matthew 7:16 that we are known by our fruits. This means that the way we behave toward others says a lot about who we are in Christ and just how much of a relationship we really do have with God whom we profess to know and love. To know God is to love God enough not to offend His holiness with unholy behaviors.

4. Let us now address the second question for guiding our understanding of the principles of knowing God, "How can we get to know God relationally and how does that knowledge change us?" We can know God relationally by having a sincere desire to be at one with Christ. Jesus says, "If you know Me you know My Father."[49] He also says, "I am the way and the truth and the life. No one comes to the Father except through Me."[50] If you know Jesus Christ the Son and have a saving relationship with Him, you know and have a saving relationship with God the Father because the glory of God was invested in Jesus from whom that glory shone with divine excellence as evidenced by His life and ministry. God is seeking to save us through Jesus Christ. Knowing Jesus then, not only draws us into close proximity to God, it also puts us in direct connection with God. If you know Christ a little, you know God just as little. If you know and love Jesus Christ a lot, then you also know and love God a lot. If you have found Jesus Christ, you have found God because it was in and through Jesus that God was present and is still working to reconcile us to Himself.[51]

---

[48] Jer 22:15-16; Mic 6:8

[49] Jn 8:19

[50] Jn 14:6

[51] 2 Cor 5:19

5. As we come to relationally know God through Jesus Christ and become acquainted with what He has done for us through the finished work of Christ, that knowledge renews us. Anyone who is in Christ is a new person because in Him and through Him, old things— our old habits and behaviors, our old sins and faults— have passed away in order that all things might become new.[52] As we have already established, change in our attitudes and behaviors begins with the Holy Spirit renewing and redirecting our minds toward God. By the power of the Holy Spirit, we become what we know and believe about God. As we respond to God's holiness and redeeming grace through Jesus Christ, knowledge of God leads us to repent of our sins as the Holy Spirit pours upon us God's forgiveness, justification, and sanctification, thus empowering us to develop through grace, a new identity, a new way of behaving and living out Christ, and therefore a new way of embracing and relating to God. When we embrace God's actions we know that moral transformation has taken place because we cannot know God and intentionally and habitually act outside of His moral framework without a deep sense of remorse.

6. The third question that may guide our understanding of the principles of knowing God is, "How is knowledge of God the basis for human excellence?" Knowledge of God is spiritual medicine for the soul as well as the impetus for moral excellence. Knowledge of God has a way of redirecting our thinking and perspective. With new perspective, the blindfold comes off and we are empowered to see rightly. When we are able to see rightly, we can act rightly towards God and our sisters and brothers. When we act rightly towards God and our sisters and brothers, we are leading excellent lives.

7. Human excellence is developed when we know God as:

- Mercy and we proceed to show mercy to our sisters and brothers
- A forgiving God and we learn to forgive those who wrong us, just as God in Christ has forgiven us
- Holiness and allow the Holy Spirit to develop in us attitudes and behaviors that are in keeping with the holiness of God

---

[52] 2 Cor 5:17

- Justice and we proceed to treat others fairly
- Truth and we learn to speak and live by truth
- Love and we proceed to love God and our neighbor
- Peace and we learn to live in peace with others
- Order and we learn to have order in our lives, relationships, and church
- Goodness and we proceed to demonstrate that goodness in our relationships with each other and in the world

8. After all, while it is the Christian hope to live eternally, we are not called to wait to be like God in the life after the resurrection. We are called to live a life that reflects the excellence of God in this life which is essentially our daily practice for living eternally with God. We were made to lead excellent lives here and now so that in living we may bring honor, glory, and praise to God who is intent on sharing His eternity with us.

9. We cannot say we know and love God when our lives are not guided by those moral attributes and principles that emanate from God. We cannot say we know God when truth is not an integral part of our way of life. We cannot say we know God when there is no love in us for anybody. We cannot say we have knowledge of God if bitterness, hatred, prejudice, and malice govern our lives and the way we respond to and treat other people. We cannot say we know God when the spirit of unforgiveness has us twisted and drenched in bitterness and revenge. We cannot say that we know God when our hearts are saturated with resentment toward others.

10. When we know God as holy, something of the holiness of God must rub off on us. When we know God, something of the righteousness of God needs to be manifested in our daily lives. When we know God, something of the goodness, something of the peace, something of the joy, something of the patience of God must rub off on us. And if we say we know and love the Lord Jesus, something of His humility and something of His obedience ought to influence us to be humble and obedient. Assuredly, knowledge of God does not leave us unchanged but ought rightly to change us into the holy image of the One who created us in His likeness and image. When God gives us

knowledge of Himself, God does so in order that we may become all that we know and believe about Him.

11. Knowledge of God leads to a new identity of ourselves in relationship to God. Our new identity in Christ inspires us to live out the Christ in us. Charry affirms that Christians are "not given a new identity and then left on [their] own, but [are] continuously led by God." Charry goes on to say: "The impetus for moral transformation comes from embracing God's actions."[53] Knowing God, who is revealed in the face of Jesus Christ and manifested in the presence and power of the Holy Spirit, is precisely what pulls us into the divine life and leads us to embrace God's action. Charry echoes this conviction when she writes:

> "The key to becoming divine is knowledge of God: knowledge of who he is, of the connection between God and us, what his expectations are for us. This knowledge confronts [us] with just how wrapped up in us God is, how intent on bringing us to himself, and where one's true identity is to be found. It is all designed to turn the head from distractions with lesser pursuits to the one goal worth pursuing."[54]

That one goal is the goal of eternal life for which every Christian believer aspires and of which God has promised us in Christ Jesus. We were made for eternity!

12. At no stage of our faith journey do we come to a state of moral goodness by our own merit. Christian formation and conformity to moral precepts are the direct results of divine grace into which we grow as we faithfully participate in the things and ways of God. Our lives are transformed through participation in worship, mission, and eschatological living because we see in worship, mission, and eschatology, a vision, something of the presence, something of the power and divine life of God that compels us to shift our focus from the pursuit of the mundane to the pursuit of God and His eternity. By

---

[53] Charry, 48
[54] Charry, 109

grace through faith, and as a working of the Holy Spirit, we absorb the qualities of God, the Object of our faith, so that we may become what we see and believe about God.

13. Knowledge of God not only awakens our awareness of God's existence, such knowledge revealed by God alone, is also intended to grab us at the very core of our being, and redirect our minds, attitudes, and behaviors toward God. Our minds are redirected to God so that through our participation in godly precepts, we are reordered to practice and reflect what is continuously fitting and proper to God's glory. As awareness changes us, it also leads us to intentionally pursue godly things. Such awareness or knowledge of God also stirs up in us thoughts and expectations of eternity. As Calvin remarked, "Knowledge ought not only to arouse us to the worship of God but also to awaken and encourage us to the hope of the future life."[55] Again, if, indeed, it is in the eternal God that we live, move and have our being, and it is, and if knowing God is eternal life,[56] then knowing God ought rightly to direct our thoughts and attention to eternal prospects so that we may diligently pursue God and His eternity, until our hope is complete and our souls find rest in Him at the revelation of His eternal glory.

14. Why then does God want us to "find" Him and therefore know Him? God reveals Himself to us and wants us to "find" Him so that we may know that we do not exist alone or without Him. God reveals Himself so that we may know that we need more than ourselves and our on again off again goodness to produce a life that is fruitful in holiness and therefore pleasing to Him. God wants us to know Him because when we know Him we will find in Him:

- The Great Deliverer
- The answer to our questions
- The solution to our problems
- The freedom from our bondage and the Savior for our souls.

---

[55] Calvin, *Institutes*, 62

[56] Jn. 17: 3

God wants us to know Him because when we know Him we will find that He is:

- The Giver of salvation
- Peace from our turmoil
- Riches for our poverty
- Light for our darkness
- Assurance for our despair
- Contentment for our anxiety and eternity for our temporality.

God wants us to find Him and know Him as our all in all and so that we may worship Him and go forth in the world as witnesses to His power and glory.

God wants us to know and experience Him so that we may develop the desire to not only taste of His goodness but also to hide in His goodness and become carriers of His goodness. The Psalmist says in Psalm 34: 8 "Taste and see that the LORD is good; blessed is the one who takes refuge in Him." To take refuge in anything you have to first know that it is there and so run to it. To take refuge in God, you must first know that He is there and that you can find safety and rest in Him. God wants you to know Him so that you may become absorbed with His goodness, nurtured by His precepts, and influenced by His holiness.

God wants you to know Him because if you know Him you will take the time to think about Him. If you take the time to think about Him, you will begin to act toward Him. If you act toward Him, you will begin to please Him. If you please Him, you are positioned to receive His blessings. If you receive His blessings, you will begin to live the divine life, which is the abundant life that Jesus came to give you (Jn 10:10).

Come taste and see that the Lord is good. In order to taste you must either slurp or take a bite out of something. I declare that God wants you to take a bite out of Him. God wants you to stop nibbling and take a big bite of all that He is. God wants you to take a bite out of:

- His Wisdom and knowledge
- His holiness and grace

- His power and love
- His goodness and mercy
- His kindness and forgiveness
- His creativity and redemption
- His sanctification and glory
- His truth and justice
- His patience and compassion
- His freedom and sufficiency
- His veracity and infinity.

These are just some of the attributes of God that He wants you to know about Him and gravitate toward. When you bite into God with faith and digest His attributes, wrap yourself into His Spirit and believe in His Christ, eternal life your soul shall have. Feeding on God fills us with the divine qualities that lead to our eternal duration. The good news today is that it has always been the divine design of God to draw us into knowledge of Him so that we can be inspired by that knowledge and drawn to repentance so that we might seek after Him and more diligently pursue His holy ways.

Having looked at knowledge as the first step in the process of spiritual transformation, let us now turn our attention to the second step, repentance.

B. Step Two: Repentance

1. The second step in the process of spiritual transformation is repentance. Repentance is our expressed sorrow for sin as well as our turning away from it. It is also our turning in joy towards God for forgiveness and empowerment to live above sin. Repentance is a direct result of the first step in spiritual transformation which is the reorientation or enlightenment of the mind through knowledge. As a result of our awareness of God, we are lovingly drawn to Him because we have come to know Him as holy and yet merciful to those of us who have made mistakes (sinned) and stand in need of forgiveness and reconciliation. Repentance is not the human choice of will. It is the Holy Spirit that makes us aware of the state

of our own sinfulness[57] and the destructive nature of sin. Knowledge of God instills within us the desire to be like Him. Because sin is diametrically opposed to everything that God is, based on what we have come to know about God, we are inspired by that knowledge to go to God in repentance so that He may rid us of sin's cruel bondage.

    2. It is God that gives us knowledge and awareness of Himself as well as awareness of our own moral state of existence. This awareness moves us to seek after God through repentance. Therefore, before repentance is our action, it is God's action and not purely the desire of the human will. As we have already seen, the human will, left alone is only capable of pursuing unprofitable things because even when it knows the difference between what is life and death, good and evil, right and wrong, the human will is bent on blindly following after destructive, mundane, and fleeting things rather than things eternal. It is for this reason that God, having given us a choice, has also helped us to make the right choice— the choice of life over death.[58] Repentance is therefore a turning away from sin and death and a turning to righteousness and life in God through the Lord Jesus. This desire to turn away from sin is a gift of grace. For, as 2 Timothy 2:25 indicates, it is God who grants repentance. We should understand, then, that repentance is a gift from God who seeks to help those who are in error, to come to their senses and find their way back to Him.

    3. It is also God that moves us to come to Him in repentance. God draws us to Himself because He is merciful and willing to forgive and convert or change the course of our lives by changing our thoughts and actions so that we may, by the help of divine grace, pursue His holy precepts (laws). Psalm 19:7 tells us that, "The law of the Lord is perfect, converting the soul..." The implication of this is that the correctness and rightness, the perfection and trustworthiness, the dependability and surety of the Word of God,[59] when heeded, brings about change in the believer's thoughts and behavior. This change moves us from the path of hopelessness and bondage to sin to a path of redemption, freedom, and hope in the Lord Jesus. We are also told in

---

[57] Jn 16: 8
[58] Deu. 30: 19
[59] Ps 19: 7-9

Romans 2:4 that it is the goodness and forbearance of God that lead us to repentance. Because we have come to know Him as goodness and mercy, instead of remaining with the guilt of sin and staying hopelessly disconnected from God, God, in His mercy draws us to Him so that He may grant us release through forgiveness.

C. Step Three: Forgiveness (Section One)
(Give It If You Want To Receive It— Matthew 6:14-16)

1. Forgiveness is a fundamental principle for Christian living and freedom yet it is one of the things holding many of us in bondage today. Most of us are fine with the intellectual principle of forgiveness and even the gift of it whether from God or from others. While we are comfortable with the intellectual principle of forgiveness, it is the actual practice of the full meaning and range of forgiveness that we have trouble with.

2. During the course of this discussion on forgiveness, I will attempt to answer the following questions and in the process find out what the Bible says about forgiveness:

- What is forgiveness?
- Is forgiveness a conscious choice, a physical act involving the will, or is it a feeling or an emotional state of being?
- By what means are we forgiven?
- Who should take the initiative in forgiveness?
- Why should we forgive those who offend us?
- How do we know that forgiveness has taken place?
- How should we forgive and should we forgive even when we do not feel like it?

3. What is forgiveness? Before we look at what forgiveness is, let us look at what forgiveness is not. Forgiveness is not forgetting. Forgiveness does not mean that we suddenly develop amnesia. People often say, "I will forgive, but

I will never forget." The truth is that while we are obligated to forgive, we are not obligated to forget. However, every time that we remember the hurt, we should also remember our forgiveness. That way, the memory of the hurt does not cause us further pain. Remembering our forgiveness whenever we remember our hurts empowers us to rise above the hurts. Remembering our forgiveness, the giving or receiving of it, means that we no longer bring up the past hurts and offenses that may cause further estrangement. Because forgiveness is the granting of pardon for sin or remission of any offense or debt, when we forgive, even though we do not necessarily forget the offense, forgiveness necessitates that we give up all claim of hurt or offense committed against us.

4. Forgiveness is not pretending as though nothing was wrong, that no offense was committed, and that no one was hurt. We should never act as though the past offense never existed or even still exists in our minds and sometimes is like a wall between us and other people. It happened. It is real. We felt offended or have offended. We are hurt or have hurt others. We should not however, continue to use past hurts and offenses as weapons against others. If forgiveness has taken place, the past is dead and buried in the past. That should mean that the past offense and hurt are dead issues. We may not be able to ignore the fact that hurt occurred; but we cannot change the past. Wishing it never happened or that it would magically go away will not make it go away. When we forgive, then, it is not the past that we are seeking to change. When we forgive we are seeking to transform the present and change future relationships.

5. Forgiveness is not conditional. We should not demand to see change in others before we offer them forgiveness. We do not wait to see what someone does before we offer pardon and seek after atonement and the mending of relationships. God did not wait for us to start doing what is right before He forgave us. We are reminded in Romans 5:6 and 8 that, "While we were still weak at the right time Christ died for the ungodly…God showed His great love for us by sending Christ to die for us while we were still sinners." Because we could not and cannot change ourselves, God forgave us so that

we might be empowered to do right before Him and before our sisters and brothers.

6. Forgiveness is not weakness. When we forgive, it does not mean that we are giving in. It takes strength to forgive. The weak are more inclined to hold grudges. Those strong in faith and grounded in the love of God should be more willing to forgive because they know that they have been beneficiaries of God's mercy and grace. Certainly, God forgiving us is not an indication of weakness but a demonstration of the power of His love and compassion for the weakened condition that sin and human offenses place upon us. Forgiveness is indeed an attribute of the strong—strong in faith; strong in love; strong in compassion and kindness!

7. Forgiveness is not to be partially given. When Jesus says we should forgive seventy times seven He was not just saying we should forgive 490 times or as many times as possible. In the Bible, seven is the number of completion. So when Jesus says seventy times seven, He is saying forgive completely. Forgive without the pain. Forgive without the malice. Forgive without the desire for revenge. Forgive in love because love makes us complete. Listen to 1 John 4: 16-18:

> "We have come to know and have believed the love which God has for us. God is love, and the one who abides in love abides in God, and God abides in him/her. This is how love is made complete in us, so that we may have confidence in the Day of Judgment; because as He is, so also are we in this world. There is no fear in love; but perfect love casts out fear, because fear involves punishment, and the one who fears is not completed [perfected] in love….

8. Forgiveness does not mean that we have lost. Yes, I concede that forgiveness empowers us to lose the anger and the bitterness that accompany the offenses and hurt. As we shall see, when we do not forgive we imprison ourselves in the stronghold of bitterness. But when we forgive, we win the freedom of the offender and our own freedom from the offense. When human relationships are affected by the wrong actions of another, it can lead to bitterness, anger, resentment, and the hurt that imprison us. Forgiving one

another therefore sets us free from bitterness and provides an opportunity for us to experience the kind of joy and goodwill that lead to the healing of our hurts. Let me give you a "selfish" reason to forgive —you will feel better! When we free ourselves from being "the offended one," we unlock our prison of bitterness and are empowered to live a life of unrestricted freedom in Christ Jesus. If Jesus did not withhold His forgiveness from us, why should we withhold our forgiveness from others?

9. Let us look at five (5) mutually inclusive keys to walking in forgiveness—Keys to forgiveness number one: We need to accept forgiveness as a command and not as a suggestion. As a command from the Lord Jesus, forgiveness is a divine principle that fixes things between us and between us and God. Jesus says, "For if you forgive others their trespasses or sin against you, your heavenly Father will also forgive you. But if you do not forgive others their trespasses and sins against you, neither will your heavenly Father forgive your trespasses and sins" (Mt. 6:14-15). Jesus says in Mt 5: 23-24, "If therefore you are presenting your offering at the altar, and there remember [not that you despise your brother or sister, but] that your brother/sister has something against you, leave your offering at the altar, and go your way and be reconciled to your brother/sister, and then come and present your offering." In other words, God does not want to talk to us about forgiveness until we have reconciled our differences with one another (Mt. 5:24). The idea here is that our hearts cannot be in the right place in prayer and communion with God when we are holding grudges against our sisters and brothers in our hearts. It is therefore not proper for us to ask something of God that we are intentionally withholding from others. Also, Jesus tells us to make things right with our brothers and sisters because the heart that harbors anger and past offense cannot be completely focused on worship.

10. When Jesus says get up from the altar and go and make things right with our brother or sister with whom there is an offense, does that mean that we are responsible for someone else's offensive behavior and grudges against us? Not entirely or at all; unless we are the cause of the offense or grudge. What we may gather from what Jesus is saying to us is that we need to have our minds and spirits at peace in order to experience true worship. It is

therefore profitable to be reconciled with those who have something against you, before you bring your sacrifices of praise before God. Regarding ownership of grudges and offensive behaviors, Jesus says in Matthew 5: 9-12,

> "Blessed are the peacemakers, for they shall be called sons/daughters of God. Blessed are those who have been persecuted for the sake of righteousness [not sin, but righteousness], for theirs is the kingdom of heaven. Blessed are you when people cast insults at you, and persecute you, and say all kinds of evil against you falsely [not truly], on account of Me. Rejoice, and be glad [that is, do not let your conscience be troubled as if you were guilty of their hostility], for your reward in heaven is great, for so they persecuted the prophets who were before you."

We may also gather from this statement of Jesus that we are to be peacemakers amongst ourselves so that our hearts will be in harmony with God whom we seek to worship.

11. We may also gather from this statement by Jesus that sometimes people will hold something against you when they should not. They will insult you, persecute you, and say all kinds of evil against you falsely. What do you do in such circumstances? Do you get up from the altar and stop worshiping just because someone feels like this about you? If that is the case you will never have time to worship because somebody somewhere seems to always have something against you or someone else. If every time you recall that somebody did you some wrong or that somebody is holding a grudge against you, you have to get up from prayer or worship, you will never finish a prayer or become fully engaged in worship. If that is the case, Jesus Himself would never have been able to worship. He was constantly opposed. The Scribes and Pharisees persistently sought to trip Him up and persecute Him. They tried to kill Him. They tried to shame Him. Was He responsible for this? Assuredly not! Not only that, He said that the same would be true for His disciples for in Matthew 24:9 He said, "You will be hated by all nations on account of My name." What Jesus is directing us to do is what is written in Proverbs 19:11— "The discretion of a person makes

that person slow to anger, and willing to overlook a transgression." In other words, get past the hurt and the offense so that you may freely worship God from a heart that is not fixed on revenge, malice, and anger, but on peace, love, joy, and righteousness. Regarding offenses and our treatment of the offense and the offender, Proverbs 24:29 also reminds us that we should not say, "I will do to such and such a person just as he/she has done to me…" Colossians 3:12-13 reminds us that, "…As the elect of God, holy and beloved, [we should] put on tender mercies, kindness, humility, meekness, longsuffering; bearing with one another, and forgiving one another, [and] if anyone has a complaint against another; even as Christ forgave you, so you also must forgive."

12. Keys to forgiveness number two: There is no limit to forgiveness. In Matt 18:21-22 we read: "Then Peter came to Him and said, "Lord, how often shall my brother sin against me, and I forgive him, up to seven times?' Jesus said to him, 'I do not say to you, up to seven times, but up to seventy times seven.…" Jesus did not mean forgive 490 times and stop, it is limitless. Forgive as often as it is needed. The question therefore becomes, "How many times do you want (or need) to be forgiven by God?" If therefore we want to be forgiven, as often as we need it from God we should offer it to others.

13. Key to forgiveness number three: Unforgiveness holds us in bondage. In order to illustrate this bondage situation that unforgiveness puts us in, let us read from Matt 18:23-35:

> "Therefore the kingdom of heaven is like a certain king who wanted to settle accounts with his servants. And when he had begun to settle accounts, one was brought to him who owed him ten thousand dollars. But as he was not able to pay, his master commanded that he be sold, with his wife and children and all that he had, so that that payment might be settled. The servant therefore fell down before him, saying, 'Master, have patience with me, and I will pay you all of it.' 'Then the master of that servant was moved with compassion, released him, and forgave him the debt that he owed. But that servant went out and found one of his fellow servants who owed him a hundred dollars. When he found him, he laid hands on him and took

him by the throat, saying, 'Pay me what you owe me!' 'So his fellow servant fell down at his feet and begged him, saying, 'Have patience with me, and I will pay you all that I owe.' 'But he would not relent. Instead, he further assaulted the man that owed him and threw him into prison until he should pay the debt. So when his fellow servants saw what had been done, they were very grieved, and came and told their master all that had taken place. Then his master, after he had called him, said to him, 'You wicked servant! I forgave you all that debt of ten thousand dollars because you begged me. Why did you not also have compassion on your fellow servant, just as I had pity on you?' 'And his master was angry, and delivered him to the torturers until he should pay all that was due to him. So My heavenly Father also will do to you if each of you, from his/her heart, does not forgive his/her brother and sister their trespasses."

What Jesus is telling us here is that unforgiveness keeps us imprisoned by our own desire to exact revenge and hurt on others even when we are guilty of the same offense. Unforgiveness tortures our minds and spirits. It blocks the forgiveness from our heavenly Father. By virtue of our own sinful behaviors, past and present, we were forgiven a debt that we could never pay back. Any debt owed to us by another person is small in comparison to what we owe God. We want to beg God for forgiveness of our debt, our sin, and our offenses, but we want to make sure that we collect on the offense of others even if they have to suffer, as long as they pay up.

14. Unforgiveness holds us in bondage because it can limit or even cut off the blessings of God for our lives. Matthew 6:14-15 makes it clear that we can block our own forgiveness. If we do not forgive, we cannot be forgiven. Unforgiveness is a sin which blocks prosperity. Unforgiveness leaves us bitter and our hearts hardened and void of grace. Hebrews 12:15 reminds us to "see that no one falls short of the grace of God; because if we do, bitterness will take root, trouble will spring up, and by it many will become defiled."

15. Keys to forgiveness number four: Forgiveness is a choice. Though a command, we can choose to forgive or not to forgive. When we forgive,

we are walking in obedience before God. When we do not forgive we have chosen to disobey God. While offenses are real and even though our feelings may be hurt by those offenses, forgiveness is not a feeling. It is a decision that is inspired by the spirit and the heart that has chosen to obey God. As a choice that is made with a heart that seeks to please God, we also make the choice to see our offender as a living spirit and not an enemy. As we choose to forgive, we must be able to also see our offender as someone that God would forgive as much as He would forgive us.

16. Keys to forgiveness number five: Forgiveness leads to reconciliation. Forgiveness makes things right between you and others and between you and God. Forgiveness as reconciliation is the act of causing two people or groups after an argument or disagreement, to become affable or neighborly again. Because of the moral compass and restored rightness that forgiveness offers us, we cannot afford to harbor the spirit of unforgiveness and bitterness in our lives. Because of the freedom that we experience from having been forgiven, we must keep our conscience clear and keep ourselves reconciled to others. Because of the burden of the offense, we cannot afford to dwell on the offense. Because of our own imperfections and frequent need for forgiveness from God, we need to yield to the command of the Lord Jesus to forgive so that we might be forgiven. Listen then to Romans 12:14-18:

> "Bless those who persecute you; bless and do not curse. Rejoice with those who rejoice, and weep with those who weep. Be of the same mind toward one another. Do not set your mind on high things, but associate with the humble. Do not be wise in your own opinion. Repay no one evil for evil. Have regard for good things in the sight of all people. If it is possible, as much as depends on you, live peaceably with all men."

And remember, always forgive your enemies, it annoys the devil but it pleases God!

17. Why should we forgive those who offend us? We should forgive because we frequently offend God and always stand in need of His forgiveness.

If we desire forgiveness from God, then we are required and must be willing to forgive others. God's treatment of us is an example of how we should treat others. Receiving God's promise of forgiveness is conditional on our own willingness to forgive. If we cannot forgive those who have offended us, we have no right to expect God whom we have frequently offended by our sins and wayward tendencies to forgive us. Forgiveness is freely given and provided through Christ and given to all who come to Him. In Matthew 10:8 we are told that what we receive freely we must freely give away. There are therefore two sides to forgiveness— the giving of it and the receiving of it. Forgiveness is a divine gift and a divine quality that must be practiced among humanity.

Forgiveness
(Section Two)
(It Is Freedom from Bondage— Ephesians 4: 32; Colossians 3: 12-14)

1. The absence of forgiveness in a person's life is a destructive bondage that causes strife, division, depression, oppression, sickness, and broken relationships including marriage and divorce. Unforgiveness is bondage because it locks us in the torture chamber of physical and mental anguish. From a spiritual perspective, unforgiveness holds us captive in the realm of demonic strongholds. We speak of unforgiveness as demonic stronghold because it is a spiritual problem that is diametrically opposed to the divine and therefore spiritual standards of God. In order to break free from such stronghold, we need to renounce the spirit of unforgiveness that holds us bondage by thoughts of revenge and malice that lead to estrangement between us and God as well as between us and our fellow humans. To renounce a behavior or practice is to give it up, refuse to participate in it, or to resign from the practice of such behavior. Whereas repenting is directed toward God, renouncing is directed toward the enemy or force that is holding us hostage. To renounce is also to bring into subjection any word or action that is contradictory to the word and

principles of God. To break free from the bondage of unforgiveness we need to intentionally declare that we will no longer align ourselves with things that oppose God. God's nature is to forgive and restore. We must therefore choose to forgive and not be held captive by our hurts and the offenses committed against us.

2. If forgiveness is to take place and our freedom from sin and human offenses obtained, we should not wait for someone to apologize. We cannot always wait for people to apologize to us before we forgive them. Some people will not even acknowledge that they have done you wrong. If they cannot acknowledge that they have done you wrong they cannot be expected to apologize for their offense. But we must proceed to forgive. Sometimes telling some people that you forgive them will cause them to feel insulted and angry even if they are the offenders. However, if you need to let it go, and you really do need to, speak forgiveness into your life and act as though the person is before you receiving it. That way you can get on with your life and live in peace without the bondage that comes with resentment and hatred, and the revenge and hurt that you feel from the offense. If healing from the hurt is to take place we need to forgive. We often say that we can do all things through Christ who strengthens us (Philippians 4: 13). Well then, forgiveness is one of those things that we can do through Christ who lives in and strengthens us.

3. Forgiveness does not mean that our sins or offenses have been overlooked or lightly dismissed. Forgiveness is not condoning wrong. By forgiving someone, we are not saying the action was ok. A wrong committed against another is never ok. When we forgive someone for example, it does not mean that we have overlooked the offense. It only means that we value the person and the relationship more than we value the offense. God values us more than the sins that we commit against Him. Therefore He forgives us so that we would not be bothered by the guilt of the sin or offense. God's forgiveness is based upon His great love for us.

4. It should be noted that when we forgive someone who has done us wrong we cannot remit or get rid of that person's sin. That is something the

person has to do with God. We forgive the offense to restore our relationship with the person; but only God can forgive the sin that has been committed. This is so because every sin is ultimately committed against God.

5. Is it okay to feel anger and to desire justice from the person who has offended us? The Bible does say that we can be angry but we should not sin (Ephesians 4: 26). This question of anger due to an offense against us presents another reason to pray for the person we need to forgive. We can pray for God to deal with the injustices. We can pray for God to bring clarity and forgiveness to an offensive situation and leave that prayer at the altar. When we pray for the offender and even for our own offense against others, we no longer have to carry the anger. Although it is normal for us to feel anger toward sin and injustice, it is not our job to judge and seek to condemn the other person.

6. From a human perspective, forgiveness does not mean that we are suddenly bosom buddies with those who have offended us. Though forgiveness makes it possible for people to be friends again, some people you forgive, but may have to feed with a long stick. We are to love everyone, but not everyone is necessarily our buddy. You will forgive some people but they may still have a clinched fist when they are around you. You can forgive some people and find that they still cut you with their eyes and push up their noses at you. You should forgive and love everyone but not everyone qualifies to be in your inner circle. No one should stay in abusive and toxic, snake infested (deceitful and conniving) relationships and situations. We should forgive but we should not position ourselves to be hurt in the future by staying close to someone who has proven again and again to be untrustworthy, unkind and downright vindictive and cruel. That being said, we should forgive everyone but always remember that a snake is snake and a rat will always be a rat. From a human perspective, friendship may grow out of forgiveness, but sometimes the best we can hope for is tolerance, forbearance, and a peaceful coexistence. Sometimes that can be done with a long stick.

7. Forgiveness compels us to let go of our pride. The action of the other person may cause you pain and deserve your anger but instead of anger, you must chose to let go of your pride and in the process of doing so, release

the offender from his or her guilt. That is the problem many people have with forgiveness; forgiveness releases people and cancels our claim to injury from another person's words or action. Many people would much rather hold something over another person. They want to hold their offender down. They want them to pay for what they did to them. They want them to hurt as much and even more than they have been hurt. Pride makes us want those kinds of exactions. But pride also sustains and even magnifies our hurts. One of the reasons we have difficulty forgiving is because it messes with our pride. Forgiveness forces us to give up our pride and sets us free from it. To forgive means to say, "What you have said or done has truly and deeply hurt me; but even though I feel the pain of what you have said and done, I have chosen to release you from penalty." As you release the person of guilt something awesome happens; you find relief from your pain. A good lesson to take away from this is that you cannot hold your offender down and expect to soar. In order to hold someone down you have to stay down with him/her. You must consciously choose to release the offender so that you too can find relief from the offense and so rise above the hurt.

    8. So then, is forgiveness a conscious choice, or an emotional response? I believe that forgiveness is a choice we make through a decision of our will, motivated by obedience to God and the command of Jesus Christ to forgive. The Bible instructs us to forgive as the Lord forgave us (Colossians 3:13). We are to bear with each other and forgive whatever grievances we may have against one another. Forgiveness is a choice that involves self-sacrifice. In order to forgive others we have to surrender our desire for revenge and retribution. We offer the offender free grace, just as God by His grace has forgiven us. Grace forgives what it cannot excuse.

    9. How should we forgive and should we forgive even when we do not feel like it? We forgive by faith. We forgive out of obedience. Since forgiveness goes against our nature, we must forgive by faith, whether or not we feel like it. Forgiving by obedience and faith means that we must trust God to do the work in us that needs to be done in order that forgiveness will be complete. I believe God honors our commitment to obey Him and by our desire to please Him when we choose to forgive. We must continue to forgive by faith, which

is our task, until the work of forgiveness is complete. Assuredly, it is God's task of working on our hearts to complete it.

10. We should forgive just as God forgives. Forgiving one another requires that we extend kindness and compassion just as in Christ, God forgives us. As noted above, we do not always forgive because we let pride get in the way of forgiveness. We say for example: "I will not let him/her do that to me and get away with it." Or, "I am not going out like that." It should be pointed out that even though God takes the initiative in offering us forgiveness and presents us the opportunity to be restored, not all of us will accept God's gift of forgiveness. Not everyone that offends you or whom you have offended will ask for or accept your forgiveness. You are however, obligated to offer them the opportunity to receive it.

11. **What then is forgiveness?** Forgiveness is the antidotal remedy that is divinely applied to our hurts and injuries and wounded relationships with God and each other so that healing, reconciliation, and atonement can take place. Forgiveness is atonement and the removal of sin. It is empowerment to rise above offense, hurt feelings and revengeful human thoughts. Forgiveness is the dispensation of grace that gives us the divine sanction to live out the Christian life. Forgiveness is God removing our wounded wings and fitting us with new ones so that we can soar above the guilt and burden of sin.

12. Because sin is burdensome, by His mercy, God releases us of it so that we may be elevated to new levels of awareness concerning His holiness as well as to new levels of relationship with Christ. Forgiveness is the taking away as well as the cancellation of our sins and offenses. The idea of cancellation is supported in Luke 7: 42-43. When our sins are forgiven , it is God's way of setting us free from the guilt and punishment of sin so that they will no longer burden us. As indicated earlier, forgiveness does not mean that our sins or offenses have been overlooked or lightly dismissed. When we forgive someone for example, it does not mean that we have overlooked the offense. God's forgiveness is based upon His great love for us. For God so loved the world that He gave His only begotten Son to atone for our sins.

13. By what means are we forgiven? We are forgiven by the sacrificial death of Jesus. When Christ died for us He literally lifted our sins upon the cross thus signifying them being taken away from us and placed upon Him. Through Christ, we are not only forgiven, we are given a new life and a new opportunity to make things right in our relationship with others and with God.

14. How do we know that forgiveness has taken place? We know that forgiveness has taken place when the reason for estrangement or disagreement between two persons is overcome by the initiative of one of those persons to restore the once good relationship. Since God is the One that prompts us to seek Him through repentance, it also means that God is the One that takes the initiative to restore us. We know that we are forgiven when steps are taken to reconcile and when the guilt of the offense no longer torments us. Regarding our relationship with others, we know that forgiveness has taken place when we no longer feel resentful toward the person whom we have offended or who has offended us.

15. Who then, should take the initiative in forgiveness? People are not always willing to take responsibility for their actions. Someone however, has to take responsibility for bringing about forgiveness. Do not offer forgiveness because you think you are the "bigger" person. Well, thinking that you are is one thing, but when you verbalize to the other person that you are the "bigger" person you are also sending the message that you are also the better person and that he or she is not. That realization, real or perceived may lead to further estrangement between you and the other person and may potentially invoke anger and resentment. Furthermore, even though you may be the person hurt, you should take the initiative to forgive because you know it is the right and godly thing to do. Remember, our sins are offensive to God but He takes the initiative in forgiving us by lovingly drawing us to Himself so that we may realize the need to respond to Him, confess our sins, repent or express sorrow for them and so receive His forgiveness. If your brother or sister sins against you as Mathew 18: 15 indicates, you should take the initiative to forgive as many times as is humanly possible.

16. Learning how to forgive others is one of the most unnatural duties in the Christian life. The command of Jesus to forgive others their offense seventy times seven is a good indication that forgiving others is not entirely easy. It goes against our human tendency to let go of hurts. Forgiveness is a supernatural act that Jesus Christ was capable of, but when we are hurt by someone, we want to hold a grudge. It is therefore not uncommon for Christians to have questions about forgiveness. Forgiveness does not come easily for most of us. We want justice and revenge. Our natural instinct is to recoil in self-protection when we have experienced injury caused by the offense of others. As we recoil, like venomous rattle snakes, we lash out and launch ourselves in defensive modes, and with words and actions intending to hurt others as we have been hurt by them. When we have been done wrong, we do not naturally overflow with mercy, grace and forgiveness. Because forgiveness poses such a challenge for us, we need to trust God with the initiation and completion of the process of forgiveness between Him and us and between others and ourselves. It is important to forgive because in doing so we discover the secret to successfully restoring our relationship with God and each other as well as for living the Christian life. As we practice the art and exercise the gift of forgiveness, we find freedom from personal and spiritual injury and bondage.

17. Forgiveness is freedom from bondage. It is freedom from hatred and malice. It is freedom from pain and anger. It is freedom from malicious thoughts and actions. Forgiveness is freedom from the spirit of revenge. Without the soul cleansing and mind regulating power of forgiveness, human relationships would be in constant states of disaster and restrictions. Without forgiveness, no matter how we try to love and please each other, because of our human faults and weaknesses, and because of the human desire to exact revenge, we would fail to love and nurture healthy relationships. With our failures to forgive, we will be left with hurts and anger. The ultimate relief from the bondage of sin, hurt, and anger is forgiveness.

18. Forgiveness is freedom from turmoil and the freedom to live in peace and walk in the holiness of God. Forgiveness is the freedom to let

go of misery and the holding on to calmness and happiness and contentment. I find that people who can forgive are usually more sweet-natured and pleasant to be around than those wallowing in resentment, bitterness and hatred. No one wants to be near to a person who is consumed with bitterness. Learn to forgive and release the sweetness of Christ in you. When we forgive others we are set free from the strangle-hold of unforgiveness. That way, we may grab hold of the freedom to follow God without the chains of bitterness and malice restricting us and choking the very life out of us. That is the power of forgiveness. It warms the human heart while cooling and taking the sting of hatred and malice and revenge out of us. Forgiveness gives us the opportunity to draw closer to God so that we may live in and by the holiness of God.

19. Forgiveness sets us free. Because forgiveness sets us free, if we do not move on pretty quickly from the state of mind that the offense and hurt bring to us, we may get stuck in our anger and bitterness. If we are stuck in anger and bitterness we really are the ones to suffer. If we do not forgive we disable our happiness for today and our future is stunted as we end up lost in the bondage of our thoughts of bitterness, revenge, retaliation and hatefulness. When we do not forgive and when we do not seek after God's power and grace to empower us to forgive, we are the ones left spiritually impaired and wounded. When in faith we surrender to God, we give God the opportunity to put His benevolence on display; thus making right what is wrong and fixing what is broken in our lives.

FORGIVENESS
(SECTION THREE)
(God's Benevolent Fixing Of Us— Psalm 51)

1. Psalm 51 is a great example of the repentant cry of a broken person and that person's appeal to the benevolence of God. This Psalm is rightly called the penitential Psalm. Other penitential Psalms would be Psalms 6, 25, 32, 38, 39, 40, 102, 130, and 143. Psalm 51 is considered the greatest of the penitential Psalms because of its spiritual underpinning and

focus. It is a Psalm of personal awareness and ownership of a wrong—sin. It is a Psalm of repentance and a cry for personal renewal. It is the deep expression of a heart that is overwhelmed by shame and riddled with brokenness caused by guilt. It is a cry of, as well as a declaration of deliverance from despair. It is an appeal by the penitent soul for the removal of sin and the restoration of joy. Verses 1-2 report the human cry for God's forgiveness. Verses 3-5 reveal that personal admission and brokenness is what makes genuine confession and repentance the basis for our appeal to God. A broken willing spirit is therefore the sinner's best preparation for renewal. Verses 6-12 outline the sinner's petition for cleansing and renewal. If we observe carefully we will see that before an answer is given, David, assuming God's merciful answer, committed himself to giving God praise. In verses 13-17 we see him demonstrating change as he commits himself to being a living witness and a walking testimony to God's goodness and mercy so that others like him can find their way back to God.

2. This psalm gives us an inside view of the mind of the repentant sinner. It reveals that the Psalmist is well aware that sin can only be adequately dealt with by God. Listen to his appeal in verses 1-2: "Have mercy on me, O God, according to Your unfailing love; according to Your great compassion blot out my transgressions. Wash away all my iniquity and cleanse me from my sin." The thing about sin is that you can try to hide it but it will only burden your soul and oppress your heart and spirit. This Psalm is the cry of the human soul who can find no peace and find no hope in the attempt to hide sin. The rediscovery of our peace and hope can only be in our admission, confession, repentance, and total dependence on the benevolent mercy of God. In this Psalm the truth about sin is therefore revealed. Sin is transgression or iniquity because it is offensive and disruptive behaviors that destroy our peace, cripple our hope, and adversely affect our relationships with each other and with God.

3. When we realize that we have sinned, we have a choice. On one hand, we can see sin for the evil that it is and repent of it. When we do, we

discover and receive the forgiveness and cleansing power of God (Jeremiah 33:8; 1 John 1:9). Or, on the other hand, we can harden our hearts and go deeper into that sin until it adversely defines and more deeply defiles us and our relation with God and each other.

4. Sin is transgression. As transgression, sin is rebellion against God. As a source of guilt, sin as an offense tends to encourage us to move further away from God. Like Adam and Eve in the garden, we tend to want to hide from God because, even instinctively, we are well aware of His holiness and the guilt of our offense makes us want to hide ourselves because of shame. That is never the right direction to go because the shame and guilt that we feel and experience because of sin can only be relieved when we seek after God. When we flirt with sin, we fall for the lie that we can control it. We cannot relive ourselves of sin. We need God for that!

5. Sin is iniquity. As iniquity, sin is perversion. Perversion is the state of changing something good to something evil. From the dictionary's perspective, iniquity means the lack of justice or righteousness. It is wickedness as in a wicked act. From the Bible's perspective, the Bible uses words such as iniquity, transgression, and trespass to indicate levels of disobedience to God. All of these words are categorized as "sin." Micah 2:1 says, "Woe to those who plan iniquity, to those who plot evil on their beds! At morning's light they carry it out because it is in their power to do it." The Hebrew word used most often for "iniquity" means "guilt worthy of punishment." Iniquity is sin at its worst. Iniquity is premeditated evil, continuing, and escalating.

6. When we give ourselves over to a sinful lifestyle, we are committing iniquity because by giving way to a lifestyle of sin, sin has become our master (Romans 6:14). As iniquity, sin pollutes the human mind. Polluted minds will only lead to more polluted behaviors. That is why when we sin and feel that we can control it, we find ourselves like David in 2 Samuel 11, in the case of Bathsheba and Uriah, doing something sinful to cover up the sin we have already committed. As disruptive and polluted behavior, sin leads to personal and relational ruins. Sin destroys our souls' relationship with God. If our relationship with God is perverted, our relationship with other

humans cannot be genuinely healthy ones either. Because of his awareness of the nature of sin and the One to whom the offence is first directed we find the sinner in Psalm 51 saying, "Against You, You only have I sinned and done this terrible thing." Here we find the sinner confessing, repenting and asking that his sin be blotted out; that he may be washed, cleansed and made pure again as he is purged with hyssop: "Cleanse me with hyssop, and I will be clean; wash me, and I will be whiter than snow" (Psalm 51:7). What he is asking for here is more than just forgiveness so far as we may be able to relate forgiveness or extend it to other humans. Just as in the Old Testament blood and hyssop purified a defiled person, so Jesus' shed blood purifies us from the defilement of our sin. As the blood of Jesus remits our sins, cleanses our souls and renews our spirits by removing our sins, the Psalmist David is not just asking for a physical cleansing. Rather, he is asking God to cleanse him spiritually as he confesses his sin. He is asking for complete deliverance from the pollution of sin. He is asking for his record to be wiped clean and a fresh start given to him. He was desperate to be set from the thought and the burden that the guilt of sin brought upon him. We therefore find the Psalmist David overwhelmed by his sin-stricken soul appealing to the benevolent mercy of God. David went to God because he knew that because of God's benevolent grace and mercy, He will not despise someone that comes to Him with a broken spirit and a contrite heart. God obligates Himself to listen and receive those who come to Him with broken and contrite hearts because He says through the prophet Isaiah in Isaiah 66:2, "These are the ones I look on with favor: those who are humble and contrite in spirit, and who tremble at My word."

    7.   Forgiveness requires that we forgive just as God in Christ has forgiven us. Forgiving one another requires that we extend kindness and compassion just as in Christ, God in His benevolence has shown us. As I have shown above, we do not always forgive or seek forgiveness because we allow pride to get in the way of our need to ask for it, receive it, and offer it. Because of foolish human pride, even though God takes the initiative in offering us forgiveness and presents us the opportunity to be restored, not all of us will accept God's gift of forgiveness. Conversely not everyone that offends you or

whom you have offended will ask for or accept your forgiveness. Nonetheless, you are obligated to offer them the opportunity to receive it. In Matthew 18, Jesus tells us several stories to help us understand forgiveness. In that chapter, we see that human beings, like sheep, are likely to make mistakes or go astray. When human relationships are affected by the wrong actions of another, it can lead to bitterness and resentment. Forgiving one another therefore sets us free from bitterness and provides an opportunity for us to rediscover and experience love, joy, and the potential for friendship that come from the healing of our hurts and the mending of our relationships. This is precisely what God does for us when He forgives us. He restores us. He renews our joy and gives us the opportunity to rediscover His great love for us.

8. Forgiveness is not something we earn. Forgiveness is God's benevolent fixing of us. God is benevolent and is therefore supremely devoted to doing good to us and for us. Because of His benevolence, God engages all His powers to promote the highest good of His people. God is eternally benevolent— not benevolent at one time, and selfish at another. God is forever benevolent; forever compassionate; forever merciful; and forever willing and able to forgive. Without change, God is benevolently the same. God is immutable. Therefore, all that He does to restore and renew us is unchanging. God is eternally benevolent and therefore eternally merciful and forgiving. Forgiveness is a gift granted us by God's grace and favor because He is a benevolent God.

9. As a gift from God, forgiveness puts us in a position of trust and obedience to God. Because we know God as the benevolent and merciful God, as we trust Him enough to go to Him in repentance expecting to receive His forgiveness, grace, and mercy, we should also seek to obey Him as an affirmation of the sincerity of our repentance. Obedience should always follow forgiveness. Otherwise, our repentance would not have the value of regret and remorse that would subsequently keep us diligent in the pursuit of a new direction of faith, obedience, and holiness. Indeed, our repentance is an indication that we are so sorry that we will aspire to no longer do the thing that was offensive in the first place. Obedience is important in the process of forgiveness because it also shows that we are willing to be influenced and

led by the Holy Spirit to obediently follow the ways of God as we learn to develop and display attitudes and behaviors that are indicative of God's forgiven daughters and sons.

10. Humans may or may not show mercy but because of His benevolent grace, God is merciful. I recently watched the trilogy of the Rambo movies with Sylvester Stallone. One of Rambo's (Stallone) friends starring Richard Crenna as Colonel Sam Trautman, was imprisoned in Afghanistan in a Russian controlled prison holding. Rambo attempted to rescue his friend but his first attempt failed. Amazed that Rambo was even able to infiltrate the security of the prison holding complex, the prison commander in charge demanded of the imprisoned friend concerning who Rambo was. He then asked, "What do you think this man is, God?" To that, Rambo's Friend Colonel Sam Trautman responded, "God will have mercy, he (Rambo) wont." It was David, the presumed writer of the book of Psalms, who, in 1 Chronicles 21 committed an offense by manipulating the census reports of Israel. In verse 8 of said chapter, David prayed saying, "I have sinned badly in what I have just done, substituting statistics for trust; forgive my sin—I've been really stupid." In verses 9-10, GOD answered by speaking to Gad, David's pastor saying, "Go and give David this message: 'GOD's word: You have your choice of three punishments; choose one and I will do the rest.'" In verses 11-12, Gad, David's Pastor, delivered the message to David: "Do you want three years of famine, three months of running from your enemies while they chase you down, or three days of the sword of God...? Think it over and make up your mind. What shall I tell the One who sent me?" It did not take long for David to make a decision about the options available to him because in verse 13 David made his choice saying, "They are all terrible! But I would rather be punished by God whose mercy is great, than to fall into human hands." Because of His loving kindness He will punish but He will also have mercy. God will be merciful because His benevolence will not and cannot allow Him to do otherwise. Like David, I would also rather be in the hands of God than to fall into the hands of humans. In the hands of my peers, because of my errors and offenses/sins I am just another unworthy person guilty and deserving of punishment. But in the hand of the benevolent God, I can find grace, mercy and redemption.

11. When trouble surrounds you, and you need to be delivered, place yourself in the hand of God because your deliverance depends on whose hands you are in.

A basketball in my hands is worth no more than $19. But a basketball in LeBron James' hand is worth a two year $42.1 million deal and over $492.1 million in his career up until 2016… It depends on whose hands it is in.

A baseball in my hands is worth about $6. But in the hand of the Los Angeles Dodgers' superstar pitcher, Clayton Kershaw, it is worth a record seven-year, $215 million. It depends on whose hand it is in.

A baseball bat in my hands is worth $80 to $175. But a baseball bat in the hands of 2013 season New York Yankees' third baseman Alex Rodriguez is worth an annual salary of $29 million. It depends on whose hands it is in.

A tennis racket is useless in my hands…But it is priceless in the hands of Rafael Nadal or Venus and Serena Williams. It depends on whose hands it is in.

A rod in my hands will keep away a wild animal and crush the head of those snakes in my life. But under the anointing of God, a rod in Moses' hands will part the mighty sea. It depends on whose hands it is in.

A sling shot in my hands is only a child's toy perhaps capable of killing small birds. But a sling shot in David's hand is a mighty weapon capable of slaying a giant. It depends on whose hands it is in.

Two fish and five loaves of bread in my hands will only offer me a couple of fish sandwiches. But two fish and five loaves of bread when put in the hand of God will feed thousands. It depends on whose hands it is in.

A jar of water is only water in my hands; but in the hand of Jesus it is the best batch of wine. It depends on whose hand it is in.

Spit and dirt in my hands are just a nasty mess. But in the hand of Jesus, they are prescriptions for the blind to see.

Nails and two pieces of wood in my hands might produce a column for a chicken coop. But in the hands of Jesus they brought down the strongholds of hell and brought about salvation for the entire world. It depends on whose hands it is in.

12. When I am in trouble, I would rather be put in the hand of God for judgment than be in the human hands. Because of God's benevolent grace, no

matter what life throws at you, and no matter the extent of your human error and sin, put yourself in the hands of God, because in due time it will all work out. Have you not heard? The God whom we serve works out everything for the good of His people! It is always God's desire to do good to us and for us. That is benevolence, driven by God's great love for us. No matter what, put yourself in the hand of God because it is never His will to see anyone perish but that all would come to Him through repentance.

13. When we go to God for forgiveness, we do so because we believe and act under the conviction and assurance that God is love. When we speak of God as love, we are not saying that God is love in the sense of fondness for His created humanity or that His love is merely an emotion as it were, fixated on and attached to the sensibility. Rather, such love belongs to the voluntary faculty of His mind that is purposefully concerned with the wellbeing and spiritual health of His created humanity. If God is love, He never has done, and never will do anything but kind and eternally benevolent deeds aimed at restoring our original state of goodness and virtue. God is therefore eternally committed to doing good as He engages all of His power to elevating humanity to its highest good. God forgives and draws us to Himself because it is in Him that the full extent of our goodness is realized.

14. God's benevolence is nondiscriminatory. The benevolence of God is dispensed to sinner and saint, young and old, and to every race alike (Mt 5:44-45; Lk 6:35). God's benevolence is a blanket affair that is more corporate than particular, more inclusive than exclusive. Because of God's forgiveness we are set free from the mistakes of our past. Because of God's forgiveness of us, we are empowered to develop the energy and to exercise the will to love again. Because of God's forgiveness of us, we are delivered from the feeling of failure and guilt that can so often lead to self-judgment and self-condemnation as well as the judgment and condemnation of others. Because God has forgiven us, we are free from guilt and the devil can no longer use our past offence and hurts to judge us or cause us to judge and condemn ourselves and others. Because of God's forgiveness of us, we no longer beat upon ourselves but are set free from such harm. By ourselves we could not and would not free ourselves from the strangled hold of sin. But because

of God's benevolent mercy, like the Psalmist David in Psalm 51, we can hear and experience joy and gladness again.

15. Because of God's benevolent fixing of us, the joy of our salvation is restored. On account of God's benevolent fixing of us, His Holy Spirit is again living within us and sustaining us. By reason of God's benevolent grace, bones that were broken, that is, relationships that have been destroyed can find reasons to rejoice again. Thanks to God's benevolent fixing of us, we can see His face one more time; and oh what joy to see His face. "Oh, I want to see Him, [and] look upon His face, there to sing forever of His saving grace; on the streets of glory let me lift my voice, cares all past, home at last, ever to rejoice!" Assuredly, God forgives us in this life so that we might be empowered to live the Christian life and walk in His holiness in preparation for living in His eternity. Because of God's benevolent fixing of us:

- New and pure hearts have been created in us
- Our lives are taken over by a new and steadfast spirit within us
- We have been delivered from the guilt and burden of sin
- Sin no longer is our master; God through the Lord Jesus is again our God and Savior
- We have new tongues to sing of His righteousness and clean mouths to declare His praise

We messed up ourselves because of sin and the world because of our disobedience. But God alone through the Lord Jesus has forgiven and saved us in order that He might reposition us for eternity.

16. We have sinned against God and each other; and God alone by His benevolent favor has forgiven and redeemed us through Christ. We allowed sin to mess up our lives and relationship with God. God alone through the Holy Spirit has sanctified us and given us a new life. By ourselves we would not and could not have gone to God. By His benevolent grace He prompts us and lovingly draws us to Himself. By His benevolent grace, through the sustaining power of the Holy Spirit God seals us. That is, God has identified

us as His own by placing the Holy Spirit in our hearts as the first installment that guarantees everything He has promised us and which is to come (2 Cor 1:22).

17. By His benevolent grace, God alone has established us in Christ. Through the Lord Jesus alone, and by virtue of His atoning death on the cross, we have received God's benevolent gift of salvation. Without Him we would be nothing. Without Him we would fail. Without Him we would be drifting like a ship without a sail on this tumultuous ocean of life. Without Him we would not be living. Without Him we would be enslaved and in bondage to sin. Without Him life would be worthless. But thank God, through Jesus, we are saved!

18. Justice demanded that we should die. But grace and mercy said, "Oh no, we have already paid the price." We once were lost but grace and mercy found us. We were blind; but thank God, now we can see. We can see because God's benevolent grace and mercy came along, rescued us, and equipped us with new eyes to see that Jesus is the light of the world. We are living this moment because of God's benevolent grace. We need to thank God and praise Him too, for saving sinners just like you and me so that we can be His witnesses in telling the world that salvation is free. There were times when we just did not do right but God watched over us all day and all night and through Jesus He has made things right. His benevolent grace and mercy brought us through and into His marvelous light. Forgiveness is God's benevolent fixing of us! **Hallelujah**!

FORGIVENESS
(SECTION FOUR)
(Forgiven People Are Changed People—2 Cor. 5: 17-21)

1. God forgives us in order to change the downward spiraling of our lives. God forgives us in order to change the way we act and live. Having said that, knowledge of God, purposeful engagement in worship, repentance, forgiveness, regeneration, studying the Word of God, Christian service, acting with kindness and compassion, and the practice

of proper behavior that brings glory to God in the world, are some of the fundamental indicators that we have been spiritually transformed. Spiritual transformation is therefore not restricted to the mind through knowledge. Transformation needs to also engage the believer's attitude and behaviors. These, essentially, are the overt evidences of forgiveness and change. Proper Christian behavior and attitude are therefore important components of spiritual transformation. Indeed, God's integrity and dignity imparted to us at creation, affirmed in us through Christ who indwells us, and sustained in us by the operations of the Holy Spirit, need to be demonstrated through Christian behaviors that reflect conformity to the ways and purposes of God. Forgiveness empowers us to live as unto Christ as we intentionally seek to demonstrate behaviors that make us proper representations of the divine nature of God in us.

2. We cannot therefore say that we have been forgiven and changed when we do not demonstrate the evidences of having been forgiven and changed. We cannot say that we are forgiven when we are still as purposefully mean and lacking in mercy as we were before we met Christ. We cannot say that we are forgiven and changed when there is no demonstrative evidence of the fruit of the Spirit in our lives. If indeed being changed or born-again is to be born of the Spirit, then we are obligated to demonstrate love, joy, peace, longsuffering/patience, kindness, goodness, faithfulness, gentleness, and self-control. When we shall have done that, we will have shown others that we have been forgiven, renewed, and transformed to bear the fruit of the Spirit, and equipped to reflect Christ in the world. These aforementioned behaviors, values, and attitudes are the results of the repentant, forgiven, and renewed or born-again person.

3. We cannot say that we have repented, are forgiven, changed, saved, and are indeed Christians just because we think we are good persons. Nicodemus was a good person and a good Jew; but he was not yet inwardly or spiritually changed, renewed, or born-again based on the New Testament understanding of spiritual transformation. To that extent, though a good person and a good Jew, Nicodemus had not yet acquired saving knowledge of the Lord Jesus. We cannot say that we are Christians because we know a few

scriptures and have a little knowledge about the person of Christ. Nicodemus knew the scriptures and was versed in the legalities of the scriptures but he did not have a saving relationship with God. We cannot say that we are Christians because we like what we have read and heard about Jesus. Nicodemus liked what he saw in Christ. It is that likeness that inspired his visit and subsequent conversation with Christ in the third chapter of John's gospel. He admired Jesus but he had not yet believed in Him for salvation. Nicodemus admired the works of Jesus but he had not yet surrendered to the transforming power that is Jesus. As Jesus teaches Nicodemus He also teaches us that to be born again, we must accept by faith the Lord Jesus Christ and allow the Holy Spirit to work in and through us to bring about all that is not only good, but also Christ-like in us. By Christ indwelling us, we are not only transformed to be good persons, we are empowered to reflect the goodness of God working in and through us to transform the world.

4. We are not Christians because we have lifelong church memberships. We are not Christians because we sing in the choir. We are not Christians because we serve on this board or that committee. We are not Christians because we are presidents and chairpersons of one committee or another. We are not Christians because we are able to teach and preach. To be Christians, to be God's children, to be the church that Christ intends for us to be, we must be born again. To be born again is to be radically changed and renewed by the Holy Spirit to accept Jesus Christ as Lord and Savior in whom we can also have a brand new start. **Hallelujah!**

5. The person and the church that have been forgiven and renewed become part and parcel of a community and fellowship where there is holiness and goodwill towards each other. This does not mean that there will not be conflicts and misunderstandings between us and other persons that we are in relationship and fellowship with. What this means is that when conflicts and misunderstandings do come up, we are more willing to forgive and find common ground for establishing and reestablishing understanding. It also means that we are more inclined to let go of offenses so that we may continue to grow in grace and proceed to demonstrate the presence of Christ in our lives by the way we act toward one another. The person that is born-again seeks

after harmony and the church that has been renewed is a place, indeed a community of people where there is harmony in the choir and a place where we find unity, peace, and sanctity in committee and board meetings. The church that is regenerated is the place where there is gentleness in Christian fellowship just because the church is supposed to be a place where born-again, blood washed, sanctified and Spirit-filled people come to worship, glorify, praise God, and lift up each other in the redeeming name of Jesus. The absence of these spiritual qualities in church members' dealings with one another may be a good barometer of the prevailing habits of disobedience. It may also be an indicator of our desperate need to draw near to Jesus and respond to God's offer of grace and forgiveness. Through forgiveness and our daily walk of obedience, we, with the help of the Holy Spirit, may progressively become children of God and so finally rise above the obstacles and natural human tendencies that have prevented us from living in the glory and abundance of Christ through whom alone a new life is possible.

6. The new life in Christ means that we must leave our old self with all of its old unchristian behaviors and our old baggage of sin behind. Having repented and having been forgiven, we are to begin walking in the newness of life which God gives us through the Lord Jesus. When we are born again, it is God, through Christ, in the power of the Holy Spirit that makes us new by changing us from the inside out. To be changed from the inside out means that our minds and hearts are first changed in order to influence the kind of behaviors that we display on the outside. Forgiveness of our sins works from the inside so that we may know how to act on the outside. With God working on us from the inside, the Holy Spirit, over time, filters out our old ways and infuses us with new ways of thinking, walking, talking, and behaving. That way, the things we used to do, we do them no more and the places we used to go, we do not go there anymore. What this means is that people who are forgiven by God ought to lead the lifestyle of the forgiven. That lifestyle is reflective of the change that comes over us as a result of having met and believed in Jesus as Savior and Lord. Having met Jesus, that is, having developed a saving relationship with Him, we should no longer behave as we did before meeting Him.

7. Through forgiveness, with the Holy Spirit reorienting of our minds toward God, and infusing us with new thoughts, we begin to progressively display the emergence of new attitudes so that even our behavior is changed to act toward God. As forgiven persons, we are changed to respond to God in faith. We are also changed to demonstrate the presence and personality of God as we relate to each other in our homes, in the church, on the job, as well as in the world. To be born again means then, that we are born from above and fitted with a new nature. It also means that we are guided by new principles, driven by new affections, and inspired by goals and objectives that are new and of eternal value. To be born-again is to have our souls fashioned by the Holy Spirit into the likeness of Christ. Indeed, changed people are expected to demonstrate love. Changed people are expected to emulate Christ and manifest the faithfulness and obedience of Christ. Changed people are forgiven people who have been made humble enough for Christ to use for the benefit of the kingdom of God. Forgiven people are changed people.

8. The question that confronts us and needs to be answered at this juncture is, "Why are we changed?" A litany of affirmations, which is by no means exclusive, would be appropriate here. Let us consider them:

- We are changed and our minds are redirected toward God so that our lives and behaviors may be reordered to practice and reflect what is continuously fitting and proper to God's glory
- We are changed and set apart so that we may learn to appropriately live for God and reflect His goodness in the world
- We are changed to love God and neighbor
- We are changed and set apart so that we may learn to live out our faith in total obedience to God
- We are changed to live the divine life of God on earth and to become passionate witnesses to the goodness, power, grace, and love of God in the world
- We are changed to become God's redemptive agents in the world

- We are changed and empowered by the Holy Spirit to spread scriptural holiness, heal broken relationships, and transform social structures as we seek to establish justice and mercy in the world
- God has changed us so that we may bring healing to those who are hurting and wholeness to those who are broken
- We who were once strangers and have become sons and daughters of God, are changed to embrace the marginalized and include those whom society has excluded
- We are changed to bring liberty and transformation to a world where human beings are stricken by sin and victimized by hopelessness
- We are changed to tell the world that in Christ they will find strength for their weakness, hope for their despair, and gladness for their mourning
- We are changed to tell everybody about Somebody who can change anybody. His name is Jesus!
- We are changed to tell the world that Christ is the Savior for anyone that comes to Him in faith, the blessing for everyone's burdens, the resurrection for every believing soul, and our hope of eternal glory
- We are changed to celebrate God for making all things right and new in our lives.

That takes us to the fourth step in the six-step process of spiritual transformation—justification.

D. Step Four: Justification

1. When someone is justified it means that the person's relationship with God has been made right and the person declared innocent. While our prior actions were wrong, because of our repentance and because of

the atoning sacrifice of Christ on the cross, we are forgiven, justified or made right before God. If we take the Psalmist David as an example, we see that although his actions were wrong, in Psalm 51 he repented and appealed to God for forgiveness. That was David's surrender and complete reliance on the mercy and compassion of God for forgiveness and relief from the burden of sin. Essentially, this means that it is only God's saving actions that can free us from the guilt of our own sins. Justification is therefore our release from a wrong action that has led to a bad condition, guilt. Justification, then, is God declaring us innocent and released from the sentence and burden of our prior sin. Despite our shortcomings, the Bible says that God justifies and declares righteous all those who believe in Jesus.[60] Since all have sinned according to Romans 3:23, our salvation is a gift from God who, through the atoning sacrifice of Jesus, and our faith in the Lord Jesus, justifies us.[61] Justification is God acting through grace to make the sinner a fully forgiven child of God. We may still remain vulnerable to sin and capable of sinning. However, through repentance and forgiveness, we are daily renewed by divine grace.

2. Justification is part of God's plan of salvation. As such, to be justified is to be put in a position of restored innocence and freedom as a result of God making things right in our relationship with Him. Justification is therefore one of the ways used by God to reconcile or draw us back to Him. Through His offer of forgiveness, justification is God making just, those who were guilty and found in the wrong. Justification is God accepting us in our wrongness and unrighteous state and making us what He wants us to be— RIGHTEOUS. We are not made righteous by our own efforts but by God's grace. By His grace, God declares and makes us righteous. To be righteous means to act rightly or to be good as well as to do good. We cannot however, become good by doing good. We must first be good in order to do good. Only a good tree for example can bring forth good fruit.[62] Certainly, we are not justified as a result of any duty or good work that we perform but rather

---

[60] Acts 13:39

[61] Rom 3:21-31 and Gal 2:16

[62] Mt 7:16-20

by our faithful response to duty already performed by Jesus Christ, demonstrated through His life, ministry, and atoning work on the cross. The works that we do, we do not do in order to be saved but because we are already saved by faith and empowered by grace to do them for the glory of God.[63] Salvation therefore has everything to do with God moving us from a state of sinfulness and the guilt of it, and imparting to us His own righteousness. God's justification of us is God empowering us to be good and therefore to do good and walk justly before Him.

3. Justification is therefore God removing our guilt and sinfulness and giving us a new start. God justifying us tells us that we count for something in His grand scheme of things. To that extent and to announce the value that God places on us, while we were still sinners, Christ died for us.[64] It follows that our justification is not something that we have paid for; nor is it something that we earn. Rather, our justification has been paid for with the life of Jesus Christ given to redeem us and therefore change our status from the condemned to the redeemed. **Hallelujah!** We are justified freely by the grace of God through our faith in the Lord Jesus.[65] Justification by grace through faith alone means that we cannot escape sin by ourselves nor can we set our life in order without faith in God's amazing grace. Abraham believed and he was justified by God.[66] Having demonstrated faith in God, by His grace, He releases us from the guilt and power of sin. Romans 3:21-31 indicates that we have all fallen short of God's glory and can only be saved by the actions of God to save us through Christ. Our salvation is therefore only made possible by God taking the initiative to redeem and correct our wrong by setting us free from the sin that puts us in a spiritually unhealthy situation from which we could not and would not free ourselves. Justification is a divine action and not a human effort.[67] Justification is God's application of the spiritual intent of His own law and love, so that by His grace, He might find reasonable grounds

---

[63] Eph 2:10
[64] Rom 5:8
[65] Eph 2:8
[66] Rom 4:3
[67] Gal 2:16

to release us from the guilt of sin and set us apart for His purpose, which is His sanctification of us.

E. Step Five: Sanctification

1. The fifth step in the process of spiritual transformation takes place at the level of sanctification by the Holy Spirit. Sanctification is God setting us apart for His purpose and for molding us into His holy ways. Sanctification may rightly be considered God's training ground for those who have been forgiven and justified by His grace and favor. At this level, we receive spiritual training in the ways of God and are drawn into His holiness by the practicing of those ways. Sanctification is God's action of pulling us away from all that we used to be and setting us aside to become all that we can be in Christ Jesus. Sanctification is God setting us apart from old habits so that we may be spiritually detoxified. That way, as we are purged of old spiritually unhealthy toxic habits, we may learn godly ways and develop godly lifestyles.

2. Sanctification is the work of God who enters humans' lives and experiences to change us and set us apart from unprofitable pursuits. God does so in order to infuse us with His power to lead new lives and for the pursuit of the divine purpose. God sets us apart from what we used to be so that we may become something new in Christ. Sanctification shifts us from the ordinary level of natural human errors in order to prepare us to live and perform at an uncommon level of spiritual and moral excellence. Sanctification is God removing us from all that we used to be and bringing us into a new state of existence and understanding so that He might progressively transform us into becoming His sanctified and Spirit-filled agents of reconciliation in the world.

F. Step Six: Moving from Glory to Glory (Section One)

1. Moving from glory to glory is indicative of our progressive spiritual ascension to the ultimate level of spiritual transformation. Before

we get into this matter of moving from glory to glory as the ultimate level of our spiritual transformation, a word about glory is appropriate. When used in the Hebrew context, the word "glory" is most exclusive to God and yet has become an ordinary word describing earthly things even in the Old Testament itself. For example, the Hebrew word for glory "kabod" is used to describe Aaron's priestly robes (Ex 28:2), the reign of kings such as David (1 Chron 17:18, 29:28), Jehoshaphat (2 Chron 17:5), Hezekiah (2 Chron 32:27) and even Gentile king Xerxes (Est 1:4). The word is also used in reference to the splendor of countries such as Moab (Isa 16:14), Israel (Isa 17:3), and Lebanon (Isa 35:2). However, while the same word for human's glory is used in reference to God's glory, God's glory is unlike human's glory. What then, is God's glory like and how is it different?

2. The Bible tells us that glory belongs to God and that human's glory comes from God and is given or bestowed by God (1 Chron 29:12; Ps 3:3). So, then, whenever I speak of our sharing in the glory of God, it should not be taken to mean that we have the same glory. Rather, that sharing is bestowed glory from God. Redeemed humanity is the beneficiary of God's glory but God is the sole Benefactor. We reap life's bounteous benefits but God is life's Benevolent Benefactor. The Bible tells us that while others freely use the word "glory," only God's name is glorious, holy, or praiseworthy (Neh 9:5, Ps 66:2, 72:19, 145:21). He is majestic and His glory cannot be shared in the sense of someone else having the same glory as in a joint CEO or co-chair.

3. When we speak of God's glory, we are speaking of His divine esteem so to speak. God's glory is God's active, pervasively radiant, and transforming presence among His people. It is our recognition of that divine and holy presence that moves us to worship and ascribe praise and glory to God. As a result, the New Testament or Greek rendition of glory is "Doxa" used to translate the Hebrew "Kabod." Unlike the Hebrew "Kabod" however, the Greek "Doxa" does not speak of the human opinion or other "worthy" human attributes based on their positions or achievements, but purely of the majestic manifestation of God through His own self-disclosures. In the New

Testament, then, the qualities of God are in themselves glorious.[68] God's glory is therefore manifested through His actions and mighty works in the material universe as well as in and through the lives of believers. When John 1:14 speaks of the glory of God that we have seen in Christ for example, the writer is speaking of the visible manifestation of God's presence that is acknowledged only by those who look to Jesus with faith[69] and recognize Him as the anointing of God. The nonbeliever does not look with faith and therefore only sees Jesus as that historical man from Nazareth.

4. The New Testament also speaks of another unveiling of God's glory. This unveiling has eschatological significance because that which has always been hidden from mortals (humanity) will be revealed to all believers in the eternity of God's glory.[70] When therefore, we think of glory, we often think of it and rightly so, in terms of the revealed manifestations and divine attributes of God. Glory is not some vague manifestation of splendor accompanied by bright lights that shine forth from God or from the believer, like that of a halo that rings above the believer's head. Glory emanates from God and is the very essence of His nature. That means that God is glory itself. His own attributes emanate from Him. The glory of God becomes real to us in Jesus Christ through whom we gain access to the glory of God and are anointed by the Holy Spirit to bear witness to His glory in the world. As witnesses to His glory, we, having been regenerated, ought to live lives that are reflective of the nature of God in whose image we were created.

5. Furthermore, while the common glory of human achievements is subjective and often ascribed glory, the glory of God is not subjective but objective. That means that the glory of God is not ascribed to Him by any human or otherwise extraterrestrial admiration and opinions. Whether we think well of God or not, it does not take away from His glory nor does it change who He is. God does not need anyone's permission or approval to

---

[68] Eph 1:6, 3:16; and Col 1:11

[69] Jn 2:11, 8;50-58; Heb 1:3

[70] Mt 16:27, 24:30, 25:31; Mk 8:38, 10: 37, 13: 26; Lk 9:26, 21: 27; Col 3:4; 1 Thess 2:12; 2 Thess 1 9; Tit 2:13; 1 Pet 4:13, 5:1; 2 Pet 1:17; Rev 15:18, 21:11:23

be God and by extension, glorious. He is God all by Himself and altogether glorious. You see, God's glory is not invested in or dependent on the human evaluation or opinion of God. God's glory is grounded in the very nature of God. God's glory is who God is. God is altogether majestic and loaded with splendor displayed through creation as well as through His loving character and divine attributes that permeate the universe. When the glory of God is manifested by God's own self disclosure, all that we humans take glory in, tend to fade into insignificance. When, for example, Moses asked God in Exodus 33:18 to show him His glory, Moses was in fact asking God to give him a fuller knowledge of the ways of God. This perspective is affirmed in verse 19 where the Lord said in response to Moses' request: "I shall make all My goodness pass before you…" Moses' request to see the glory of God was one way of asking to see the goodness of God so that he may diligently seek after it in the pursuit of holiness. Moses was therefore not just seeking to know of God, he also wanted to become acquainted with the ways of God.

6. Now then, our moving from glory to glory is therefore indicative of our progressive acquaintance with the ways of God as well as of our becoming more and more God-like. It is our pursuit of that goodness of God that we have been transformed to seek after. In 2 Corinthians 3:18 the Apostle Paul speaks of us on a journey toward glory whereby we are being transformed from glory to glory by the Spirit of the Lord. What the Apostle is saying is that by means of the Holy Spirit working in us, we are not only reflecting the glory of the Lord; we are also being progressively moved into increasing degrees of that glory. Many scriptures in the New Testament speak to this weighty matter.[71] By virtue of a saving knowledge of God and as a result of our relationship with Jesus, the majesty of God's divine splendor enters our lives and is now permeating our being, thus changing our lives and moving us to a closer proximity of what God is like and who God wants us to become. Romans 8:29-30 puts it this way:

---

[71] Rom 2:7, 10, 5:2, 8:17, 30; 2 Cor 4:17; Phil 3:21; Col 1:27, 3:4; 1 Thess 2:12; 2 Thess 2:14; 2 Tim 2:10; Heb 2:10; 1 Pet 1:7

"For those God foreknew He also predestined to be conformed to the image of His Son, that He might be the firstborn among many brothers and sisters. And those He predestined, He also called; those He called, He also justified; those He justified, He also glorified."

The message of 1 John 3:1-2 is that we who have taken notice of the presence and actions of God and believe in His Christ, will enter as well as live in the presence and glory of God, which is the ultimate manifestation of our spiritually transformed personhood.

7. When therefore we speak about growing in grace or moving from glory to glory, we are at the same time talking about growing in love and spiritual maturity and moving toward perfection, which is the human pursuit of the perfection of God. Make no mistake about it; our pursuit cannot and will not lead to any personal discoveries regarding the glory of God. Since it is God who governs our hearts, minds, and will, it is God alone by the power of the Holy Spirit, who is all the time drawing us into His glory and perfect life. Christian perfection therefore implies God's love and holiness that are being made perfect in us as a result of God's indwelling and sanctifying grace that keeps our hearts tuned to His holy ways.[72]

Step Six: Moving from Glory to Glory (Section Two)

1. Perfection, the goal of spiritual transformation, is the result of total surrender to the perfect will and purpose of God. It is God's overarching and perfect love manifested through His grace and forgiveness given to us through Christ that sets the agenda and tone for our Christlike actions in the world. God's overarching love also helps to shape and establish our Christian priorities. Our priority is always to put God first, love Him with all of our hearts, minds, souls, and spirits, daily seek after His eternal kingdom, love our neighbors, and engage in personal witnessing to the love of God in the world. That way, when the Lord Himself

---

[72] 1 Jn 4:12

shall have descended from heaven with a shout, with the voice of archangels, and with the trumpet of God, we shall be caught up together to meet our blessed Savior to live with Him in the presence of His perfect love for all eternity.[73]

2. By virtue of our redemption, Christ has effectively reintroduced us to the life and glory of God. Surely the glory of God that indwells Christ also extends to Christian believers through faith in the redemptive and reconciling work of Jesus Christ. Since we have been brought into union with God by the reconciling work of Jesus, we are also kept in that union by the unitive power of the Holy Spirit. Because we are in union with Christ, we are participating in that glorious manifestation now through the present reign of God and the present operations of the Holy Spirit. On this earth we have been redeemed to extend the glory of God in the world. Right now we are being transformed to become more like Jesus in preparation to live in the eternal glory of God.

3. Our becoming Christ-like or more like God should not be taken however, to mean that we are acquiring deity or becoming divine. Instead, it should be taken to mean that we are destined to be eternally permeated by the love, grace and glory of God and His Christ. The very notion that we have fallen short of the glory of God, as attested to by Romans 3:23, is an affirmation that we were created to aspire toward that glory and are indeed destined to attain to that greater glory because it is God's eternal design for us. Yet, in a real sense, it is not we who attain, but rather, God who brings His redeemed people into the reaches of His eternal glory.

4. Remember now that we are not necessarily sharing the glory of God as much as we are being drawn into His glorious and eternal presence. From the perspective of eternity, our moving into the glory of God is God indwelling us to the extent that He bestows upon us and saturates us with His divine life. This divine saturation of us suggests that in eternity, we will no longer need to reflect God as required in our earthly existence. Instead of us being reflections of God as we did in the world, in eternity, it will be God perfectly permeating us with His divine life and glory as we are eternally and finally drawn into His divine life. Moving from glory to glory is therefore

---

[73] Jn 14:3, 17:24; 1 Thess 4:17

our becoming absorbed into the eternal life of God. Our becoming absorbed in the divine life of God is, in a real sense, progressively happening now as self gives way to the indwelling of the Spirit of glory[74] who influences our thoughts and directs our actions in ways that are pleasing to God. That way, we are empowered to act god-like in this world and, in eternity, we shall be like Christ in His eternal glory. Listen to the words of Philippians 3:20-21:

> "...Our citizenship is in heaven. And we eagerly await a Savior from there, the Lord Jesus Christ, who, by the power that enables him to bring everything under his control, will transform our lowly bodies so that they will be like His glorious body."

5. According to 2 Corinthians 5:4, the One who has prepared us for this very thing— eternity, and our living in His glory— is God. He has made it so that our mortal bodies will become swallowed up by His divine life. While Paul speaks of this mortal body taking on immortality,[75] I prefer to speak of us taking on eternal duration because in my view there is only One Immortal and Invisible and He is God! Yet, by His permission and the counsel of His own will, He shall fit us with eyes to behold Him in His eternal glory.

6. Moving from glory to glory is about the completion of our spiritual transformation. Moving from glory to glory implies our being shifted from one degree or level of glory to another. At this present level, we are growing in grace as the Holy Spirit sustains and progressively works in us, bringing us into a greater awareness of God. At another level, the futuristic and ultimate level of eternity, it will be our eternal basking in the presence and glory of God. I say we shall bask or live in the glory of God because we will have no glory of our own. If indeed we dwell in and share the life of Christ here on earth, we shall dwell in His glory when He returns to receive us unto Himself and for eternity. This is the message of Colossians 3:4. It speaks of completeness, the triumph of God and His kingdom, the victory of Jesus and our completion in Him. Consequently, the Christian who lives in Christ

---

[74] 1 Pet 4:14

[75] 1Cor 15:53

now, shall live in the glory of God and have fellowship and eternal communion with Him.[76]

7. Our moving from glory to glory should therefore be taken to mean that we are caught up in a process whereby we are progressively learning more of the ways of God and learning more of His love and will. In this process of growing and becoming, our human self-will accumulatively gives way to the will of God which ultimately leads to our spiritual growth and maturity. I speak of our "becoming" as a process because Christians are not supposed to be at the same level of Christian maturity as they we were the day they came to the Lord Jesus. Owing to the Spirit in us progressively drawing us into Christ, we are expected to increase in love, in the same wisdom and knowledge as did Christ, and in many more areas of godliness and favor.[77] Put differently, we were saved, redeemed, and set apart (sanctified) from our old self and other bad habits and influences, so that God can impart Himself to us. That impartation is God giving us the opportunity and the grace to develop knowledge of Him. As we grow into that knowledge, we learn more of God and as we learn more of God we are elevated to higher levels of understanding, love, grace, faith, and favor. This is indicative of our advancement or succession to glory.

8. Our moving from glory to glory is also our moving toward perfection. With God as the standard toward which we aspire, we are moving from one level of perfection to another so that we might find completion in Him who is our perfection. We may never be perfect in this life. However, in this life, we are to aspire toward perfection. Our standard of moral perfection is God. Our goal, indeed the goal of the Holy Spirit and God's design for us, is for us to grow in grace and seek always to be like Him. Because God's design for us is that we grow in grace, we should never be the same as when we first met Jesus, or when we first confessed and accepted Him as Savior and Lord. Indeed, the love of God is working in us to elevate us to higher standards of virtue and righteousness. Our growth in Christ is not attained by ourselves. It is reached by God working in us to make us like Him. As we develop to

---

[76] 1 Cor 15:22-28

[77] Lk 2:52

become more like Jesus and therefore more like God, we also become less and less creatures of the "now." As creatures of the "now" we are limited and burdened by the fleeting circumstances and sufferings of time in the process of becoming citizens of God's eternal kingdom. Time, even with its limitations, is therefore preparing us for a greater and eternal glory. That is what Paul means when he says in Romans 8:18: "I consider that our present sufferings are not worth comparing with the glory that will be revealed in us." And again in 2 Corinthians 4:17: "For our light and momentary troubles are achieving for us an eternal glory that far outweighs them all." The Apostle Peter chimes in when he echoes this affirmation in 1 Peter 4:13: "But rejoice that you participate in the sufferings of Christ, so that you may be overjoyed when his glory is revealed."

9. In this life, the more we behold the presence and power of God in our lives, and as we surrender to that power working in us, the more we are elevated to become like Him. In addition, the more we contemplate the truth that has been revealed to us concerning the purposes of God for us, the more our thoughts, affections, and actions will become infused with the ways and actions of God. The more we are aligned with the will of God, the more we are transformed into His likeness. That is the eschatological hope of glory of which Romans 5:2 speaks. Indeed, Christ in us is our hope of eternal glory (Col. 1:27). The awesome realization of who God is, and what He is doing in us to transform us and bring us into His eternal glory, moves us to ascribe glory to God through worship and praise. This is the subject of the following chapter.

Chapter Three

Christian Worship

Prayer:

Dear Lord, thank You for coming where we are. We are moved by Your desire to have fellowship and communion with us. We give You honor, glory, and praise because You are worthy. We thank You for inviting us to worship and for stirring up our faithful response to You. All that we know You have taught us through the gift of Your Son Jesus Christ. Continue, we pray, to enlighten our minds. By the inspiration of You Holy Spirit, empower us to live and worship You because we know that You are our Creator, Redeemer through Christ Jesus our Lord, and Sanctifier through the power and authority of the Holy Spirit. Teach us we pray, to differentiate between sincerity and pretense in worship, and move us by the Holy Spirit to worship You so that what we do and say will be in Spirit and in truth and for your glory. This we pray in the name of Jesus, Amen!

Suggested Scripture Readings:
   2 Kn 17:36; 1 Chr 16:29; Ps 29:2; 99:5; Mt 4:10; Jn 4:24; Rev 14:7

Hymns:
"Open The Eyes Of My Heart Lord"
"Be Thou My Vision"
"Holy, Holy, Holy…"
"O Worship The King"
"To God Be The Glory"
"Joyful, Joyful, We Adore Thee"
"O For A Thousand Tongues To Sing"
"We Have A Story To Tell To The Nations"

1. Overview

This chapter is an examination of the correlation between proper knowledge of God and proper worship of God. Proper knowledge and worship of God have to do with knowing and worshipping God as He exists in unity with, and as He manifests Himself through Jesus the Son, in the presence and power of the Holy Spirit. The God whom we worship is, and should always be understood as Creator, Redeemer, and Sanctifier. Knowing God the Father as Creator, who reveals Himself through Christ the Son as Redeemer, and through the Holy Spirit as Sanctifier, is critical for our understanding of the dialogue that takes place between God and us in worship as well as in our life experiences.

True worship begins with recognizing and responding to God as He exists and is manifested through the Son, in the power of the Holy Spirit. Worship that is true is worship that is in response to God as He exists, not as we desire Him to be. Otherwise, we would be worshipping a god after our own making and design rather than the God who made us after His own likeness.

Worship, indeed, the Christian life, is a process of transformation that begins with an engaged understanding of the unity of the Father, Son, and Holy Spirit. An engaged understanding of the unity of the Father, Son, and Holy Spirit is necessary because understanding how the Father, Son, and Holy Spirit work in our lives and worship will lead us to embrace the fullness of God who is intent on having a relationship with us. Our worship of God is both a communion and a participation in the already perfect worship and service of Jesus the Son to God the Father. In worship, the Holy Spirit facilitates and empowers our worship, while Jesus the Son, is our Mediator and High Priest and therefore the medium of our worship dialogue with God. This ongoing dialogue in worship and our motives for worship will form constituent parts of this portion of our conversation.

2. What is Worship?

1. Worship is a divine initiative and event. It is an event in which God the Father comes to us and draws us to Himself, through Christ, in the power of the Holy Spirit to bless us with His presence and pour upon us the gift of participation in His Word, life, and work. Worship is the human recognition and proclaimed praise response to God who first reveals Himself to us and empowers us to participate in His communal life. As a result of our knowledge gained through God's own self-revelation,[78] we are moved to surrender and bow down to the awesome power and presence of God. Upon discovering who God is, we are inwardly inspired to offer Him what He is due— worship!

2. Since worship is a divine initiative and a human response to a divine invitation, worship is communion with God. Our transformation and journey into eternal life begins with our knowledge (discovery or, preferably, awareness of God) and subsequent worship, communion, and fellowship with God. Indeed, to know God is to have eternal life.[79] If knowing God is eternal life, our worship, fellowship, and communion essentially become an eternal series of praise and adoration of the One who created us.

3. While we gather in buildings and locations to worship, worship really takes place in the human heart and mind where nothing else matters but God. The worship encounter takes us to an intimate yet not isolated place, where we are summoned by God to have fellowship and communion with Him. Worship is a place of the heart where we, having surrendered ourselves to God, can, in spirit and truth, lift up holy hands and worship God with sincere and uninhibited praise. Such sincerity does not come from buildings and decorative surroundings. Such sincerity comes from the deep place of the human heart: that moral proclivity, disposition, and inclination to believe, feel care, and respond to God with passion, love, and sincere adoration. Today,

---

[78] See chapter two of this text— Six Steps for Understanding Spiritual Transformation for a discussion on the ways and importance of knowing God.
[79] Prov 8:35; Jn 17:3

God is still seeking such people to worship Him.[80] As a heartfelt response to God, worship is a gift of participation, whereby believing worshippers faithfully participate in the already perfect and acceptable worship of the Son to the Father. Indeed, before it is our worship it is the worship of the Son to the Father.

4. Worship is all that the body of Christ does in faithful response to God's invitation and gift of participation with the distinct purpose of giving glory to God. Consequently, whether the human response to God is in the celebration of the formal liturgy, in deeds of devotion and commitment to God, or in the demonstration of mercy and love toward our fellow human beings through mission and service to the community, when it is done for the glory of God, it is worship.

5. Worship therefore becomes an enriched spiritual experience with God and an occasion to witness to others about His mighty power, grace, and love. Worship is essentially a spiritual experience whereby we encounter God who receives our praise and worship, transforms our lives, and brings us, body, mind, and spirit into alignment with His will and purpose.

3. Knowledge of God and True Worship

1. Our journey with God begins with our recognition and knowledge of who He is— GOD! He is the all-powerful, all-knowing, the everywhere present God, Defender, Provider, Healer, Protector, merciful, just, Creator, Redeemer, and Sanctifier. Worship is the manifestation of our recognition and response to who God is. For, how can we not bow down before the One who made the heavens and the earth? How can we not bow down in holy reverence before the One who is the First Cause of our existence and the Source of our salvation?

2. While our faith journey begins with an awareness of God and spills over into worshipful adoration of God, and while the Christian life begins in and through the activity of God who calls us together and meets us

---

[80] Jn 4:23

in worship, the "formal worship setting" is not the only place where God meets us. For many people, their most real experiences and encounters with God are related to times of personal needs, tragedies, and, perhaps, even in those cases of despair and hopelessness. In those moments, when our own efforts fail, and when our resources and expertise do not seem able to deliver us, we are often compelled by circumstances to throw ourselves at God's mercy having tried everything else only to have it fail us. However, it is not only in tragedy that God comes near to us. God also comes near at those times when we are most receptive to Him, and are not necessarily compelled by circumstances but are motivated purely by our awareness of Him as well as by our love for Him. Furthermore, even those who might have experienced God apart from the formal worship encounter, are drawn to communal worship because they are seeking to offer up gratitude and communal praise with those who have also experienced the God who delivers them in their times of distress.

3. In crisis, tragedy, or when driven by despair, we may go to God for ourselves; but in worship we go to God for God. Worship, as we shall see, is therefore a time when we respond to God for God. When we respond to God through worship, something wonderful happens to us and we leave the worship encounter with some of the benefits that come from responding to and encountering God. Having truly worshipped God, we leave the experience feeling renewed, invigorated, and alive. But then, that is what happens when we put God first and allow our life-giving source to renew His life-giving power in us. Worship renews and changes us. I therefore believe that worship is an important starting point in the Christian journey with God.

4. Since it is in the context of our historical and empirical existence that we come face to face with the Object of our faith, we need to begin with worship as a place where we are summoned to respond to God. As we respond to God, we are also summoned to act upon His Word, and live in the world to bring Him glory through worship and Christian service. It is in life, including those aforementioned tragedies and unfortunate circumstances, as well as in worship that God meets us through Christ and

transforms us through the operations of the Holy Spirit so that we may think godly thoughts, pursue godly actions, and follow a lifestyle that affirms our transformation.

5. Our knowledge and subsequent worship of God is the beginning of a remarkable journey with God that leads to our progressive transformation and subsequent eternity with Him. A number of writers[81] support the view that Christian worship is founded upon Christian truth and knowledge of God. This knowledge is grounded in the understanding and reality of God who is revealed through the Son in the power of the Holy Spirit. As such, God in worship needs to be understood in terms of the unity of the Father, Son, and Holy Spirit. Understanding God's descent and ascent, presence, and continuous work among us in worship and daily life is fundamental to our understanding of God. This understanding is also important to the development and maintenance of our faithful response and proper attitude toward worship that is directed toward God. Because God is made known in Christ who mediates our praise to God, and because God's mighty works are daily manifested through the activities of the Holy Spirit, in worship it is right and acceptable to ascribe praise to the Father, Son, and Holy Spirit— the initiator, inspiration, facilitator, and sustainer of our passionate worship.

6. Knowledge of God leads to informed and proper worship of God. This knowledge must be grounded in our understanding of what worship is, as well as the power that draws us into the recognition of the worthiness of God for worship and adoration. Knowledge of God who is known as Father, manifested through the Son as Redeemer and the lifter of our worship, and as Sanctifier, in the person of the Holy Spirit, must form the basis of our understanding if our worship is to be in spirit and truth. Since knowledge is the bedrock of understanding and sense making in the human construct, having proper knowledge of God may result in worship which is meaningful

---

[81] See for example, Charry, By the Renewing of Your Minds, 1997; John Macquarrie, Principles of Christian Theology (New York: Charles Scribner's Sons); Bishop Frederick Hilborn Talbot African American Worship: New Eyes for Seeing (Fairway Press, 1998); Torrance, Worship and Community, 1996; James White 1998, The Forgotten Trinity: Recovering the Heart of Christian Belief (Minneapolis, MN: Bethany House Press, 1998).

instead of one that is done without understanding. Worship without understanding becomes self-centered and routinely meaningless weekly or bi-weekly episodes. If our worship experience is to be of lasting value to us as worshippers, then we need to truly know, understand, and concentrate on the worship process so that we may truly focus on God and make sense of our worship experience. Yes, worship requires concentration. Otherwise, we are merely engaged in mindless routines. Mindless routine is not worship. Certainly, it is not worship that is directed to God. Assuredly, God deserves our thoughtfulness and the engagement of our minds and spirits in worship.

7. Understanding the worship process may therefore lead to a real, living, and participative experience through Christ who taught us, and the Holy Spirit who stirs us to respond to God's invitation to worship. Charry makes the point that, "unless educated to grasp God's majesty and grace, we should fail to understand God properly and be moved to virtuous living as a consequence."[82] White also insists that "if we have defective knowledge, or worse, if we have wrong information and have been deceived, our worship is either lessened [due to simple ignorance], or it is completely invalid…"[83]

8. Valid and sincere worship is the kind of worship that reaches to the Father through the Son in the power of the Holy Spirit. Outside of that knowledge, indeed, outside of that channel of ascent and holy descent in worship, from God to God, through Christ in the power of the Holy Spirit, our worship would not and cannot ring true! While I do not believe that worship is something that is taught but rather, experienced, it is perfectly acceptable for worshippers to be nurtured and informed concerning what worship is. That way, they may develop reverence for the worthiness of God as well as appropriate responses to the prompting of God in worship. With appropriate knowledge of the worship process, the pastor, worship leaders, and the rest of the congregation may be mutually elevated and inspired to know and experience God in worship through an engaged understanding that is manifested

---

[82] Charry, 115
[83] White, 194

through cooperate, purposeful, and sustained praise. As Brown observes, "through instruction in the meaning of worship, encouragement to participate will come of itself."[84]

9. While perfect knowledge is not required to worship God, our desire to worship should always be driven by what we have come to know about God. Our desire to grow in the grace and knowledge of God, and our deep love for Him should also continue to inform our worship experience. The importance of knowledge cannot be overstated because as Jesus indicates, knowledge does indeed go beyond true and meaningful worship to encompass eternal life (John 17:3).

10. Without knowledge, we cannot participate in the divine life. Knowledge leads to understanding. Knowledge also prompts us to respond to and participate faithfully in worship that is meaningful, true, fitting, and directed to God. As White posits, "knowledge does not save (that is the error of Gnosticism); but true worship does not exist without knowledge."[85]

4. WORSHIP: A DIVINE INITIATIVE AND A HUMAN RESPONSE (SECTION ONE)

1. The tendency to think that worship is something that we worshippers initiate and therefore "do" is a common misconception that leads to common and often routine worship. We do not do worship; we participate in what God is doing for us and to us and expressly through us for His glory. Our worship should always be a response to what God is doing. Because worship is something we think we are responsible for initiating and doing, we are too often content with "going to church" on Sunday mornings, singing our songs, reading and listening to the

---

[84] Edgar S. Brown, (1967). "The Worship of the Church and the Modern Man." In <u>Liturgical Renewal in the Christian Churches,</u> (Ed. Michael J. Taylor, pp. 197-221), Helicon: Baltimore-Dublin, 219

[85] White, p. 195

scripture, praying for ourselves and perhaps a few other people, listening to the sermon if we are not distracted, and depositing our money, while impatiently waiting for the benediction so we can go home, and tend to something more "important" or perhaps more "interesting" that we also "do." **Worship is not about us. Worship is all about God!** Worship has its origin and completion in God who alone is worthy of our worship and praise.[86]

2. Because we think that worship is something that we initiate, we go into worship trying to invoke and call forth the presence of God through our so-called prayers of invocation. **We do not call God to worship. God calls us to worship**. It is not God that we need to invoke. Instead, we should ask God to invoke our awareness of His presence. Before we get to "church" for worship, God is already there. It is therefore our awareness of God that we need to ask God to invoke. Worship is a divine initiative whereby God Himself attracts the human attention and invokes the human response through thanksgiving and doxologies of praise because of who He is, what He has already done, and what He promises to do.

3. Worship is an event in which God comes to us and draws us to Himself through Christ in the power of the Holy Spirit. God takes the initiative and comes to us because He wants us to know Him and His holy ways. God comes to us because His goal is to have us caught up in the nearness and revealed divine drama of His holiness so that He might restore His dignity that He imparted to us in creation. This goal is an integral part of God's plan for our salvation which is forever engraved in the life and ministry, death, resurrection, and ascension of Christ. To that extent, to be in Christ is to take notice of the nearness of God and His unfolding plan for our salvation. The notion of being caught up in the drama of God is a reflection of the Christian life that is surrendered to, and therefore ordered by God. Accordingly, as we are enabled by the Holy Spirit through grace, what we "do" in worship and mission while living in the hope of Christ's return, we do and live with the expressed backing of the Father, Son, and

---

[86] Rev 19:10; 22:9

Holy Spirit. These Three, working as One, are deeply and persistently engaged in developing in us the gifts and graces we need to respond to God and for living lives that are pleasing to Him.

4. As the Holy Spirit enables us to recognize the nearness and initiative of God, He also helps us to respond faithfully to that nearness with worship. Worship as a divine initiative means that God makes the first move. Because God makes the first move, God is not merely the Object of our worship; God is also the Subject, and if the Subject, the "content," and if the content, the sole reason for our worship and praise. Because God is not only the Object, but also the Subject of our worship, the language and every aspect of our liturgy should be filled with praise for the One who thinks enough of us to call us to Himself for worship and communion.

5. As a divine initiative, it is God, by the inspiration of the Holy Spirit that stirs within our hearts the desire for communion and fellowship. As Matthew 15:8-9 and Mark 7:7 indicate, worship that is not from the heart, or in spirit, is vain worship. Worship that is true is worship that is informed and motivated by our knowledge or awareness of God who takes the first step toward us. Worship that is in spirit is worship that is from the heart if only because the Holy Spirit of God inspires such worship.

6. The misconception of worship as something that we do and initiate is one that has carried over into the act of worship itself and needs to be corrected. Undoubtedly, the human contribution to worship through buildings, furniture, praise, musical instruments, songs, ingenuity, intelligence, networking, the applications of computer technology, and the full range of human skills and experience cannot be denied. However, when we conclude that our contributions and the tools we use to "do" worship are the things that make worship what it is, worship becomes our own sensational and emotional enjoyment. When we get to that stage, it is a clear indication that our worship is degenerating into idolatry.

Worship:
A Divine Initiative and a Human Response
(Section Two)

1. Worship is likely to become idolatrous when it is no longer our response to God and His divine initiative, but a projection of our learnedness and egos, our theatrics, our know-how, our personal achievements, our own self-centered aspirations, and our human abilities aimed at satisfying our own emotions and desire to entertain the masses. Worship that is focused on human achievements rather than the inspiration of the Holy Spirit is an indication that we have become spiritually bankrupt. The richness of our worship is only realized when we are connected to the richness and abundance of the overflowing grace of the Holy Spirit who gives worship substance, depth, purpose, and lasting value. That richness and abundance of the Holy Spirit is further enhanced when our worship is inspired by the majesty of the Son of God, Jesus Christ, who mediates our worship to God, the Father. Our ascent to God, the Father, is only made possible through Christ the Son in the power of the Holy Spirit. Without the Holy Spirit moving and stirring us up and without Jesus Christ mediating and lifting our worship, our prayers and praise would not go above the ceilings of our sacred sanctuaries.

2. If we think that worship is something that we do, we are, above all persons, most bankrupt because we are also saying that the only priesthood is our priesthood, the only offering is our offering, and the only intercession is our intercession.[87] Conceivably, perhaps it is because we have settled for a human-centered view of worship that we are so easily driven to weariness and are ready to leave the worship service as soon as we arrive "at church." Because of this human-centered view of worship that seems to have a grip on worshippers' approach to the worship event today, we have become satisfied with being mere spectators watching the ushers usher, observing and listening to the choir sing their songs, and watching the worship leader lead the worship service while hoping that the pastor gives a very brief sermon that

---

[87] Torrance, *Worship and Community*, 1996

does not necessarily challenge us on any level. At the same time, we observe others doing "their thing," we are anxiously watching the clock or peeping at our watches, and sometimes making it obvious as we impatiently wait for the moment to leave our "holy sanctuaries," believing that we have done our exacted Christian duty for the week. As Bishop Talbot correctly points out, "There should be no spectators [in worship] but only participants in a congregation... [as] the people of God [are] gathered together around the Word and the Sacrament"[88] for the expressed glory and praise of God. Christian worshippers ought not to be spectators but active and lively worshippers faithfully and enthusiastically responding to God's invitation and vibrant participants in what God, in the power of the Holy Spirit, is doing in worship.

3. Worship, it must be stressed, is not a spectator event or something that we leisurely and mindlessly observe. Worship is an encounter with God that we respond to and participate in freely and out of love for God. Worship is not homage that is exacted from us. Worship is the faith inspired human response to God's action upon us. Because worship is our response to the action of God upon our hearts and spirit, worship is truly a gift of communion and participation. Worship, like our salvation, is God's gift before it is our task. Because it is God's gift, like our salvation, Christ in worship is both our High Priest who offers Himself for us, and our Intercessor who sits at the right hand of God continuously interceding on our behalf. Worship is true only when we recognize that Christ is "the one true worshipper, the one for the many, who, through His representative humanity, includes all humanity in Himself."[89] Our participation and response to God's initiative in worship is our participation in the worship of Son to the Father.

4. Our response in worship is what Thompson calls "a response to a response."[90] Ours is a response to a response because in worship we are responding to the Holy Spirit who prompts us to be worshipful imitators of

---

[88] Bishop Frederic H. Talbot, <u>African American Worship: New Eyes for Seeing</u>. (Fairway Press, 1998), 81-82

[89] John Thompson, <u>Modern Trinitarian Perspectives</u> (New York: Oxford University Press, 1994), 100

[90] Thompson, 100

Christ who has already responded to God and offered up the perfect worship to God the Father. It is only when the Holy Spirit draws us, and only when Christ the Son, our High Priest and Mediator, facilitates our worship and praise before God the Father, that our worship reaches God. Only then is worship true, sincere, and acceptable to God. The implication here is that our worship of God is aided and facilitated by the Holy Spirit and mediated to the Father by Christ. This understanding of worship is critical to any meaningful participation in the worship encounter.

5. In worship, then, our participation and response are gifts of the Holy Spirit. Outside of that initiative by God the Father and outside of that priestly intercession by Jesus the Son, and outside of that inner urging by the Holy Spirit, who aids our worship, our worship experience would fail to be worship that is true and therefore acceptable to God. Worship that is true is worship that is based on knowledge of God, inspired by the Holy Spirit, and has become an outflowing product of the human mind, spirit, and a heart that truly loves God. If we fail to recognize that it is God who calls us to worship, that it is Christ the Son who mediates our prayers and praise to the Father, and that the Holy Spirit is the inspiration and facilitator of our worship, worship will only be a routine gathering with the appearance of worship but lacking the power to please God and transform us.

6. By extension, our response to God's initiative with our kneeling at the altar, and our communion at the Lord's Table are gifts of the Holy Spirit. Our response and participation are gifts of the Holy Spirit because the Holy Spirit is the One who both bears witness to Christ and His worship to the Father. The Holy Spirit draws us to respond and participate in the worship of our Creator God. Jesus says in John 6:44 "No one can come to Me unless the Father who sent Me draws [him/her]..." Indeed, "Christ is not known and believed on the ground of human testimony but only on the basis of the testimony that comes from God Himself."[91] Whether we view worship as devotion, reverence, respect, admiration, adoration, or love for God, unless

---

[91] Thomas F. Torrance, "Come Creator Spirit for the Work of Renewal of Worship, Doctrine, and Life," in <u>Liturgical Renewal in the Christian Churches</u>, ed. Michael J. Taylor (Baltimore-Dublin: Helicon, 1967), 135; See also John 10:29

God takes the initiative, and unless our response is one of faith in the Lord Jesus, and unless we are prompted by the Holy Spirit, such worship is fundamentally flawed. Without divine initiative and inspiration, human worship would be reduced to mere appearances, theatrical performances, and unfulfilling routines.

7. If worship is to be more than appearance, exacted homage, and a cluster of routine theatrical procedures, we need to urgently recognize that it is God who lovingly makes the first move in drawing us to Himself. We also need to grab hold of the understanding that it is Christ who mediates our worship. If our worship experience is to have the desired effects of pleasing God and transforming us, it is imperative that we realize that it is not by our know-how but by the power of the Holy Spirit by whom worship is facilitated and sustained. The vitality of worship is therefore invested in our knowledge of the One who not only lovingly draws us to Himself, but who is also the very source of true worship and sustained praise. If that truth is lost in our human theatrics, worship never really begins at all.

8. When in worship, we allow Jesus by His example and knowledge of the Father[92] to inspire our worship of God, worship is likely to become more meaningful for us. Also, when we submit to the mighty working power of the Holy Spirit to draw us into fellowship with one another, our worship experience will become one that we are eager to be part of. Such realization may even potentially make us more open to spending quality time with God. When we get to that place where quality time with God matters, our worship experience has the potential to be so uplifting and so fulfilling, that we would probably forget about ourselves, forget that we are wearing watches, or even that a clock is on the wall somewhere in the sanctuary. Assuredly when God shows up and shows out in the power and presence of the Holy Spirit, time, and indeed, our own inconveniences, will be of little or no consequence. When God invites us and when the Holy Spirit shows up, it is time to lift up holy hands and magnify the Lord because Sunday morning is **Hallelujah** time!

---

[92] Jn 15:15

9. While worship requires our response and participation, and while the things we bring to worship are important contributions to the worship experience, we need to leave room for God to surprise us. When God, not our fine buildings, when God, not our finely tuned musical instruments, when God, not our human expediencies, when God, not the sounds of our own voices and oratory skills, becomes the real center of our worship, worship will be an experience where we never know what is going to happen next. But then, whatever happens, because we let God have His way, we believe it will change us and position us for the next level of relationship with God.

10. The things that we bring to the worship encounter, such as our fine buildings, finely tuned instruments, human expediencies, and oratory skills, are all together good. However, they should never be used to override the presence, goodness, and power of the Holy Spirit of God in worship. When in worship, the emphasis is placed on those things and how good we are at utilizing them, our worship experience at best, will remain shallow and repetitive patterns. Let us always remember dear friends that the real agent in our worship is not human invention, skill, or experience. The real agent in worship is and always will be Jesus Christ who, in and through the presence and work of the Holy Spirit, leads us in worship, lifts our praise, mediates our prayers, and receives and presents our thanksgiving to God.

11. The Holy Spirit who invokes within us the need and the desire to respond to God's initiative, and moves us to rely on the sole priesthood of Christ, also gives life/vigor and meaning to our worship of God. As Hebrews 8:1-2 affirms, Jesus is the one true medium, High Priest and Minister of Christian worship and Sacraments. As our sole Mediator and High Priest, Jesus Christ is the only perfect and acceptable offering in worship offered up to the Father. As worshipping sons and daughters of God then, what we do in response to God's call to worship is really our participation in what is an already acceptable and perfect offering of the Son to the Father. This understanding ought to grip us like a vice and take hold of our minds and spirits if our participation in worship is to bring glory to God, have real and enduring spiritually transforming value to us, and draw us into the communal life of God.

5. Christian Worship as Communion and Participation (Section One)

1. The Bible is filled with references to the communal and participative nature of worship. Though worship, as noted above, is service to God from the heart and an expression of our love and relationship with God,[93] worship is also communion with God expressed by and through our fellowship and communion with other worshippers. Worship is communion with the Father through Jesus Christ our blessed Lord.[94] It is our sharing in the like-mindedness of Christ toward God the Father[95] as well as our sharing and fellowship in the Holy Spirit.[96]

2. Worship, as communion, our sharing in the Word and Sacraments, and in the life and ministry of Christ, is most appropriately celebrated in the spirit and context of the Christian community. If indeed we conclude that worship is a responsive act of the Christian community, then the profession of our faith needs to reflect the communal nature of God who lives and works in unity with the Son and the Holy Spirit. As the Father, the Son, and the Holy Spirit exist and work as One in a communal relationship, we, through the Holy Spirit, are drawn into that communal life to be one with God. Worship, then, is the expression of this communal and participative relationship initiated by God.

3. In what, then, are we participating? We are participating in the life, worship, and ministry of Christ to the Father. In worship we are also participating in the life and mission of God. Through the finished work of the Lord, Jesus, through whom and by whom we are reconciled to God, and by whom our personhood is restored, we are also sharing in the communal life and dignity of God. As we share in the communal life of God through the Son, in the power of the Holy Spirit, the realization of that communion and fellowship

---

[93] Ps 111:1; Mt 18:20; Lk 24:33; Acts 1:4, 14; 2:1, 4:31, 14:27, 16:13, 20:7, 1 Cor 11:33
[94] 1 Jn 1:3; 1 Cor 1:9
[95] Phil 1:5
[96] Phil 2:1

ignites our awareness of the value God has placed on us. For those of us who have come to this realization, it has become a powerful means of spiritual and behavioral formation. As a direct result of that awareness, we now have the capacity to develop a deeper sense and value of our restored personhood. Consequently, we are encouraged and inspired to reflect the dignity of God implanted in all of us. With God inviting into, and stirring within us desires for fellowship with Him, and in view of our realization of His divine dignity invested in us, holy thoughts are ignited in us and contemplations of eternity come into our focus. As we conform to the revealed purposes and nature of God, the Holy Spirit daily directs our minds to things eternal so that we may pursue the divine purpose and destiny that we have been called to.[97]

Christian Worship as Communion and Participation (Section Two)

1. If worship is communion and participation, the communion and the fellowship that we share with God in worship needs to spill over into the Christian community. It is in community and through Christian fellowship and communion, which is our time of sharing with God and with each other, that worship finds true faith expressions and affirmations. Discovering the worthiness of God and proclaiming and sharing that worthiness through Christian witness and praise reports, are precisely what we are called to do. Such proclamation is not restricted to the formal liturgy.[98] If we believe that God's worthiness for praise is restricted to an isolated place and time, we run the risk of making worship temporal, fixed to a set context in time, departmental, separate, and far removed from other areas of our lives.

2. Christian worship and fellowship are not only Sunday morning events. They are daily encounters and experiences with God as well as opportunities

---

[97] 1 Tim 6:12; 1 Pet 5:10

[98] See chapter five of this text for a detailed discussion on the relations between worship and Christian mission/service

for us to fellowship with one another. As a pastor, one of the things that continues to concern me is the verbal exchange or greeting between fellow worshippers and between worshippers and the pastor, following the worship service. It is almost as if we are saying goodbye until next Sunday. One of the most common expressions that I continue to hear is, "See you next week." Without realizing it, we do not always make ourselves available for sustained fellowship and communion with each other. The truth is, far too often, we do not see some people for midweek fellowship, prayer, and Bible study. No room is made in our busy lives for sustained fellowship with each other. Where sustained fellowship with one another is disabled, communal and participative praise of God is also disabled. Because of our willingness to settle for occasional contact with other believers, opportunities for worship and shared fellowship and communion are reduced to casual meetings, until perhaps "next Sunday;" providing of course, that we do not decide to take next Sunday off from church.

    3. Worship should never be compartmentalized nor should it be an occasional experience. There is no sustained communion in that. Far too many believers are content with being C.M.E. Christians— because they only show up on Christmas, Mother's Day, and Easter. We have made worship so departmental, occasional, and seasonal, that we continue to ignore the need for continuous participation and communion not only with each other, but also with God. Such practice will only result in the retardation of our spiritual growth in Christ. Worship should never be restricted to an isolated weekly or seasonal event. Worship is continuous communion. As believing Christians, we need to urgently find ways at working to enhance true, sincere, and lasting fellowship. Otherwise, all that we are left with are casual exchanges on Sundays or other days that we may gather for potluck dinners, fish fries, yard sales, or if we decide to show up, perhaps to push an agenda, at committee "meetings."

    4. As a Christian and a pastor, I have painfully observed the absence of sustained fellowship in the Christian community. I often observe Christians coming together for social events but not necessarily socializing; always meeting through "church meetings" but seldom having a meeting of the minds and

getting to know each other through lasting fellowship and purposeful communion. After going to the same church for many years, some Christians still do not know each other's names. As a people worshipping together (in community), we ought to know each other well enough to at least know each other's names. Sadly, that is not always the case. If we are to move beyond casual, weekly, monthly, or seasonal encounters, we need to be intentional about developing meaningful and lasting communion and relationships with fellow believers. As indicated above, if proper and meaningful worship is the result of knowing God and having communion with Him, then meaningful relationship with fellow worshippers will only emerge through our intentional efforts to know and understand each other.

5. Perhaps if we were to acknowledge that we will spend eternity in heaven with each other and with Christ, we would begin to develop the good sense of fellowshipping together so that we can begin to have "a little heaven down here." We can begin with intentional demonstrations of true love and sustained fellowship and communion with other worshippers. If we treat each other as strangers and cannot stand to be around each other in our temporal state of existence, how are we going to stand spending eternity with virtual strangers? It is conceivable, then, that just knowing that it is God who comes to us and invites us into fellowship with Him and with each other through worship, we may be more intentional and excited about giving more of ourselves to the worship experience, to each other, and to every area of the church's life and ministries.

6. When we understand worship as relational, participative, and an overflow of our fellowship and communion with God and with each other, we may become more serious about being in alignment with each other as well as being in alignment with the will of God. We may also be inspired by that understanding to create and sustain an environment that is conducive to safe, healthy, and realistic relationships with fellow worshippers. As we faithfully bring all of ourselves, body, mind, and spirit, to the worship experience, we may also learn through our daily living out of the liturgy and our continuous communion, to extend compassion, empathy, and love to one another. Being a Christian is not a departmental or seasonal affair. Assembling with

fellow believers for worship, prayer, Bible study and fellowship, should not be a part-time aspiration but a frequent realization and manifestation of the communal God in us.

7. The point to remember is that worship is central to our lives. Because worship is not temporal but continuous, the worship experience needs to impact all of our lives beyond the formal gatherings on a given day of worship. If worship is communion and participation, a dialogue is necessary to sustain that communion and participation. Let us now turn our attention to a discussion of the dialogue and channel of mediation in worship.

6. Worship as a Dialogue: The Channel of Mediation

1. Because worship is communion and participation, it becomes essentially a dialogue between God and human beings. Understanding how this dialogue takes place is critical for our understanding of worship. James Torrance identifies this dialogue as a double movement of grace.[99] This implies a sort of back and forth exchange between God and us. Thompson speaks of this dialogue as the twin thrust of faith from God to humanity and humanity to God, a movement from above to below and vice versa.[100] This double movement of grace, indeed, this twin thrust of grace and faith, is a dialogue between the Creator and His created and believing sons and daughters that is mediated by the begotten Son, Jesus Christ and facilitated by the Holy Spirit.

2. This dialogue begins and ends with God. It is therefore from God to God, through Christ, in the power of the Holy Spirit to humanity, and from humanity through Christ our High Priest, in the power of the Holy Spirit to God who initiates the dialogue in the first place. This means that God has the first and the last word in this double movement of grace and faith. This

---

[99] Torrance, James B. <u>Worship, Community and the Triune God.</u> Downers Grove: InterVarsity Press, 1996.

[100] John Thompson, <u>Modern Trinitarian Perspectives,</u> 1994

movement is initially a God-humanward movement. In our response of faith to the outreaching grace of God, we then have a human-Godward movement. In this human-Godward movement, humanity reaches out to God the Father, through the Son, and by the Holy Spirit.

3. Grasping this essential principle of the channel of mediation is necessary for our understanding of God's flow of grace to us in worship and life. In both the movements from God to human and from human to God, it is God who initiates and sustains that dialogue. That dialogue or holy conversation we have with God in worship and daily living takes place in the power of the Holy Spirit and through Jesus Christ our Mediator and High Priest. The Holy Spirit, as it relates to communication between God and us, is like a live telephone line that keeps us connected with the Father and the Son. I am happy to report that this line is never busy. We are never put on hold. We are never stalled or delayed by electronic menu choices and dropped calls. And, thank God, because Jesus lives in us, it is a local call; no roaming charges! Furthermore, because worship is a dual affair, a dialogue if you will, between God and us, God always keeps His line of communication clear and absolutely free and open so He can hear us when we call.[101] **Hallelujah!**

4. True worship, true prayers, and true praise are emphatically God-centered and channeled through Christ in the power of the Holy Spirit. Though this medium of communication may sound formulaic in tone, it is the proper medium for understanding and sustaining our dialogue with God— from God, through Christ, in the power of the Holy Spirit to us; and from us in the power of the Holy Spirit to Christ who mediates us to God. In worship our holy conversation with God begins and ends with God; yet it is always continuous and refreshingly sustaining.

5. Because of the mediatory role of Jesus and the sanctifying and sustaining power of the Holy Spirit, the place where God meets us is not merely in the external forms of worship, but in places of the heart, mind, and spirit. Worship becomes something spiritual when the human heart is engaged in the process. Worship is effectual and spiritually transforming when our conversation with God goes through the proper channel— by the Holy Spirit,

---

[101] See Jeremiah 33:3

and through Jesus Christ who mediates our worship and praise to the Father. The desire to hear from God should always motivate us to worship.

7. Motives for Worship (Section One)

1. We are motivated to worship God first of all because we recognize who God is and because God invites us to. Our coming together as a congregation or in small groups for worship is therefore in response to God's invitation. As the Holy Spirit enables us to recognize who God is— Creator, Redeemer, Sanctifier, Sustainer of the universe, the One that is high and lifted up and shining in the light of His eternal glory— we are motivated and constrained by that realization to offer up loving reverence through worship and praise.

2. We are moved to worship God because we experience God taking hold of us as the First Cause and at core of our existence. Our desire and act of worship is a direct response to the fact that we are aware that God is God and that He is God all by Himself, needing no one's permission to be God. We are motivated to worship God because we recognize that by Him and for Him all things and peoples were made. Recognizing God to be the self-existing One, possessing life in Himself, and the First Cause of all created things, we are moved to worship and bow down before this most awesome and praiseworthy Being. Such an awesome power, transforming, holy and irresistible a presence, God, cannot be ignored!

3. We worship God because we are moved by the Holy Spirit to celebrate God. All that God is, everything that He has done through Jesus Christ for the redemption of our souls, and the manifold ways that He has manifested Himself in our lives, are worthy of celebration. Worship is therefore an occasion set aside in response to, and in celebration of God. In worship we celebrate God's faithfulness and the enduring friendship into which He has drawn us.[102] This friendship we have with God is the result of His overflowing love

---
[102] Bishop Talbot, <u>African American Worship</u>, 1998; see also Jn 15:15

and our faith response to that love that is manifested through trust and obedience.[103] Friendship is indicative of closeness and mutually valued personhoods. This friendship we have with God through our Lord Jesus Christ has placed us in a permanent state of restored personhood and dignity which we had lost through disobedience and sin. Our friendship with God and the restored dignity and value that we have obtained from God are the direct results of the atoning and reconciling work of Jesus Christ on the cross at Calvary. Reconciliation is indicative of restoration. We are moved to celebrate God because we recognize that He has restored us from our fallen state, mended our brokenness, and gifted us with His love demonstrated by His mighty act of salvation through the Lord Jesus.

4. Love motivates us to worship God. Our worship and celebration of God is our faith response and our living sacrifice of praise to God for His outpouring love, grace and favor. Celebration as used in the worship context is, and should always be indicative of love that is expressed through exuberant praise. When we think of the goodness of the Lord God, and what He has done for us through Jesus Christ, our souls, our hearts, and our voices should cry out, **Hallelujah**, thanking God for saving us! Given the involvement of God in our lives, and given the extent that He has gone in order to redeem us, passive and silently "sophisticated" observance of the worship process almost seems like an expression of ingratitude directed to God. God is worthy of our active and passionate worship and exuberant praise.

5. We worship and celebrate God with joyful shouts of praise because we are aware of His involvement in getting us through some of life's greatest challenges. Shouting and praising God in some churches is still an emotional hot button issue that tends to divide people who should not be divided at all. Some people go to church to have a quiet time while others do so to verbally voice their praise in joyful celebration of God. People shout because when they look back over their lives, they see where they should have been dead but God kept them alive. They see where, with all the problems and drama they have had in their lives, they should have lost their minds, but God kept them sane. All week they may feel like nothing at home and nothing at work but

---

[103] Jn 15:14

when they get to church, the presence of the Lord, coupled with the understanding that God is seeking fellowship and communion with them, makes them feel like they are somebody; worthy persons. They shout because they are overjoyed and filled with praise for God because they realize that God thinks enough of them to care, bless, and deliver them from their distresses. The Lord God is worthy to be praised! **Hallelujah!**

6. In life and in worship, praise does three, though not exclusive, things. One, praise manifests the presence of God. Two, praise takes the attention off ourselves and the circumstances in our lives and places the attention on God. And, three, praise confuses the enemy. Praise sends the enemy running with no time to pack. Since praise manifests God's presence, we also realize that praise repels the presence of the enemy, satan. An atmosphere that is filled with sincere worship and praise to God by humble and contrite hearts is disgusting and absolutely disturbing to the devil. Wherever God's praise lives and wherever the name of Jesus is lifted up in praise, the devil cannot stay there. The devil fears the power that is in and comes from the name of Jesus. The devil might show up but he cannot tarry there because praising God and lifting up the name of Jesus, is to the devil, what kryptonite is to Superman. God inhabits the praise of His people. But the devil cannot live where there is praise. Having trouble in the church? Start praising God there. Having trouble in your home? Start praising God there. Having trouble in your relationship? Start praising God together. Start praising God in the midst of your situations and the devil and all the haters, backbiters, and forces of evil will get so discombobulated that they have to leave your space and return your peace. As darkness flees when light shows up, so the devil and the forces of evil flee when praise is in the atmosphere.

MOTIVES FOR WORSHIP (SECTION TWO)

1. I want to make it abundantly clear that while a shout of praise is usually a spontaneous expression of joy and praise response to the

extraordinary blessings of God, no one should be compelled to shout or made to feel that they are ungodly if they do not shout. While for some worshippers just showing up is believed to be a sufficient demonstration of gratitude to God, and while shouting may not be necessary for the work of God to be accomplished, praising God is some worshippers' way of verbalizing their gratitude to God for what He has done. It is faith that releases the blessings of God so even if you shout, just for the sake of shouting, without faith it is impossible to please God. When you shout therefore, make sure faith is in the shout. When you shout make sure it is God that you are glorifying and not drawing attention to yourself. Because God actively loves[104] and cares for us, we are motivated to respond to Him with active and vibrant and joyful praise and worship.

2. We should never belittle or disparage those who elect not to verbalize or articulate their praise. While we should not belittle those who come to church to have a silent moment with the Lord, I do believe that the worship experience is an opportunity for those who are so moved, to get really excited about God. After all, the Word by which the worshipper's convictions are guided tells us to:

> "Make a joyful noise unto the Lord…Serve the Lord with gladness; come before His presence with singing. Know that the Lord, He is God; it is He who has made us and not we ourselves; we are His people and the sheep of His pasture. Enter His gates with thanksgiving, and into His courts with praise. Be thankful to Him and bless His name. For the Lord is good; His mercy is everlasting, and His truth endures to all generations."[105] **Hallelujah!**

Psalm 150 also calls on worshippers to praise God with every fiber of their being and with every available instrument. Now, if God commands us to make joyful noises as we come into His presence, our insistence on having quiet time during the worship experience seems a lot like disobedience to

---

[104] Jn 3:16
[105] Ps 100

the will of God and His expectations of us in worship. God obviously loves it when we verbalize our praise of Him with thanksgiving. Worship is not for our quiet downtime. Worship is an up time; a time for lifting up God with joyful and celebratory praise.

3. For those who may want to insist on having quiet times during worship, they should not, however, get mad when "Sister So and So" and "Brother So and So" get really joyful and happy in the Lord. When we hear others verbalizing their praise of God in worship, we ought to encourage them because we do not know what things they have had to put up with and the troubles through which God has brought them. In worship we should not hide or cover the righteous and mighty deeds of God with our silence. Instead, we should speak of the goodness and faithfulness of God in verbalized and exuberant praise. In worship and in our daily lives we should not conceal the loving-kindness and truth about God from the great assembly of those whose lives He has also touched.[106] Praise is never silent. Praise is the verbalized and joyful sounds in the worshipping congregation in response to the goodness of God. When I think of the goodness of Jesus, and all the he has done for me, my soul cries out **Hallelujah!** Thank God for saving me!

4. Some of us just love to praise God. This does not mean that those who elect not to verbalize their praise do not love God. It is however, a joyful and empowering experience to give God praise. As soon as a few hearts begin to stir with joy and gratitude, and as soon as a little praise gets started, and as soon as a little prayer wheel begins to turn, before you know it, the Holy Ghost sets our hearts on fire for Jesus and we cannot help moving and grooving to the power and rhythm of the Holy Ghost. By His power we praise the Lord. By His power we shout **"Hallelujah!"** By the grace and power of the Holy Spirit, we send up mighty praises to God; our help in ages past, the keeper of our souls in the present time, and our hope for years to come. Worship is an experience, then, where God meets His people and we never quite know what is going to happen. But when the Holy Spirit manifests Himself and begins to stir up our souls, something always has to give. In worship, self has to give way to God. In worship, if it is to be true and spiritually

---

[106] Ps 40:10

transforming, the human action has to give way to the actions of God. In worship fear and pride ought to take second place to praise.

5. As the old spiritual says: "There ain't no harm to praise the Lord." Some of us, even though we profess our love for God, are sometimes a little reluctant to verbalize our praise of God for fear that we may disturb or offend the "silently sophisticated worshipper." If allowed, our sense of personal pride, the fear of disturbing others, and our own misplaced sense of dignified behavior in worship, will muzzle our praise of the One who alone is truly worthy of our uninhibited praise. Pride and the fear of expressing our passion for God in the company of others, have contributed much to the silencing of our praise to God. The result is impassionate religious and ritualistic routines. What God, the source of our strength, deserves is passionate worship and praise! **Hallelujah!**

6. We are motivated to worship God because He is our strength. As a pastor, I have had occasions to observe some of our more experienced (senior) members, many of whom had reasonable excuses to stay home. However, because of their love for God, they show up and show out for God with profound expressions and desire to worship and praise God. I recall this particularly sweet and most committed lady, "Mother Drew," whom I met in 1998 and pastored form 1998-2000. She was 91 years old. She was a communion steward in a local church that I served in Burlington, Iowa. Coming in for the Sunday morning service, with feet inflicted with arthritic pain and stiffness, she would literally use her hands to pull her way up about an eight or nine-step stairway in order to get into the sanctuary. Slowly but surely, Mother Drew would make her way into the sanctuary. When it was time for worship however, she was a picture of liveliness and a Spirit-filled soul. Another lady, I called "Grandma Bevel" at about age 93 was an example of lively praise. I was her pastor in Des Moines, Iowa from 2000-2005. Using a four-prong walker, and hardly able to make it up another set of seven to eight steps of stairway to the sanctuary, she would enter the worship experience with an appreciable joy for the Lord. When she got caught up in worshipping God everything about her changed. During the singing of praise songs, this wonderful lady, who could hardly make it up the stairs, would stand up and move with a holy

grove that would cause younger and able-bodied "silently sophisticated worshippers" seeking to have a quiet time in worship, to ponder their own silence and indifference to the worship, glory, and praise of God. In God, these most senior members found strength and came to "church" expressly to worship and praise God with every ounce of energy in their bodies. They are true examples of the joy of the Lord being their strength. When they came to worship God, in those moments of worship and praise, their pain and discomfort never seemed to stop them. They inspired me!

7. Some of us may not always have the energy to move all week because of sickness in our bodies. But come Sunday morning, because of our desire to be in the presence of the Lord, we walk with a special walk and move with a special purpose. When we recognize the nearness and presence of God in our lives, come Sunday morning, we have a new walk because the Holy Spirit puts pep in our step, clapping in our hands and holy moving in our righteous grooving. We are motivated to worship God because when life presses us down, God through Christ, in the power of the Holy Spirit, supports us when we are falling, lifts our spirits, and takes us to levels of enjoyment in Christ that we could not reach by ourselves. The power that compels and motivates our worship is the conviction that the Holy Spirit is coming, has come, and will already be there ("at church") when we get there, to be our strength in lifting King Jesus just a little higher with praise!

8. We are motivated to worship God because we also recognize that in Him, our value is elevated and our personhood is liberated. Have you ever considered the change in your life and status when you are gathered with other Christians to worship God? During the course of the week, your secular associates in the work place for example, may underappreciate your value. But, come Sunday morning during "church," your value or worth takes on more than chronological, statistical, or economic significance. Your transition from Monday to Sunday takes on a radically transforming spiritual significance.

9. Let us consider for a moment how worship changes and affirms our human value. The person that works in a secular setting during the week is often considered to be just another person; just another statistic, and just another employee that is being used to boost a company's economic bottom line.

But come Sunday morning, the janitor becomes known as the chairperson of one board or another; the maid or nurse's aid is recognized as the president or director of one committee or another. Come Sunday morning, your sons and you daughters become your brothers and sisters in Christ. During the work week, everybody who is called by every name except a Christian, in the world's attempts to undervalue his/her worth and belittle his/her human dignity in the work place, becomes "Mr. This" and "Mrs. That;" "Brother John" and "Sister Mary." All week, you may not count or even be considered to be much. Sometimes you are overworked and underpaid. Sometimes your dignity is crushed. Sometimes you are undervalued and underappreciated. Sometimes you may be treated as though your personhood does not matter. But when God draws you into fellowship with Himself, you know you are somebody in Christ Jesus and your bruised dignity is restored and your human value is elevated. That is the result of being in the presence of the Lord and the radically transforming effect of true worship. You and I are radically transformed by our worship encounter with God because fellowship with God moves us from a place of lowliness to a place of honor; from a state of misery to a state of comfort; and from a state of fear and uncertainty to a place of faith and blessed assurance. In worship, when we proclaim the worthiness of God through praise, God reciprocates by restoring our bruised dignity and elevating our human worth. **Hallelujah!**

Motives for Worship (Section Three)

1. The experience of God's presence and help in our lives all through the week motivates us to assemble together so that we may jubilantly gather up our joys and our concerns in a bundle of praise as we testify to others about our experience with God. All week long, the right words may elude us, but come Sunday morning we are inspired to "talk" with a special talk because we know who we are and to whom we belong. We are inspired because we know who God is, who we are in Him, where we

have been, where God has brought us from, and the purpose and destiny He has establish for our lives. Regardless of what we go through during the week, for true worshippers, come Sunday morning, knowing what God has already done and has promised to do, our whole outlook on life changes. For us as worshipping people, Sunday morning has special significance because we are changed to worship and gather up our praise to God.

2. We come together to worship God because in His presence we have assurance and acceptance. Though we may feel rejected and sometimes dejected during the workweek because of some poor working conditions and sometimes because of the not so kind bosses and people we have to work with, come Sunday morning, we know that when we assemble ourselves for worship, we are accepted and embraced by our kind and compassionate God. Because of that assurance and acceptance that we feel and experience in the presence of God, indeed, in the secret place of God's tabernacle, our affections for the Lord find uninhibited expressions. We feel uninhibited in the presence of the Lord because God Himself moves us into such close proximity to Him that it becomes a place where faith becomes stronger than fear. That place is a secret place;[107] and God Himself invites us there. It is a place where trouble is checked at the door, so to speak, and is not granted access. It is a secret place where the devil cannot come.

3. When worship is a part of our lives and our hearts are in tuned to God, we feel secure in the presence of God. We feel and experience a deep sense of security when we gather to worship because sincere worship only takes place when we are at one with God. Our sense of security comes from the knowledge that in that secret place, we are wrapped up and tied up in Jesus and caught up, as it were, in a divine experience with God through the effectual working of the Holy Spirit. Because worship is that secret place of the heart where we meet God in faith and praise, we have a deep sense of security because the door to our heart is opened to God alone and closed to the forces of evil and the things that so often trouble us. In that secret place, nothing and no one matters but God. When we worship God, we do receive

---

[107] Ps 27:5, 91:1

sweet relief from our troubles and renewed strength to face the challenges and troubles in our lives. That motivates us to worship!

4. Based on who we know God to be, and the benefits that He bestows upon us when we lavishly praise His holy name, many of us are enthusiastic about worship and do not necessarily wait for Sunday morning to "have church." For some of us, a formal moment is not enough and so worship becomes a lifestyle. When worship becomes a lifestyle, evil and trouble of every kind may still taunt us, but they cannot and will not have dominion over us. Sure, the forces of evil will come knocking at the doors of our hearts and minds. Nonetheless, in light of the fact that we are, or should be, all season, everyday worshippers, there is no room for the devil to come in and take up residence. As the Negro-Spiritual affirms, "De devil can't catch you in your min' if you keep it stayed on Jesus."[108] The devil does not like to see God's children pray or hear them in praise. Truly, reading a Bible chapter, saying a prayer, and putting praise in the atmosphere, will keep the devil away.

5. We are motivated to worship because God matters. In worship, when we become aware of the presence of the Lord and are made one with Him by the power of the Holy Spirit, nothing else matters but God. Not our problems; not our pain; not our trials; only God. That is why some of us receive freedom from the devil, deliverance from our pain, and supply for our lack when we put God first and worship Him because He matters. Worship is a place therefore, where we put God above ourselves and where our circumstances, personal desires and ambitions decrease so that He may increase in our lives.

6. Here is a joyful report! We are the objects of God's love and redeeming grace! God, who is high and lifted up, lovingly bends to receive our praise! God, who is holy, comes to us in the person of Christ.[109] In love, He reaches out to us in our sinful existence so that He may transform us. He draws us into communion with Himself, and empowers us with the authority of the Holy Spirit to overcome the power of sin. That awareness moves us to worship. The realization that we are the objects of God's love and redeeming

---

[108] From "Woke Up Dis Mornin', in <u>Songs of Zion</u>, Abingdon Press, 1981, No. 146
[109] 2 Cor 5:19

grace, encourages our obedience, stirs up our faith, and invokes our exuberant praise for God who loves us enough to allow His only begotten Son to die for us. **Hallelujah!**

7. We are motivated to worship God because we recognize that through Jesus Christ, the grace of God comes to us with hope and the promise of eternity. This awareness of hope is an act of God, who, through Jesus Christ, mends our brokenness and lovingly pulls us away from a downward spiral of personal despair, and places us in a state of hopeful resolve. Gloria Gaither puts it this way:

> "Something beautiful, something good;
> All my confusion He understood;
> All I had to offer Him was brokenness and strife,
> But He made something beautiful of my life."[110]

This is indeed that wonderful exchange of grace, whereby Christ takes our broken and unfulfilled lives, intercedes on our behalf before the Father, sanctifies them, and in return, makes us complete and fulfilled in Him. **Hallelujah!** What a Savior!

8. We are motivated to worship and glorify God because we recognize that in life, worship, and witness, the Holy Spirit takes us, broken earthen vessels, and replenishes and transforms us into the heavenly treasures of God's holiness.[111] The replenishing and renewing of our souls and the contagious holiness of God to which the Holy Spirit exposes us, equip us with the desire and motivation to constantly seek after God's holiness in worship as well as in faithful and obedient service in the world. Indeed, the Holy Spirit transforms us, weak, otherwise insignificant and insufficient human beings into instruments of power, so that even when we are weak, through Christ who died for us, we are strong.[112] Worshippers are therefore motivated to send up praise and thanksgiving to God because of who He is, and also in response to God's salvific act of love demonstrated through

---

[110] "Something Beautiful" United Methodist Hymnal # 394 (Eighth Printing, 1993)

[111] 2 Cor 4:7

[112] 2 Cor 12:9-10

Christ. Through Christ's own self-offering love on the cross, we are drawn into the recognition of God's intent and mighty act of grace demonstrated towards us.

9. Consequently, the cross should not be viewed as a sacrifice that seeks to satisfy the anger of an offended God. Rather, in a more glorious sense, the cross should be viewed as the only offer of forgiveness, redemption, and life from a loving and merciful God. The life of Christ given for the believer becomes a renewing work of God's grace. Our living out of the Christian life is therefore contingent on the love and restored presence of God in our lives. The recognition of who God is, His salvific act on our behalf, the holiness into which God has drawn us, and the good and perfect gifts He has bestowed upon our lives, churches, and ministries, have led us to worship and praise God. We therefore join the Psalmist who moved a motion in favor of God's praise urging us to:

"Praise Him in the sanctuary
Praise Him for His mighty acts
Praise Him according to His excellent greatness
Praise Him with timbrel and dance
Praise Him with stringed instruments
Praise Him with loud cymbals
Praise Him with clashing cymbals
Let everything that has breath praise the Lord
Praise the Lord."[113]

10. John Layton seconded that motion when he penned these words of praise:

"We'll praise the Lord for He is great,
And in His presence angels wait;
All heaven is swelling with His praise,
Shall we not, too, our anthems raise?

---

[113] Psalm 150

O we will praise Him,
O we will praise Him,
O we will praise His holy name!
O we will praise Him,
O we will praise Him,
O we will praise His holy name!

We'll praise the Lord for He is wise;
His wisdom shines through all the skies;
The earth He measures with a span,
And crowns us with His image, man.

We'll praise the Lord for He is just,
And in him we may ever trust;
Princes and kings may turn aside,
But God by right will e'er abide.
We'll praise the Lord for He is true;
His word the same all ages through;
Earth, sea and sky may pass away,
But firm God's truth will ever stay.

O praise Him for His name is love,
And from His glorious throne above
He bends to welcome our weak praise;
Shall we not, then, our anthems raise?"[114]

Surely, God is worthy of the praise from His created people and universe. In that universe, God's sons and daughters, empowered by grace, which is God's own divine assistance to us, are moved to acknowledge God's worthiness of praise.

---

[114] John T. Layton, We'll Praise The Lord, in <u>African Methodist Episcopal Church Hymnal</u>, 1984, No. 60

If true worship comes from our understanding or knowledge of God, then it is essential to have knowledge and understanding of the liturgy that directs our attention to the only true God who is worthy of our worship and praise. Let us now turn our attention to the liturgy of worship. Our conversation will focus on selected components of the liturgy of worship. Here we shall also examine the purposes of the liturgy, and the implications of living liturgical and doxological lives.

Chapter Four

The Liturgy Of Worship

Prayer:

Enter my heart anew today, oh Lord. Fill my heart with desires for You. Fill my thoughts with contemplations of Your merciful ways. Fill my mind with Your Word. Touch my tongue dear God, so that my mouth shall speak aloud what my mind is already aware of and what my heart desires to show forth in praise. Guide me in every area of my life so that I may bring glory to Your holy name by all that I do to serve You. This I pray in the precious name of Jesus, Amen!

Suggested Scripture Readings: Ps 150; Mt 5:16; Rom 12:18, 15:17-19, 27; Gal 5:25; 1 Pet 1:12-19

Hymns:
 "O Worship The King"
 "Worship His Majesty"
 "Open The Eyes Of My Heart Lord"
 "One God, One Faith, One Baptism"
 "O Come, O Come Emmanuel"
 "It Is Well With My Soul"
 "Fill My Cup Lord"
 "I Know It Was The Blood"

1. Overview

Since it is in worship that many practicing Christians are made aware of liturgical forms and practices, without being exhaustive, selected liturgical forms and practices will be discussed. The goal is to foster understanding of the theological and doctrinal imports of the liturgy in worship. I also set out to show how practicing worshippers might be aided by the liturgy in their understanding of God. Certainly, when the content and purpose of the liturgy are understood, the potential for worshippers discovering meaning and reaching greater levels of intentional participation becomes a more realistic goal. Such understanding may also have spiritually transforming benefits. When we understand the purpose and design of the liturgy, the potential for meaningful and intentional worship may also become attainable. Since understanding of a process often leads to sense-making, and even a greater degree of participation in that process, understanding the liturgy and its purpose in worship has fascinating possibilities and may lead to worshippers' renewed awareness of God to whom the liturgy ultimately points.

Discussions of liturgical components will be limited to the call to worship, preaching, Baptism, Holy Communion, and the doxology. In our discussion on the call to worship, we shall see that long before the pastor or worship leader calls us to worship, God has already done so. The invitation and call to worship is God's. We are simply carriers, distributors, and faithful respondents to it. As pastors and worship leaders, our task, at best, becomes a reminder for worshippers to respond to the call of God who comes near and draws us through the Holy Spirit to worship Him. The call to worship is a point at which the Holy Spirit rather than the pastor or worship leader calls forth a scattered people to lift high their united praise of God in the true Spirit of worship.

Discussion on preaching, as a word from the Lord, is intended to show how preaching is a change agent. As such, we shall see that preaching is both a source of information as well as a channel of inspiration and change. As a source of information, preaching encourages change by informing the mind and stirring up the human intellect. As inspiration, preaching speaks to the human heart in order to invoke the right attitude for living out that change.

Regarding Baptism and Holy Communion, it is my intention to show how, through the sacraments of Baptism and Holy Communion, God is intent on giving us new starts, and having sustained fellowship and communion with us. The goal is also to demonstrate how relentless God is about drawing us into communion with Him. How God the Father works in unity with the Son and the Holy Spirit to achieve that goal will constitute critical components of our discussion and subsequent understanding.

In our exploration of the doxology, I seek to show that the doxology is not limited to the worship ingathering and the context of formal worship. The doxology also extends beyond the formal liturgy to encompass the way we live our lives as witnesses to the power and grace of God. I will argue then, that the doxology and the benediction should rightly be considered precursors for continuous Christian living, mission, and service to God in the world, rather than being thought of as liturgical proclamations that worship has ended.

Based on an informative and practical paradigm, our discussion of the liturgy is intended to promote the development of a synthesis of worship, liturgical practices, pastoral leadership, and worshippers' response. The objective is to encourage mutual elevation of laity participation and pastoral leadership through the recognition of, and a working toward, a common consensus on the purpose of liturgical practices.

2. The Purpose of the Liturgy

1. What is the liturgy and what is its purpose? The liturgy is a method, a form, or a structural arrangement used to guide and give order to public worship. These methods, forms, or structural arrangements are usually developed, prescribed, and practiced by a church, denomination or a religion based on that church or religion's traditions and religious practices. Some synonyms or terms used in place of the liturgy are: Order of service, religious ceremony, ritual, rite, worship service, and mass.

2. The liturgy is a coming together of selected forms, words, and actions that are designed to open the worshipper's awareness of God and the selected sequences of that particular worship service. We commonly call these sequences "order of service" because of the prescribed sequential liturgical formats that a church or denomination may have adopted. One of the benefits of an order of service is that it creates commonality as it relates to drawing worshippers' attention to the same area of focus in worship. By extension, such commonality also helps in bringing together all the people's voices and responses as one voice, united to lift God's praise. Such order helps to minimize and, at best, eliminate the potential for confusion. In other words, the order of service helps to promote an engaged and synchronized understanding and worship of God. The liturgy is an instrument or vehicle of worship that is therefore used for the preservation of unity in worship as well as source of edification that leads us primarily to the recognition of God and God's operation in worship. In a real sense, the liturgy is a channel through which the dialogue of worship is sustained between God and His worshipping people.

3. As we have already established, God initiates worship. Consequently, the liturgy begins with God. That makes God the primary Liturgist. As the primary Liturgist, it is God that speaks and acts toward and through His people. This means that in worship, both the initiative and the response are God's actions. Shafer agrees that:

> "...The people's liturgy is their response to God's encounter with them. The response is theirs, but it is also God's. He evokes their response by His own actions and words. He also continues His work and His liturgy through the words and deeds of worshippers."[115]

4. Within the context of the Sunday morning worship service, the liturgy is a sort of disclosure of pastoral intent that seeks to deepen the

---

[115] Floyd Doug Shafer, <u>Liturgy: Worship and Work</u> (Board of Christian Education of the United Presbyterian Church USA, 1952), 2

worshipper's receptivity and openness to God. However, before the liturgy is some indication of pastoral intent, because of its doctrinal formulation and theological affirmation, the liturgy of worship helps to make clear to worshippers who God is. Though the pastor is the liturgical leader within the context of the formal worship service, the only person capable of directing worshippers' to the spiritual depth of worship and liturgical intent is the Holy Spirit.

5. The Holy Spirit is therefore the inspiration and director of the liturgy. Through the liturgy, the Holy Spirit arouses our faith, enlightens our minds, brings us into a necessary awareness of God, and inspires and directs our worship of God. Through the presence and work of the Holy Spirit, the liturgy is given life, vitality, and purpose. Due to the liturgy's doctrinal imports, as a working of the Holy Spirit in our hearts and minds, as we worship, we are given not merely a glimpse of God; we actually experience God's presence in and around us. After all, it is to God that the liturgy is designed to point us. The liturgy is therefore a sort of icon and should therefore be understood not only for its structural, instructional, orderly, and organizational values, but primarily for its spiritual and iconic value, which is to point us to God.

6. The structure of the liturgy should be such that it not only makes us aware of who God is and His presence among us; it should also encourage us to become caught up in the outpouring life and activity of God in worship. The liturgy is able to lead us to an understanding of who God is because elements of the liturgy are formulaic and doctrinal expressions of the Church's traditions and faith. These formulaic expressions of faith and ascriptions of praise may be found in elements of the liturgy such as the call to worship, the Apostles' Creed, the doxology, and other doctrinal choices that the church may elect to use in that church's affirmations of faith. By these doctrinal faith expressions, worshippers are aided in their ascription of praise to God. The liturgy of worship may also serve as a medium for promoting Christian holiness and devotion for clergy and lay alike. This can be achieved through mutual participation in an engaged and synchronized understanding of God and the worship process.

3. Selected Liturgical Components of Worship

A. The Call to Worship: A Reminder and Preparation for Worship

1. The call to worship is a component of the liturgy that may be used to draw our attention to the event of worship. The call to worship helps worshippers to uniformly recognize that not only is God already present, but also that He is worthy of our attention, and ready to receive our adoration and praise. The call to worship is essentially a greeting that may be formal or informal. Whether formal or informal, the greeting should be an explicitly Christian one that seeks to invoke worshippers' attention to the presence of God in the content as well as the context of worship. The call to worship may be a brief conversation, a sort of responsive dialogue (which is most commonly used), a monologue, a song, or scriptural sentences. Whatever the pastoral or congregational preference, the call to worship should always seek to draw our attention to God. The call to worship is also a reminder for us to renew our fellowship within the Christian community as together we diligently seek to actively participate in the worship of God.[116]

2. When then, does the worship service really begin? In my opinion, worship never really ends. What we begin in formal worship, as we shall see later, ought to spill over into other areas and times of our lives. Since it is the formal worship service and its liturgical contents that we are speaking of here however, the formal worship service really begins when people begin to gather in response to the call of God for fellowship and communion. This does not necessarily happen at the moment we gather in the physical context of worship, 'the church," or at the moment we get ready to launch what has become our formal worship service within the confines of the sanctuary. If our minds are at all focused on God, and if we have developed a lifestyle of worship, our preparation begins long before we get to "church." Certainly

---

[116] See Appendix 5, for samples of Calls to Worship that may be used throughout the Christian Year

before the pastor or worship leader calls the people's attention to worship in the local church, God's universal invitation is already issued by the effectual and pervasive working of the Holy Spirit. That way, worshippers everywhere are lovingly reminded of the experience that awaits them at their respective formal ingatherings for worship and praise. I believe it is a good practice to be prepared for worship in advance of Sunday morning and not just moments before our established time for formal worship.

3. Because worship requires preparation, the entire family should be engaged in the preparation process. In those cases where families with young children are likely to be rushed on Sunday mornings in preparing for worship, I have advised parishioners to delegate responsibilities to the older children and engage them in helping the younger ones get ready. I also encourage them to begin getting ready for worship by determining what they are going to wear to church in advance of the day of worship and to involve the younger ones in the process of picking out and preparing their outfits. The objective is to inspire interest and ownership of the process. Certainly, it is not the garment or what to wear that is important. It is the interest and attitude that such engaged preparation invokes and nurtures. In the process of getting ready in advance of the actual worship encounter, both parents and children may learn to develop and advance an attitude for worship. I also believe that we should get some of the preliminaries out of the way prior to the day of formal worship. We should for example get clothes and shoes laid out and ready; get the younger children organized; get our Bibles, purses, and car keys put in place; and prepare our checks, tithes and offering envelopes in advance. If we take the time to put these things in place, we increase the probability of saving preparation time just before we leave for church, getting to church on time, minimizing anxiety, and freeing ourselves from the activities that can so easily interfere with one's spirit and enjoyment of worship.

4. A period of preparation, a day or two before our actual day of worship, may also serve to develop as well as nurture our faithfulness, passionate anticipation, and desire for worship. Preparation also helps us to form and develop worshipful attitudes. The human interest is peeked when we take time to prepare for events such as vacation trips, a social event, Christmas, a

birthday celebration or a wedding or wedding anniversary. Advanced preparation for worship can also be a good way for directing our energies and anticipation for faithfully responding to God's invitation and call to worship.

5. The call to worship, then, is the point at which the Holy Spirit, through the pastor or worship leader, calls forth God's people for intentional and passionate worship. The call to worship is designed to invoke our acknowledgement, gratitude, and reverence, for the presence of God who comes to us and meets us for fellowship and communion. Our coming together for worship is both an inward and an outward spiritual gathering of the people of God. It is an inward gathering because worshippers come in and assemble themselves, united in spirit for worship. It is an outward gathering because having worshipped, we depart with grace and boldness to witness to the saving power of God in the world, which is our active worship.

6. We are called for inward gathering for three reasons. The first reason is to glorify and worship God. The second is to seek fellowship with others and to encourage each other's faith and spirit. The third reason is to be inspired and equipped by the worship experience so that we may become effective witnesses to the love and mercy of God in the world through intentional Christian discipleship. It is by our coming together for worship that we are equipped by the Holy Spirit and infused with power and desire to go out and serve as we are mandated by Christ and reminded by the preached word to do.

B. Preaching
(Section One)

1. Preaching is an integral part of the liturgy of worship. Preaching is the proclamation of the Good News of God's salvation in Christ and a reaffirmation of God's presence and eternal promise. The preached word is a word of salvation that brings hope, peace, joy, transformation, and life to the spiritually dead.[117] Preaching is God's way of promoting Christian values for daily living. It is the goal of preaching to inform, inspire, convict and stir up within the hearer, awareness and reverence for God.

---

[117] Jn 5:25

Preaching is also intended to hold us accountable for the holy reordering of our lives. To that extent, the preached word is both content and (holy) confrontation that requires the human response of faith and obedience.

2. The primary task of preaching is to change the human heart by drawing people's attention to the Good News of God's redeeming love, mercy and grace through the Lord Jesus. By extension, preaching has six major (mutually inclusive) functions. These are: (1) To invoke awareness; (2) to be a change agent in the process of interpreting and encouraging faith; (3) to re-present Christ; (4) to hold us accountable to God and to each other; (5) to encourage discipleship; and (6) to offer hope.

3. The first role of preaching is to invoke awareness. Preaching is intended to bring us into an intentional awareness of our Maker. The purpose of preaching, before it is anything else, is to draw awareness to God and encourage His praise. The task of the preacher is a commissioned one. That means that the preacher speaks only because God has spoken. The basis of preaching is the revelation that God has addressed to us in the Bible concerning Himself. The goal of preaching is therefore to draw our awareness first to God. Assuredly it is God who has called us and it is God who has promised to use preachers and preaching to accomplish His purpose and bring glory unto Himself. The ultimate purpose of the preached word is therefore to glorify God and to cause listeners to catch a glimpse of God's glory so that they may become transformed by it. To that extent, preaching is designed to save the human soul (Mark 16:16). Preaching also helps to invoke the human awareness of sin and the need for repentance. Preaching encourages the human intellectual and spiritual search for God so that we may discover and receive the forgiveness and salvation that He offers us through faith in the Lord Jesus. When the minister preaches to believers, it is intended to nurture, redirect our attention toward God, and remind us to show mercy, exercise justice, and walk humbly before God. When the unbeliever is the focus of a particular message, preaching is intended to make them aware of Christ as well as to draw them into a faith response to the atoning sacrifice of Christ on the cross for their redemption. Preaching is designed to encourage us to always contemplate those important and fundamental issues of life and

eternity— repentance, forgiveness, grace, mercy, justice, love for God and neighbor, life, death, and eternity.

4. The second role of preaching is to be a change agent in the process of interpreting and encouraging faith. By the life transforming power of the Holy Spirit, the preached word is a life changing agent.[118] It is the task of preaching to bring about transformation or change in people. Preaching brings about change in the way people think and act toward God and neighbor by reminding them of the moral designed God is established for us to follow. In order to do so, preaching directs the human focus to God and things of eternal value so that we may realize worthy alternatives to those humdrum human pursuits and interests that we would otherwise pursue. These pursuits of the mundane may have nothing to contribute to the advancement of our spiritual lives and purpose; but left alone, we would follow them to our detriment. Preaching therefore helps to shift our focus from ourselves and our individual pursuits, and directs us to God and His divine will and purpose for our lives. Preaching encourages change because it seeks to bring together, interpret, and translate all other areas of the liturgy of worship and the human life experiences, so that they may be seen and interpreted in light of the holiness of God and what His expectations of us are. That way, people are guided into putting their faith in God, finding new directions for their lives, and making choices that are of eternal value. In some measure, preaching empowers us to see the presence and involvement of God in other areas of our lives beyond the context of our formal day of worship. The awareness of God's presence in other areas of our lives may help to change the way we think and behave on a day to day basis. Put differently, preaching challenges us to not only live and act holy on Sundays and within the context of formal worship, but also daily and in every area of our lives. The preaching event is therefore another opportunity in worship for molding behaviors and for developing faith and understanding of the Lord Jesus. That makes preaching a channel that God also uses to bring about clarity and change in people's belief, attitude and behavior. Consequently, before preaching becomes the preacher's task, it is God's task. Because preaching is God's task manifested

---

[118] 2 Cor 3:6

through the faithful and committed preacher, preaching becomes a call to, as well as an offer of, forgiveness and sanctification by the Holy Spirit.

5. The third role of preaching is to re-present Christ. As we encounter God in the Living Word,[119] preaching becomes a re-presenting of Christ. By the preached word, Christ is presented and encountered. Our obedient and faithful response to the preached word is therefore our faithful response to Christ and a sort of rededication to Him. As preaching is a re-presenting of Christ to the believer, it is also a presenting of Christ to the non-believer for the sake of invoking their faith response. For, how shall they call on Him in whom they have not believed? And how shall they believe in Him of whom they have not heard?[120] Through the effectual work of the Holy Spirit, the Carrier and Enabler of the Word, and by the One in whom the Creative Word, the Living Word, the written Word (Verbum), and the proclaimed word (verbum) are embodied, Jesus Christ, the proclaimed word becomes a lively word by which God speaks to us. By the action of the divine Word, and by virtue of the Holy Spirit working through the anointed preacher, Christ is made present. It is not the preacher however, that makes Christ present. That task is only accomplished by the Holy Spirit. Through the Holy Spirit working in those who both preach and listen to the preached word from the Lord, the preached word is recognized as coming from God and working effectively in those who believe.[121] So, how then is Christ made present in the preached word? Christ is made present by the preached word because preaching is a testimony of His birth, ministry, redeeming grace, death and atoning sacrifice, resurrection, ascension and intercession, and His faithful promise to come again.[122] This makes preaching a carrier of both the content and substance of the Christian faith, Jesus Christ. When therefore we heed the preached word and accept it as having a divine source, or as coming from God through the human agent, the preached word makes Christ present, thus

---

[119] Jn 1:1

[120] Rom 10:14

[121] Deu 18:18; Jn 8:26, 12:49, 14:24; Acts 3:22; 1Cor 9:16; 2 Cor 5:18; Eph 3:8-10; 1 Thess 2: 13; 1 Pet 1:12

[122] See Jn 14:3 for example regarding Jesus' promise to return

invoking holiness in all of us who believe and respond to that presence with true faith.

6. The fourth role of preaching is to hold us accountable to God and to each other. In order to do so, preaching encourages and nurtures our faith and obedience and reminds us to exercise love for God and each other. The preached word holds us accountable and encourages our commitment to our covenant relationship with the Lord. Preaching does so by encouraging the human spirit, nurturing obedience, and by reminding us to act rightly toward God and neighbor. Preaching promotes obedience and love for God and others by reminding us to dedicate ourselves and our resources to God, the cause of the Gospel of Jesus Christ, and the nurturing and safeguarding of human personhood and dignity. As an agent of nurture, preaching offers healing and support to God's hurting sons and daughters. By doing so, the preached word is a constant reminder of God's love for us in Christ. Preaching reminds us to show forth our love for our neighbor in response to God's love towards us in order that we might act on the decision to live right in the world as proof that we have indeed been renewed in Christ. As a reminder, preaching calls us to walk in holiness with God so that we may honor our covenant relationship with Him. Because preaching feeds us with the word, holds us accountable, and calls us to honor our relationship with God, preaching is a sort of "soul food" upon which our minds and souls feed so that we may grow in grace and in the knowledge of God's love.

7. The fifth role of preaching is to encourage discipleship. Preaching calls and challenges us to Christian discipleship thus effectively pulling us away from the temptation to be complacent and passive worshippers. Preaching is our reminder to witness to the world concerning the presence and grace of God that we experience in worship. Preaching is a source of encouragement by which we are regularly reminded to reach out and impact other persons by our Christian lifestyle[123] for the sake of the kingdom.

8. The sixth role of preaching is to offer hope. Preaching is designed by God to advance the cause of righteousness, touch human lives, and to transform the human existential conditions with love, kindness, compassion, and

---

[123] Mt 5:14, 16

hope. Preaching, in light of, and despite the existence and extent of human suffering and uncertainty in the world, has the task of lifting up and mending fallen and broken humanity. This is accomplished when the preached word is built on scripturally sound information and offers spiritual directions that empower people to turn to the God of faith so that they may find hope and meaning for their lives with eternity always in mind. To that extent, the preacher and preaching become standard bearers of hope by encouraging people to develop faith filled relationships with God who is "faithful and will not allow the temptations and nuances of life to be more than we can stand, but will show us a way out so that we can endure"(1 Corinthians 10:13). Preaching is designed to lead people to Christ so that He, in the power of the Holy Spirit, may lift them up to God, the source of human life, hope, and dignity. People need to know that God is on their side. Reminding people of this should always be the mission of those whom God has called and anointed to preach.

Preaching
(Section Two)

1. While some may have chosen to preach, others are called and anointed by God to do so.[124] That being said, if preaching is to be effectual, those who preach need to be called, sent,[125] and have a personal relationship with Christ. The bottom line is that we cannot effectively and sincerely preach Him with whom we do not have a saving relationship. It is important to know Jesus personally because preaching is a personal and experiential testimony of the redeeming power of God's grace by the preacher who himself/herself has not only heard, but has also experienced Christ. Preaching therefore relates the preacher's understanding and experience of God to others with whom God is seeking communion and fellowship.

2. For preaching to have the desired impact of bringing about awareness and change in the human life and condition, the preacher and those who

---

[124] Mt 20:16

[125] Is 6:8; Jer 1:4; Amos 7:15; Jon 1:2; Acts 13:2, 26:16; Rom 10:15; 1 Cor 9:16; Heb 5:4

hear the word, cannot settle for faulty theology. Faulty theology is theology without Scriptural basis and therefore without divine mandate. Theology without Scriptural basis and divine mandate is purely driven by human pretext, presumption, and presuppositions. Neither can we settle for the rough edges of human theatrics and faulty traditions to inform the preaching event. What faulty tradition and theatrics will do is nullify the effect of preaching and theological understanding for our lives.[126]

3. Before the word is preached, if it is to have the desired effects, it must first be God's Word and revelation imparted to the preacher by the Holy Spirit. Indeed, the preacher preaches because God has spoken. The preacher receives that divine Word and revelation through hours of prayers, study, meditation and discernment. This way, the preached word becomes a witness to the Living Word, Jesus Christ. Those who preach and teach can only reach others when the Holy Spirit Himself transforms their spoken words into life and power. That makes the Holy Spirit the sole Anointer working through the preacher as well as within the hearer. That way, the delivery as well as the hearing, receiving, and receptiveness to the preach word may have the desired results. The Holy Spirit is also the One who moves us to respond to Christ who is made present through the proclaimed word. The preached word has life because by the Holy Spirit, the interaction between the Word of God and the human word is established thus impacting the responsiveness of the preacher to God as well as the receptiveness of the hearers to the preached word.

4. Our receptiveness to preaching is often an indication of our own understanding and encounters with God. It is not by the eloquence and power of the preacher's delivery that we are moved. For, as Jesus says, "No one can come to Me unless the Father who sent Me draws them to Me."[127] People's failure to respond to preaching is not necessarily the problem of preaching nor is it the problem of the preacher. It is the condition of the human heart and the lack of receptiveness on the part of the hearer to the presence and work of the Holy Spirit. If we take the preaching ministry of

---

[126] Mt 15: 6; Mk 7:13

[127] Jn 6:44

Jesus for example, we will see that notwithstanding the miracles that accompanied the preaching of Christ, the majority of those who heard Him rejected Him and His message. The Parable of The Sower is a very pertinent illustration of the different kinds of responses to preaching.[128] In this parable, Jesus stresses the fact that people respond differently to the preached word. Preachers and preaching styles may be a little or a whole lot different, but the seed, the Word of God, is always the same. Though the seed, the Word of God, may be the same, the people never receive the Word of God the same way.

5. As scriptures attest, many people can listen to the same message but leave with totally different takes or interpretations of it. For example, while some respond with saving faith, others will leave the experience filled with rage and animosity toward the preacher and as miserable as they were before hearing the word.[129] This is especially true if the preached word touches on any covert, and, or overt behaviors that may cause the listener concern due to having his/her conscience challenged. The attitude with which we approach preaching may therefore determine whether or not preaching directs our attention to God who moves us to repentance. Without God acting in us and without our faith response to that action in us, the preached word will not have the desired effect on us. Our preaching, our hearing, and our response to the preached word, are actions of God. It is not by the might or the power of the preacher's delivery or by the human ability to hear or accept the preached word, by which we are drawn to God through repentance. We are moved to repentance and drawn to God by the wonder-working power of the Holy Spirit who internally stirs, convicts, or makes us aware of sin and our need for righteousness.[130] The power to draw us belongs to God and God alone. It is God who exercises His sovereign power to save by lovingly drawing us to Christ. By ourselves we would fail to respond with saving faith. When we have encountered God, or when we are diligently responding to Him and His actions on us, His Word, proclaimed through the preacher, can

---

[128] Mt 13:1-23; Mk 4:1-20; Lk 8:4-15

[129] Lk 4:28-29; Heb 4:2

[130] Jn 16:8

find a place in the soil of our hearts so that it may bring forth the desired fruits of righteousness.[131]

6. Preaching in and by itself cannot change us. Such change is the work of God alone. What preaching does is invoke our awareness and need for God. Preaching prepares us for what God is getting ready to do. Preaching prepares our hearts and minds to receive God by redirecting our minds, our thinking, our conduct, our feeling, and our decisions toward God, and the finished work of Jesus Christ. However, it is only when God moves in us through the Holy Spirit that we are moved to respond to God's action in us. The word that is faithfully preached should therefore be faithfully received. When the word is faithfully received and not just merely heard, as a working of the Holy Spirit who lives within us[132] the word is planted deeply in our hearts[133] so that it might edify and build up our faith and obedience.

7. Merely hearing the word is never enough. We should never be content with just hearing a good sermon. The hearing of the preached word needs to be accompanied by faith so that the word of truth may be believed and so work in us to change us for the better in Christ Jesus.[134] Faith is important because only those who believe in the Lord Jesus Christ can understand God's truth[135] and so communicate it with conviction, authority, and Holy Ghost power. When we respond to the preaching event and meet it with faith, we are empowered to discover God by His own self-disclosure, experience His power to save, and because we believe, we are gifted with redemption as we begin our journey into God's eternity.[136]

8. Preaching is both a challenge and a source of comfort and assurance for the preacher as well as for those who hear and respond with faith to the preached word. As a component of worship, preaching brings us into an awareness of the presence of God, confronts us where we are, and challenges

---

[131] Mt 13:8, 23; Heb 4:2

[132] Rom 8:9,11

[133] See for example Mt 13:18-23

[134] Heb 4:2

[135] 1 Cor 2:6-16

[136] Heb 4:2-3

us concerning where we ought to be in terms of our faith and moral positions and walk with God. Preaching also encourages, comforts, and assures God's redeemed yet broken and hurting people. Through the message, God calls the redeemed and those seeking Him, to become caught up in this exchange between God and the preacher, and between the preacher and the congregation, as together we become engaged in worship and praise. This means that the preaching event is not a monologue but a spiritual and participatory dialogue whereby the sermon engages the Holy Spirit and the preacher, as well as the preacher and the congregation in the preaching and hearing of the word. Assuredly, preaching is a conversation, a verbal exchange, a dialogue that engages God and the preacher and the preacher and the hearers of the word. The preached word is a word from the Lord. It is a conversation in which we both hear from and respond to God with our confessions of faith as we are moved to repentance. Preaching therefore ignites our faith and prepares us for repentance and Baptism into that new life in Christ.

C. The Sacrament of Holy Baptism

(i) Overview

Baptism and Holy Communion are the two Sacraments practiced by most Protestant churches. A Sacrament is a special act of worship that was instituted by Jesus. Sacraments are means of grace. They are means of grace because they are ritualistic forms and practices that direct our attention to God's gracious acts of redemption, mercy, love, and life transforming presence in our lives as well as in the world. Sacraments are means by which God's love and grace are imparted to us. God's love conveyed to us through Jesus Christ is intended to transform us. We do not believe that the sacraments have some sort of magical powers to do so. What we do believe is that the sacraments of Baptism and Holy Communion are channels through which God makes grace available to those, who by faith, receive them and accept His Christ as their Savior and Lord.

Participation in these Sacraments does not automatically make us holy. Participation in these Sacraments helps to stir up our awareness and makes us receptive to the availability of God's divine grace and love. Our response of faith to God's love makes us receptive to the holiness and righteousness of God from whom alone righteousness comes. Our righteousness is attributed to us by faith through grace.[137] Baptism therefore initiates us into a grace-filled relationship with God. Holy Communion keeps us in faithful fellowship as the Holy Spirit works in us to remind us of the sacrifice of Christ on the cross as well as to draw us into habitual, yet faithful communion with the Father and the Son and with each other.

(ii) What is Baptism?
(Section One)

1. Baptism is a Christian Sacrament involving the ritual application or use of water. Baptism as a Sacrament or religious rite of consecration is an inward as well as an outward affirmation of the believer's new faith commitment to Christ. As such, Baptism is an outward expression of the inward grace we have already found in Christ. If Baptism is an outward expression of inward grace, then it is a mark of distinction between those who are in a covenant grace-filled relationship with God through faith in Christ, and those who are not. While Baptism is the outward application of water, it also signifies our inward spiritual cleansing and newness in Christ. Water Baptism may take the form of immersion, pouring, or sprinkling. While there are different opinions about the forms or methods of Baptism, since it is not the water that saves, but grace and believing faith in the shed blood of Christ, I do not believe that it is worthwhile to engage in a pointless debate about the methodologies and forms of Baptism.

2. Baptism, before it is ours, is first the Baptism of Christ. When, therefore, we are baptized, we are participating in the Baptism of Christ who, in the Jordon River, was baptized in the first place, for all who would believe. Our Baptism is therefore a gift of participation. Our participation announces our agreement and alliance with Christ as well as our commitment to pursue the examples of holiness that He has established for us.

---

[137] Rom 10:3; Phil 3:9

3. Baptism is a sign or public indicator of our submission to Christ, as well as an indication of who we have become in Christ. As a result of that submission, the Holy Spirit takes over, consecrates, and directs our lives while uniting us in Christ, the hope of our eternal glory.[138] As a sign or indicator of who we have become in Christ Jesus, Baptism is a seal and an expressed covenant of our unbroken bond with Christ. Baptism as a sign or a seal is indicative of God's stamp of approval in the securing of our salvation. Baptism also emphatically indicates who we are and to whom we belong. When we speak of Baptism as a seal therefore, we are speaking of a sort of divine approval of our faith confession, repentance, and justification whereby God stamps or gives us His seal of acceptance, approval, and assurance of salvation.

4. In conjunction with water Baptism, we are also baptized in the Holy Spirit. To be baptized in the Holy Spirit means the coming of the Holy Spirit upon us to cover, indwell, surround, and draw us into the divine life of Christ.[139] The Baptism of the Holy Spirit that began in full force on the Day of Pentecost continues to be a means by which God sanctifies, covers, and anoints or empowers us for His purpose. The notion of continuation does not imply that we have a need to be re-baptized by any means or in any form. This only means that the Spirit continues to indwell and develop Christ-like principles in us throughout the different stages of our spiritual journey and development. It may also be taken to mean that every now and then, because of our human failings, we need a fresh anointing of the Holy Spirit at different stages of our lives and growth in Christ.

5. Baptism is the beginning of the believer's union with Christ. Implied by beginning is a new life in Christ. Terms such as new birth, rebirth, new creation, newness of life, regeneration, and new self are sometimes used to describe this new beginning of the believer's union and journey with Christ.[140] Baptism therefore marks our new birth, regeneration, or spiritual

---

[138] Col 1:27

[139] Mt 3:11; Jn 1:33; Acts 1:5, 2:1-4; 1 Cor 12:13

[140] Rom 6:4; Cor 5:17; Gal 6:14-15; Col 3:9-10

rebirth.[141] As new creation or new birth, Baptism is essentially the beginning of our faith journey and a new relationship with the Lord. Christianity is therefore about having a new and transformed heart that draws us into a reconciled and loving relationship with God. A new heart means that we have a new beginning. With a new heart and a new beginning we are empowered to think differently and therefore to act differently towards God and our fellow humans. As new birth, Baptism signifies the start of something new with Jesus. To be regenerated or reborn is to start over with a spiritual perspective and a new way of living out the divine life. Baptism therefore marks our moving away from our sinful and unforgiven state to a forgiven state of existence whereby we have been set free from the constraints of sin in order that we might experience the liberty of God's grace and favor.

6. Regeneration or rebirth is not our work; it is a gift. Regeneration is God's conversion of us. Regeneration is God placing in us a new heart or moral affinity that is tuned to Him and, as a consequence, a heart that is inclined to pursue holiness.[142] Regeneration is God's implantation of a new nature in us through our repentance and His forgiveness and justification of us. Repentance signals that we are ready to be changed because it is the recognition of our sinfulness, an expressed desire to turn away from it, and our declared intention to turn toward God for forgiveness and a fresh start. Forgiveness is empowerment to move away from and live above that which we have repented of. God's justification of us, as we have seen in chapter two, is His declaration of our innocence. It is God making radically right what was radically wrong, thus restoring our relationship with Him and lovingly giving us a new start. Having been restored through regeneration or newness of life, this newness is sustained and nurtured by Christ through the Holy Spirit working in our lives to keep us always mindful of the redeemed persons we have become in Christ. This means that the Holy Spirit is essentially the believer's life coach on a faith journey that is destined for eternity.

---

[141] Jn 3:3, 5
[142] Ezekiel 11:19; 2 Cor 5:17; Gal 6:15

What is Baptism?
(Section Two)

1. How then, does rebirth or regeneration take place? And which comes first, faith or regeneration? Let us address the second question first. Faith comes first. The Bible says faith comes by hearing and hearing by the word of God.[143] We are also told that when we believe in our hearts that God raised Jesus from the dead, we are saved.[144] We learn from the Bible that God makes us wise and ready for salvation through faith in Christ Jesus.[145] Regeneration therefore springs from our faith awareness. The moment you are drawn by God to believe, you are saved. God prompts us to faith and our faith response shows that God's word has fallen on good soil.[146]

2. Let us now address the question of "How does rebirth or regeneration take place?" First, God prepares our hearts for repentance when we are moved to respond to Christ by our faithful hearing of the preached word. Remember now, faith comes by hearing, and hearing by the word of God. God uses the preached word then, to set us up for repentance as our thoughts are influenced to consider our sinful ways as a prelude to our urgent need for Christ as a result of what we have heard.[147]

3. Second, upon hearing the preached word, the Holy Spirit stirs us from within so that our cognition would invoke our thoughts; our thoughts would then lead to the contemplation of righteousness. Our contemplation of righteousness then leads to subsequent and right actions. Such actions are manifestations of our turning toward God in true repentance and faith. That act of the Holy Spirit in us is what enlightens us or makes us aware of God. Our awareness of God and all of His holy ways, set against our state

---

[143] Rom 10:17
[144] Rom 10:9
[145] 2 Tim 3:15b
[146] See Mt 13:18-23 (23 in particular)
[147] See the discussion on preaching above

of unholiness, moves us to embrace God so that we may, by the grace of God, seek to follow Him and walk in our newness of life or regenerated state thereafter.

4. Third, because of our awareness of God and His holiness, we are moved to bow in humility and confess our sins and shortcomings before Him. We are therefore reborn when our hearts become influenced and drawn to respond in faithful surrender. As we surrender to God, and give way to the working of God's available grace in us, we are gifted with the opportunity to start over and so become new persons. We become new persons when the old self and its sinful ways become subdued and old habits die, giving way to a new life of righteousness. When by grace we are empowered to turn away from sin and receive Christ in our lives, the new persons that we have become in Christ come alive to righteousness. Our coming alive to righteousness has much to do with God lifting our burden of sin through forgiveness, which empowers us to live the Christian life. Our restored relationship with God also gives us the freedom and joy of access to the divine favors of God. As new or regenerated persons in Christ, and with our hearts now humbly turned to God, we are changed to be Christ-like and therefore to reflect the righteousness of God.

5. Fourth, regeneration comes when our attention is redirected to Christ and His atoning sacrifice on the Cross at Calvary. With our awareness turned toward Christ, which is our belief that Christ died for us, and by our asking Him to be our Lord and Savior, God lovingly draws us to Himself and surrounds us with His redeeming and sanctifying power. Upon our acceptance and confession of Christ, and upon opening our hearts to receive Christ, God through the Holy Spirit begins to live in us,[148] thereby transforming us into saved, redeemed, and new persons in Christ.[149] God forms us into new persons and consecrates us at Baptism as a result of the Spirit indwelling us and molding and reshaping us into the likeness of Christ. This reshaping of us helps in redirecting our thoughts to things above. Things above are

---

[148] Rom 14:7-8; 1 Cor 6:17, 19-20
[149] Mk 16:16; Lk 12:8-9; Jn 6:47; Rom 10:9, 13; 1 Jn 1:9

indicative of things that are holy, of spiritual and eternal value, and are therefore pleasing to God.

6. Again, rebirth or regeneration is not our work, it is God's work. It is not by our works of righteousness but according to God's grace and mercy that we have been saved by the redeeming gift of Christ and renewed by the transforming power of the Holy Spirit.[150] Regeneration is the work of God because regeneration begins with a divine initiative and influence upon the human heart and will. That holy influence on the human will takes place when God lovingly draws us to Himself and keeps us diligent by His empowering grace. The Holy Spirit then progressively works in us to bring about or invoke our desire to surrender to God and the willingness to faithfully pursue the will of God.

7. This matter of divine initiative or God's holy influence is important for our understanding of divine grace in the process of our salvation. The unredeemed or natural nature in us is incapable of responding to God or accepting His will without the stimulation of the Holy Spirit and the gift of divine grace. Surrendering to divine and spiritual influences is not part of the natural person's makeup. The natural, as opposed to the divine and the spiritual, is more inclined to rebel against God rather than come into alignment with or surrender to God. It is by God and His holy influence upon us that we are moved to believe, accept His will, and come to Christ.[151] Our salvation is therefore an act of God. God alone created the universe and us, and God alone can save us though the Lord Jesus. God alone has forgiven and redeemed us through Christ. God alone through the Holy Spirit has sanctified us and God alone has given us a new life. It is grace that prompts us. It is grace that draws us. It is grace that redeems us. It is grace through the sustaining power of the Holy Spirit that keeps and seals us. By grace, God alone has established us in Christ Jesus.[152] Because it is God and not us, all that we do, even our response of faith, becomes a gift of response to the salvation that God offers us through Christ.

---

[150] Tit 3:3-8

[151] Jn 6:44

[152] 2 Cor 1:21-22; Eph 4:30

8. Regeneration or rebirth is therefore God's gracious and benevolent fixing of us.[153] Our rebirth or regeneration can therefore only take place when God divinely and supernaturally acts upon and within us to change our thoughts, influence our hearts, and subdue our human will. We are simply just faithful respondents and very privileged recipient souls of the pervasive love and grace of God. None of it is our works. The Bible says in Romans 9: 16 that: "It is not of him/her who wills nor of him/her who runs, but of God who shows mercy." This does not mean that we should not will, and choose, and hope, and aspire to reach the mark in Christ Jesus. We must will in order to do and we must aspire in order to run the good race of faith and in order to attain to higher levels of spiritual growth in Christ. However, our human will by itself will not and cannot lead us to salvation. We need God's help to receive it and we need God's help to sustain our new walk with Christ. Everything concerning human salvation begins and finds completion in God. It is God's will to have mercy; and it is only when we come into alignment with the will of God that we are moved to desire and therefore receive God's mercy.[154]

9. You may be asking, "What then does the Apostle Paul mean when he says in Philippians 2:12, 'work out your own salvation with fear and trembling?'" The apostle is not at all suggesting that we can achieve our own salvation by the quality or quantity of our work and efforts. What he is saying by the term "working out" is that our daily action should be an out-showing, an out-working, a manifestation, or a translation of our salvation and that inward grace we received from Christ. That working out is actually a reminder that we should demonstrate, through words and deeds that we are indeed saved to the glory of God. It is only as God works in us that we, by the grace of God, are empowered to work out, that is, display the grace that is in us through deeds of righteousness and justice and mercy in the world. That way, others may see and come to glorify the God that changes us to reflect Him in the world.

10. Because it is God who wills to save us and because it is God who shows mercy, we deserve none of the credit for our redemption. Assuredly,

---

[153] Tit 3:5-7; Jas 1:16-18
[154] Rom 9:16

we humans cannot act redemptively on our own behalf. The natural self and the stubborn human will in us only serve to pull us down and away from God. The Spirit of God in us is what pulls us upward and always toward God. We do need God to do for us what we cannot do for ourselves. We need God to redeem us! Redemption, which is our spiritual reclaiming by God as well as our renewal in Christ, who paid the price to redeem us, is the work of God. By the power of Holy Spirit, God also acts upon us to reclaim and change us for His eternal good. The Holy Spirit of God then, is not to be partially credited with our new life and nature. The Holy Spirit is to be totally credited. It is He who makes us aware of our sinful state and need for Christ. It is He who draws us to Christ.[155] It is He who turns our thoughts toward God so that we may contemplate His holiness. My dear friends, our salvation is of God and not of us. God deserves all of the glory, worship, praise, and thanksgiving.

11. When we are baptized, we are baptized into Christ. As a work of the Holy Spirit who enters our lives at our point of belief and at Baptism, our hearts are sealed and engrafted into Christ so that we can be partakers of the righteousness of God and His eternal kingdom. According to Scripture, without regeneration it is impossible to go to heaven.[156] As indicated in our discussion on the first step toward spiritual transformation in chapter two, we are not Christians nor are we heaven bound because we are privileged with lifelong church membership. We are not Christians bound for heaven because we sing in the choir, serve on a particular board or committee, are presidents and chairpersons in a church, or because we are able to teach and preach. To be Christians, indeed, to be God's children, to inherit the kingdom of heaven, we must be born again.[157] To be born again is to become dead to sin and our old way of living, as we are renewed and made alive in the resurrected Christ. Being dead to sin implies that sin no longer has control over you. Being alive in Christ therefore means that Christ now has control over you. That is why we say that Jesus Christ is Lord. Jesus becomes your Lord when you have surrendered your will and learned to walk in His holy

---

[155] Jn 16:8-11
[156] Jn 3:3
[157] Jn 3:5

precepts through faith and obedience. He is your Savior because He died to redeem you. He is your Lord because He now leads and directs and controls the destiny of your life and the eternity of your soul.

(iii) Baptism and the Death and Resurrection of Jesus

1. Baptism is often viewed as an imitation of the death and resurrection of Jesus. This is so because Baptism, particularly when immersion is the standard form followed, is symbolic of our being buried with the old self as we are submerged underwater. Baptism is also symbolic of the resurrection of Jesus on account of the baptized person being raised from under the water as a new person with Christ. Going under the water or having the water poured or sprinkled means that the old self dies and must necessarily remain dead in order for the new person in Christ to emerge and live a grace-filled life. To become a new person in Christ, our self-will has to be crucified or subdued so that the life of Christ may be resurrected anew in us. That way, the will and purposes of God are given priority over the human will. Baptism is therefore a spiritual death to sin and a spiritual resurrection to a new life in Christ. Romans 6:6 informs us that our old person is crucified with Him (Christ) so that the body of sin might be destroyed and so that we should no longer serve sin. Having been crucified with Chand by cause of our faith in His resurrection, it is no longer we who live, but Christ who now lives in us.[158]

2. Through Baptism, the believer is united with Christ in His death and is raised to a new life of faith in His resurrection. Colossians 2:12 tells us that we were buried with Christ at Baptism but we were also raised with Him through faith in the working of God who raised Him from the dead.

3. At our Baptism, emphasis is not so much on the act, but on the result. The result of Baptism is our new identity in Christ. For the Apostle Paul, Baptism places the believer "in Christ" through the Holy Spirit.[159] When we are baptized, we are sharing in what Christ has already accomplished for us.

---

[158] Gal 2:20
[159] Rom 6: 3; 1 Cor 12: 13; Gal 3: 27; Col 2: 12

Because we are baptized in Christ, external variables such as race, gender, nationality, and social standings are of no significance.[160] This essentially means that individuality is diminished and community is affirmed and increased because we are baptized into the Community of Faith. To live in Christ is to live in oneness with Him in a community without boundaries. The new Christian cannot be nurtured in isolation. He or she is nurtured in community where the faithful take responsibility for lifting up and nurturing each other in Christ without regard to race, gender, nationality, or social standing. Essentially, the Holy Spirit, through Baptism, removes us from a state of isolation and individualism and draws us into a life of communion with the Father and the Son and with each other. At this juncture I shall now turn my attention to addressing two concerns, the Baptism of children and circumcision.

(iv) The Baptism of Children
(Section One)

1. Should children be baptized? This matter of whether or not children should be baptized is one of the issues that I have always had to address as a pastor. I do not believe that it is my place or anyone else's place to say that children should not be baptized. To say that children should not be baptized, is to also say that children are not deserving of Baptism and therefore not deserving of divine grace and fellowship in the family of Christ and the communion of God. I certainly believe that they are deserving! Baptism as an act of faith is our sharing in the Baptism of Christ to which I personally believe that children have access to.

2. As a believer and practitioner in the liturgical faith practices of the church, I do not feel obligated to justify the Baptism of children to anyone. After all, it is God's prerogative to accept and receive His children without the restriction of age or any other human variable. I believe that God's grace is available to all people without regard for age, gender, or race specifications. Furthermore, no one has the right or the authority to restrict the dispensation and working of God's grace. It is my conviction that the availability of grace

---
[160] Gal 3:28

for salvation is accessible to children in whom also, the spirit of God dwells and for whom Christ was baptized and also died to redeem.

3. Here are some questions to consider as we contemplate the matter:

    a. Are children not part of God's kingdom?
    b. Were children also not made by God to share in God's eternity?
    c. Do children not have the right and access to the kingdom of heaven?
    d. Did Christ not die so that children too may live?
    e. If we say that the Baptism of Christ was our Baptism, was Christ not also baptized for children?

Assuredly, the promise and gift of eternal life is to the believing parents and their children, and as many as the Lord God, the Author and Giver of eternal life gives such a gift.[161]

4. Let us highlight for a moment a few Scriptures that speak to the Baptism of households. In Acts 16:15 we are told that Lydia and her household were baptized. We are also informed by Acts 16:33 that a Philippian jailer and his entire family were baptized. In Acts 18:8, Crispus, a ruler of the synagogue, believed on the Lord and he and his household were baptized. The Apostle Paul reports in 1 Corinthians 1:16 that he also baptized the household of Stephanas. While these texts do not make reference to infants or children, the inference seems plausible. It is also clear that none of these texts speak of the Baptism of couples or a man and his wife. They speak of the Baptism of households of people or entire families making it highly probable that young children were part of those households and families and were therefore included with those baptized.

5. While children may not be able to make independent choices for Baptism, it is not our adult responsibility to deny them Baptism. To deny them Baptism would be a futile attempt to block and compromise the pervasiveness and redemptive grace of God. That has been an improbable attempt

---

[161] See Acts 2:39

resulting in denominational conflict and a breakdown in denominational dialogue on the issue of the Baptism of children.

The Baptism of Children
(Section Two)

1. Some base their objection to children's Baptism on the grounds that children have not developed the cognitive ability to understand the spiritual significance and faith principles of Baptism. I wish to emphasize that human salvation, including that of children, is not limited to an understanding of the Sacrament of Baptism. Our salvation is totally dependent on faith in the salvific act of Christ and the pervasiveness of God's grace. Implied here is that the grace of God cuts through and transcends race, nationality, human cognitive development, and certainly age. The truth is, even as adults, we are by no means experts at understanding the supernatural workings of God in Baptism.

2. Baptism is a gift of grace that is not made effectual by human understanding but by the human faith response to the grace of God offered to us through Christ. Furthermore, our Baptism is not of any greater value due to our intellectual applications, as much as it is by the effectual workings of faith and the transforming power of the Holy Spirit. As our discussion of the Holy Spirit and the effects of Baptism in the section below will disclose, because the effects of Baptism are the work of grace and not of human intellect or works, we have no real basis for arguing against children being beneficiaries of divine grace. Indeed, Christ by His death and resurrection has redeemed all of humanity including children who are also destined to share in God's eternity. Jesus has affirmed this when He says: "Let the children come to me, and do not forbid them; for to them belongs the kingdom of heaven."[162]

3. Mental capacity and cognitive development are not prerequisites for salvation. While children may not have yet developed the mental capacity to make independent choices for Baptism, it is the Christian parents' responsibility to develop in their children those tendencies that are Christ-like and

---

[162] Mt 19:14; see also Mt 18:3-4; Mk 10:14-15

therefore pleasing to God. Christian parents, having been baptized and having themselves experienced Christ, and having been changed by the effectual working of the Holy Spirit in their lives, have the right and the responsibility, can, and should make the decision to baptize the child. It is also their responsibility and that of the faith community to see to it that the child is taught and encouraged to grow in the ways of Christ through intentional demonstration of Christ-like living.[163] When the child is old enough, that child may be encouraged to make public and intentional confession of Christ and affirm her or his faith through confirmation.

4. If we were to look back at circumcision in the Old Testament for example, we will see that the male child did not make the decision to be circumcised. The decision was always made by the parents who themselves were in covenant relationship with God. Jesus Himself was circumcised when He was only eight (8) days old.[164] **I rest my case!**

Let us now turn our attention to a discussion of the question of whether Baptism is a replacement for circumcision in our covenant relationship with Christ.

(v) Baptism: A Replacement for Circumcision?

1. What is circumcision and what is the religious importance of the practice? Circumcision was the practice of Judaism where the removal of the male's foreskin[165] was a precondition for acceptance in the Hebrew worshipping community followed by ritual washing. Circumcision was not unique to the Hebrew tradition. Before it was a Hebrew practice, it was a common practice in the Ancient Near East. It became a practice in the Hebrew community and culture when God used it as a sign to distinguish the people of the Abrahamic covenant. Circumcision was therefore an initiation rite as well as a sign of covenant with God as seen in Genesis 17:10.

---

[163] Deu 4:9, 6:7, 11:19, 31:13; Ps 78:5; Prov 22:6; Is 28:9, 38:19b; Jn 21:15; Mt 19:14; 1 Thess 2:11

[164] Lk 2:21

[165] Gen 17: 10-14; Lev 12:3; Lk 1:59, 2:21

The rite of circumcision, as Genesis 17:11 indicates, was also a ritualistic essential and an indication of a person's determination to walk uprightly before God. Circumcision was used as a mark of the Hebrew covenant with God and was practiced and passed down from fathers to sons and renewed with each generation. This was to emphasize the continuous nature of their covenant relationship with God. Cutting away the foreskin was symbolic of cutting away dependence on their own flesh and placing that dependence on God for their future posterity as well as prosperity.

2. With the exception of ritual washing for purification, there are no parallels to Christian Baptism in the Old Testament. Neither was the term Baptism used to describe ritual washing. Baptism, as we have come to know it, was first instituted by John The Baptist who demonstrated a bold religious innovation. This was innovative to the extent that neither the term nor the practice was used in the Hellenistic world[166] or in Judaism. Baptism was innovative and indeed revolutionary because John The Baptist was calling the people to do more than perform a physical act of circumcision. John The Baptist was calling the people to repent and turn wholeheartedly to God in true faith. Baptism in John The Baptist's scheme of things became a public demonstration of one's commitment to walk in righteousness and with a heart for God. Consequently, it was not merely the ritual of Baptism that had merit. Merit was fundamentally found in the demonstration of changed lives and behaviors that emerged from repentance and forgiveness and from developing a heart or moral propensity for God.

3. John's Baptism, picked up by the Early Church, influenced no doubt by Jesus' acceptance of it, took on new spiritual significance including Baptism as union with Christ and the Baptism of the Holy Spirit. While Baptism may be considered a replacement for circumcision as a means by which members are initiated into the community of faith,[167] circumcision is not however, a parallel to Christian Baptism. Christian Baptism is of more far-reaching spiritual significance. In circumcision a piece of flesh, the foreskin of the male pe-

---

[166] The Hellenistic world or culture has to do with ancient Greek civilization characterized by their learning and practices during the late 4th to 1st centuries BC.
[167] Acts 2:41

nis, was removed after the child was born[168] but in Baptism the entire "body of flesh," that is, the human tendency that is in conflict with the holiness and divine will of God, is removed.[169] Also, according to Old Testament reports, while circumcision was a male oriented practice, which excludes the female gender, the New Testament practice of Baptism is more inclusive in its spiritual purpose and intention.

4. Baptism in the New Testament is a reflection of the same emphasis on covenant relationship as was circumcision in the Old Testament with one fundamental difference. The difference is that Baptism emphasizes changed behaviors and lifestyles resulting from a new spiritual birth, rather than a physical or bodily adjustment. The spiritual value of Baptism is reflected in the fact that unlike circumcision, which is a removal of physical flesh, the body of flesh that is put off at Baptism is the old sinful existence which is laid aside and must die in order for Christ to live in us and for us to live for Christ. In Colossians 2:11, Christ is shown to have made circumcision unnecessary. This is so because Christ is the fulfillment of what is typified in the ritual rite of circumcision. By extension, Christ accepting and having been baptized indicates a new trend and condition for a new life in Him. Salvation is therefore not by ritual observation but by conformity to a life in Christ in whom we are both circumcised and baptized into the family of God. For, as Colossians 2:17 affirms, the substance of the believer's life is not mere ritualistic observation, but Jesus Christ.

5. Actually, even in the Old Testament, true righteousness was never found in circumcision but in walking obediently with God. Certainly, it was not by Abraham's circumcision that he was declared righteous but by his faith in God.[170] It is not by our Baptism that we are declared righteous but by our faith and obedience to God. Through faith and obedience, we are changed by the transforming power of God to walk in His righteousness. Salvation is not found in rituals. Salvation is found only in Christ in whom our future

---

[168] Gen 17:11 (In Abraham's case this took place when he was already old since he had not yet come to know God).

[169] Col 2:11-12

[170] Gen15:6

posterity and prosperity are invested through faith in His redeeming sacrifice and grace. Where circumcision is used in the New Testament in reference to the new believer in Christ, it is not in regards to confidence in the flesh.[171] Rather, it is in reference to the heart that is transformed by the Holy Spirit as we put off the old person (flesh) that we were and put on the new person (the Spirit) whom we have become in Christ.[172]

(vi) The Holy Spirit and the Effects of Baptism (Section One)

1. To be baptized is to receive the Holy Spirit because Baptism marks the Spirit's entry into the Christian's life.[173] As the Holy Spirit came upon Jesus, symbolizing His spiritual anointing at His Baptism in the Jordan,[174] so does the Holy Spirit come upon and indwell the believer at Baptism, to anoint and empower that believer for his or her faith journey. While we believe that there is one Baptism and therefore **do not re-baptize**, this anointing of the Holy Spirit at Baptism is not a onetime, never again experience. For the duration of our Christian life and journey, we are likely to receive fresh anointing and renewing of the Holy Spirit for particular tasks that we may be given.

2. Though we are baptized once, we are never left alone. At our onetime Baptism, not only does the Holy Spirit come upon us, the Holy Spirit draws us to, and engrafts us into Christ, thus initiating and establishing or securing our union or saving relationship with Christ. Therefore, we are not just introduced to Christ at Baptism never to have further contact and exchanges with Him. The Holy Spirit does the double duty of initiating our contact and keeping us in touch with Christ for the duration of our faith journey. For the duration, the Holy Spirit's empowering work is to sustain in us the desire for Christ in our pursuit of His righteousness. Our growing in

---

[171] Rom 2:29; Phil 3:3
[172] Col 3:9-10
[173] Acts 2:38
[174] Lk 3:22

Christ is therefore a continuous process of spiritual formation and transformation into the likeness of Christ,[175] with the ultimate goal of eternity with Him. At Baptism, then, we receive the gift of the Holy Spirit as a pledge of sanctification and a guarantee of accompaniment into our final inheritance as sons and daughters of God.[176]

3. Through Baptism, the Holy Spirit is the believer's point of contact and entry into intimacy with God. The Holy Spirit is the One who quickens our awareness and draws our attention to Christ.[177] As we respond with faith in the Lord Jesus Christ, He gives us true knowledge of God through His revelation of the Father.[178] We are therefore baptized in the name of the Father, and of the Son and of the Holy Spirit because these Three work together as One for the attainment of the believer's salvation and union with Christ.

4. As a work of the Holy Spirit, Baptism signifies forgiveness. Having confessed and repented of our sins before God, and having accepted Jesus Christ as Lord and Savior, and having been baptized by water and with the Spirit, we are forgiven and our relationship with God is mended. Our broken relationship with God is mended as we are reconciled to Him by the atoning blood of Jesus. Our conviction, confession and repentance of sin must therefore necessarily precede Baptism.[179] We do not get baptized and then confess and accept Jesus Christ as Lord and Savior. We do not get baptized and then repent of our sins. Acknowledging, confessing of our sins, and accepting Christ lead us to participate in His Baptism for us; thus signifying our agreement with who He is and what He has already done for us. When we acknowledge our sins we are confronted with the need to repent. That is, we express sorrow before God for our sins, turn away from a life of sin and turn toward a new life in Christ as forgiven, changed, or transformed children of God.

---

[175] 2 Cor 3:17-18

[176] Eph 1:14; 2 Cor 1:22

[177] Jn 16:13-14

[178] Mt 11:27; Jn 15:15

[179] As indicated in the Book of Acts, Baptism follows conversion. See Acts 16:15, 33 and 18:8 for example

5. It is the Holy Spirit that draws our attention to Christ, urges us on to repentance by convicting us of sin, and making us aware of the value of righteousness.[180] As we repent of our sins, confess Christ as the Son of God, and accept Him as our personal Lord and Savior, as a gift of grace through Baptism, we are forgiven and redeemed.[181] The Holy Spirit then acts upon us as we confess and are forgiven and baptized, to sustain our restored relationship with God. This is precisely what reconciliation is. It is the mending or restoration of our broken relationship with God and therefore our being brought back into fellowship, communion, and a right relationship with God, which is achieved by faith in the atoning death of Christ.

6. Through Baptism, and by the infusing power of the Holy Spirit, Christ who indwells us, permeates our hearts, minds and souls, and unites our entire being with the life of God. That is reconciliation and our union with God. By the sanctifying power of the Holy Spirit, who transforms and renews our minds (the result of our new spiritual birth), we are directed through faith and obedience to conform to the holy ways of God. To seek Baptism is therefore an expression of our desire to seek after God and to have union with Christ through whom and by whom our broken relationship with God is mended.

The Holy Spirit and the Effects of Baptism
(Section Two)

1. When we are baptized, it is not the water that saves or washes away our sin. That is the work of atoning grace through faith in the shed blood of Jesus Christ, and the soul cleansing power of the Holy Spirit. As the Apostle Peter writes in 1 Peter 3:21: "There is also an antitype which now saves us— Baptism (not by the removal of the filth of the flesh, but the answer of a good conscience toward God), through the resurrection of Jesus Christ." This answer of good conscience toward God is the Christian response of faith in the redeeming power of God. Accepting

---

[180] Jn 16:8
[181] Mt 10:32; Rom 10:9-10

Baptism means that we have accepted God's offer of grace and forgiveness and reconciliation offered to us through Christ. Forgiveness then becomes empowerment for us to live again as God intended us to.

2. As a work of the Holy Spirit, sanctification also begins with our Baptism. This means that we are called and set apart. We are not set in isolation from others, but set apart for God's use of us. We are also set apart for the Holy Spirit's grooming of us so that we may grow in our faith walk, knowledge, and relationship with God. The whole of the Christian life must therefore be seen as conformation and growth into the life of Christ. By our Baptism which is our new birth, we effectively become sons and daughters of God.[182] For, having been drawn into communion with Christ, we share in the sonship and daughtership of Christ[183] by whom we are justified by grace through faith.

3. Forgiveness, justification, regeneration, and sanctification, though distinct, are therefore related terms used to describe the process of our new life in Christ. Repentance, forgiveness, and justification make possible our freedom from the guilt of sin. Justification leads to regeneration whereby we are set free from the power and guilt of sin to begin a new life of liberty in Christ.

4. Our renewed life in Christ is the result of our justification through faith and forgiveness, which is our freedom from the guilt and bondage of sin. It was a state of guilt and bondage that we could not escape from by our own efforts. As Calvin puts it: "[Human beings are] so held captive by the yoke of sin that [they] can of [their] own nature neither aspire to good through resolve nor struggle after it through effort."[184] Freedom from the guilt of sin is the direct result of the outflowing of God's redeeming grace and power within us to rise above sin. By God's forgiveness of us, and by the sustaining presence of the Holy Spirit in us, we are empowered to resist and overcome sin. However, while we are no longer slaves to sin, we must continue a lifelong

---

[182] Jn 1:12-13; Rom 8:14-16; Gal 4:6

[183] Rom 8:23

[184] Calvin: <u>Institutes of the Christian Religion,</u> (ed John T. McNeill) Book 1, v. xx, (Philadelphia: West Minister Press), 309

struggle against it.[185] Though we may have a lifelong struggle with sin, by divine grace, sin shall not have dominion over us.[186] For, the Holy Spirit, who touches our lives at Baptism, is always present to aid us in overcoming sin while empowering us to live lives that are pleasing to God. Furthermore, in our struggle with sin, and in the event that we fall into error to it, we have an advocate in Jesus Christ, the propitiation for our sins, and the One who lives to intercede with the Father on our behalf.[187] By virtue of our repentance, Christ's atoning sacrifice for the forgiveness of our sins, and as a result of the intercessions of Christ and the sustaining presence of the Holy Spirit, who is our help on our faith journey, we are gifted with the opportunity to progressively resist sin and so grow in grace. Furthermore, God's prevenient grace is available to guard our souls from presumptuous sin

5. I believe that prevenient grace is God's merciful pre and post intervention in our lives. Prevenient grace is divine grace that precedes human decision and error to sin. It exists prior to and without reference to anything humans may or may not have done. As human beings are likely to become corrupted by sin and the effects of it, prevenient grace allows us to appeal to God's gracious provision of grace, mercy and freedom already in place. By God's prior provisions of grace, we are prompted to choose God and His gifts of forgiveness and salvation over that which debilitates us, sin. This divine intervention makes it possible for us to respond to God's love, thus preventing the forces of evil from dragging us farther away from the eternal love of God. Prevenient grace may therefore be considered God's way of pulling us to Himself with the compelling greatness and power of His love, so that life's circumstances, evil and worldly influences cannot separate us from Him.[188] With the aid of God's prevenient grace, we have the divine help we need in time to endure the process, as we are lovingly carried and safeguarded on our journey toward our eschatological goal. That way, though satan may buffet

---

[185] Rom 6:12
[186] Rom 6:14
[187] 1 Jn 2:1-2, 4:10
[188] Rom 8:35

and sin may abound, neither will be able to circumvent God's prior safeguarding of our souls.

6. I further believe that prevenient grace is God's proactive action on believers' behalf intended to safeguard our souls from presumptuous sin. By God's prior empowerment, which is really what prevenient grace is, and does, sin does not have dominion over us.[189] As sin is warded off by grace through our faithful response to God, the Holy Spirit working in us makes our words, thoughts, and actions consistent with the will of God and therefore, acceptable to God.[190] Consequently, our expressions of faith, confessions of Christ, our repentance, God's forgiveness of us, our regeneration, our justification, and our sanctification by the Holy Spirit, are all grounded in the prior empowerment of God's grace.

7. One of the promises of God is to never leave nor forsake us. Because God has promised to never leave us, prevenient grace becomes God's abiding and preventative presence within us. That way, we, having been regenerated or born again,[191] may no longer be powerlessly led into the habitual practice of sin. Prevenient grace is therefore the actions of God working in us to prevent sinful tendencies, as well as to empower us to rise above sin. This does not mean that we are no longer vulnerable to sin. However, as the apostle John indicates, in the event that we fall into the error of sin, "we have an Advocate with the Father, Jesus Christ the righteous"[192] to plead our case before the Father.

8. Here we see an outpouring of God's grace at two levels. At the first level, God has before time proactively provided an Advocate to plead the believer's case.[193] On the second level, because we have fallen short of God's glory, God has provided Jesus Christ as the propitiation (atoning sacrifice) for our sins.[194] The availability of grace or God's abundant forgiveness is not an

---

[189] Ps 19:13
[190] Ps 19:14
[191] Jn 3:3, 5-8
[192] 1 Jn 2:1
[193] Heb 7:24-25; Rom 8:34
[194] Rom 3:23-25

excuse to intentionally sin. To sin intentionally, would be an abuse of divine grace. Even though we are called into liberty through Christ, such liberty should not be used as an opportunity for the flesh[195] because human freedom is not a license to be morally reckless. As we wait in anticipation for the return of our Redeemer, some of us may be tempted to sin and some of us may fall into sin; but we are never too far beyond God's abounding and sufficient grace.[196]

(vii) Baptism: An Opportunity to Grow in Grace (Section One)

1. Being forgiven, justified, regenerated, and sanctified, and having been baptized do not by any means suggest that we are automatically perfected. While perfection is the ideal goal, in our imperfection, the perfect God through His Holy Spirit is always there to lift us up when we fall, correct us when we err, and forgive us when we sin and turn to Him in repentance. Our repentance, God's forgiveness and justification of us, coupled with our being set apart (sanctified) for the Holy Spirit's grooming of us, imply that we have been changed and positioned to grow in holiness.

2. While we are obviously changed, and while very often the change is sudden, growth in Christ is still a process. The Christian life is a changed life that is caught up in a series of progressive experiences and growth in Christ. Our encounter with God does not mean the sudden perfecting of us. Rather, our encounter with God takes us on a progressive faith journey in the pursuit of the righteousness and perfection of God. For some people, change is immediate as in the case of the Apostle Paul in the ninth chapter of the Book of Acts. Let us remember however, that Paul was not ignorant of God or of Christ for that matter. What Paul found was a new channel and a new cause for utilizing and directing his zeal after the persecuting Zealot encountered the fire baptizing Christ. The fire baptizing Christ won, and Paul submitted.

---

[195] Rom 6:1-2; Ga. 5:13; 1 Pet 2:16
[196] Rom 5:20; 2 Cor 12:9

Let us remember also, that Paul himself had challenges as he sought to live out his changed life. In his own words:

> "For what I am doing, I do not understand. For what I will to do, that I do not practice; but what I hate, that I do…But now, it is no longer I who do it, but sin that dwells in me…for to will is present with me, but how to perform what is good I do not find…O wretched man that I am! Who will deliver me from this body of death?"[197]

3. However, notwithstanding his own deficiencies, Paul also grew to discover the sufficiency of God's grace.[198] For others, whom Peter calls newborn babes,[199] continuous feeding on the word of God becomes essential for growth in Christ. Change and/or our conversion may indeed be sudden and often obvious, even to observers; but our growth in Christ is always a process of kneeling at the altar in earnest prayer, repenting, and seeking forgiveness, strength, and faith in order that we might continue to live lives that please God.

4. Faith takes time to develop. Faith takes time to mature in us. It took Abraham about twenty-two years to see the realization of what was promised Him by God, his son Isaac. It was not God that took time to fulfill His promise. It was Abraham who needed time to grow in faith and therefore be in a position to be the father of faith to Isaac and to us. It took Joseph about seventeen years to come into the realization of the visions he had and believed since boyhood. Yet in order to reach his vision he had to survive a pit at about seventeen years old, being sold into slavery in Egypt, and a period of false imprisonment, before he got to the palace, a position of power and responsibility. It took forty years in the wilderness for the remaining Hebrew people to come into the maturity of faith and some still did not make it because they did not demonstrate the necessary faith shift and obedience connection with God during their sanctification period. Some, including Caleb and Joshua

---

[197] Rom 7:15-24

[198] 2 Cor 12:9

[199] 1 Pet 2:2

had to delay their promise trying to encourage the faith and obedience of those who were slow in recognizing, believing, and obeying God. Growing in grace takes time.

5. While in some cases change is truly sudden, for some of us, it takes a while to grow in faith and rid ourselves of bad habits and certain sins that seem to "have our number." Old habits, and the old self or mindset that housed them, must be sufficiently despised and torn down in order for us to completely turn away from them and build a new life in Christ. The old self is to be despised and turned away from because it did nothing more than drag us down to the depths of hell and away from the arms of God who loves us. The new self, the person we have become in Christ is to be loved and cherished and nurtured and guarded and built up. The sinful things you used to do and take pleasure in before turning to God should therefore no longer be of value to you. If they are, you need to consider if you have truly repented of them.

6. Though we are changed, we still need to resist the temptation to lie, to steal, to gossip, to commit adultery, to commit fornication, to hold grudges, to harbor resentment, to envy others, to practice prejudice and every other form of divine prohibitions. Now, sin of any kind and at whatever level, is always forbidden. Sin should always be vehemently resisted, despised, and never spoken of lightly. Psalm 97:10 for example, tells us that we who love the Lord should hate evil.[200] When you are saved and by error fall into sin, you should feel so violated, that you are driven to your knees in earnest and urgent repentance before God, whose forgiveness we seek through Christ to rid us of the detestable burden and violation of sin. Not only should we feel personally violated, sin must be more vehemently detested because sin is a violation of God's holiness and an offense to our relationship with God.

7. Even though as humans we still have the capacity to sin, there should be no desire in us to sin. Sure, temptation will come; but the redeemed of God are empowered by the Holy Spirit within us to reject it[201] and let God take full control of our lives. It is by resisting sin that we learn to overcome the power of it. It is by overcoming sin with the help of divine grace that

---

[200] See also Ps 34:14, 101:3; Prov 8:13; Amos 5:15; Rom 12:9;
[201] See Lk 4:1-13; Eph 4:27, 6:11-13; Jas 4:7

we learn to walk and grow in Christ and not stay subjected to the enslavement of sin.

Baptism: An Opportunity to Grow in Grace
(Section Two)

1. Again, being born-again or regenerated does not mean that we have suddenly arrived at perfection. What it means is that we have begun our new faith journey with God. It is a journey on which we learn, in time, to let go and let God take total control of our lives. That is why growing in grace is a constant process of repentance and forgiveness and surrendering to God. If we were made perfect all at once, we would not have the need for additional grace. Because we are not perfect, God knows we need His grace, which is His perfect help, to aid us in our imperfection as we seek to grow in Christ. Thanks be to God! His grace is available and sufficient for all of us.[202] **Hallelujah!**

2. While regeneration marks the beginning of our new journey with God, it is not the end of our growth in Christ. Our growth in Christ is a lifelong commitment and pursuit. Sometimes you may even fall into error. However, if you have truly given your life to the Lord, He is gracious and merciful to all who turn to Him in repentance. Above all else, when we fall into error and turn to God in sorrow and repentance, our Advocate, Christ Jesus, mediates our cause before God.[203] The good news then, for you and me today, is that our God is able to save to the uttermost those who come to Him through the Lord Jesus who lives to make intercessions for us.[204]

3. Growing up in Christ takes time. Sometimes you fall and sometimes you are made to cry but if you have made the Lord your Savior, through faith in Him, He will pick you up and dry your weeping eyes. Furthermore, Proverbs 24:16 tells us that the righteous person may fall but gets back up again. We may fall because of error, but God, by His divine grace and favor,

---

[202] 2 Cor 12:9

[203] 1 Jn 2:1

[204] Heb 7:25

has made provisions for us to rise through repentance and forgiveness. We rise to seek after God because we love God and are miserable when we are far away from Him. We rise because we know that God loves us and that His mercy is available. We rise, not by our own abilities, but by God's redeeming and uplifting grace, we rise. **Hallelujah!**

4. I have more good news for you! In the event that you fall into sin, God forbid, if you do not continue in unbelief, you will be grafted in again because God, by whom you were called into fellowship through Jesus Christ, is faithful.[205] Remember that! On your faith journey, be encouraged by the knowledge that God is always able to bestow His grace upon you. This does not mean that you should intentionally sin so that grace may be bestowed.[206] The intentional practice of sinning by Christians is ruled out by virtue of our salvation and the very implications of our Baptism. God does not need us to intentionally provide Him opportunities to bestow His grace.[207]

5. Although we are saved, we are still growing and becoming more of Christ and all that God purposed us to become. Because of our human inclination, with which we have to daily struggle and resist, every now and then, God by His Holy Spirit in us may have to nudge us and gently urge us along the way so that by His grace we may arrive at the place of holiness and maturity in Christ. Maturity in Christ takes time and is attained by our submission to the Holy Spirit who teaches and inspires us to pursue and develop godly ways. We can also develop our awareness of Christ by studying the Bible, engaging in prayer and meaningful spiritual discussions, and participating in Christian fellowship.

6. If you are a newborn in Christ in spiritual training, you can keep in training and develop your faith by aligning yourself with those who are more mature in the Lord and further along than you are. You can also keep your focus on Christ by associating yourself with a Bible believing, Bible preaching, and Bible teaching church. It is also beneficial to align yourself with faithful Bible study and prayer groups. That way, faithful and mature Christians can

---

[205] Rom 11:23-24; 1 Cor 1:9
[206] Rom 5:20, 6:1
[207] Rom 5:8

encourage you to develop the gift of faith.[208] Faithful and intentional training in the ways of God can also get you the spiritual nourishment that will allow you to steadily grow in the Lord Jesus. And remember dear friend, God will come wherever you are in your growth in grace to give you more grace to run this race and rise to new levels in your relationship with Him. God will do that for you because He loves you and is intent on bringing you all the way into His glorious eternity.

7. Understand then, that God is intent on seeing you through to the completion of His good work in you.[209] God has not brought you this far to leave you now. Because God is intent on saving you, God has put in place a twofold provision to restore you and me just in case we fall into error and violate our baptismal vows and our relationship with Him. The first provision that God has put in place is that He has provided Jesus as the One who appeases (propitiates or satisfies) divine justice by sacrificial means on the cross at Calvary. The second provision which God has put in place is that He has appointed the ascended Jesus as Advocate to plead our case before Him. Jesus secures your pardon for two reasons. The first is that you believe in Him.[210] The second is that Jesus has already satisfied God's requirement for your salvation when He offered up Himself on the cross. You and I could not pay the price for our own redemption because of our unrighteousness. However, because of His righteousness, Jesus was the acceptable and perfect sacrifice to satisfy the justice of God and so procure our forgiveness. Jesus has already taken upon Himself, your sin and my sin, your grief and mine.

8. I have more good news! As we continue to grow in Christ, remember that when God looked at Jesus on the cross what He saw was our sins. Now, when God looks at us, even in our imperfection, He sees the perfection and righteousness of His only begotten Son, Jesus, because Jesus now stands between God, the Father, and us, pleading our case and covering our sins. That makes Jesus our go-between. God loves you and sending Jesus Christ, His only begotten Son into the world to die for you on the cross, is evidence

---

[208] 1 Tim 4:14; 2 Tim 1:6

[209] Phil 1:6

[210] Jn 3:16; Rom 5:8-9

of that love. God loves you enough to forgive you when you sin and by His sustaining grace, picks you up when you fall and puts your life back on track. That is good news! Yes, faith takes time to develop. But if your faith, no matter how small, is anchored in the Lord Jesus, He will aid you as you grow into God's holiness and ultimately bring you into the realization of His promised eternity.

9. Assuredly, Baptism marks the beginning of a process of transformation with the divine goal of gradual recovery whereby Christ brings us into the fullness of God.[211] I am therefore affirming with you that faith in Christ followed by Baptism marks the beginning of a process of your spiritual renewal and growth in Christ. By the Holy Spirit working in and through us, we are regenerated, sanctified, made into new persons and are being transformed and elevated in the Spirit of God who is progressively shifting, modifying, and repositioning us as He moves us from glory to glory.[212]

10. As new creatures in Christ, then, the Holy Spirit helps us to be good since we cannot be good all by ourselves. The Holy Spirit helps us to avoid evil inclinations, resist the self-will in us, and resurrect us from our death in sin to a new life in Christ. This means that the Holy Spirit is the One who helps us in our conversion from sin to a fruit bearing life of holiness in Christ. Now, the fruit of the Spirit as outlined in Galatians 5:22-23 may not always be evident in the believer's life but they are always there, dormant perhaps, but always there. The good news for us is that through Baptism, we are identified with Christ,[213] and if Christ is the True Vine to which we are attached or engrafted, and by grace through faith we are, we have the help that we need in Him to become His fruit bearing branches as we seek daily to live and walk in the Spirit.[214] As we live and walk in the Spirit, our value and personhood are daily restored.

---

[211] 2 Pet 3:18

[212] Rom 6:4; 2 Cor 3:18

[213] Gal 3:27

[214] Gal 5:25

(viii) *Baptism and Our Restored Personhood*

1. By the Holy Spirit's entry in our lives at Baptism, we are renewed and our human dignity and personhood are restored by virtue of our new life in Christ. When we intentionally demonstrate the presence of Christ in us, our true value and personhood become more pronounced. Through Baptism and our restored relationship with God, and as a result of the Holy Spirit drawing us into union with Christ, thus forming us into the image of Christ, we are reconstituted as redeemed persons in relationship with God. Since God was in Christ reconciling the world to Himself,[215] being formed into the image of Christ also means that we are on our way to becoming new persons in whom the dignity of God is restored. What this means is that our personhood and human worth are realized only when we are in a right relationship with God in whom we live, move, and have our being.[216] Since it is in God that we live, move, and have our being, outside of God we fail to be truly human beings, the offspring of Being (God).

2. Volf observes that "in order to become a person, one must be freed from the restrictions of the biological hypostasis. Hence, this process of becoming a person can come only from the direction of God and as a total eschatological transcending...of biological existence."[217] The Apostle Paul puts it this way: "I have been crucified with Christ; it is no longer I who live, but Christ who lives in me; and the life which I now live in the flesh (the biological hypostasis and existence), I live by faith in the Son of God, who loved me and gave Himself for me."[218] If we are to have liberty in Christ and walk in the dignity of God's holy ways, the natural self needs to be crucified[219] and disciplined and brought under the reign and authority of Christ in whom our personhood is invested.

---

[215] 2 Cor 5:19

[216] Acts 17:28

[217] Mivoslav Volf, <u>After our Likeness: The Church as the Image of the Trinity</u> (Grand Rapids, MI/Cambridge, UK: William B. Eerdmans Publishing Co., 1998), 101

[218] Gal 2:20; Rom 6:6

[219] Gal 5:24

3. Our faithful acceptance of Christ and our desire for Baptism grow out of the recognition that our lives are incomplete, our value inconsequential, and our purpose uncertain, without a spiritual reorientation toward God. Wainwright agrees that "Baptism as the sacrament of death and resurrection...symbolizes the radical reorientation and transformation humanity needs, which only God can bring about...."[220] Our reorientation towards God signals the reshaping of our character and restoration of our human dignity and personhood fashioned after the moral image or moral DNA of God. It is that moral DNA in us that necessitates behaviors which are reflective of the holiness of God. Change in our character is important because a difference in our character also means a difference in our conduct. So, then, the Holy Spirit is not only our change agent; the Holy Spirit also works in us to restore the divine qualities that God created in us. Baptism is therefore another divine action of God that grounds our Christian identity and gives shape to our Christian character and personhood. By this action of God, the eschatological reality of Christ is transferred to all believers. The implication of this is that through Baptism, the Holy Spirit of promise grants us hope of eternal life and seals us for the day of redemption.[221] You and I were made with eternal values, weaved with eternal fibers, and infused with the divine DNA of God. God is intent on restoring that eternal value, moral fiber, and that divine DNA (personhood) that has been oxidized, distorted, negatively mutated, and cripplingly impacted by that destructive spiritual free radical we call sin.

4. Through Baptism, the holiness and dignity of God that descended upon Christ in the Jordan, descends upon us by the gift of the Holy Spirit at our Baptism, marking the beginning of that process of our spiritual transformation, empowerment, and restoration. This means that the new life of holiness we now live is the result of the restored dignity of God in us. It is the Spirit of God in us that equips us to lead holy lives. To understand this better, let us always remember that Christ by His death reconciles us to God. The Holy Spirit, by His presence and transforming power, shapes our personality and character making us more and more like Christ each and every day of our faith journey.

---

[220] Wainwright, 74

[221] 2 Cor 1:22; Eph 4:30; Rev 7:4

The Holy Spirit shapes our personality and character by keeping us steadfast and mindful of the goodness and holiness of God so that we may daily pursue them. The descent of the dignity and holiness of God on us at Baptism also means that Christian identity and dignity are grounded only in the righteousness and excellence of God. Our new state of living in Christ Jesus opens to us new opportunities for spiritual elevation. The invitation of Christ to feast at His Table and to commune with the Father, Son and Holy Spirit as adopted sons and daughters of God is a good indication of that opportunity and privilege. Our feasting at the Lord's Table and the spiritual significance of it will now capture our attention.

D. THE SACRAMENT OF HOLY COMMUNION

(i) Overview

The objective here is to help us develop an understanding of the meaning and purpose of Holy Communion. I also hope to help us see Holy Communion not merely as an event with historical significance that we cognitively remember. At a deeper relational level, the celebration of Holy Communion becomes for us an opportunity for our "re-membering" with Christ. Implied by our "re-membering" with Christ is our spiritual reconnection and renewal with the One who died for us. That way, our participation at the Lord's Table becomes a sort of renewal of our membership in the body of Christ as well as the renewing of our covenant relationship with Him. (Some Scriptures to consider as we pursue this area of our study of the Sacrament Holy Communion are: Matthew 26:26-30; Mark 14:22-26; Luke 22:14-20; 1 Corinthians 11:23-34).

(ii) What is Holy Communion?
(The Passover at a Glance)

1. Holy Communion is the Fellowship Meal of Christ's New Community established by Jesus Christ, signifying a New Covenant (New Testament). The origins of Holy Communion go back to the Passover Meal. The first Passover Meal took place just prior to the enslaved

Hebrews' departure from Egypt. The blood from the sacrificial lamb from the Passover Meal was plastered on the doorposts and beams where the Hebrew people resided as instructed by God to Moses who transmitted this information to the Hebrew population. The purpose was to offer those households, with the blood-plastered doorposts, protection from the angel of death, who, upon seeing the blood, would "pass over" those households— hence the term "Feast of the Passover." This notion of an angel of death should be seen purely for its historical value and within its historical context in Egypt. The plastering of blood on doorposts was not an ongoing event. It was a onetime occurrence that is memorialized and has become embedded in the religious reflective or memorial exercises of the people who experienced and benefited from that one time event.

    2. This practice of the Passover would become both historicized and traditionalized into the Hebrew and subsequent Jewish culture and tradition under the banner of Israel. During every ensuing Passover Meal the people of Israel would remember they were once slaves in bondage in Egypt. Having been liberated, and given a promise of fruitful abundance by God, they began a journey that took them through the wilderness. For forty years they wandered in the desert and were led to the Promise Land. This land was believed to be a land "flowing with milk and honey." It was so called because the land there was fertile, yielding great fruits, vegetation, and flocks of animals. Each time they ate the Passover Meal they would call to remembrance who they were as a people of long ago. In their eating of the Passover Meal, they fellowshipped, became one with that bondage people, recognized their freedom and expressed their gratitude to God. The Passover was for them, a typology of redemption and freedom.

    3. This typology and the ultimate hope of redemption find fulfillment in Jesus Christ, the true Passover Lamb that takes away the sins of the world.[222] According to Mark 14:12, Luke 22:7, and Matthew 26:17, the Last Supper with Jesus and His disciples was the day the Passover lamb would have been sacrificed. The Gospel of John however, indicates that Jesus was crucified or offered

---

[222] Jn 1:29

up on the cross during the celebration of the Passover.[223] John's account seems plausible. It is highly probable that Jesus would have eaten the Last Supper with His disciples the night before the actual Passover since on that day He would have been offered up as the Passover Lamb. It was significant that the death of Jesus should coincide or synchronize with the actual Passover; more so, than would the eating of the Passover Meal with His disciples. This position is supported by the words of Jesus in Matthew 26:2: "You know that after two days is the Passover and the Son of Man will be delivered up to be crucified." His death represents the fulfillment of the Hebrew/Jewish Passover.

4. During His own ministry, Jesus did in fact participate in several Passovers. His last was when He instituted what is now known as the Lord's Supper (Holy Communion). During the meal, Jesus offered Himself as the Passover Lamb for the redemption of the world. There He took bread, gave thanks, broke it and gave it to His disciples saying, "This is My body which is given for you; do this in remembrance of Me.[224] In the same manner, after supper, He took the cup and having given thanks He said: "This is My blood of the New Covenant, which is shed (poured out) for many for the forgiveness of sin."[225]

5. Jesus' Passover Meal with His disciples and the breaking of the bread and lifting of the cup became new symbols of the new Exodus. So, as we eat and drink of Christ, we look back and believe in the person of Jesus and all that He has done to free us from the bondage of sin. We look back in time and remember when we were under the bondage of sin and how we have been redeemed and liberated from such bondage by the sacrificial death of Jesus, the new Passover Lamb. We celebrate in the present, as we affirm God's covenant with His Church. We look forward with hope and rejoice with thanksgiving to a future where our happy reunion with Christ will be manifested.

6. Holy Communion, like Baptism, is a Sacrament instituted by Jesus at the Last Supper. These two Sacraments are the two Sacraments practiced by so-called "Protestants." Holy Communion is also known as The Lord's Supper or Holy Eucharist. Because of the diversity and richness of Holy

---

[223] Jn 19:14, 18:28

[224] Lk 22:19

[225] Mt 26:28

Communion, and because of the wealth and breadth of meanings associated with Holy Communion, we cannot speak adequately of it. By faith we believe that as Baptism is a sign of our commitment and new relationship with Jesus, a seal of our guaranteed salvation, and our sanctification or setting apart by God for God's use and glory, Holy Communion becomes our reconnection with Christ and the feeding and nurturing of our souls and spirits.

7. By faith we have resolved that the Sacrament of Holy Communion is the meeting place for renewal and reconnection with Christ for all who believe and confess His Sonship and Lordship. This meeting place takes place in the human heart where we respond to the Lord's invitation to a spiritual feeding and nurturing of our souls. Holy Communion, as we shall see later, is more than a calling to memory of a given historical moment in time. Holy Communion is an enacted as well as a reenacted experience that keeps Christ present for us and in our lives because it is our continuous sharing in the life, death and resurrection, as well as our active proclamation of His ascension and promised return. Holy Communion is also our faithful appropriation of all the benefits of the passion of Christ— forgiveness, redemption, justification, sanctification, spiritual empowerment and health, sound mind, and prosperity in all of its forms. Holy Communion is therefore, appropriately, a celebration and expression of gratitude to the One who died, has risen, and has promised to come again, Jesus, the Christ.

(iii) The Symbolic Value of the Bread and the Wine / Grape Juice

1. The table that we set, along with the elements, the fruits of the vine (the bread and the wine/grape juice), that we put on the Lord's Table, in and by themselves are only of symbolic value. However, when, in the mighty name of Jesus, the pastor or priest invites the presence of the Holy Spirit, the Holy Spirit shows up. When the Holy Spirit shows up, and gets involved, He releases His sanctifying and consecrating power and grace upon the elements and upon us. By that action of the Holy Spirit, we believe that the elements and we obtain spiritual significance and they effectually become for us, the body and blood of our blessed Lord. Therefore,

it is not the pastor, the elder, or the priest that consecrates the elements of Holy Communion; it is the Holy Spirit! We break and give the bread, but it was Christ whose body was broken and given for us. We lift the cup and pour the wine/grape juice; but it was Christ that was lifted to the cross and whose blood was poured out for the remission of our sins. We pray over the elements of the bread and the wine/grape juice; but it is God in the power of the Holy Spirit that performs the consecration.

2. The broken bread represents the broken body of Christ. The cup (wine/grape juice) represents the shed blood of Christ. Our sharing at the Lord's Table through the eating of the bread and the drinking from the cup is our sharing of Christ. The mediatory action and sanctifying presence of the Holy Spirit empower us to be faithful and obedient participants at the Lord's Table. We are empowered to be faithful and obedient because the Holy Spirit brings to our remembrance the love of God demonstrated on the cross through Christ on our behalf. That love, demonstrated by the sacrificial giving of Christ, constrains us and invokes our faithfulness and obedience in response to such great love given by Christ who gave up His life for us. Holy Communion is therefore our sharing in the atoning death of Christ.

(iv) The Holy Spirit at Work in Holy Communion

1. At the most celebrated and venerated of all Christian sacraments, the Holy Spirit is present and actively uniting us with the Father and the Son and each other. By our faithful participation in Holy Communion, like an invisible and gentle gravitating force, through the inspiration of the human thought and will, the Holy Spirit lovingly pulls us away from ourselves and the mundane things of life and draws us into fellowship with the Father and the Son, and with one another. By the work of the Holy Spirit that renews and transforms us, Holy Communion becomes a medicine of immortality to all that faithfully receive it.

2. Because we are sharing in the body and blood of Christ, we are essentially sharing in His incarnation and communion with the Father. Consequently, through Christ and the Holy Spirit working in us to bring us

into conformity with the ways of God, we are essentially becoming God-like. Becoming God-like does not mean that we are becoming little gods. Becoming God-like implies conformity to and therefore reflections of God-like qualities. This is indeed the eternal purpose of God and the destiny of all believers— the restoration of the personhood and the holy life-giving breath by which God created us.

3. Through the Holy Spirit, God meets us in worship, descends on us at Baptism, communes with us through the sacrament of Holy Communion, and summons us to respond in faith, obedience, and thanksgiving through a committed life in Christ. As a result of our faith in Christ, and by reason of our faith response to feast at the Lord's Table, we become recipients and beneficiaries of the passions of Christ, our Chief Celebrant (High Priest) and Mediator. As our High Priest and Mediator, Christ lifts the inconsistencies of our faith and obedience to the Father, sanctifies them and in return, gives us grace for our weakness. This act of grace gives us the privilege of access to feast at the Lord's Table where we are spiritually fed and divinely satisfied and renewed.

(v) Holy Communion as Satisfaction for Our Souls

1. As we eat the consecrated bread, the body of Christ, and drink His shed blood symbolized by the grape juice/wine, we are drawn into the life-giving power of Jesus who died to satisfy the justice of God. When God's justice was satisfied, so also were the souls of all who believe Him for salvation. Our communion with Christ brings enduring satisfaction to the believer's soul because He, upon whom we feed and drink, is the Bread of Life in whom we will never hunger or thirst.[226] As we drink of His life-giving blood, we receive new life because Christ becomes for us a fountain of living waters that will never run dry.[227]

2. Holy Communion brings fulfillment and satisfaction to those who hunger and thirst after righteousness.[228] As a result of the righteousness of

---

[226] Jn 6:35
[227] Jn 4:14
[228] Mt 5:6

God invested in Christ, and by virtue of our faith in Christ upon whom we feast, and who dwells in us, there is a sense of Christ in us filling, restoring, and satisfying our souls. The notion of our souls being filled and satisfied comes from the awareness of our renewed connection with Christ and the assurance of our salvation. Our satisfaction is further pronounced by our capacity to understand ourselves as transformed persons in communion with God and therefore restored persons in a saving relationship with Him. That assurance is a rewarding and satisfying conviction which words are not adequate to convey.

(vi) The Spiritually Restorative and Transforming Effects of Holy Communion

1. The restorative and transforming effects of Holy Communion come from our deep sense of the nearness of God and the communion that we have with the Father, Son, and Holy Spirit. As we commune with God, and renew fellowship and communion with our believing brothers and sisters in Christ Jesus, we also experience a refreshing of the Spirit that comes from God embracing us. As the Holy Spirit pulls us away from self, He also pulls us away from our worldly pursuits and the daily nuances of life. As the Holy Spirit does so, He also turns our minds toward Christ. As our minds are turned toward Christ, we then develop new visions of ourselves as persons in communion and fellowship with God through the Lord Jesus. The very notion that God wants to have fellowship with us restores our sense of worth. Our sense of value is restored as we become aware that God thinks enough of us to want fellowship and communion with us. That realization is also powerfully transforming because the awareness of God's love for us makes us want to change, humble ourselves before Him, and seek by God's help, to become more like Him.

2. Holy Communion is restorative because it is a constant reminder to us that we matter to God. When God created us, He filled us with His eternal value, which is His breathing in us, thus making us living souls. Because of the sin of disobedience, we elected to lower our worth as we lost sight of

our eternal value. However, God's love for us is far greater than our offense against Him. Because of God' great love for us and His infinite capacity to forgive, He forgives and restores His own divine value in us when He sent His only begotten Son into the world to atone for the sin that separated us from Him. By His sacrificial atonement, Christ redeemed us, restored, and elevated our human worth and dignity, which God had invested in us in the first place.

3. Faithful partaking of Holy Communion is spiritually transforming and restorative because Christ, who mediates our worship and our sharing in Holy Communion, also presents us with Himself to the Father by the unitive function of the Holy Spirit. Unitive implies bringing together or uniting. The unitive work of the Holy Spirit is therefore the power and action of the Holy Spirit that unites us with the Father and the Son as He brings us into fellowship and Holy Communion. This sense of being in fellowship and communion with God is powerfully transforming. Without the Holy Spirit drawing us into fellowship and communion with the Father and the Son, we would not, by the influence of our own will, seek fellowship with God; nor would we develop any affinity to His holy ways to which we have been wonderfully exposed through Christ. It is this exposure, indeed, this awareness, that changes the way we think, behave, and have become in Christ. Our becoming is a redefinition of who we are in Christ Jesus.

(vii) *Holy Communion Redefines Who We Are in Christ*

1. As already stated in the case of our Baptism, as a result of our communion with God, our personhood and eternal value can no longer be defined by human divisions of race, gender, nationality, and social positions. Rather, our personhood and eternal value must now be redefined by our relationship and communion with God. Indeed, "the Son of God became our brother that He might lift us up into that life of wonderful communion."[229] Through Jesus Christ, God has adopted us as His sons

---

[229] James B. Torrance, <u>Worship and Community</u>, 84

and daughters.[230] Regarding a redefinition of who and what we have become in Christ, Galatians 4:7 affirms that we are no longer slaves but sons and daughters, and if sons and daughters, we have become heirs of God through the Lord Jesus. Consequently, God is now our God and Father and we have become His people,[231] sons and daughters, upon whom He looks lovingly and daily bestows mercy and grace.

2. Our human differences of race, nationality, ethnicity, and social standings no longer matter because through Jesus, we have all become adopted sons and daughters of God. The idea of adoption is a metaphor borrowed by Paul[232] from the Roman legal system. The importance of this is the authority that adoption gives to the child's father or new family. The adoption gives the child a new family and a new name. Therefore, when God the Father adopts us, we have new names, and a new family, the family of God, thus redefining who we have become in Christ. Accepting Christ as our Savior through whom God adopts us, implies that old debts and obligations have been cancelled. We are no longer under the obligation of our "old parents" and habits of sin and the devil, because our alignments have been changed and we are now under the parenting of God our Father. Under the Roman's legal system, the father was considered owner of the adopted child and was further considered to have the power to control the behavior of such a person. The adopted father not only had authority, he had an obligation.

3. What this means for us who are adopted by God is that God, not us, and certainly not sin, God alone has authority and dominion over us. It also means that we owe no allegiance to our old masters— sin and the devil.[233] Now that Jesus Christ has paid the price for us, we owe allegiance only to God the Father. That is an opportunity for praise and thanksgiving. **Hallelujah!**

4. Being adopted by God also means that all that He has is ours, and all that we have become, we owe to Him. On God's part, what this means for

---

[230] See for example, Rom 8:15-17; Gal 4:5-7; Eph 1:5
[231] Jer 31:33; Heb 8:10; Jn 1:12; Rom 8:15, 9:25; 2 Cor 6:18; Gal 4:6; Eph 1:5-6
[232] Rom 8:15, 23; 9:4; Gal 4:5; Eph 1:5
[233] Gal 3: 26-4:7

us is that God has committed Himself to guiding us so that our behavior can bring credit to His name. Indeed, the death and resurrection of Christ that we celebrate, redefine who we have become in God. We are the righteousness of God because God made Him who had no sin to be sin for us, so that in Him we might become the righteousness of God.[234]

(viii) Holy Communion: A Re-presenting of and A "Re-membering with" Christ

1. On every occasion that we come to the Lord's Table for Holy Communion, the Holy Spirit ministers Christ to us. Our participation in Holy Communion, while not a repetition of the crucifixion of Christ, or the reenactment of His life and ministry, is a re-presenting of the finished work of Christ by the Holy Spirit. As the Holy Spirit ministers Christ to us, Christ in His ascension lifts us before the Father of grace and mercy. That way, we are never left on our own, but as often as we eat and drink of Christ, the Holy Spirit re-presents Him to us and reconnects us to Him as He progressively draws us into the communal life of God the Father.

2. The work of Christ on the cross that we commemorate through Holy Communion is not just a moment in time that we remember; it is an experience that we live. Because of the Holy Spirit's re-presenting of Christ, we also relive and renew our experience of Christ every time we gather for the Lord's Supper. The re-presenting of Christ makes Holy Communion a dynamic event since it is not an event that is stuck in time immemorial but an experience that embraces the dimensions of the past act of Christ on the cross, His present operation in our lives through the Holy Spirit, and the future manifestation of His promise of eternal communion with us.

3. When we come to the Lord's Table, then, we do not do so merely to remember a date and time in history. We do so to celebrate Christ and remember how our sins which were many have been washed away by His precious blood. Through Holy Communion, we experience our past, present, and eternal destiny wrapped up in the eternal Son of God. By the Holy Spirit

---

[234] 2 Cor 5: 21

re-presenting Christ to us and by our partaking of Christ, we are empowered to embrace that past with faith, celebrate the present operations of Christ in our lives and church with passion, and look to the future with glorious hope for the return of Christ.

4. Holy Communion is therefore more than the celebration or memory of an event of spiritual significance or historical proportion. As we celebrate and participate in Holy Communion, our understanding of the traditional rendering of "In Remembrance" should be taken to mean "re-membering" as in reestablishing our relationship with Christ and our membership in the body of Christ. This means that as often as we partake of Holy Communion, we are reconnecting or reestablishing or renewing our commitment to Christ. The implication of this is that we are not only participating in this process to remember the historic Jesus, but at a deeper level, we do so to reestablish our spiritual connection with Jesus through whom and by whom God and believing humanity are reconciled. To "re-member" or reconnect with Christ may therefore be taken to mean that the power of the Holy Spirit of grace has reestablished our union with Christ as well as restored our membership in the body of Christ.

5. Furthermore, when we speak of Holy Communion as a memory, it is not merely a cognitive recalling of an event. It is a spiritual reconnection with the person and finished work of Christ whereby the Holy Spirit brings the act of the cross and its significance for us to memory.[235] This bringing to our recollection happens when we are moved to contemplate all that Christ has accomplished— His life, ministry, death, resurrection, ascension, intercession, and His promise to come again.

(ix) Holy Communion and the Forgiveness of Our Sins

1. The universal invitation to the Lord's Table was given by Christ the night before He was offered up as the Sacrificial Lamb. There He invites His disciples and us to eat and drink of Him for the remission of our sins. At Holy Communion, God summons our hearts and draws us

---

[235] Jn 14:26

to respond in faith to Christ who becomes present at the Lord's Table to take away that emptiness caused by sin, so that He might fill us with an abundance of pardon, grace, and love. As reconciled people, Holy Communion is our celebration of divine grace and favor, as well as a celebration of forgiveness.

2. The invitation to the Lord's Table is still a call to repentance and at the same time an invitation to receive forgiveness and atonement. It is an invitation to receive forgiveness because in it Jesus says, "This is my blood that is shed for many for the remission of sin." That invitation has formed the theological and liturgical basis for the invitation most commonly used by the Church:

> "You who have repented of your sins and are living in love and unity with your brothers and sisters, and earnestly seeking to follow the ways of God, Christ has invited you to His table. Therefore, draw near with faith to receive this holy Sacrament to your comfort, as we make our humble confessions to Almighty God, meekly kneeling."

3. Holy Communion is an affirmation of our forgiveness and reconciliation with God and each other. Assuredly, we who are invited to the Lord's Table are the forgiven and regenerated (baptized) sons and daughters of God. We approach the throne of grace empowered by the Spirit of forgiveness and we come to the Lord's Table with the same confident assurance that we are the forgiven, redeemed, and reconciled people of God.

4. By our sharing in the Holy Communion, and by the illuminating Spirit of grace, all generations of the faithful and expectant Church have learned to see and know themselves to be a people whose sins Jesus nailed to the cross, not in part but the whole. **Hallelujah!** Through Holy Communion, we recognize in the event of the cross that Christ confessed our sins, bore our pain, paid the price that we could never pay, and made a New Covenant between God and us, signed with His own blood. Holy Communion is a re-presenting of Christ and therefore a reminder to us that Jesus took upon Himself the sins of us all, and has given us back our lives, no longer sinful lives, but thank

God, repentant, converted, forgiven, regenerated, justified, sanctified, and reconciled lives. What a wonderful exchange of grace! Oh to grace how great a debtor daily, we are constrained to be! It is this realization that fills our hearts with thanksgiving as we approach the Lord's Table to feast upon Christ.

(x) Holy Communion as an Opportunity for Thanksgiving

1. Let us quickly recap what Holy Communion is for us. Holy Communion is Christ coming near to us. It is our sharing of Christ who is continuously re-presented to us by the Holy Spirit. Holy Communion is our "re-membering" or reconnecting with Christ. It is nourishment for our souls. It is spiritually restorative. It redefines who we are in Christ Jesus. Holy Communion is an affirmation of our forgiveness and it is an opportunity for thanksgiving.

2. When we consider all these and other benefits of the Passion of Christ, Holy Communion presents us with the opportunity to recount the great deeds of God with profound gratitude. Our invitation to the Lord's Table is an invitation to fellowship and commune with God as well as to express our gratitude for what God began in creation, has done through Christ for our redemption, continues to do through our sanctification by the Holy Spirit, and waits to complete in Christ on that Great Day.[236] We gather at the Lord's Table to express our deep gratitude because Holy Communion is our constant reminder of what God has done for us through the Lord Jesus Christ, by releasing us from the stranglehold of sin and all that once enslaved us.[237]

3. We are thankful because Jesus, having secured our salvation through His death, has given us the assurance of victory over death by His resurrection. Additionally, He also fills us with hope by His promised return to receive us into eternity. Holy Communion therefore has eschatological significance to those of us who not only remember, but also believe on the Lord

---

[236] See Phil 1:6
[237] Gal 4:6-7

Jesus Christ and earnestly live with the expectation of His triumphant return. Indeed, the Holy Spirit who knows all the deep things of God[238] assures us that at the final resurrection, all of God's called-out and chosen people,[239] will receive and fully experience every benefit belonging to God's heirs,[240] to the honor and glory of God. Such affirmation moves us to magnify God with thanksgiving and doxological praise. **Hallelujah!**

E. THE DOXOLOGY

(i) What Is The Doxology?

1. The doxology is a statement of glory ascribed to God. It is an important component of the Christian liturgy that is used for aiding worshippers in ascribing praise and glory to the Father, Son, and Holy Spirit. A doxology is a hymn or formula of praise to God. Many doxologies are found in the Bible, such as in Romans 16:27, Ephesians 1:3, 3:21, and Jude 1:25. These are known as Biblical doxologies.

2. We also have what are known as the Lesser and Greater Doxologies. The Lesser and Greater Doxologies are two responsive forms that originated in the 4th century and are still being used in the liturgies of many Christian churches. The Lesser Doxology, also known as The Gloria Patri is rendered: "Glory be to the Father and to the Son and to the Holy Ghost; as it was in the beginning, is now, and ever shall be, world without end. Amen." The Greater Doxology, known as the Gloria in Excelsis Deo, is an early church expansion of the song of the angels in Luke 2:14: "Glory to God in the highest, and on earth peace, goodwill toward men!" The Greater Doxology is rendered:

> "Glory be to God on high, and on earth peace, goodwill toward men. We praise You, we bless You, we worship You, we glorify You, we give thanks to You for Your great glory. O Lord God, heavenly King;

---

[238] 1 Cor 2:10
[239] 1 Pet 2:9
[240] Rom 8:23

God the Father Almighty; O Lord, the only begotten Son, Jesus Christ; O Lord God, Lamb of God, Son of the Father, that takes away the sins of the world, have mercy upon us. You, who take away the sins of the world, receive our prayer. You that sit at the right hand of God the Father, have mercy upon us. For You alone are holy; You alone are the Lord; You alone, O Christ, with the Holy Ghost, are most high in the glory of God the Father. Amen!"

3. The doxology is fundamental to Christian worship because it is a constant reminder to us of the majesty, power, and glory of God. Even though the doxology is not an instrument of holiness, by virtue of its doctrinal affirmations, practicing its applications may be useful in guiding Christian believers to a clearer and deeper understanding of the holiness and majesty of God. From a structural, theological, and doctrinal perspective, the doxology announces and teaches us the essential unity of the Father, Son, and Holy Spirit. Doxologies help worshippers who are paying attention to these doctrinal affirmations to understand how the Father, the Son, and the Holy Spirit are actively engaged and working in the believer's life and worship.

4. The doctrinal affirmations of the doxology also help in our understanding of how worship becomes a dialogue that connects us to God and God to us. This dialogue takes place through the channel of the Holy Spirit.[241] The Holy Spirit makes Christ present in worship and reminds us of His worthiness as the One who offered up the perfect sacrifice for our redemption. Christ, our Mediator, then lifts our worship and praise to God. It is by Christ the Son, and our emulation of His perfect worship of the Father, that our worship becomes acceptable to God the Father. These Three, Father, Son, and Holy Spirit, to whom we ascribe our balanced praise in worship, work as "One." When we speak of God in three Persons, therefore, we are saying that God the Father is Creator. Through the Son He manifests Himself as Redeemer. And, through the glorious and effectual work of the Holy Spirit, God's glory and sanctifying power are forever manifested and made present. This knowledge is essential for

---

[241] Please refer to chapter three, Christian Worship, section 6, Worship as a Dialogue: The Channel of Mediation

Christians not only to shape our minds as worshippers, but above all, to help us understand how God the Father, works through the Son, and manifests Himself in the sanctifying power of the Holy Spirit, in order to change our lives, bring about our redemption, sanctify us for His purpose, draw us into His holiness, and to daily anoint and prepare us for His eternity.

5. Doxologies are useful for the Christian worshipper at four levels of theological understanding. At the first level, doxologies impress upon us an awareness and reminder of the majesty, glory, and power of God and His worthiness for praise. At the second level, doxologies aid our understanding of the manifestations of God's operations and the essential unity of the Father, Son, and Holy Spirit who work inseparably in creation and for our redemption and sanctification. At the third level, doxologies in their theological applications may invoke the worshippers' awareness of the manifold goodness of God's divine compassion and grace. At the fourth level, doxologies are useful in aiding worshippers' understanding of the channel through which God's grace and mercy descend to us— from the Father, through the Son, in the power and manifestations of the Holy Spirit to whom we also ascribe glory and praise. When we say, for example, "glory be to the Father and to the Son and to the Holy Ghost," we are doctrinally affirming the essential unity and praise of God's divine nature and manifestations as Creator, as Redeemer in Christ, and Sanctifier through the effectual work of the Holy Spirit.

6. The ultimate liturgical and theological objective of the doxology is to empower believers to reach up to God through understanding and therefore with purposeful praise. Again, that understanding should be based fundamentally on knowledge of God as He exists as Creator, Redeemer, and Sanctifier. As a component of the liturgy, and as a result of its doctrinal formulation, the doxology also enables us to have clarity regarding the ascent and descent of divine grace in worship and daily life.

7. In worship, when used in the preliminary or opening stages of formal worship, the doxology is an announcement of celebration. When used at the conclusion of formal worship, particularly when it immediately precedes the benediction, the doxology becomes our marching orders to go forth into the world to serve and glorify God through intentional service in the context of

community. Worship is always an opportunity to celebrate and be thankful to God who empowers us through His Holy Spirit to live doxological lives.

(ii) Living Doxological Lives:
The Liturgical and Doxological Nature of Christian Living
(Section One)

1. Living doxological lives is really about practicing what we preach. The glory that we give to God in our words should extend to the glory we give to Him by the way we behave. The doxological formulas to which we prescribe, and the glory of God that we lift up in formal worship, need to spill over in and through our daily lives so that worship becomes a living experience for us. Our lifestyle outside the context of the formal worship ought to become our daily liturgy as we seek to become what we know and believe about God. This daily liturgy of which I speak is the liturgy of life; a life that brings glory to God by the choices we make and the way we conduct ourselves in the world. Living a doxological life requires that we represent God well, not only on the day of our scheduled worship services or for the duration of our "set in stone" one hour or however long the worship service may last. We should be intentional about representing God well on a daily basis. After all, God is God on other days than those days that we set aside for our weekly formal gathering for worship.

2. Knowledge of God ought to cultivate in us the desire to bring continuous praise to His name by the way we live our lives in the world. When Jesus says, "Let your light so shine before [mankind] that they may see your good works and glorify your Father in heaven,"[242] He is giving the Christian community a mandate for acting out their faith conviction in the world through worship and praise and a lifestyle that draws attention to the goodness and glory of God.

3. Our daily liturgy is the way we live our lives as beneficiaries of God's goodness and as witnesses to His mercy and grace. The way we live should be such that people are drawn to God because of the way we conduct ourselves

---
[242] Mt 5:16

even when we think the pastor or fellow church members are not around to see and hear us. The life that privately and publicly conducts itself in accordance with the will and purposes of God is a doxological life. The life we live, in response to the God we encounter in worship, needs to be an ongoing and overflowing expression of God's glory and praise in the world. If indeed we believe in the excellence and infinite goodness of God, and if, indeed, we believe in His holiness and manifested activity in our lives, then it behooves us to live excellently for God in the world. That way, the liturgy of worship finds expression not only through our holy words, but also through our holy actions.

4. While liturgical observations are not necessarily indicators of holiness, proper observation and practice of the liturgy may induce holiness. Practicing a liturgical lifestyle entails the living out or manifesting in the world, the God that we confess and glorify in formal worship. Intentional observation and practice of Christian liturgy, advanced by our knowledge of God and acquaintance with His ways, should inspire us to live out our faith in the context and dynamics of human encounters. That way, the Christian life becomes what Charry calls "a tutorial in the art of holiness."[243]

5. Participation in the liturgical practices of worship as a custom not only has faith and tutorial values, it also has behavioral values for life. Consequently, what we learn of God in worship ought to inform and influence the way we live our daily lives. The liturgy therefore becomes a sort of behavioral reminder of who we are and the way God requires us to live our lives. Our lives should be lived in a way that draws attention to the holiness of God in us. That way, our demonstrative behaviors may appropriately represent and honor God in the world. Based on the understanding that knowledge of God shapes and influences worshippers' faith response to God, the same may be said of our understanding and practical application of such knowledge to our daily lives. If correct knowledge of God leads to a proper understanding and worship of God, then it is reasonable to affirm that such knowledge when applied to our daily lives can also invoke proper behaviors that bring glory to God.

---

[243] Charry, 105

Living Doxological Lives:
The Liturgical and Doxological Nature of Christian Living
(Section Two)

1. We begin to lead doxological lives when, having learned the ways of God, we are moved by what we learn about God to display those ways in our dealings with others. When, for example, we give to others the same love, mercy, compassion, and forgiveness that we receive from God, we are extending God's glory in the world. When our practical demonstrations of these attributes become a lifestyle for us, they also become daily exercises of praise and manifestations of glory to God.

2. The liturgy of worship is not only to be recited, it is to inform our faith, inspire our hope, and influence our actions. The liturgy, performed by words, needs to be translated into action in order that we might glorify God by our words and by our behavior. The liturgy of word is our offering of praise and adoration to God in formal worship. The liturgy of action is indicative of the life we live in the world that is reflective of justice and mercy and compassion. That way, our liturgical lives effectively become visible representations of God's justice, mercy and compassion in the world. It is in the world that the duet between faith and works finds expressive harmony. It is imperative then, for our faith to spring into action so that what we do through obedience and faith may become lively expressions of praise offered up to God.[244]

3. We live doxological lives when we are empowered by the Holy Spirit to effectively and faithfully participate in God's redemptive and liberating acts in the world. When we become engaged in spreading Scriptural holiness, sharing the good news of salvation, healing relationships, showing mercy to our neighbors, feeding the hungry, transforming social structures and changing lives, we are living lives that glorify God. It is that type of living that really reveals the extent of our sharing in the life and ministry of Christ. We cannot say we have worshipped God if we believe that the worship service or the formal liturgy ends with the doxology and the benediction. If

---

[244] See for example Jas 2:14-20

congregational renewal is to mean anything, then the way we live beyond the confines of our sanctuaries must necessarily be an outflowing of the love, grace, and mercy of God that we experience in worship.

4. The community of faith, the Church, is not only a worshipping community as it relates to formal worship; it is also a working community that should be actively seeking to bring glory to God by the way we live and behave in the world. As such, we are called to worship God as well as serve Him in the world in our pursuit of holiness and the discovery of spiritual formation. Such pursuit and discoveries can only be realized by our intentional pursuit of God in worship and in life. The ultimate goal of worship, as Bishop Talbot resoundingly attests, is to "see God high and lifted up...and for the people gathered through revitalized worship experience to disperse and seek intentionally to live out the liturgy of worship in the world."[245]

5. The human pursuit of holiness is ignited by our awareness of the holiness of God which is grounded in worship, and finds active expressions through our intentional living out the liturgy of worship in the world through acts of righteousness. Now, while we may discover faith in the context of formal worship or by other life experiences and encounters with God, the world is the stage on which faith is lived and where righteousness is practiced and developed. Our influence in the world is therefore largely dependent on the extent to which we live out or practice our faith in the world.

6. Without our intentional pursuit of active service we run the risk of worshipping only in words and not with active, expectant, and participative faith. Our worship of God and our activity in the world are therefore continuously inseparable gifts of grace. When we ascribe glory to God through the expressive means of the formal liturgy of words, we are worshipping God. When we minister to the needs of others, we are living the liturgy and therefore demonstrating God's actions of grace and mercy in the world. We truly reach up to God with praise when we reach out and give of ourselves and our possessions to others through service and love that change lives. If indeed, we are pleased to share in spiritual blessings we ought also to find pleasure

---

[245] Bishop Talbot, 62

in the sharing of material things.[246] The message here is that whether in formal worship or through Christian living, the actions and life of all Christians should be a continuous liturgy and a doxology regardless of the context that we find ourselves in.

7. True worship never really ends. That would be an anticlimax of the Christian experience. True worship is continuous because the formal liturgy ought always to translate into Christian discipleship and actions that bring glory to God. The life that is continuously doxological is a life inspired by the Holy Spirit to move from the preaching and the hearing of the word, to the living of Christ in the world. In both His worship and service to the Father, Christ brought glory to God in the world.[247] To glorify God in the world is to make His name great and reveal His true character so that those seeking Him may come to know Him through us as we have come to know God through the Lord Jesus. As Jesus came into the world to reveal and fulfill God's design for humanity, so should we, by grace, reveal Christ and fulfill His design on our lives by living lives that truly reflect the holiness of God as we are empowered by the Spirit of grace to do so.

8. Our doxological living is only made possible by the empowering Spirit of grace. By ourselves we cannot and would not do what is right and fitting for God's glory. The same Spirit that inspires our worship is the same Spirit that inspires our daily living and behavior, making it possible for us to practice what we preach. Our daily exercise of faith and therefore our cumulative growth in holiness is not so much the result of our own strength, ability and goodness, as much as it is the faithfulness of Jesus Christ and the providential care of divine grace. Torrance says it best when he writes:

> "It is Christ the object of faith who holds on to us and saves us even when our faith is so weak. The Christ in whom we believe far exceeds the small measure of our faith, and so the believer finds…security not in poor believing grasp of Christ but in the gift of grace…

---

[246] Rom 15:27

[247] Jn 17:4

It is not therefore upon the strength of our faith that we rely but upon the faithfulness of Christ."[248]

9. From the narrow and "secured" confines of our places of worship, God has called and anointed us to go forth into the world to live doxological lives. By the help of the Holy Spirit, we are empowered to influence the world by living exemplary lives, doing deeds of kindness and showing compassion for broken humanity. It is in the world that faith is practiced and where the true meaning of Christianity and a doxological life are manifested.

10. Speaking of the true meaning of Christianity and a manifested doxological life style, the story of the Good Samaritan in Luke 10:25-37 comes to mind. This certain Samaritan became known as the Good Samaritan because he demonstrated what it means to live a liturgical and doxological life. What the Good Samaritan did on that Jericho Road, is precisely what God requires of us, and exactly what Jesus did for all of us as we traveled on our personal Jericho Roads. In this story, we have Jesus putting the hammer down and holding the so-called religious community accountable for their moral obligations and the performances of those obligations, or lack thereof. Here we see Jesus calling out the pretentious, exposing superficial religion, and establishing in purely practical terms, the true meaning of religion and what it means to live doxological lives.

Living Doxological Lives:
The Liturgical and Doxological Nature of Christian Living
(Section Three)

1. There, on that unforgiving Jericho Road, the doxology of praise through service of love and mercy spilled over from an unlikely source. As the story goes, "a certain man went down from Jerusalem to Jericho and fell among thieves who stripped him of his clothing, wounded him, and departed leaving him half dead." "A certain man…" No reference is made of the wounded man's race; no mention is made of his nationality

---

[248] Thomas F. Torrance, <u>Scottish Theology</u>, 1996, p.58

(unless otherwise implied from the Jerusalem reference); and nothing is said of his religious affiliation. Jesus made no such reference because He probably wanted to avoid prompting His listeners to think about the situation in terms of the labels we put on people. Those labels— national, ethnic, social, economic, political, and religious, variables— that so often influence the way we respond to and treat others. Jesus avoided those labels and points of reference because it was more important for those listening to pay attention to the fact that the beaten man was a human being in need.

2. On the Jericho road, this "certain man" laid there after being beaten, robbed, and left half dead. Later, as the story indicates, a priest passed by perhaps coming from the place of worship, the synagogue. Upon seeing the man lying there, beaten up and half dead, the priest passed by on the other side without offering any assistance. Not even a prayer! Still later, another religious person, a Levite came by. He stopped and checked probably out of curiosity, but he too went on about his business without aiding the "certain man" in need.

3. Perhaps the priest and the Levite convinced themselves that the situation was none of their business. Both the priest and the Levite professed to be good men by reason of holding sacred offices and being frequent worshippers. They taught the law but suppressed the spirit of it. They taught others about loving God but they did not practice what they taught. They knew of duty but did not have the devotion to it. They were expected to show mercy to the wounded man but they turned a blind eye. They were expected to have compassion but they were cold and indifferent. They were expected to aid people in misery, but they proved to be miserable pretenders. Motivated by their own status and self-preservation, these two religious persons went on their way leaving a fellow human to suffer and die on the side of the road. Perhaps they wished they had not passed by when they did. That way, they would not be held accountable for their gross neglect of a moral responsibility. But they did neglect a moral responsibility; and would probably use religious and cultural practices to justify such gross dereliction of duty.

4. The unlikely source of blessing and compassion, a certain Samaritan, came along that same Jericho Road. When he saw the wounded man, without concern for his own safety, this certain Samaritan stopped and showed compassion. Motivated by someone else's need, touched by humanity, and inspired by God's pervasive grace, this certain Samaritan proceeded to do a good work. He knew that if the situation was reversed he would not want to be passed by and looked upon with contempt, but with compassion. This stranger's heart was overflowing with divine love. Without showing any concern for his own comfort and safety, he took off his garment and covered the wounded man. The oil and wine that he took for his own use and convenience, he used to anoint and refresh the suffering man. The mule he had for his own transportation, he put the wounded man on it, and led him to the safety of an inn (hotel). There, he took care of the wounded man. When he had to leave, he paid the current expenses, left the wounded man in the care of the innkeeper, and promised to take care of any additional expenses when he returned from his business trip. What a practical doxology!

5. The story of the Good Samaritan was prompted by a young lawyer seeking to justify himself in a previous discourse with Jesus when he asked, "…Who is my neighbor?" The young lawyer asked the question of "Who is my neighbor?" Jesus answered with the demonstration of how to be a neighbor. Jesus' own life exemplified a good neighbor and a doxological life. At some point in our lives all of us have had to travel on our own rough Jericho Roads. On our Jericho Road we were in despair when Jesus came to our rescue. On our Jericho Road He saw us dying, and He stopped by to give us life.[249] On our Jericho Road He saw us victimized by the condemnation of sin and He took on our case.[250] We were wounded and He healed us.[251] He found us naked and in sin; and by His grace, He covered us with His robe of righteousness. We were beaten up, robbed by sin, and left half dead when Jesus left the glory of heaven and came where we were, opened the doors of heaven

---

[249] Jn 10:10, 15;11:25
[250] Is 53:6
[251] Is 53:4-5

and made provisions for us at His own expense by dying to redeem us, and promised to come again.

6. Someone, undoubtedly a beneficiary of grace and mercy, once testified: "I am wretched and undone. Too mean to live and not fit to die. I had no shoes on my feet, no clothes on my back, and no money in my pocket. But Jesus met me on my Jericho Road. He picked me up, cleaned me off, turned me around, and planted my feet on higher ground. Jesus, how sweet the name! He is my bread when I am hungry; my water when I am thirsty; my doctor in the hospital room; my lawyer when I am falsely accused; and my conscience in the pool room; Jesus, how sweet the name!" Jesus was a living and walking doxology of praise and glory. He expects us to go and do likewise!

Living Doxological Lives:
The Liturgical and Doxological Nature of Christian Living
(Section Four)

1. The story of the Good Samaritan is an indictment. It is an indictment against having religion without conviction and concern for the human condition. It is an indictment against having a form of godliness without the power to live as children of God. It is a call to practice what we preach. All around us there are people who are stricken by hunger, paralyzed by ignorance, dehumanized by poverty, victimized by racial prejudice, afflicted by despair, deceived by drugs, infected by the demon of alcohol and infectious diseases, beaten up by circumstances, and left half-dead. You may say, "What is all that to do with me? My family is safe and quite alright." It has everything to do with you. They are your neighbors and you do need to care. They are our neighbors and we should no longer be content with passing them by on the other side. Their conditions are opportunities presented to us in order that we might get involved, change their lives, and so bring praise and glory to God by our deeds of kindness, compassion, and empathy. That my friend is what it means to live doxological lives. Today Jesus is saying to all of us that

kneel at the altar to worship, "Rise, go, and do likewise." Go and care for the dying. Go and rescue the perishing; snatch them in pity from hell and the grave. To live in the service of love and mercy is to live a life of active praise to God.

2. A doxological life is a life that is dedicated to the lifting up of the fallen and downtrodden who, in not so "secure" a world, have been stricken and beaten down by misfortune and sin and need to be rescued and restored. The liturgical and doxological nature of life implies living in the world to lift up fallen humanity to the honor and glory of God who first lifted us in Jesus Christ. As God's grace continues to move us from glory to glory on our journey into God's eternity, we need to stop, show that we care, and help others along their journey.[252]

3. If, on your way to heaven, you see others standing by the road with life's heavy load, it is your Christian duty to give a helping hand. As you continue your walk with God, if you see others falling by the way, it is your Christian duty to stop and say "You are going the wrong way." As sons and daughters of God, we are obligated, for the sake of God's glory, to show a little kindness. The kindness that we show every day will help someone along the way. If we try a little kindness, soon we will overlook the blindness of narrow-minded people on their narrow-minded streets.[253]

4. On that Jericho Road, God did send help from likely sources to help the man beaten up and left half-dead in the form of two religious persons and worshippers, a priest and a Levite. However, they neglected their assignment. Since God is always intent on lifting up fallen humanity, what the expected helpers refused to do, God used a stranger to do. As practicing Christians, we are derelict in our responsibility to the fallen, the downtrodden and the victimized when we turn blind eyes to their sufferings. God is determined to help and He is waiting for you and me, His hands, His feet, and His voices to move, to reach, and to speak in the world. We are always to serve God in the world so that His glory may shine forth in it. As believing sons and daughters of God, living a life of praise demands that we move our lives and faith from

---

[252] Rom 15:1-3; Gal 6:1-2; 1 Thess 5:14-20; Heb 4:16

[253] From Glen Campbell's song, "Try A Little Kindness" (1970)

the safe confines of our formal worship settings and make ourselves vulnerable for the sake of the kingdom of God. We can do so by backing up our faith with kindness even in rough neighborhoods. It is in those neighborhoods that God has called and sent us to put our faith in action. It is there that God's people are hurting. It is there that they desperately wait for us to show up and show them the way to Jesus so that they too can find hope in Him.

5. Christ has taught us that love for God should not be restricted to formal worship alone, but needs to extend to serving those who are deprived, hurt, excluded, abandoned, and avoided by others. We are not only called to worship in order to express our gratitude for what He has done for us. Having experienced God in worship and life, we are also called to a life of demonstrative faith which is our obligation to God and His alienated people everywhere so that they can also come to experience God's grace and favor.

6. In worship and daily living, our doxology ought to become continuous confession, adoration, thanksgiving, devotion, and service. That way, we offer up continuous praise to God for allowing us in worship to come into His holy presence, and for anointing us to go forth into the world, to be witnesses to His holiness, goodness, mercy, and grace. In worship God reorders our lives so that we should no longer live for ourselves but for God and others through the active demonstration of mercy, and the promotion of justice, love, and compassion. A doxological life is attainable when the praise that begins in worship, spills over into our daily lives and service.

7. The singing of the doxology and the pronouncement of the benediction do not signify the dismissal or conclusion of worship. Neither are the doxology and benediction suggestive of surrender or retreat into isolation. They signify that having been drawn into the presence of God through the reconciling power of Christ as we are empowered by the Holy Spirit in worship, we are being sent out with the mandate and full backing of the Father, Son, and Holy Spirit to witness to the power and love of God in the world. Having been empowered by a new vision of God in worship, the benefits of God's goodness ought rightly to motivate us to live for God in the world. For all practical intent and purposes, the doxology and the benediction are the Christian's mandate to go out into the world with the blessings and assured

presence of God, to faithfully practice and proclaim what we preach from the pulpit and shout about from the pews. Bishop Talbot has offered a rather wonderful synthesis between worship and the living out of that worship in the world when he writes:

> "To encounter the One who is "high and lifted up," to confess and to accept forgiveness demand the radical response to the God who is in the world through service. Christian worship seeks to evoke such a response from each worshipper… Lives which have been graced by God's self-giving love issue forth in acts of compassion, justice, hospitality, mercy and love. Lives that have been "gifted" by the unmerited and undeserved grace of God, and initiated by God, respond not merely in gratitude but also in obligation. Clearly, it is God's saving work in our justification that liberates us for valid ethical efforts."[254]

8. Indeed, as worship spills over in our daily lives and encompasses our daily activities, a doxological life demands that the Christian shines his/her light in a dark and lonely world. Our task as believing Christians is to make conspicuous the love and compassion of God in the world and shine our light so that darkness may be dispelled. By doing so, it is the expectation that lives bent down under the burdens of life, be lifted up; and humanity pushed aside and left behind in the dark crevices of the world, be embraced and brought into the marvelous light of Christ. That way, people may be moved by faith to believe and claim Christ as their Lord and Savior. That way, upon claiming Him, they too can become recipients of all the benefits of His grace and passion. When by grace we live and work to make the world a better place, we are living doxological lives. Jesus lived a doxological life. Having worshipped and served the Father, even by His service to others, Jesus says in John 17:4: "I have glorified You on the earth. I have finished the work which you have given Me to do." To glorify God is to do His work in the world and make His goodness known in all the earth.

---

[254] Bishop Talbot, 83-84

9. To conclude that the celebration of the liturgy of worship ends at the singing of the doxology and the pronouncement of the benediction is to mummify worship. We mummify worship when we presume to wrap up and put that holy and spirit-filled experience on hold until such time when we elect to show up "for church," perhaps "next Sunday" to revive or resuscitate our worship. We serve a living God whose activities in our lives, the church, and the world, are never concluded or put on hold because the God we serve, and who keeps us, will neither slumber nor sleep.[255]

10. Worship is continuous. If worship is to mean more than kneeling at the altar, or just showing up on Sunday mornings to go through the motion and get our emotions soothed, then the conversation that begins at the altar needs, in practical ways, to continue in every area of our lives and activities. If indeed we kneel at the altar to confess and receive the redeeming love of God in Christ Jesus, we need to allow grace to develop in us the humility to also kneel in obedience and purposeful service in the world. Through our service of love, kindness, and compassion, we may continuously and fittingly bring glory to God. Worship never ends. Worship is God's perpetual desire for us. It is God's divine invitation for us to come into His presence for empowerment so that we will be filled with holy energy to actively glorify Him in formal worship and by our intentional service in the world.

11. Moving from the liturgy of worship to the liturgy of life and service is not a transition into a different compartment of our lives. Rather, it is a continuous act of verbalized praise translated into active service and praise. Assuredly, the grace that God bestows on us requires and invokes praise as well as service. If, indeed, it is by the coming together for worship that faith is manifested, it is also by our service to others that our faith finds validation when it becomes faith that works. As Wainwright affirms for example, "In worship we receive the self-giving love of God and the test of our thankfulness is whether we reproduce that pattern of self-giving in our daily relationship with other people."[256] The way we live our lives therefore becomes a sort of test of our faithfulness and commitment to our worship practices. Our

---

[255] Ps 121:4

[256] Wainwright, 422

actions do validate our words. Worship and service are indeed inseparable companions on the Christian's faith journey. As in worship the grace of God embraces us, so also in life and service His grace accompanies us to empower and rejuvenate us as we serve the Lord in the Church and in the world. To that service, which essentially is the extension of worship through Christian mission, we now turn our attention.

Chapter Five

Christian Mission

Prayer:

Heavenly Father, I praise You today because You are God and worthy of praise. As I contemplate going out into the world today, give me the desire and develop in me a deep sense of commitment to serve You through serving others. Empower me so that I may willingly offer myself in service to my fellow humans as I witness to Your glory in the world. By Your indwelling Spirit, ready me I pray to face the challenges and accept the opportunities You present me to reach up to You by reaching out to others. O Lord God eternal, please empty me of myself and all contemplations of my own desires and accomplishments. Ready me with Your quickening power, surround me with Your presence, and infuse me with Your grace so that I leave nothing undone that You require of me today. Help me to put others and their needs and aspirations before me and my own needs, and to put You always before all. Grant me the boldness to speak Your Word as I go forth to make disciples for Christ. Lord, I declare my love for You. Move me by Your Holy Spirit to declare my love to my brothers and sisters through the demonstration of mercy and justice before those that I encounter today. As I interact with others in my service to You in the world, help me by Your Spirit to align my actions in the world with the words and faith that I have confessed in worship, so that I may be fully Yours in all that I do and say. For these and all of Your mercies I pray in the name of Jesus, Amen!

Scripture: Isaiah 49:3-4; Luke 4:18-19; 24:47-49; Acts 2:1-4

Hymns: "A Charge To Keep I Have"
"Come Holy Ghost, Our Souls Inspire"
"How Shall They Hear The Word of God?"
"Go Make All Disciples"
"We Have A Story To Tell"
"Pass It On"
"Spirit Of The Living God"
"Breathe On Me Breath Of God"
"Where He Leads Me I Will Follow"
"This Little Light Of Mine"

1. Overview

This chapter is an examination of Christian mission. Attention will be given to an examination of the dual and continuous relations between Christian worship and Christian mission. The coming and necessity of the Holy Spirit for mission will be discussed. The Holy Spirit, as we shall see, is God's gift of power for Christian mission and witness. Consequently, Christian mission is the working of the Holy Spirit. Using scripture references, we will promote the belief that God is a missional God. As a missional God, He is the God that sends. As a consequence and an imperative, our holy and worshipful confrontation or encounter with God in worship becomes an opportunity for our sanctification and empowerment for mission. How the conviction of faith developed in worship spills over into corresponding demonstrations of faith through Christian mission; how participation in Christian mission leads to the spiritual formation or shaping of the Christian's life, character, and growth in Christ, and the importance of building relationships for doing Christian mission, will also be critical components of this level of our examination.

2. What is Christian Mission?

1. Christian Mission is faith in action. It is our faithful participation in God's mission of life transforming love in the world. Christian Mission is the active articulation and outpouring of our worship experience in a world where the Holy Spirit is present and working in and through us to make mission a worshipful and life transforming experience. As it was the love of God that sent Christ on His mission to redeem humanity, mission for us is not an extracted obligation. Mission is something that we participate in because we love God, and are joyful about participating in the ministry of Christ in carrying out God's mission to the world.

2. God's mission began in creation. Creation was God's first act of grace and a manifestation of His giving of Himself to humanity. Assuredly, God's existence is not for Himself but for His creation, that is, us! God's act of grace, which began in creation, is an overflow of His love that reaches out. The grace and love of God, reaching out from creation, began with the purpose of redemption and sanctification and will ultimately lead to our final consummation in His eternity. Consummation implies final restoration of the image of God invested in us at creation that became distorted because of our original sin of disobedience but was restored by the redemptive sacrifice of Jesus.

3. Our engagement in Christian mission means that we are God's witnesses to the world. As witnesses, we are also representatives of Christ to the world. Therefore, when other people see, hear, and speak to us and become engaged in our lives, they must necessarily be able to see and hear God in us because we are essentially transcripts of God and our Lord Jesus in the world. "Let your light so shine before men that they may see your good works and glorify your Father in heaven" is not just a Christian cliché. It is Christ's sending and endorsing us as witness bearers of God in the world. Christian mission is our response to the God that reaches out and our intentional engagement in the restorative purpose of God.

4. Christian mission is God making visible in the world, through our proclamation and service, His Word, actions, and intention to lift up fallen humanity. As we offer up our praise in response to God in the formal worship, in mission, by the demonstration of compassion and the deeds of kindness that we are empowered to perform, we are proclaiming the reconciling mercy of God to the world. As Christ made God present by dwelling among us, revealing the heart and compassion of God through His life and service to us, so we, the redeemed and sanctified of God, ought to make Christ present through our sanctified life, behavior, and witness in the world.

3. The Relations Between Worship and Christian Mission (Section One)

1. The primary functions of the Church are worship and mission. In both worship and mission, we are responding to, as well as sharing in, the one and the same worship and ministry of the Son to the Father. This necessary duality between worship and mission needs to be affirmed and sustained because liturgical renewal and missional renewal are one and the same.

2. Worship therefore becomes a sort of precursor of a movement in which God comes to us and shakes us free from all the constraints of life and our own cares and preoccupations. Having shaken us free of our natural constraints and preoccupation with ourselves, the power and grace of God are imparted to us in order that we might be equipped for Christian mission and the giving of ourselves in service to the world. That way, the God that we worship in word is also the God we worship through our faithful service. If God is to be given priority in our lives, He must be engaged in every area of our lives. We cannot put worship in one compartment and mission in another as though they are distinct and therefore separate. The very notion of a disconnected transition between worship and mission suggests separation of the liturgy of worship and the liturgy of mission or service. Since the liturgy is both God's word and action that invoke the human response, a continuous dialogue between worship and mission must be affirmed. There can be no separation between our life of worship and our life of service.

3. From a Biblical perspective, to profess Christ through worship and not live Christ in the world makes that profession false. Isaiah 48:1b indicates that we swear by the name of the Lord, make mention of God, but do not sincerely live for God through truth and righteousness. In Ezekiel 33:31 we are told: "They come to you as people do, they sit before you as My people, and they hear your words, but they do not do them; for with their mouths they show much love, but their hearts pursue their own gain." Jesus warns in Matthew 7:21 that: "Not everyone who says to Me, 'Lord, Lord' shall enter

the kingdom of heaven, but [he/she] who does the will of My Father in heaven." And again: "Why do you call Me 'Lord, Lord,' and do not do the things which I say?"[257] Listen also to the word in Titus 1:16: "They profess to know God, but in works they deny Him, being abominable, disobedient, and disqualified for every good work." Clearly, there is a connection between the liturgy of words and the liturgy of service. Words of praise need to be accompanied by actions that bring praise and glory to God. Our words are confessions of faith. Our works of service are evidence of our saving faith. As 1 John 3:18 entreats us, we should not love in word alone but also in deed and in truth. Our commitment to Christian mission, which is the Christian's work, is therefore a demonstration of the sincerity of what we profess in worship.

4. As we encounter God in worship and in life, we are empowered by that encounter to be witnesses. Such encounter, indeed, such disclosure of God to us, cannot and should not be kept secret. We cannot help speaking of and witnessing to the things that we have seen and heard.[258] Inasmuch as Christ became the expressed presence of God to us and for us through obedience and service to the Father, we ought rightly to become Christ in action to and for our neighbor. As Christ restores us and brings us back into a good relationship with God, by His life and atonement, which is His work of reconciliation, so we ought to be witnesses to the world, seeking diligently and faithfully to bring the world into redeeming fellowship with Christ by the authority of the Holy Spirit working in and through us. Indeed, it is to us, the Faith Community that Christ has entrusted the ministry of reconciliation.[259]

5. I am certainly not contending that worship is to be used as a tool for preparing us for mission. Worship is expressly designed by God for us to acknowledge and verbalize His worthiness for praise. What I am seeking to affirm is that whereas worship is a moral and praiseworthy activity that brings glory to God, Christian mission is our moral or ethical response and obligation to God. Mission is our ethical response and obligation because

---

[257] Lk 6:46
[258] Acts 4:20; Mt 28:19-20
[259] 2 Cor 5:18-20

it is morally expected and acceptable to God. Christian mission is therefore worthy of our time and attention because by our faithful engagement in mission, we bring honor and glory to God while changing and elevating the human condition. God does not grant us a worship encounter and experience of Him so that He may leave us to contain a secret. He meets us in worship with the message that He is God. He fills us with mercy and saving grace, pours into us a fresh anointing, and sends us as public witnesses with a message of redemption and hope that must be told.

6. Every true worshipper ought to be a true public witness. The Bible nowhere encourages secret or private discipleship. The confessions that are made in worship should therefore be confirmed and proclaimed not only by our words, but also by our actions. That way, what we proclaim in words finds expression through our daily service as we diligently seek to make disciples for Christ to the glory of God. Webster makes the point that:

> "Worship and mission are different ways of making the same proclamation, the one in and to the church, the other in and to the world, both indispensable. The Church came into being as a result of the proclamation of the Gospel. The church lives by that proclamation and for it. Proclamation is central to [the church's] worship and to its mission. There is no either-or; it is all one."[260]

7. This dual purpose of worship and mission may be best understood as a sort of double or shared expressions of God's love in worship through praise and in the world through active Christian mission that brings Him glory. The love that we express for God through worship and praise needs to extend to loving God by our active service in the world. As we express love and worship to God through formal worship, we also need to show our love for Him through service to the world. Indeed, through worship and Christian mission we are seeking to glorify the same God.

---

[260] Douglas Webster, "The Mission of the People of God," in <u>Liturgical Renewal in the Christian Church</u>, ed. Michael J. Taylor (Baltimore-Dublin: Helicon, 1967), 184

The Relations Between Worship and Christian Mission (Section Two)

1. To cultivate disparity between our worship in word and our worship through service and Christian mission is to create an unhealthy imbalance between what we confess in the formal worship and what we do and practice in the world. The beloved disciple, John, agrees for example, that anyone claiming love for God in worship but does not complement that declaration of love for God with corresponding love for one's neighbor, is a liar.[261] The Christian's motivation for mission is, in the first place, inspired by love for God. In the second place, our love for God must necessarily be translated into love for, and identification with our neighbor. Since Christ identified with us and all of our human failings so that He might change the direction of our lives, we also need to identify with the human needs and conditions around us so that by the transforming power of the Holy Spirit, their lives will be redirected to God. This is the task of Christian mission.

2. As Christians, we are called to be both worshippers and witnesses. We are not one or the other. The faith that is planted in worship ought to bring forth its fruit in mission.[262] There might be slight variations in the language or the tone of the conversation we employ between worship and mission; but the "Subject" is always the same. Put differently, our word and our action should always be directed to God and His Christ. Ultimately, the things that we do and say in worship and mission are about God, to God, for God and His eternal glory. God is the Object, Subject, content, and sum total of our worship, praise, and mission.

3. Worship and mission are not discontinuous; they are a continuous duet and a perpetual dance. The dance floor may change, but the dance continues to the same music of love and grace, mercy and pardon, healing and atonement, adoration and glory, worship and praise as unto God! Worship

---

[261] 1 Jn 4:20
[262] Mt 7:17; Jn 15:8,16

informs and plays the joyful tunes that inspire and move us to go out on the dance floor to serve. If worship is the music that inspires, then mission is the dance floor where our inspiration finds practical expression through service that brings glory and praise to God. Sometimes the harsh realities of mission, the dance floor, may leave us exhausted and physically and emotionally spent. However, because we are committed to God's mission, those harsh realities only serve to push us back into worship where we joyfully go before God for a refreshing sound of music and a fresh anointing of the Holy Spirit. Returning to worship for a refreshing is for our continuous worship and praise of God. Worship is our sacrificial music to God and empowerment for our souls and service to the world.

4. In worship, then, we sing God's praise, and in mission the liturgy of work becomes sweet music to our souls because we rejoice in the fact that God is making use of us. When we please God in worship, and cause God to smile by our sincere praise, God refills us with a double portion of His love and a fresh anointing of the Holy Spirit. In so doing, when we go back into the world to witness to the awesome power of God, we are sufficiently refueled and energized for the task, the enduring dance. This going in for worship and going out for service is indicative of that continuous dance between worship and mission, that continuous duet between faith and works, and that endless communion between the liturgy of worship and the liturgy of service. Since God's faithfulness has no end, our worship and service to God must necessarily be unending and therefore continuous.

5. Full and complete Christian discipleship calls for the incorporation of both worship and Christian mission. In other words, if Christian worship does not lead to Christian mission in the world, we have only halfway served God. If, therefore, worship and the liturgy answer the indicative question of "What is right praise in giving glory to God?" then mission needs to answer the imperative question of "What principles lead to right work that brings glory to God?"

6. Mission is an imperative extension of our worship. To that extent, not only is God worthy of our verbalized praise in the formal worship, He is also deserving of the praise of our daily work (obligation) proclaimed through

our service in the world.²⁶³ Wainwright agrees that, "[It is] in worship [that] God addresses us at the personal root of all our works; [and] the hearing of the Word in faith liberates us for service in the world."²⁶⁴ Mission and worship are one and the same because the church that worships is also a witnessing community. As Wainwright further posits:

> "Liturgy has both ethical presuppositions and ethical consequences. If positive correspondence is lacking between the vision and the values celebrated in worship and the practical attitudes and behavior of the worshippers before and after the liturgy, then either practical ethics must have progressed beyond the conscious and the formulated ideal, or else, and in the much more likely other direction, a question-mark is put against the sincerity and effectiveness of the worship. Or, if that way of putting it appears unacceptably moralistic: failure of correspondence between liturgy and ethics amounts to an undesirable separation between the sacred and the secular."²⁶⁵

The Relations Between Worship and Christian Mission (Section Three)

1. In Christ Jesus, word (the ethical presupposing) and work (the ethical consequences) are inseparable. Jesus is the Word that became flesh in order to work with and among us in the world and in the context of our empirical existence so that we may behold His divine glory.²⁶⁶ There is no Christian mission without our Christian presence in the world. Our service to God and the manifestations of God are not by any means restricted to the confines of our sacred sanctuaries and formal worship. In order

---

²⁶³ 1 Pet 2:5,9
²⁶⁴ Wainwright, 412
²⁶⁵ Wainwright, 399
²⁶⁶ Jn 1:14

for our service to be effectual, and in order for the manifestations of God revealed to us in worship to accomplish what God intends, we must be the carriers of God's love, mercy, and grace to the world.

2. To affirm our love for God without demonstrative faith, or faith that works, is to promote both lazy as well as cheap grace. Grace is neither lazy nor cheap. Grace is not cheap because grace paid for our sins with the valued life of the only begotten Son of God.[267] Grace caused a worshipping and missional Christ to do, through obedience, the work of the One who sent Him; even when He was rejected, despised and persecuted. In John 8:42, Christ knows Himself to be the Divine Messenger and affirms that such awareness leads to active labor of love (service): "I must do the works of Him who sent Me while it is day, for the night is coming when no one can work."[268]

3. Every Sabbath, the historical Christ entered the synagogue to worship the Father and departed to lift up fallen and broken humanity. Whether in the temple where they gathered to worship or in the fields where they labored, when Jesus encountered the downtrodden, and those victimized by sicknesses and demonic spirits, He worked to bring them deliverance. The woman bent over with infirmity that Jesus healed in a synagogue on the day of worship is a good example of worship and service being locked in an irresistible divine dance that brings glory to God.[269] God who acts in worship is the same God who acts through us in mission to bring glory to His holy name. Here are a few scriptural testimonies of service in the world bringing glory to God:

> "As He (Jesus) was getting into the boat, the man who had been demon-possessed was imploring Him that he might accompany Him. And He did not let him, but He said to him, 'Go home to your people and report to them what great things the Lord has done for you, and how He had mercy on you.' And he went away and began to proclaim in Decapolis what great things Jesus had done for him; and everyone was amazed" (Mk 5: 18-20).

---

[267] 1 Cor 6:19-20; 1 Cor 7:23
[268] Jn 9:4
[269] Lk 13:10-17

Once again:

"…Jesus said to him, 'Receive your sight; your faith has made you well.' Immediately he regained his sight and began following Him, glorifying God; and when all the people saw it, they gave praise to God" (Lk 8:42-43).

And again:

"But, so that you may know that the Son of Man has authority on earth to forgive sins,'— He said to the paralytic—'I say to you, get up, and pick up your stretcher and go home.' Immediately he got up before them, and picked up what he had been lying on, and went home glorifying God. They were all struck with astonishment and began glorifying God; and they were filled with fear, saying, 'We have seen remarkable things today'" (Lk 5:24-26)

4. If indeed we are followers of Christ, we ought to be vehicles for the living presence of Christ in the Church as well as in the world. If by our formal worship we lift up the name of the Lord God, then by our intentional service in the world God expects us to lift up fallen humanity to His honor and glory. Our formal worship and public witness are not separated but are intricately linked and therefore continuous. The writer of the book of Hebrews sheds some light on this continuous exchange between worship and mission when that writer declares: "Therefore by Him let us continually offer the sacrifice of praise to God, that is, the fruit of our lips, giving thanks to His name. But do not forget to do good and to share, for with such sacrifices God is well pleased."[270]

5. As Christians, then, we show love for God at two levels of human existence. These two levels are the place where we meet God in Christ to worship, and the place where we meet humanity in the world to serve. The appropriate Christian response to Christ is to faithfully continue the worship of the Son to the Father and to share in His ministry to the Father through our witness of His redeeming love in the world. That way, people may see in

---

[270] Heb 13:15-16

Christ their purpose for living, the answer to their perplexing questions, the hope for their salvation, and the fellowship for their loneliness.

6. Through Christian mission we become Christ to the world. I recently received an anonymous correspondence from an associate. I was touched by the content of the correspondence and believe that it is a relevant illustration of who and what we should be to the people we encounter on our faith journey. The correspondence reads: "...Some businessmen/salesmen were hurrying through the airport trying to make their flights home after a hectic week away. As they ran by a fruit stand, one of their briefcases accidentally knocked over a display of apples. None of them stopped. However, when they got to the departure gate, one of the men said to another, 'Call my wife and tell her I'll be on the next flight.' He then turned around and went back to help the young woman whose apple stand had been accidentally overturned. When he got there, the young woman was crying as she struggled to gather her scattered supply of apples. The salesman knelt down and helped in the gathering of the apples and reorganizing of the display. As he did, he noticed that some of the apples were bruised. He set those aside; and when he and the young woman had finished putting her apple stand together, he took $40 out of his wallet and gave it to her saying, 'Please take this for the damage we did.' He then asked her, 'Are you OK?' Through her tears she nodded yes. As he started to walk away, she called out, 'Mister . . . are you Jesus?' She could not see him because she was blind. But she heard and felt the presence of Jesus in this man's kindness and compassion."

7. Like the man in the above story, we need to exemplify Christ in the world. Not only should we know Christ; we need to be Christ to the world. Are you Jesus? Are we....? Are you Jesus? Do we live our lives in ways that people see and hear Jesus in us? In the ways we serve and care for people, do we show His love and reflect His life of kindness and compassion? Do we demonstrate His grace? Perhaps the only Bible some people may read is the story of Christ in us displayed through our behaviors, kindness, and compassion. We need to carry that story of Jesus and tell it well, with faith and conviction. It behooves us, the worshipping faith community, to urgently

become walking billboards for Christ so that the world may see Him in us and come to rely on His redeeming grace.

8. Because worship and mission are not distinct, we are not only praisers that eat at the Lord's Table and find comfortable places to rest when the worship service is "over." We are also praisers that work. Through worship we continue Christ's praise of the Father. Through mission, we work to extend God's love to the world. In so doing, the Word of God in worship becomes the action of God in the world. If indeed, the Word of God, as the first chapter of the gospel of John affirms, is Jesus Christ, it means that all that Jesus says and does is the Word and action of God. That makes worship and mission one and the same! In His divine and human natures Jesus embodies both Word and work because in Him, and through Him, God was speaking and working to reconcile the world to Himself.[271] Indeed, the Word became flesh that He might work.

9. If the world is to take the Church seriously, the Church needs to live up to the demands of the Gospel imperative. That Gospel imperative is to live for and disclose Christ to the world by our words and our deeds. The Gospel demands that we share what we know and experience about God as well as practice what we preach and profess from our pulpits, choir stands, and pews. To be taken seriously and remain the authentic voice of salvation and hope in the world, the Church needs to both preach Christ and live Christ. One action is not separated from the other. The Church is indeed, a worshipping and witnessing community through which God's love is extended to the world.

10. The objective of worship and mission is for us to intentionally share in all that Christ the Son has done in worship and service to bring glory to God. By our faithful sharing in what Christ has already done through worship and mission, we learn the art of holiness. The art of holiness is learned when we become humble students of the Holy Spirit by whom we are Spirit-fed with the Word, and Spirit-led in the world, to walk in God's holy ways as living examples for the world to follow on their way back to God.

---

[271] 2 Cor 5:19

11. In worship we celebrate God's forgiveness and in mission we extend that forgiveness to our brothers and sisters. As the Holy Spirit lifts our voices in praise and worship and confers God's forgiveness upon us, He also helps us to pray, and empowers us to forgive others as we have been, and still need to be forgiven. As the Lord holds our hands and leads us to His Table for Communion and fellowship, so should we in mission hold the hands of alienated people and bring the excluded into Christian fellowship. As we bow before God in worship and adoration, let us in obedience willingly bow before Him in service as we carry out our Christian duty to God and to our neighbor.

12. Every Christian has his/her liturgical duty to perform within the congregation and outside of it. The full meaning of the formal liturgy is therefore lived out and accentuated by the Christian's daily witness, which is the living of the liturgy of worship in the world through service. Shafer puts it this way:

> "Formal liturgy tells the worshippers that they are a work of God in order that they may do the works God expects of them. Thus they are equipped [in worship] and directed to fulfill their daily liturgies [through Christian mission] …A worshipping church is also a church working in the common affairs of life. Christians worship in order to work because they have worshipped…Liturgy does not divide Christ; it adores Him in order to serve Him, and it serves Him because it adores Him."[272]

Worship is continuous. It is expressive of the mighty and dynamic Word and works of God, which are daily experienced afresh, graciously adored through the sweet music of worship, and wonderfully displayed on the dance floor of Christian mission where the Holy Spirit comes into our hearts and into our midst to aid us in our mission to the world.

---

[272] Floyd D. Shafer, <u>Liturgy: Worship and Work</u>, 15

4. The Coming and Necessity of the Holy Spirit for Mission (Section One)

1. Let us first attempt to address the matter of the Person of the Holy Spirit. Who is the Holy Spirit? Human language cannot adequately wrap itself around the Holy Spirit. It is in humility that I speak of Him; trusting His power in me to give me utterance and clarity. Know then, that no matter what I say about Him and no matter what you think about Him, He is much more. Who is the Holy Spirit? The Holy Spirit is the third Person of the Godhead. This means that the Holy Spirit is of the divine nature of God and therefore proceeds from God (Jn.15:26). He is called Spirit because He is like the wind that cannot be restricted by time or space. He is God's unseen but always manifested-presence and power in the life of those who believe. The Holy Spirit is the One who makes us aware of Christ and our need for Christ (Jn. 16: 8).

2. As the third Person in the Godhead, the Holy Spirit has divine attributes. As such, the Holy Spirit is eternal (Heb. 9:14). He is omnipresent (Ps. 139: 7-10); meaning that He is present everywhere. He is omnipotent (Lk.1: 35); meaning that He has all power. He is omniscient (1 Cor. 2: 10, 11); meaning that He is all knowing. As Person, the Holy Spirit teaches and speaks (Rev. 2:7). The Holy Spirit is our guide (Jn. 16:13). The Holy Spirit is our comforter and help (Rm. 8:26). As Person, He can be grieved (Eph.4: 30) by our unchristian conduct and behavior. As Person the Holy Spirit possesses the attributes of mind (Rm. 8:27) will (1 Cor. 12: 11) and of feeling (Eph.4: 30).

3. The Holy Spirit, contrary to what some believe, is not a New Testament phenomenon. The Holy Spirit was before there was time. The Bible says in Genesis 1:2 that the Spirit of God moved upon the face of the waters and was therefore the creative agent in creation. As the creative agent of God in creation, the Holy Spirit is the Lord and Giver of life. The Holy Spirit is not a New Testament phenomenon. He acted in the Old Testament and is still acting in the New Testament. The difference between the manifestation

of the Holy Spirit in the Old Testament era and the New Testament era is that, in the Old Testament, the Holy Spirit is often reported to have come upon a special person to empower that person for a special assignment, work, or mission for God. In the New Testament however, the Holy Spirit not only comes upon the church and the Christian believer, He also takes up residence within the Christian believer and the Community of Faith, the Church.

4. On the Day of Pentecost, the Holy Spirit descended upon, and entered the life of the Early Church in a new and powerful way. The Holy Spirit has been poured upon the Church and into the life of every believer in order to make present the risen Christ, while quickening, uniting, sanctifying, and renewing the Church for mission. The Holy Spirit has come to give purpose to our lives, and authenticity and power to our witness. Without the Holy Spirit, everything we are and everything that we do in mission would become shallow, pointless, and wearisome routines. It is by the operation of the Holy Spirit that our mission has purpose and value. It is by the Holy Spirit's transforming influence that people can see value in what we do and find purpose for their own lives. The Holy Spirit is God's divine agent and power for mission. Christian mission is a responsibility that human beings, left alone, cannot accomplish. For that reason, Christ promised to send us the Helper; and He came with quickening power. To do God's work, we need God's help.[273]

5. In Christian mission, our primary goal is to win souls for Jesus as we encourage the unchurched and the unredeemed to believe in Christ for salvation. Since our mission is first and foremost the mission of Christ, we must be careful to allow Him to be our "way maker," and the bearer of light in a darkened world. For our mission in the world where darkness abounds, we need the Holy Spirit to turn on the light of Christ in us and around us. That way, Christ, the Light of the world, may shine forth and shine on us and through the darkness. For mission in the world where there are many confusing mazes, we need the Holy Spirit to go before us so that we might obtain clarity of mind and find our way through life's mazes. Without the Holy Spirit, everything about us and what we do would remain in darkness and confusion. We would stumble because of the darkness and no one would be

---

[273] Jn 14:16; 15:26

able to find his/her way. But thanks be to God, Jesus is the Light of the world and the Holy Spirit is on assignment to lead us by that Light.

6. Through Christian mission, God has called and empowered us to shine our light in the world. Through Christ Jesus, the light in us, and by virtue of His love and the light of divine kindness, the debilitating effects of the world's darkness may be removed. Surely, before Christ came into our hearts, we who have become witnesses to the light and power of God, once lived in that darkness.[274] By Jesus coming into our hearts, we have been removed from our prior condition of darkness and have been brought into the marvelous light, which is Christ Jesus. Christ the Son, coming into our hearts as light on the one hand, is to enlighten our minds concerning God the Father so that we may no longer walk in ignorance. On the other hand, He has done so that we may become His light bearers in the world. We have been changed to reflect and proclaim that Light but we are not that Light. The Light that shines in and through us is not our own. We are only witnesses and carriers of that Light.[275]

7. The Holy Spirit, as the Spirit of illumination, is the pervasive light of God in the world. By His illuminating power, we are drawn into the Light that is Christ. And by His enduring presence in our lives, the light of Christ remains lit in us and therefore shines through us for the world to see and come to glorify the God and Father of our Lord Jesus Christ. The Holy Spirit enlightens our minds and brings illumination and understanding to our worship and mission. Without Him we would stumble in darkness. By the presence and work of the Holy Spirit, Christ, the Living Word, Christ the Light of the world, becomes the lamp of God to our feet and a light to our pathway.[276]

8. Since the goal of Christian mission is to make disciples for Christ by bringing people into awareness and saving faith in Jesus and fellowship with God, we essentially have to witness to lost and broken people. In order to witness to lost and broken people, we cannot employ an attitude of

---

[274] Eph 5:8; 1 Pet 2:9

[275] Jn 1:8

[276] Ps 119:105

self-righteousness and indifference. While we are in the world but not of the world,[277] we cannot win souls for Christ by isolating ourselves from the world or cause those to whom we witness to feel like they are merely our assigned projects. People with moral failures and spiritual weaknesses do not need our indifference and judgment. They need our love, forgiveness, compassion, and mercy. Since it is human nature to think less of others, the Holy Spirit in us becomes the power of love and compassion that cancels out any human tendency in us to be indifferent and judgmental. The love and compassion that we impart and sow into the lives and spirit of others eventually become the seeds that the Holy Spirit develops in them so that they may grow into saving knowledge of the Lord Jesus.

9. The realization that we are saved through Christ and empowered by the Holy Spirit to do the work of God in the world does not mean that we should exalt ourselves above the people that we think are not saved. We have been saved to reach people for Christ. In order to do that, we must serve them with humility and with the measure of love and grace that we ourselves received from the Lord.[278] We should serve with humility because we should never think of ourselves more highly that we think of those whom we are anointed to serve.[279] We should serve with love and a deep sense of mercy because that is what it takes for us to distinguish between the persons we serve and the sin we seek to pull them away from. The Bible has time and again affirmed that while sin is intolerable to God, God loves and seeks to redeem the sinner.[280] The human condition has never been deterrence for the grace of God; it should not be deterrence for us. The human condition has always been an opportunity for grace to intervene because where sin abounds, grace abounds in more abundance.[281] The unmistaken realization that while we were still sinners God demonstrated His love

---

[277] Jn 17:16

[278] Jn 3:16; Gal 5:13-14

[279] Rom 12:3; Phil 2:2-4

[280] Mt 9:13; Jn 3:16; 1Tim 1:15

[281] Rom 5:20-6:2

toward us by sending Christ to die for us[282] ought to cancel out any selfish and self-righteous orientations that we may be holding on to.

10. As a gift to us for mission, the Holy Spirit turns our attention from self and redirects our lives and attention toward God and those we are called to serve. That way, self-will, with its pride and personal desires, gets out of the way of Christian mission and the cause of the Gospel. As we go forth to serve, we should seek after the Holy Spirit of grace to help us avoid preoccupation with our own ambitions. With personal feelings, egos, and selfish ambitions in check, Christ's own self-giving love becomes the only means by which the world is won.

11. In our service to the world, our goal should never be to win the world for our credit, to fulfill the local church mission drive, or to meet goals for percentage membership increases for the year in our local churches. Any success in mission should not go to our credit because the task of mission and the work of reconciling the world are not ours. The Holy Spirit in us carries on the work of Christ in the world. Indeed, Christ has already done that work. Already, Christ alone has gone before us to bring our mountains low and to lift up our valleys. Christ alone has already straightened crooked places. Christ alone has already made rough places smooth.[283] We do not move the world. We do not bring the world to Jesus. The Holy Spirit in us moves them to respond with faith in the Lord Jesus.[284] We are just the human instruments that God equips and uses to reach unredeemed humanity. If they see us saved and representing Christ with dignity and purpose, by the transforming power of the Holy Spirit, they will be encouraged to come to Christ for salvation so that in Him, they too can find hope and purpose for their lives.

---

[282] Rom 5:8

[283] Is 40:4; 45:2

[284] Jn 16:8

DR. WALKER WALKER

THE COMING AND NECESSITY OF THE HOLY SPIRIT FOR MISSION (SECTION TWO)

1. In mission, without the Holy Spirit imparting Christ to us and to those to whom we witness, we would focus on ourselves, our wisdom, our experience, our abilities, and our expertise. While those qualifications are good to have, what God really needs are our brokenness, our humility, and our availability. In Christian mission, the human channel is only the means by which God, through the Holy Spirit, bears witness to Himself. God has the wisdom, and God certainly has the power to bring about His purpose. The grace and power of God will always take care of everything else that God wants to get done through us. The Holy Spirit is the One that sanctifies us for mission, equips us with the gifts to do mission, and bestows upon us the grace we need to accomplish the task.

2. When we believe it is our ability that matters most whether in worship or in mission, "we violate the holiness of the Spirit by resisting Him in His self-effacing office and confusing Him with our own spirits."[285] Torrance stresses that: "It is only when God's own self-witness is heard that the world will believe."[286] This point of view resonates well with the declaration of Jesus Christ who says in John 6:44: "No one can come to Me unless the Father who sent Me draws him/[her] and I will raise him/[her] up at the last day." It is by God's self-witness and effectual power of the Holy Spirit that the world hears, acknowledges, responds to, and comes to God through the Lord Jesus. Consequently, as worship is a gift of the Holy Spirit, mission is also a gift of the Holy Spirit imparted to us. Through the Holy Spirit, God implants the desire for mission in us and infuses us with the will and passion for Christian mission. It is also the Holy Spirit that moves people to respond to the One to whom we bear witness in the world. The attainment of divine purposes is never a human accomplishment; it is always a divine one. Our becoming God's voices and instruments for mission in the world is the action of the Holy Spirit who draws us into Christ so

---

[285] Torrance, "Come Creator Spirit…," 142
[286] Torrance, "Come Creator Spirit…," 143

that He may impart to us His own mission to Creator God. As we respond to the indwelling of the Holy Spirit, then, we are raised up to become obedient, lively, and obedient witnesses for Christ in the world.

3. Obedience is important for Christian mission because it makes Christian mission effectual. Without obedience to God we cannot effectively witness to His goodness in the world. Without obedience we would become too easily broken and discouraged and far too willing to surrender in retreat from the rigor, challenges, and tests that accompany Christian mission in the world. Obedience to God keeps us steadfast because it is not ourselves that we aim to please. Our aim is to please and honor God through our witness of Christ who engages us in His own obedient life and ministry. Even in those moments when the most obedient among us become discouraged, the Holy Spirit becomes our strength when our strength deserts us. When our human spirit is broken He is the mender of our broken spirit. When it seems like our legs cannot take us any further and we have no one to lean on, we have God's gift of the Holy Spirit to prop us up on every leaning side and to strengthen our faith.

4. The faith that we have in Christ and the task of mission that we have been given, are gifts of the Holy Spirit. Without the Holy Spirit we would not and could not live out the divine life on earth through Christian service. As we work to bring others to Christ, our own lives become active demonstrations of faith, daily confessions of our own shortcomings, and our need for grace becomes increasingly real. Through the Holy Spirit who daily bestows grace upon us, we become living examples to our fellow humans of what the grace of God can do to redeem even the worst of us. It is indeed by God's gift of forgiveness and by the power of the Holy Spirit that we are empowered to rise above our own shortcomings and become transformed, faith-inspired, and bold witnesses for God in the world.

5. God gives the Holy Spirit to us because without the Holy Spirit, our mission, like our worship without the Spirit, would become, at best, our own inventions and works, and not the works and manifestations of God. God alone has the power to make our work effectual, and God does that very well through the Holy Spirit. The Holy Spirit alone is invested with

the power to cause human thought, cognition, speech, liturgy, witness, and participation, to contemplate the divine activity and purpose, receive Christ by faith, and so become participants in God's divine plan as active witnesses to the life changing power and grace of God in the world. That grace empowers us to serve.

6. As we serve God through Christian mission in the world, despite the challenges and sometimes the discouragement that accompany such mission, the Holy Spirit encourages our hearts with the guarantee of God's eternal promise.[287] The Holy Spirit also keeps us focused on eternity, and His abiding presence becomes a sort of foretaste of that divine glory.[288] In that promise and foretaste, our faith finds resolve as we are bestowed with the necessary grace and divine encouragement to press through the challenges of mission and our own daily life challenges. As God came near to us in Christ, giving us a glimpse of Himself, so the Holy Spirit comes close and actually indwells us. The Holy Spirit indwells us not only to give us a momentary foretaste or glimpse of what the joys of heaven are like, but also to sustain in us that divine longing that keeps us wanting to do more for Christ. By the indwelling of the Holy Spirit, we are imbued with the desire to reach for more of Christ, diligently seek to become all that we can become in Christ Jesus, and daily keep our minds fixed on His promise of eternity, .

7. To that extent, Christian mission has eschatological significance. In as much as the Holy Spirit is engaged with our lives in Christian mission, our participation in mission becomes an opportunity for our spiritual shaping, character building, and repositioning in readiness for eternity. As the Holy Spirit keeps us focused on the task at hand, we are also filled with hope that is inspired by our having pleased God through faithful service as well as by the promise of eternity. Without the hope instilled in us by the Holy Spirit, the stress and difficulty we encounter in Christian service would cause us to bend under the stress and force us to retreat, perhaps in isolation, as Jeremiah attempted in search of personal relief. Though at times tempted to despair, Jeremiah's faith in the God of the covenant encouraged him to hope for a new

---

[287] 2 Cor 1:22; 5:5; Eph 4:30
[288] Eph 1:14

and better future.[289] Whereas Christian mission can sometimes be a struggle, we find resolve in the knowledge and experience that when the Holy Spirit adds His power to aid us in our struggles, our mountains are brought down, our valleys are pulled up, crocked places become straight, and rough places become smooth. As God's gift to us, the Holy Spirit is our staying power for every hour.

5. THE HOLY SPIRIT AS THE GIFT OF POWER FOR CHRISTIAN MISSION

1. God has given us the gift of the Holy Spirit to empower us for ministry. The purpose of the Holy Spirit for worship and mission is to draw us into the holy breath and life of God. The operation of the Holy Spirit in our lives and in the Church is the quickening power that transforms us into a Spirit-filled Community of faith that is actively engaged in worship and the ministry of Christian mission and service to the Lord.

2. No ministry should be attempted without the anointing of the Holy Spirit. For that reason, after His resurrection, Jesus told His disciples not to go anywhere or attempt to do anything except tarrying in Jerusalem until they received power from on high. The Acts of the Apostles should really be called the Acts of The Holy Spirit. He was the power behind every word that they preached. He was the power behind every act of healing that they performed. He was the power and presence of God for every miracle they experienced. He was the presence and grace of Jesus Christ that gave them hope and the faith to endure every persecution. He was and still is the power that causes every soul to turn to God for salvation. I submit that if we as persons and if we as a church are to realize our ministry goals and objectives, we need to recognize that the ministries within the church are not ours. They are the ministries of the Holy Spirit. It is the Holy Spirit that speaks (1 Tim. 4:1). It is the Holy Spirit that teaches (1 Cor 2: 13). It is the Holy Spirit that bears witness to the power of God (Rom 8:16). It is the Holy Spirit that

---

[289] See Jer 20:1-18

makes intercession (Rom 8:26). It is the Holy Spirit that distributes the gifts for ministry (1 Cor 12:11). It is the Holy Spirit that invites the sinner to come to Christ (Jn 16:8; Rev 22: 17).

3. God has given us the gift of the Holy Spirit so that we may become empowered and effective participants in the ministry of Christ. Without the Holy Spirit in us, we would not and could not do the work of God. Without the Holy Spirit in us we would not and could not reach out in love and compassion to people in need all around us. Without the Holy Spirit we cannot live for Christ because He is the Power in us that enables us to know and live like Christ. Without the Holy Spirit we cannot please God. The Holy Spirit is the One that opens ours eyes to the ways and purposes of God, strengthens our faith, and bestows upon us the grace we need to please God. In worship and our daily Christian living, the Holy Spirit is the real power in all that we do to bring God glory and praise. It is by the inspiration and power of the Holy Spirit that our worship and service please God. If we are to be the church that God intends for us to be, I declare that we need to submit to and obey the Spirit of God. Indeed, according to Acts 5: 32, the Holy Spirit is given to those who obey.

4. Human wisdom, strength, and ability, alone, cannot accomplish the work of God. Doing God's work requires God's divine power. Jesus says, "Behold I send the Promise of My Father upon you; but tarry in the city of Jerusalem until you are endued with power from on high."[290] That Promise is the overflow of God's power from on high, the Holy Spirit. The outpouring of the Holy Spirit in us is empowerment for Christian mission. Through the Holy Spirit, believing Christians are empowered to hear, believe in, understand, witness to, and respond to the Lord Jesus in the world by the articulation of our faith in His redeeming grace. Because of the presence and power of the Holy Spirit in our lives, church, and community, every occasion of communion with God becomes an occasion for God to empower us by His outpouring of Himself. The power to know, understand, receive, and effectively articulate Christ to the world is the power the Holy Spirit.[291] He is our source of truth. He is our source of wisdom. It is He that teaches us and

---

[290] Lk 24:49

[291] Jn 16:13-14

creates in us an understanding of faith concerning Christ.[292] As our source of power, the Holy Spirit came to give us the advantage.[293] When the Holy Spirit descends upon us and indwells us He gives us the advantage because He effectively becomes our Advocate, our guide, our hands, and our voices, by which the world is persuaded and therefore moved to seek after Christ.[294] Without the Holy Spirit, we could not possibly understand the scope of the kingdom of God,[295] aspire toward it, or participate in its mission. The mere notion of the Holy Spirit as our Helper[296] gives us the advantage over our own weaknesses and the resistance that accompanies Christian mission.

5. As our gift of power, the Holy Spirit is authorized to draw our attention to Christ and furnish us with the gift of impartation. That way, we are equipped to impart what we know and believe about Christ to others as we bear witness to His redeeming love in the world. Remember now, we are just witnesses and instruments of God's redeeming gift of grace, caught up as it were, in the cause or mission of God to proclaim His Good News.[297] Through the Holy Spirit, and by virtue of His creative, redemptive, and sanctifying power, God makes use of us in mission in order that He might bear witness to Himself in the world.

6. As our worship is first the worship of the Son to the Father before it is ours, so our mission and witness are the mission and witness of the Holy Spirit before they are our mission and witness.[298] It is He who testifies of and administers Christ to us.[299] It is He who comes forth from God[300] and comes to us with His quickening power to facilitate our mission and it is He that returns our sacrifice of service to God, for God's good pleasure and glory. As

---

[292] Jn 15:26-27
[293] Jn 16:7
[294] Jn 16:8,13
[295] Jn 16:11-12
[296] Jn 16:7
[297] Lk 24: 48-49
[298] 1 Jn 5:6-10a
[299] Jn 16:13-14
[300] Jn 15:26

Scripture attests, "...it is God who works in you both to will and to do for His good pleasure."[301] It is only by our recognition that it is God who uses ordinary people to perform extraordinary things to His honor and glory, that we can become humble and purposeful contributors to the kingdom purposes of God. All that we do in mission is by God's permission, God's power, God's authority, and for God's eternal glory.

7. On the one hand, then, God deserves our love and demands our service. On the other hand, God is the source of our ability to both love and serve Him. The point to understand here is that whatever we do as believing daughters and sons of God, whether in worship, Christian mission, or by our eschatological lifestyle invoked by the expectation of the return of Jesus, it is God that engages and makes use of us. God engages us and makes use of us so that He may develop in us the capacity to become effective Christ bearers in the world, to His glory and praise. As we demonstrate our willing faith and obedience in the service for God, the Holy Spirit supplies us with the impetus to respond to God and infuses us with the power to serve Him. The Holy Spirit also facilitates our service by working in and through us to turn our weak and feeble service into strong and acceptable praise unto God.

8. In mission, the Holy Spirit is for us, the life sustaining power of God. The power to serve and the power to please God is the power of the Holy Spirit. Living, serving, and pleasing God have more to do with the Holy Spirit acting in us and through us than they do with our own action toward God. You see, left alone, our human will and tendencies would not be compelled to respond to God. What they will do is compel us to seek our own interests and pleasure. However, with the Holy Spirit indwelling us, we are changed to become more amiable to God; more pliable for Him to fashion us and make use of us, and more inclined to please God. By the Holy Spirit the Church lives, and moves[302] to fulfill its mission in the world for the expressed pleasure and glory of God. It is by the presence and help of our missional God that we, as witnesses, and those to whom we witness, are daily confronted, sanctified, and empowered to witness and respond with faith to the saving power of Christ.

---

[301] Phil 2:13
[302] Acts 17:28

6. God Is a Missional God Confronted and Sanctified for Mission (Section One)

1. God is a missional God because He is the God that sends. God sending Christ into the world, and His subsequent sending of the Holy Spirit to continue His witness to us, are the highlights of God's divine missionary deployment and activity. The Bible is filled with evidence of the dialogue between the human encounter with God and God's sending of the human agent to proclaim and witness to that encounter. Noah, after his encounter with God, was moved by godly reverence and obedience to go on a mission of building an ark as specified by God.[303] Abraham, after encountering God[304] went on a mission of faith and righteousness, became the father of faith for believers, and, as a result, was reckoned by God to be righteous.[305] Moses, having encountered God in the burning bush, was sent by God on a mission to liberate the enslaved Hebrews.[306] Isaiah, having been confronted with the incomparable holiness of God, shining in the light of His glory in the Temple,[307] was sent on a prophetic mission[308] of calling a nation back to God. The Early Church, having experienced Jesus, His life and miracle working ministry, and having encountered the crucified and resurrected Christ, was commissioned and deployed on a mission that has since set the world on fire for Christ.[309] God is a missional God.

2. A new mission is always preceded by a new vision, a restored consciousness or a new awareness of God. Our encounter with God draws us first and foremost into an attitude of worship and praise. We are confronted and sanctified for mission because what we receive from God in worship and

---

[303] Gen 6:13-22; Heb 11:7
[304] Gen 12:1-9
[305] Gen 15:6; Rom. 4:3
[306] Ex 3:2-10; 4:18-31
[307] Is 6:1, 7-8
[308] Is 6:9
[309] See Mt. 28:19-20

life, we are also empowered to give back to Him by our service to the world through Christian mission. God confronts us in order to transform us. God transforms us in order to send us. God gives us a vision so that we may understand His mission. Worship opens our eyes to that vision; mission keeps that vision in perspective. Willimon makes the point that, "the vision of our faith is not static but is a constantly unfolding, transforming reality, which is the working out of God's purposes."[310] So that whether we encounter God in worship or in life, the vision of our encounter with God stirs up our faith, and subsequently becomes an active response to God's self-disclosure which is understood and lived through our mission to the world.

3. We should never take God's self-disclosure for granted. We are changed by it. The Christian life is a journey of transformation, transition, and progression that begins with the recognition of who God is, and what He requires of us. The experience of God's self-disclosure transitions and repositions us for service. As we come face to face with God's own self-disclosure in worship and by our life experiences and encounters with God, we are changed by it. We are also constrained by the experience to progressively become what we know and experience about God. We are also encouraged by the experience to proclaim and mirror the holiness of God in the world.

4. Since the Christian life is a lifelong journey of transformation and repositioning by the Holy Spirit of grace, the question that immediately confronts us is: "What is the Christian's response to God who confronts us with His grace?" After responding to God's invitation to worship, and after being empowered by the knowledge of His grace and purpose for us in Christ Jesus, and after recognizing the value God has placed on us by reconciling us to Himself through Christ in the power of the Holy Spirit, our response ought rightly to be one of love, worship, proclamation, witness, and humble service.

5. In the fourth chapter of the Gospel of John, it was the Samaritan woman's encounter with Christ that led her to depart with a burning desire to share the good news of her face-to-face encounter with the Christ. That encounter moved her to witness of the Christ when she passionately announced: "Come,

---

[310] William H. Willimon, The Service of God: How Worship and Ethics Are Related (Nashville, TN., Abingdon Press), 65

see a man who told me all things that I ever did. Could this be the Christ?"[311] The Samaritan woman may rightly be considered the first missionary in the New Testament era. In addition, it was the wonderful encounter of the Risen Christ that also led Mary Magdalene[312] and the other Mary to go spread the first good news concerning the resurrection of Christ.[313] The significance and role of women in the propagation of the Gospel of Jesus Christ should therefore never be undervalued. Mary Magdalene and the other Mary were the last to leave the cross, the last to leave the buried body of Christ, and the very first to witness the empty tomb. To these two women, the angel gave the first news of the resurrection: "He is not here; for He is risen like He said."[314] These women were also the first to encounter and bow down in adoration of the risen Christ. It was the glorious experience of encountering Christ and the wonderful reality that Jesus is alive, that inspired the first Christians to claim the world as a pulpit for spreading the Good News of Jesus Christ.

GOD IS A MISSIONAL GOD CONFRONTED AND SANCTIFIED FOR MISSION (SECTION TWO)

1. Christian believers are motivated to become witnesses for Christ in the world because what we know about God we have also encountered and experienced in Christ. The experience of the resurrected Christ, and the manifold ways that God has manifested Himself in our lives, are encounters and experiences that we are compelled and constrained to share with others. We do not have the capacity to store up or contain such good news. The prophet Jeremiah, having encountered God,[315] became weary in ministry because of the people's resistance and treatment of him. In his failed attempt at self-pres-

---

[311] Jn 4:29
[312] Mk 16:9-10
[313] Mt 28:9-10; Jn 20:15-18
[314] Mt 28:6
[315] Jer 1:4-9

ervation, the prophet Jeremiah tried to keep himself from proclaiming God to the people. He confessed however, that the presence and force of the word and experience of God, locked in his heart, was like fire shut up in his bones.[316] The Apostle Paul says, "Woe is me if I do not preach the Gospel."[317]

2. We must proclaim and therefore release what God has deposited in us because we do not have the capacity to contain God or what He has deposited in us. We must proclaim Him and speak of His goodness. God does not reveal Himself to us for us to keep secrets concerning who He is and what He is doing. God reveals Himself to us because He trusts us to do with the information what He purposes for us to do. Having an encounter with God is more than a privilege. It is an awesome responsibility. God's revelation of Himself equips us for Christian mission. God confronts us so that He might sanctify and send us out for mission.

3. God confronts us and reveals Himself to us for a reason. My sense is that the design God has placed on us as a result of our encounters with Him in worship or in life, is to furnish us with the evidence of His existence and transforming work so that we may become His change agents in the world. God reveals Himself to us so that as we witness to the world, we can speak of Him with intelligence because we know that He exists. God's self-disclosure is also designed to equip us with the necessary boldness and authority we need to present Him to the world. Our encounter with God is so riveting and so absolutely life transforming, that we are literally compelled by the encounter to tell somebody about God.

God Is a Missional God
Confronted and Sanctified for Mission
(Section Three)

1. Our encounter with God is contagious by design and every encounter with God is a formula for spreading a compelling testimony. The

---

[316] Jer 20:9
[317] 1 Cor 9:16

contagious nature of our witness is such that as the Holy Spirit empowers us to proclaim the Good News, those who hear and believe our witness, are soon inspired by the grace of God to live and experience God in their lives as they themselves become witnesses for God. Surely, the Good News of salvation is one that is received and given on a continuous basis. The work of God is abundant and He always needs laborers to reap the harvest.[318]

2. Our encounter with God is for the conviction and building up of our faith and witness. According to 1 Peter 2:9, we are called and sanctified or set apart for mission so that we "may proclaim the praises of Him who called [us] out of darkness into His marvelous light." Our encounter with God and our subsequent conviction about God inevitably lead to corresponding faith that becomes active through our service to God in our mission to the world. Assuredly, the person, indeed the church that truly encounters God, becomes a worshipping church as well as a church that reaches out. A church that worships inevitably becomes a missionary and evangelistic church. A worshipping and missionary church is a church that has encountered God, is filled with the burning desire to share that experience, and sets forth to do so with conviction and Holy Ghost power.

3. Having encountered God, and having been transformed by His redeeming grace in Christ Jesus, through mission, we become demonstrative evidence of His grace in the world. The evidence of grace so freely given to us, finds expression through corresponding acts of kindness, healing, and atonement, as we carry out the mission of the church. The life that is transformed by the grace of God is a life that is faithfully given to Christ through service of love, in response to the self-revealing and self-giving love of God in Christ Jesus. If our encounter with God is indicative of who we are called to be in Christ, then mission becomes the imperative of what we are called to do. We are called and empowered to do the work of an evangelistic and missional church in the exercising of our gift of participation in the mission of Christ. Because our participation is a gift, we are essentially giving to the Lord what is already His own.

---

[318] Mt 9:37-38

4. Since what we are called to do is a gift, we must be careful not to think that we are the ones changing the world. We are God's agents of change in the world, but it is God that does the work of changing the human heart by the effectual work of His Holy Spirit. After all, our giving of ourselves will always be measured by the extravagant self-giving of Christ. By the oblation of Christ, we have been set free and gifted by God in order that we might offer our gifts at the altar in worship and ourselves in mission. Had our service not been a gift of participation, and if our efforts were not sustained by our faithfulness and love for God, we would be easily driven to despair and our missional efforts would be inconsequential. Furthermore, anything less than our unconditional faithfulness would be grossly inadequate. Our task is to proclaim the message of salvation as we leave room for the Holy Spirit to do the work of convicting and converting souls for Christ. As the mission of Jesus the Son was to bring people to God the Father,[319] our task is to bring people to Jesus so that He might mediate their cause, satisfy their spiritual hunger, and lift them up before God the Father of abundant grace.

5. As we carry out mission with Christ, we need to urgently recognize that people outside the conventional church also have a deep spiritual hunger. Since many will not come to "the church," we, the church, must go wherever they are so that we may reach those who hunger and thirst for righteousness. While God may indeed confront us or grant us an encounter with Him wherever we are, existentially, the operations of God and His sending of us to do mission, are not restricted to the narrow confines of our sacred sanctuaries. Indeed, the workings of the Holy Spirit of grace are so pervasive, that they cut through and transcend our existential denominational boundaries, nationalities, races, social standings, cultures, ethnicities, and personal residences.

6. To restrict the working out of God's purpose to a particular place or surrounding, such as where we regularly gather to worship, would be a presumptuous attempt to restrict and domesticate the operation of the Holy Spirit. As the whole earth is full of the glory of God, so is His Spirit everywhere working and lifting up humanity in every corner of the earth with the gift of God's pervasive and redeeming grace. To believe otherwise would be

---

[319] Jn 14:6

to make light of our own conviction that God was in Christ working to reconcile the world to Himself.[320] Assuredly, the God we serve is always acting everywhere within the framework of His created universe and human experiences across nations and ethnicities so that He might bring all of us under His sovereign rule and care.

7. Since Christian Mission emerges from an assignment that springs out of our recognition, interpretation, and application of our encounter with God, our missional engagements ought rightly to give us a worldview. God's purpose in His encounter with us is to invite us into His divine life so that He may empower us for His mission of transforming the world by the outpouring of His Spirit on all flesh.[321] God is intent on redeeming the world. As God confronts us, even as He comes to us in Christ Jesus, His self-disclosure to us is so that we may go forth in His Spirit to proclaim the Good News of salvation. What we know and have experienced of God and His Christ, must be proclaimed on every hill and in every valley until the entire world is confronted with God's Christ, before whom every knee shall bow and every tongue shall confess, that He is Lord to the glory of God.[322] Right now, God's sanctifying activity is taking place in the world where the pervasive grace of God is working to redeem fallen humanity. If we are to faithfully exercise our gift of participation in the mission of Christ, we can no longer hide behind the curtains of our own insecurities or behind safe and secure confines of our churches' walls. We must be willing to make ourselves vulnerable as well as available for mission with Christ in the world where the rubber hits the road. It is in the world that real mission takes place.

8. We are confronted so that we may be equipped to go forth into the world with a message of redemption and hope. If we do not go, how shall they call upon Him in whom they have not believed? If we do not go, how shall they believe in Him of whom they have not heard? If we do not go, how shall

---

[320] 2 Cor 5:19
[321] Joel 2:27b-29
[322] Phil 2:10-11

they hear without a preacher?[323] Indeed we are confronted, empowered, and sanctified by our encounters with God so that we may become His faithful and lively witnesses in the world.

9. Have you encountered the risen Christ? If you have, what are you doing with the evidence of that encounter? Every encounter and every experience you have of Jesus Christ in your life is indicative of God giving you a testimony, a story to tell. If you have experienced Jesus Christ in any area of your life, you have a story to tell and the world is waiting to hear it.

Do not keep it to yourself. Under the anointing of the Holy Spirit, go and tell your story. Go tell everybody about Somebody that can save anybody. His name is Jesus!

7. Practicing Christian Mission and the Shaping of the Christian Life

A. Christian Mission as Character Building and Spiritual Formation

1. Our Christian mission, much like Christian worship, helps in the formation of our spirituality. Christian mission is an activity whereby a continuously marvelous exchange happens. Very often in the mission field, God takes our hardships and weaknesses and our failures and our frustrations, and transforms them into relief, strength, successes and confident assurances. These changes and affirmations that we experience in our faithful efforts to serve God, gives us a deeper appreciation for God. It also gives us a sense of the divine possibilities that are already part of God's design for our lives and eternal destiny. Meaningful participation in Christian mission may lead persons to more deeply contemplate their divine value and purpose. The very realization that God is making use of us in His mission to redeem the world is spiritually transforming. Inasmuch as worship does not leave us

---

[323] Rom 10:14

unchanged, neither does committed participation in Christian mission leave us unchanged. We are shaped and changed for the better by the things we participate in with Christ.

2. Practicing Christian mission helps our spiritual formation at two levels. As a work of the Holy Spirit, at the first level, practicing Christian mission opens our minds and hearts to God and makes us aware of what God is doing to transform and restore us. At the second level, practicing Christian mission progressively remodels our attitude and character as the Holy Spirit draws us into the life of Christ. In a true sense, we become what we practice with Christ. Practicing Christian mission is transforming because in mission as in worship, we learn more about God. We learn about God in mission because even in the fields of labor and love, God meets and strengthens us for the task He has given us. The very notion that God is with us influences the way we think and behave.

3. In the mission field where real mission takes place, character is also molded. Character is formed and developed in Christian mission because in mission, we become vulnerable, we are often challenged, rejected, and ridiculed, as we open ourselves to others. As we go through those experiences however, and as God sustains and preserves our worth and dignity in the mission field, we become stronger and better persons. In the practice of Christian mission, our character is formed and our lives are spiritually transformed as God daily works in us to graciously take away our rough edges; replacing them with humility and grace. As we labor in mission, surrounded by its challenges, rejections and acceptance, frustrations and encouragements, our character is developed and our faith in God grows as we endure and come to depend more on God's grace to direct and strengthen us. Character is molded in the mission field because as we labor for God, His sustaining presence encourages us and gives us the internal spiritual fortitude to stay diligent. Character and faith are further developed as God gives us strength to carry on through the hardships, His assurance to keep hope before us, forgiveness for our failings, and His grace and love for the hate and resentment that we encounter. These all together empower us to daily renew our commitment

to God, confront and meet our life challenges, and learn more and more to entrust our future to His eternal care.[324] As Shafer indicates:

> "Only the daily liturgy (that is the liturgy of service or mission) provides the time and the opportunity for the fullness of life in Christ in the works of God. Here there are no staged conditions and no easy answers. Here life is sometimes happy, often frustrating, and frequently raw. Under such conditions Christ achieves His ministry. In our similar circumstances Christ teaches His followers how frail they are. He teaches them how much they need Him. More than that, in such daily living Christ gives Himself to His followers. He, Himself, is their intelligence and their strength in meeting challenges of life."[325]

4. Transformation happens in mission when the Holy Spirit opens our minds to the realization that we are of value to God. When our value is acknowledged and affirmed by God's presence and use of us, we are virtually compelled to adjust our lives and bring them into alignment with the will of God. Not only does God call and empower us in order to make use of us, He does so in order to transform and renew His value in us. God making use of us also reminds us that we belong to Him. He reminds us in Isaiah 43:1-2 that we belong to Him; He knows us by our names; and He stands ready to defend and protect us. Having called and sent us, God also promised that He will be with us. God has promised that when we pass through the waters, He will be with us. He has promised that when we walk through the rivers, they will not overflow us. God has assured us that when we walk through the fire, we shall not be burned, nor shall its flames scorch us because He, the Lord our God is always with us.[326] We are not just statistics to God. We are His daughters and sons that He values and accompanies in order to defend, empower, and protect.

---

[324] 2 Tim 1:12

[325] Shafer, 57

[326] Is 43:1-3; Mt 28:20

5. The knowledge that we belong to God and are sharing in the ministry of Christ is a powerful source of spiritual transformation and opportunity to grow in Christ. The realization that God is interested in us and that He is making use of us in His grand scheme of things ought to change us to walk before God in faith and obedience. Having been changed to walk in faith before God, we must also do so in obedience as we work with Him to change the world. Working with God under the empowerment of the Holy Spirit, implies intentionally giving of ourselves and possessions to others and finding opportunities to touch and change the lives of the broken through love, kindness, compassion, and hope. Participating in these acts of kindness brings us into a state of spiritual maturity or growth in Christ.

6. Christian mission shapes the Christian life because wherever and whenever the Holy Spirit of God is present and working in us, change is inevitable. Through the presence, anointing, and nurturing influence of the Holy Spirit, we experience spiritual transformation and growth as we diligently pursue the task of Christian Mission. Christian mission also draws us into deeper dependence and saving relationship with the Lord Jesus. Through Christian mission, we also grow to appreciate and develop more meaningful working relationships with those with whom we participate in Christian mission. Since forming and developing Christian character does not take place in isolation but in community, practicing Christian mission requires the building of relationships.

B. Christian Mission and The Building of Relationships: The Four Levels of Interrelated Christian Relationships

1. Christian mission is built on four levels of interrelated Christian relationships. Effective Christian mission requires the building of Christian relationships. Building Christian relationships is based fundamentally on the building blocks of love, peace, joy, patience, justice, understanding,

compassion, and respect.[327] These are also the foundational principles upon which human relationships are built. Developing relationships demands mutual respect and the safeguarding of the dignity and integrity of those with whom we partner in mission. In the pursuit of Christian mission, the dignity and integrity of those whom we serve should also be guarded. By the help of the Holy Spirit, we learn in mission as we do in worship, to see each other as gifts from God in whom God's dignity is implanted. When we learn to see others as God sees them, even with our knowledge of each other's weaknesses, we are empowered to look at each other with new eyes; through the lenses of love, acceptance and respect. With new eyes, we are gifted to see that notwithstanding our faults and weaknesses, all of us are gifts from God and are therefore worthy of love, respect, support, understanding, and encouragement. We are witnesses to God's love in the world only to the extent that we love and respect one another.[328] Indeed, our Christian faith and commitment to Christ demand that we take the other person seriously and treat each other with respect as we seek to show reverence to God. One manifestation of the grace of God in us is the extent of our love and esteem for others.

2. As we engage in Christian mission, our growth in Christ is practically facilitated by Christian networking and relationships. O'Connor[329] identifies three levels of relationship that Christian mission is built on. At the first level of relationship, she speaks of our need for others who are further along the way than we are. It is there that the shepherd is shepherded. At the second level she talks about the need for our peers. At this level we have opportunities to share the day-to-day events of our lives and experiences, hold each other accountable, and mediate healing and forgiveness. At the third level, O'Connor suggests that we need those who are not quite where we are in spiritual awareness and growth. This is the level where we have our "little flock which is ours to feed

---

[327] See Gal 5:22-23

[328] 1 Jn 4:7-11

[329] Elizabeth O'Connor, Journey Inward Journey Outward (New York, Ebanston & London: Harper & Row, Publishers, 1968)

and nourish."[330] I have advanced these three levels and added a fourth level. This fourth level is the level where sheep produce more sheep. I believe that these respective levels wonderfully impact the shaping of the Christian's life as we participate in the mission of Christ. Let us examine these respective levels.

3. **Level One: Where the Shepherd Is Shepherded**

The first level of relationship upon which Christian growth is built is on the level where the paradox of service becomes evident. It is here that the shepherd is also the sheep that looks up to and depends on others. Every now and then, the shepherd needs to be shepherded, that is, spiritually fed, led, nurtured, enlightened, criticized, corrected, affirmed, encouraged and empowered. At this first level of relationship, as we participate in Christian mission, we rely on those who are further along the way than we are, to help us along. We may be as educated and knowledgeable as those to whom we look for directions; but they are often more experienced and spiritually mature than we are. Considering their maturity in Christ, and as a result of their experience in Christian ministry/mission, these persons— pastors and lay persons alike—are suitable sounding boards and dependable sources of knowledge. They may also help us clarify concerns and values, check assumptions that we might have, and explore with us alternative ways and the consequences of decisions that we might make. They are also wonderfully placed in our lives as big sisters and brothers for giving us hints, offering guidance and support, making suggestions, encouraging our faith and efforts, facilitating our leadership decisions, and holding us accountable. Having been there and done that, they are well equipped for mentoring us, holding us accountable, and encouraging and directing us in the use of our time, gifts and graces. They also help us in our understanding of where we are in our growth process and how aligned we are with where God desires us to be.

4. **Level Two: Where We Participate in Missions with Our Peers**

At the second level of Christian networking and relationship, we are engaged in missions with our peers. It is here that we find people helping people just like themselves. When people experience frustrations, concerns and other life events, it is customary for them to turn to their peers. This is probably

---

[330] O'Connor, 110

due to the level of comfort and trust that exists between people who are similar and are at the same level of experience and understanding. At this level, our peers may offer practical understanding and assistance in the carrying out of our missional goals. Our peers can also offer us the empathy, understanding, and practical support that we may need. With our peers, we can share the day-to-day events and experiences of our lives. We can also share with our peers concerning our discoveries, areas of challenge, discouragement, concerns, our joys, and our hopes and aspirations. At this level, our peers also hold us accountable, mediate healing and forgiveness, and remind us of who we are in Christ Jesus. Our peers also help to sustain and encourage our faith through prayer and shared experiences.

5. **Level Three: Where We Shepherd and Tend to Others**

At the third level we minister to and nurture those who are not quite where we are in spiritual awareness and growth. At this level, we have what may be rightly considered our own little children[331] to mentor, inform, encourage, nourish, and nurture in the ways of Christ. It is at this level that intentional mission and Christian discipleship take place. It is here that we give of ourselves to others and become neighbors to the marginalized and excluded of society. At this level in our attempts to reach out, we obligate ourselves to crossing cultural boundaries and demonstrate solidarity with those who suffer wrong, are alienated, and are in need of a friend and a Savior. At this level of Christian mission we become role models as our lives, our attitude, and our behavior become models of holiness and teaching tools for educating and lifting up those who are not quite where we are in terms of our experience, understanding, and faith. Here we also become advocates and sounding boards for those we are seeking to empower, serve, and lead to Christ. By nurturing and setting good examples for our own little flock, they are given a glimpse of the Christ in us so that they may see what they can become in Christ Jesus.

6. **Level Four: Where Sheep Produce More Sheep**

At this level of relationship disciples are made. It is often believed that pastors or shepherds of the flock are exclusively responsible for church growth and increased memberships. Shepherds do not however, produce

---

[331] 1 Jn 2:1,2; 3:18

sheep. Sheep produce sheep. Jesus was acutely aware of this church growth principle when by the Great Commission,[332] He sent His disciples, the sheep, into the world to minister to and bring in more sheep into His kingdom. Inasmuch as it is the pastor or shepherd that equips the church and sets the tone for God's people to become engaged in church growth and ministry, the task of reaching people is that of the sheep. Church members are therefore the best means for meeting and greeting and sharing their experiences of the local church to which they belong. In addition, they are also well suited to share their own life changing experiences of Christ. People do have an affinity to respond to and align themselves with people who have experienced the fellowship into which they are seeking or being encouraged to be a part of. Ultimately, while we may plant and water whether as shepherd or sheep, it is God that gives the growth.

7. The point to remember about these levels of relationships in mission is that when we are engaged in ministry with Christ, we are better and stronger together than we are apart. As we participate in Christian mission, these levels of relationships are necessary for our spiritual growth and transformation. At each level of relationship that we develop in mission, we discover that in Christian mission we are shepherded at the same time that we are shepherding; we are giving and we are receiving; we are listening and hearing while we are being listened to and heard; we are giving attention as we ourselves receive attention; and we are learning as well as teaching. At these four levels of relationship, we grow in Christ as our focus shifts from our personal interests to the interests, joys, and concerns of others— those we serve as well as those with whom we serve. As we surrender our own interests and desires, we grow in faith. As we risk ourselves for the kingdom and glory of God, which is our mirroring of the self-giving sacrifice of our blessed Lord, the Holy Spirit forms us into the image of Christ. That way, our encounter with Christ does not leave us unchanged or idle. Instead such encounter engages us to become engaged in God's mission to the world, where the Holy Spirit is still working to transform the lives of God's people in diverse ways and places.

---

[332] Mt 28:18-20

Chapter Six

Diversity And Christian Mission

Prayer:

Merciful and loving God, equip me as I go forth in the world to serve Your people. Give me the grace and a heart filled with love so that I may accept and love all persons without regard for what they look like or where they come from. My heart is opened and my mind is fixed on bringing glory to You today. Empower me therefore to embrace the differences that You have created so that I may celebrate the richness of your diverse world and diverse people. This I pray in the precious name of Jesus, Amen!

Hymns:
   "All Things Bright And Beautiful"
   "All People That On Earth Do Dwell"
   "We Are One In The Spirit'
   "When We All Get To Heaven"
   "Make Us One Lord"

Scriptures: Jn 17:20-23; 1 Cor 12; Eph 4:1-16

1. What is Diversity?

1. Diversity is the existence of differences encompassing a rich array of religious, national, ethnic, gender, cultural, age, and generational variables. Whether we know it or not, or even willing to accept it, there is a silent revolution taking place in contemporary churches, communities, hospitals, prisons, and pastoral care facilities all over the world. As the Apostle Paul indicates in Ephesians 4, God's new society will be characterized by new standards. One of these new standards is unity in diversity.

2. Diversity is a biblically endorsed phenomenon. As 1 Corinthians 12 and Ephesians 4 indicate, unity is rooted in diversity and is therefore a healthy and normative framework for doing ministry and carrying out the mission of Christ. Indeed, there are many gifts but one Spirit, a variety of ministries but one Lord; a multiplicity of outcomes but one common work— the work of salvation, the work of healing, atonement, reconciliation, and redemption. God Himself works all things for and in all people.[333] For, at last, in Christ there are neither Jews nor Greeks, slave nor free, male nor female; for they are all one in Christ Jesus.[334]

3. Not everyone is open to or willing to recognize, accept, and honor the changing trends and richness and value of diversity in our society today. Those who do, open themselves to the possibility of experiencing the richness and multifaceted expressions of God in the world. Indeed, our worship and mission in both their diversity and unity are encounters and experiences of the one true diverse God who is Creator, the Redeemer, known in the face and person of Christ, and whose diverse works continue to be manifested in the power of the Holy Spirit. Some people may have to be taught, trained, or perhaps moved by God's grace before they can understand and accept the sweeping phenomenon of diversity.

4. If we desire to become culturally relevant, however, diversity is a reality that ought to be acknowledged, embraced, and promoted. The promotion

---

[333] 1 Cor 12:4-6

[334] Gal 3:28

of diversity should be the task of the Church and other religious institutions, healthcare, and other social service organizations that are embedded in God's diverse cosmos. In light of the prevailing and manifold human differences, diverse human experiences, cultural practices, dreams, and expectations, that we are bound to encounter at different levels of our services and faith journey, we need to develop meaningful methodologies for creating and sustaining unity in worship, mission, and service to others.

5. As Christians, we are essentially a diverse people. We are called and sent on a mission by a diverse God, to bear witness to His Christ in a diverse world, and to prepare a diverse people, with diverse needs, diverse issues, and diverse questions, for eternity in God's diverse kingdom. As we do so, we need to be mindful that human differences are not to be scoffed at or merely tolerated. They are to be respected, and celebrated. Worshipping and serving with diverse persons in diverse communities is the task of all Christians— pastors, worship leaders, laity, missionaries, pastoral caregivers, clinical pastoral care educators, and healthcare providers. Because we serve a diverse community, if we are to make any serious impression on the pluralistic society to which we are called to be witnesses for Christ, our missional goals need to be directed at inclusiveness rather than exclusiveness.

2. The Mission of the Church in a Diverse/Pluralistic Society

1. A diverse and pluralistic society is one in which we have people with different ethnic origins, cultural orientations, religious views, and political preferences. It is a society that is comprised of people from a variety of nationalities and ethnic backgrounds who ought not only to be tolerated, but accepted, respected, and loved.

2. The vocation of the Church in a pluralistic society is to mediate the reconciling love of God and create and nurture inclusive communities that live under the power and authority of the resurrected Christ. Working in a diverse and pluralistic society demands that the Church

develops ways for discerning and appreciating the richness and diversity of God's universe. That way, we may be more equipped to appropriately respond to the demands of the Gospel and its implications for human life in its diversity. Discerning the richness and diversity of the Gospel of Jesus Christ as we actively participate in the spreading of the Gospel, may purposefully shape our lives while impacting the lives and convictions of those to whom we witness. As we participate with Christ in mission, we should always remember that He came to receive and embrace "whosoever will."[335] As believing people called by the title of Christ, Christians, we need to urgently seek ways to emulate the richness of a diverse God and Creator of diversity.

3. As the church is enriched by the diverse manifestations of God, so should our witness and service be enriched by our embracing of the oneness of a diverse humanity. Knowing the diverse manifestations of God as Creator, Redeemer, and Sanctifier, along with the many diverse attributes that our experiences of God have revealed, we cannot affirm the oneness of the Father, Son, and Holy Spirit if we deny the oneness of humanity. As we seek to diligently disciple and nurture a diverse world in the ways of Christ, we need to bear in mind that all persons are God's sons and daughters, made in God's moral likeness and image.[336] As God in diverse ways is revealed in Christ as Redeemer and manifested in diverse ways by the Holy Spirit as Sanctifier, humanity also exists in many forms, whether they may be racial or gender, religious or creedal, cultural, or generational. I do not believe that we can please God who is always doing a new thing[337] if we are not willing to accept and adapt to the new and increasingly diverse and overlapping human experiences through which God continues to reveal Himself.

4. Our failure to adapt, without compromising our faith and loyalty first to God, may render us left behind and culturally irrelevant. Since God has created humanity with such rich diversity, which is a reflection of His own nature and richness, we need to adapt and develop diverse methods or

---

[335] Jn 3:16, 7:37; Rev 21:6, 22:17

[336] Gen 1:27

[337] See for example Is 43:19, 48:6; Jer 31:31; Mt 26:28; Rev 21:5

approaches for doing ministry. The adaptation and application of diverse methods for worshipping, witnessing, nurturing, and discipling, may keep us relevant as we seek to lead diverse peoples to God, without regard to color, creed, social and economic standings in society, or political orientations.

5. Diversity is an important component of worship, mission, and life. Given the far reaching impact of diversity on the Christian life and worship, and since worship as a human response to God is also expressive of the diverse human experiences of God, diversity as a moving phenomenon and a fixture in our lives and cultures, cannot be ignored or avoided without rendering our religious practices and us irrelevant. Diversity in worship is also crucial because of the variety of human needs and desires for God, as well as the diverse human desires and expectations that are brought to bear on the worship encounter.

6. In worship, wherever Christians are gathered in the spirit of oneness, it should always be a place and an opportunity for people to bring their entire existence and diverse experiences to the worship of a diverse God. That way, our existence, experiences, and expectations can be communally shared, identified with, and gathered up in one bundle of joyful praise. Certainly, it is in worship that we bring our experiences gained through life and mission, to pray over, share in times of fellowship, celebrate in times of achievements, sorrow together in difficulties and disappointments, share our joys, express our prayer concerns, and lift our praise together in the spirit of Christian love. In worship and in mission, even those who are held captive by cultural biases, experience some sense of freedom when persons, though diverse, raise a common voice in praise and worship of the one God and Creator of a diverse humanity.

7. Regardless of who we are, what denominations we belong to, what schools we and our children go to, what color our skins are, what neighborhoods we come from, none of us has a monopoly on God. Assuredly, the Gospel we preach, and the Christ we proclaim cannot be effectively proclaimed in the world if we continue to hold fast to a culturally biased expression of the Gospel of Jesus. God loves all of us and is eternally accessible to all people. It is my conviction that Christ did not come for one select and

exclusive group, nation, or race. Christ came for the diverse many, and for all. Christ came to gather up the "whosoever wills" of this world, and died to redeem God's diverse sons and daughters everywhere. Consequently, our Christian witness, if it is be authentic witnessing, must be the kind of witnessing that manifests the authentic Christian Christ, and proclaims and makes visible what the kingdom of God is.

8. God's kingdom is a diverse kingdom. It is a kingdom where all of humanity in its diversity is reconciled to the one God through the one Redeemer, Jesus Christ and sustained by the one Holy Spirit. God's kingdom is a kingdom where wounded humanity can experience healing. It is a kingdom where human brokenness is mended. It is a kingdom and a state of existence where opportunities are always presenting themselves for building bridges and breaking down the walls that separate God's diverse sons and daughters. Indeed, that bridge has already been built with the atoning and reconciling blood of Jesus through whom and by whom a diverse people can find their way back to God and back into healthy and transforming relationships with fellow humans. As we embark on our mission of reconciliation, forgiveness, and atonement in the world, we must be willing to accept and embrace human diversity.

9. Because of the human failure to accept and celebrate differences, some of us are still afraid to "go through Samaria." Between 1993 and 1998, I pastored a church in a small college town called Edwardsville in Illinois, Wesley Chapel. The church's pianist, Irene Davis, lived in East St. Louis about seventeen miles slightly north, northwest of Edwardsville. East St. Louis is a city located in St. Clair County, Illinois, directly across the Mississippi River from St. Louis, Missouri. East St. Louis is wedged between Illinois and St. Louis, Missouri. It was a predominantly black neighborhood at the time and neither state seemed to have paid enough attention to the city; so it was left underdeveloped and lacking resources for growth. Irene Davis was the most committed and faithful church musician I have ever known. She did not drive and was always dependent on someone to take her to church. For years that was the volunteer task of another prominent member of the church, Jessie. Jessie became ill and was no longer able to pick up our musician. A meeting

was called to discuss alternative arrangements. Several members remarked, "I will lend someone my car to drive there to get her, but I personally am afraid to go to East St. Louis." Since no one else seemed willing to go, and because I know the value of music for worship, I volunteered to drive there to pick up our musician. I did so for just over three years before Jack Turner, a faithful brother, friend, and godfather to my daughter Jhameek, took over the responsibility. Based on the fears expressed in that meeting, one would expect that everywhere he or she goes in East Louis, something bad is always happening and is therefore threatening to his or her life and wellbeing. For the three years that I drove there to pick up our musician and attended church functions and conferences, I never had a bad experience. What I found were alienated people longing perhaps to be acknowledged, claimed, and regarded as persons with value much like the alienated people of Samaria in the time of Jesus.

10. According to Scripture, Jesus was on His way to Galilee but felt an urgent need to go through Samaria.[338] Though He was on His way to Galilee, that urgent need to go through Samaria was not based on a shortcut nor was it based on any geographical consideration for getting from one point to another. Jesus' desire was a divine compulsion to bring healing, atonement, and the message of salvation and acceptance to a culturally and religiously alienated people.

11. Jesus Christ journeyed and tarried and gave of Himself in places and to people where it was neither customary nor safe to do so. It is to these places that God is calling and sending us to risk ourselves for His kingdom. It is there that God is calling and sending us to build bridges and tear down walls of segregation and divisions so that Jews and Samaritans can once again drink from the same well; so that blacks and whites can drink from the same water fountain, get the same educational opportunities, and be judged and accessed by the same laws; and so that all of God's children can kneel at the same altar to pray. Until all of us learn to kneel at the same altar, break the one bread, drink of the one cup, and rise up together as one people, to witness to the one Savior, unity and diversity will continue to elude us.

---

[338] Jn 4:1-26

12. We cannot wait until we get to heaven to honor diversity. Our failure to honor diversity here on earth is a good indicator of the extent and authenticity of the faith we confess, but fail to practice. We cannot confess and affirm the oneness of the Triune God while we continue to deny the oneness of humanity. We cannot claim to love and serve Jesus Christ, when we continue to alienate ourselves from those for whom Christ has also died, just because of their race or gender. Authentic faith and authentic Christian witnessing take place in an authentically diverse world, where an authentic and diverse God sent an authentic and diverse Christ, to die for a broken and diverse people. It is to these diverse peoples that God has called, anointed, and sent us to care for and prepare for a diverse kingdom where He lives and reigns eternally.

3. Diversity and Pastoral Care

1. People were not created to go through hardships and sicknesses and heartaches alone. I believe it is imperative for us as Christians, as pastors and pastoral caregivers, to aid people in understanding that God is intent on elevating them and restoring their health, human worth, and their dignity though healing and fellowship with Him. Sometimes people are so sick, they are driven to despair and just need someone to help them connect to their divine source so that they may discover faith, and find comfort and hope. As we diligently seek to serve others, our challenge is to allow Christ to work in us and through us to empower the diverse people to whom we minister to see God in their lying down and in the rising up, in their sickness and in their healing, in their brokenness, and in their wholeness.

2. As caregivers and facilitators of wholeness, our objective should always be to make it possible for the sick, the suffering, the disabled, and the dying, to come to the knowledge that God cares and is intent on relieving them of their condition. They like all of us, also have the desire to know that God is the source of their healing, the mender of their brokenness, and

the source of their salvation. To that extent, we should not be content with merely asking patients "how they are," we should go a step further by reminding them of who they are in God's grand scheme of things. The goal, despite their existing condition, is to validate their human worth, elevate their personhood, safeguard their dignity, and give them purpose and hope. People need to know that even while dying, they matter!

3. If by our compassionate presence and prayers we are able to nurture the sick into recognizing God and claiming their own value in Him, forgiveness, healing, health, and even dying in hope, can become attainable goals. When people are able to recognize their value in God, hope supported by faith, even in the midst of dying can be a powerful source of healing and eternal resolve. As believing Christians we can offer healing and resolve to dying people and their families in a number of ways. First, we can do so by offering love and compassion as we witness to those that are dying and facilitating or aiding those family members who are coping with death and dying. Second, we can do so by empowering them to face death and sicknesses with hope based on the understanding that medication and medical treatments and even dying are means that God also allows to bring them gracefully back to Himself. Most certainly, those who die in Christ are not lost to death. Yes, they may die a physical death, but they live through the Spirit in Christ, the Resurrection and the Life.[339] So then, even in the midst of dying, hope is not to be withheld. Hope never dies and should therefore always be affirmed and nurtured in those who are grasping for it. Indeed, hope, even in the face of death, will not disappoint, because our hope is in the resurrection of Christ who has conquered death. Surely, He who was dead now lives. This hope is also grounded in the eternal promise of God to raise up those who believe in His Christ. I believe this recognition can be a powerful source for faith formation as well as empowerment for suffering and dying people seeking to cope with their conditions, claiming their healing, and for living their last days in dignity and hope. While it is perfectly OK to acknowledge and affirm the state of the person's health or condition, I do not believe it is proper to use the human condition to dismiss the human dignity and value by

---

[339] Jn 7:39-40, 44; 11:25-26

speaking despair into the person on top of what he or she is already enduring. Hope safeguards the human value and dignity. This is not false hope; rather, it is purposeful utterances for and into the human spirit, dignity and worth, which transcend the human condition.

4. As pastoral caregivers, our task is to help people get in touch with God. If we fail to help people who are open to spiritual pastoral care in general, and people of faith in particular, to get in touch with God, pastoral care has not taken place. Of course, we would have made our rounds and filled our visitation quotas. However, without connecting people with God, we would have failed miserably as pastoral caregivers.

5. The people we visit need to be seen as more than quotas that we quickly fill from our visitation lists. Several years ago, while I pastored this local church in Des Moines, Iowa, I was called by a member of the church. She wanted me to visit her brother who was admitted to the hospital, the Iowa Medical Center. They were both on the membership list but were not in regular attendance. For the five years that I served that church, neither one of them came to church any more than two or three times. This was my second call from this member requesting that I visit her sick brother in the hospital. I promptly responded on both occasions. When I got to the hospital recovery room where the brother was placed this time around, he had an older friend visiting. Upon my arrival, in seemed they were both in conversations about a number of issues concerning things happening within the city. Lying in his hospital bed engaged in conversation with his friend sitting on a chair, the sick man seemed to have been coming along well in his recovery. I greeted them both but made an effort not to change the direction or tone of the conversation. I got involved in the conversation when I was prompted with a question from the patient who actually recalled me visiting him about eighteen months before in that same hospital. With a smile, I told him we need to stop meeting like this. All three of us responded with laughter. After about ten minutes into my visit with this gentleman, another pastor from the city, whom I had not met before, walked in. The entire tone of the visit was changed. The moment he walked in, he said "hello," took off his hat, quickly shook our hands, and said: "I can only be here for a short

time. There are some other people I need to visit and then I need to go to the office to get ready for a meeting." He pulled out a pocket Bible, quickly read a few verses and said a "quick" prayer. He then said "take care" and he was gone. His "quick" prayer became his immediate benediction and permission to depart.

6. Depending on the physical condition of a patient, I do not believe that we should spend excessive amounts of time in the hospital room exhausting a patient with extensive conversations. I do believe however, that quality time should be spent with patients, especially when they request the visitation and have the desire for conversation. Quality time does not however, mean extensive time. Quality time is time taken to show patients that they matter and that you really care enough to not only show up, say a "quick" prayer, and hurry away, but enough time to honor them with warmth and hope and considerate and purposeful prayers. Quality time spent with those whom we visit helps them know that they are valued. Conversely, our busy rush may cause them to feel as though they are inconveniencing us and that they do not really matter. Let us not forget that patients are persons with desires, with hope, with expectations, and with spiritual questions. As such, we need to treat them as persons worthy of our time, love, and nurture. God does not send us to hospital rooms just to show up and fill visitation quotas. God sends us to manifest His presence so that hopeless people may find hope; that sick people may claim healing; and that dying people may claim life or die in dignity, and with the hope of God's eternity imprinted in their minds and hearts to the praise and glory of God.

7. Diversity is also critical to the pastoral care process because it makes us deeply aware that the spiritual, physical, emotional, mental, and medical conditions that so often impact human beings are not limited to any one gender, race, culture, or ethnicity. As we exercise Christian service through pastoral care, we need to understand that regardless of the person's race, age, gender, religion, or political orientation, the compassion of God does not know any boundary. If God's outreaching love has no boundaries, neither should the love and compassion of those who profess to know Him and are in service with Him.

8. Whether or not we like it, or whether or not we are willing to accept it, our churches and health care facilities are increasingly becoming diverse places and institutions. Churches and healthcare facilities are increasingly becoming more and more populated by diverse persons, staff, as well as members/patients/clients. Since that is the case, one of the challenges to us as pastors, and pastoral caregivers, is the challenge of establishing and maintaining flexibility and relevance without abandoning the tradition that has guided our faith, convictions, and pastoral care methodologies. To develop and maintain flexibility and relevance, while embracing inclusivity in our attempts to reach God's hurting sons and daughters, we need to develop a balanced repertoire and inclusive approaches in order to address, without prejudice, the real issues that impact the human condition. Diversity can be as exciting for mission and pastoral care as it is for worship if we do not take our overt or covert prejudices to the pastoral care processes.

9. My advice is for us not to go into ministry and or pastoral care situations with preconceived notions of what the situation is or what the outcome should be. To do so, we open up ourselves to rigidity and irrelevance, while ignoring the need that we are called to address in the first place. Let the context of the visitation dictate our response as well as the content of our conversations and prayers. That way, our communication exchanges and prayers will emerge from our understanding of the needs and demands of the prevailing physical, medical, spiritual, emotional, social, and cultural variables that are part of the lives of the people for whom we are called to care. If we ignore these and other prevailing variables that are nested in these culturally diverse contexts in which we offer pastoral care, we may find ourselves failing to respond appropriately to the human need and condition. If we fail to respond appropriately, we may become unresponsive to people's needs. We may also find ourselves answering questions that are not being asked, and sending up prayers that are not requested or relevant to the existing human condition, experience, need, and expectation. Without our openness and understanding of the prevailing cultural and social variables that are brought to bear on the situations and contexts of our visits, our visits and prayers will only be impersonal and generic engagements at best.

10. To enhance our diverse ministries and pastoral care methodologies and approaches in diverse settings, we need to take time to develop some understanding of prevailing multicultural demands and practices in the context within which we serve. All churches, institutions, hospitals, or nursing homes, as well as the homes of those recuperating, have their own unique cultures and demands that are brought to bear on pastoral care responses and must therefore be understood and respected. As we continue to practice Christian mission in the midst of diverse cultures and peoples, it is advisable for us to acknowledge that cultural differences do exist. If we fail to acknowledge, embrace, and respect cultural differences, our presence and efforts cannot have any impact on those we should be caring for. When we fail to acknowledge, embrace, and respect diversity, ministry and pastoral care stop and any potential impact from our presence and effort is nullified. Only when we acknowledge, embrace, and respect the existence of diversity are we empowered to proceed to learn about those differences that are brought to bear on our ministries and pastoral care encounters. When we acknowledge, embrace, and respect prevailing diversity, we put ourselves and others in positions of relevance and empowerment to make sense of our cultural encounters, to become wiser by the experiences, and to emerge from those experiences mutually transformed and elevated.

11. Let us look back at the areas we have already covered. So far, we have lifted up and discussed the prospect of our being made for eternity and God's design on us for eternal duration. We have outlined and examined the implication of the six selected steps in the process of our spiritual transformation. We have defined and examined worship and the implications of knowledge of God for faithful worship and active participation in Christian worship. We have discussed the liturgy, selected components of it, and their imports for pointing us to God, developing and nurturing holiness in us, as well as what it means to live doxological lives. We have discussed the dual and continuous dialogue between worship and Christian mission, their implications for spiritual formation and transformation, and the importance

of building relationships for carrying out Christian mission. We have also looked at some important considerations of diversity for effective and relevant Christian mission and pastoral care. Let us now turn our attention to eschatology and the importance of eschatological living for spiritual formation and transformation.

Chapter Seven

Living Eschatologically

The Impact of Eschatology on Our Spiritual Formation and Transformation

Prayer:

Most holy and eternal God, as I/we wait for the return of Your beloved Son and my/our blessed Savior, Redeemer and Lord, I/we pray that You would give me/us patience in waiting. Renew in me/us the motivation to serve others and shine Your light in a darkened world. Let my/our waiting be an opportunity to develop perseverance, faith, obedience, and the desire to actively serve You. Mold me/us into the likeness of You Son and draw me/us into Your divine life so that I/we may be positioned and ready for your promised eternity. In the name of Jesus I/we pray, Amen!

Prayer:

Dear God, eternal and loving You are. You have taught us to love because You first loved us. Implant in us Your Spirit of love so that we may love You and others as You have loved us. Help us today to give a little more of ourselves to others through service, concern, and love for Your people wherever they may be and in whatever station in life, circumstances may place them. As You lifted us through Your Son Jesus Christ, empower us to lift up others so that they too may come to know the love we have found in Christ. As we go through this day with the mind to serve You by serving others, grant us grace. Prevent us from falling into the temptation to withdraw ourselves from service because of the hate and meanness around us. With Your love firmly fixed in our hearts, give us the boldness to enter every situation and life's challenges depending on the sufficiency of Your grace to get us through. Assure and sustain us wherever and whenever we may be despised and rejected. Give us, dear God eternal, the gift of gratitude and appreciation for those who embrace us in our efforts to make disciples for Christ. Hear and deliver us we pray and we will be careful to give You all of the glory and the praise. This we pray in the name of Jesus, Amen!

Scriptures:
Ps 43:5; 98:9; Dan 7:13; 12:13; Mt 24:30; Mk 8:38; Lu 5:24; 12:37, 40; Jn 14:3, 8, 28; Acts 24:15; 1 Cor 2:9-12; Phil 3:20-21; Col 1:5; 3:1-4; 1 Th 4:16; Tit 2:13; Heb 6:18-19; 1 Pet 5:4; 1 Jn 3: 2; Rev 1:17; 7:9-17

Hymns:
"My Hope Is Built On Nothing Less"
"Blessed Assurance"
"Jesus Keep Me Near The Cross"
"The Strife Is O'er, The Battle Done"
"I Want To Be Ready"
"When We All Get To Heaven"
"O, Come, O Come, Emmanuel"
"Jesus, Joy Of Our Desiring"
"Soon And Very Soon"
"Lead On King Jesus"
"Lord, Lift Me Up And Let Me Stand"
"I'll Fly Away"
"Beams of Heaven As I Go"
"Love So Amazing"
"Love Divine All Love Excelling"
"Love Lifted Me"

1. Overview

Two of the most anticipated events in Christendom are the Advent of Christ and His promised return. Every generation before and since Christ has lived and died in anticipation of His coming, and now His promised return. The anticipation of both events has motivated people to live a lifestyle that is in a constant state of readiness and perhaps for some, a state of uncertainty.

In this chapter, I will offer a critical analysis of eschatology and its impact on the believer's faith formation and spiritual transformation. My objective will be to show how the nearness of God which is wrapped up in our anticipation of the return of Jesus Christ, leads ultimately to the formation of attitudes and behaviors that are pleasing to God. How that formation and or behavioral adjustment lends itself to the believer's spiritual transformation and growth in Christ will preoccupy us at this level of our discussion.

While eschatological themes such as life after death and judgment may be referenced in our discussion of eschatology, it is not my intention to investigate or develop these eschatological themes. My objective, without being exhaustive, is to examine the implication of eschatology for Christian living today. In general terms, I will focus on how our spiritual transformation is impacted by the hope that is invoked by the eschatological promises of Scripture as they relate to the return of Jesus Christ and our glorious future with Him.

How the promised return of Christ stirs up the human response to devotion and commitment to God, and how that anticipation moves us by the aid of the Holy Spirit to engage ourselves in continuous worship and the demonstration of mercy and love toward our neighbors, in anticipation of the return of Christ, will be important to our examination and discussion. Also, how eschatology consistently challenges us to actively engage ourselves in the making of disciples for Christ, rather than conforming to passive waiting and individual pursuit of piety, will form critical components of our consideration. It should not be presumed however, that Christian deeds, whether by devotions to God or the extension of mercy and love to our neighbors, are coerced by any threat of judgment or hell as it relates to the end times. As believing people, we continue to worship God and work through mission and

Christian witnessing in the "meanwhile," because we are motivated by love for God and our neighbor. How the liturgy of worship and mission finds continuous expression and purpose in our anticipation of the greater glory, and how that anticipation leads to the spiritual transformation of the Christian life will constitute our probing of eschatology. The intriguing implications of a realized eschatology and eschatology expected, as they relate to the paradox of time and eternity, will grab our attention. Also, how Jesus Christ and the hope that His resurrection instills makes Him an alternative to a world view of the human condition of hopelessness and despair, will form the overall backdrop of this chapter.

As noted above, eschatological hope should not cause us to become lost in our personal quest for an undetermined place beyond the here and now. Instead, such hope should keep us grounded in Jesus and become for us a continuous source of inspiration and joy for virtuous living in the present. Living eschatologically should therefore be taken to mean living joyfully in the present based on the glorious blessings and grace of God already experienced, and faithfully serving God and participating in the mission of Christ, in anticipation of His return. Such anticipation and active engagements also give opportunity to the Holy Spirit who is all the time seeking to cultivate our spiritual formation as He works to spiritually transform, empower us to serve, keep our hope alive, bring forth the fruit of His Spirit in us, and to position us for eternity.

2. What Is Eschatology?

1. Knight defines eschatology as the "language of promise which offers a future to those who respond to God's grace with faith."[340] I agree that on one level, eschatology is the language of promise which offers a future. That makes eschatology essentially the theology of hope. However, as the theology of hope, eschatology is more than talk or language expressing future hope. While

---

[340] Henry H. Knight III, The Presence of God in the Christian Life: John Wesley and the Means of Grace (Lanham, MD & London, Scarecrow Press, Inc., 1992), 69

hope is profoundly embedded in the human personal expectation and desire for something better, it is not simply something better that we hope for. On another level, then, eschatology moves us from the language of promise concerning our future "reward" to real expectation regarding the return of Christ who made the promise in the first place. That way, Christ, the Object of the promise, has more prominence in our minds than our conversations about our expected reward. When Christ becomes the focus of eschatology, the promise shifts from our expected personal reward, and more appropriately become an inherited gift of eternity. With our focus on Christ and His promised return, eschatology essentially becomes a lifestyle rather than a mere conversation.

2. With our focus shifted from talk about a future promise to real expectations concerning the Object of the promise, and even though eschatology is an expectation that is oriented toward the future, the very implications of eschatology instill within us the urgent desire to become engaged in the continuous activity of Christ in the present time. Such activity includes our faithful and continuous worship of God, as well as our active Christian discipleship in the here and now. At this level, then, talk becomes activity and a lifestyle. Our engagement in worship and intentional Christian discipleship (mission) makes eschatology more than talk about a future. Eschatology is a lifestyle.

3. Eschatology as a lifestyle is founded on three premises. These are: (1) Christ's promise to return (2) our belief in the promise and our expectation of His return and (3) the hope we have in the fulfillment of the promised eternity with God. Hope inspires moral actions and principles that are oriented toward the Object hoped for. In consideration of this hope that is oriented toward Christ and the future glory, these moral actions and principles keep us grounded in the present experience of faith and propel us to deeds of holiness. I am in agreement with Knight when he says "the believer not only lives and walks in eternity, but begins to live the life of eternity, the life of love which characterizes the kingdom of God."[341] This life of love which characterizes the kingdom of God must be taken to mean a life that is manifested through deeds of holiness and therefore a life that serves. This life that serves is one driven by love that reaches up to God and out to humanity (our neighbor).

---

[341] Henry H. Knight, lll, 71

This life is not lost in the rhetoric of hope and the grandeur of a glorious future but is actively engaged in God's transforming and reconciling work in the present, with that glorious future always in mind.

4. It is my position that even though eschatology relates to a promise which offers a future to those who respond to God with faith, this is not a future that is separated from the present. Our future glory with Christ cannot be separated from our present activity with Him. The present finds its fulfillment and completion in the future; but they are both inextricably parts of God's activity now. Consequently, the significance of our present worship and service to God should not be lost or overshadowed in our quest for a place, condition, or better, a state of existence beyond the here and now.

5. Because our present time with Christ is not divorced from our future with Him, to keep our heads stuck in a future heaven without any earthly grounding would be to neutralize the very purpose of eschatology. That purpose is to transform human attitudes and behavior in the here and now in response to God's nearness, and in readiness for our Savior's glorious return. Through the Holy Spirit who works in us to accomplish the work of God, and by our faithful response to God, as well as our diligent service in the here and now, we are aided in our development and preparation as we anticipate that future manifestation.

6. In the content of this book, eschatology is not viewed as the expectation of gloom and doom, destruction and condemnation, and a coming judgment with apocalyptic and Armageddon proportions that are so often projected to mark the end of time as we know it. Rather, eschatology, as a result of the lifestyle that it invokes, is presented in this book as a hope-filled expectation of the promises of eternity with God, given by a faithful Savior. The conventional view of eschatology as being marked by the final events of the world and of mankind, colored with the notion of death and judgment that warrant an urgent response of individual holiness, should not form the basis for our understanding here. That response would be a response of fear rather than faith that is grounded in love and holy reverence for God. While eschatology does have to do with the ultimate destiny of mankind and the culmination of all things, eschatology is not stamped with a condemnatory

period. Certainly, eschatology is not stamped with a condemnatory period for those who believe, but with an exclaimed future hope and glory with Christ based on His promise.

7. Eschatology literally fills us with existential hope by giving us something glorious to look forward to. Otherwise, all of us would walk around without existential purpose. The glorious hope that eschatology invokes also makes us want to do better and become better persons. Eschatology as a source of hope and expectation serves the purposes of aiding us in repentance and empowering us to live the Christian life as forgiven children of God. At the same time, eschatology also moves us to pursue moral actions that are pleasing to God as we stand before His judgment and grace in time, yet in anticipatory hope of eternity. Eschatology ignites thoughts of a glorious future but it also moves us to active service as unto God while we look with hope to the return of Christ. As 2 Peter 3:14 reminds us, our looking forward to the return of Christ should be a period of diligent waiting and the exercise of holiness nested in an atmosphere of peace and void of reproach. Our belief in the end-time or second coming of Christ should therefore invoke our present faithfulness, stir us to active service, and saturate us with expectation; hope.

8. Certainly, our belief in and anticipation of the second coming of Christ should not disable us from performing active service. On the contrary, it should empower and inspire us to active service of love. Our anticipation and hope therefore become powerful incentives for our dedication and earnest thriving to walk in the will of God in the here and now as the Holy Spirit works in us to ready us for God's eternity. In keeping with our persistent faith, obedience, dedication, and earnest thriving, the Holy Spirit lovingly takes hold of us, develops Christ-like behaviors in us, and enables us to grow in grace and the perfection of Christ.[342]

9. I believe that the content of eschatology ought to be existentially taught, believed, and lived in every moment of our earthly lives. After all, it is by our expectation of the return of Jesus that the past and our present experiences find meaning and fulfillment. Put differently, the past, the present, and the future confront humanity of every age and generation with the

---

[342] 2 Pet 3:18; Heb 6:1

message of God's forgiveness and grace and the necessity for obedience to God's divine will.

10. Consequently, in the content of this book, eschatology is viewed and presented as a moral model that inspires Christian believers to aspire through grace to live holy before God in every living age. That model is not based on fear but on love and faithfulness. That model is also not based on a figment of the human imagination as it relates to an unknown destiny. Rather, that model is based squarely on the word of Christ who promised to come again as attested to in Scripture. While eschatology definitely has to do with profound change in the present socio-historical and cosmic order as we know them, our focus for the present discussion is the radical impact of eschatology on our spiritual formation and transformation. Our focus will therefore be fixed on how the Holy Spirit, through our faithful and obedient response to the promise and nearness of Christ's return, shapes and readies us for the eternal kingdom of God. In this regard, eschatology is definitely a source of transformation and hope.

3. Eschatology as a Component of Spiritual Formation and Transformation (Section One)

1. Eschatology is an essential component of spiritual transformation by virtue of the futuristic expectations concerning the return of Christ and eternity with God that such expectations invoke. On the basis of our expectations, which are really responses to the promises of Christ, the Holy Spirit works in us to shape our attitudes, and keep our minds fixed on things of eternal value.

2. As we were created in the image of God, thus expressing the divine intent and the possibility of human communion with God, eschatologically, the likeness of God is a moral likeness into which God intends His redeemed sons and daughters to grow. Spiritual transformation is therefore a shift from

self and human endeavors and limitations to a process of spiritual reorientation toward the divine life and God's unlimited grace and possibilities. What this means is that as we seek to imitate Christ in time, the Holy Spirit is forever shaping and reshaping our human character in readiness for residency in God's eternal kingdom. The manifestations of the Holy Spirit in and through our lives are indications of God's active presence in us and throughout the Christian's life and work.[343]

3. Implied by spiritual transformation in a narrow sense, then, is a process of renewal in the Christian attitude and behavior that are being directed by the Holy Spirit toward God's eternity. In a broader sense, the term is used to mean that we are being changed for communion with God through Christ in the empowerment of the Holy Spirit. Communion and fellowship in the divine life of God takes place in our hearts and is manifested through all three spiritual components of spiritual transformation— worship, mission, and eschatology. Communion and fellowship are nurtured by hope as we are progressively moved by the Holy Spirit toward the glorious eschatological achievement of God's purpose for redeemed humanity, eternal life. To that extent, the final resurrection and our ultimate transformation into the eternal glory of the Lord Jesus, becomes our decisive stamp of approval.

4. This hope in Christ, who promised to return, continues to be a source of nurture and spiritual formation for us. By virtue of our faithful expectation and hope in the return of Jesus, eschatology gives shape to our Christian attitude and behavior and ignites our imagination concerning the possibilities of our glorious and eternal destiny. As a result of our informed way of thinking that is influenced by our conviction concerning the return of Jesus, eschatology also influences our Christian conduct, character formation, and attitude toward God and neighbor. Change in our conduct and character, which is our spiritual formation, comes as a result of change in our belief, thinking, and expectation. Eschatology properly interpreted and taken seriously, then, ignites our imagination and motivates our faithful efforts for reverencing God and valuing the worth of humanity. Assuredly, as we seriously contemplate the finished work of Christ, eschatology sort of urges us to

---

[343] 1 Cor 12:3; Gal 5:22-23

live lives that reflect the purpose of His death and resurrection. As we are eschatologically constrained to contemplate the atoning death of Christ, His resurrection and promise to come again, our outlook on life changes and getting our lives in order becomes an urgent priority.

5. At this stage of our becoming or being transformed to be more like Jesus, a set of new variables take over our outlook on life and eternity. Here, our entire outlook changes from the hopeless and the temporary; and from acceptance of the mundane and fleeting things of life, to the hopeful and the eternal. At this stage, eternity takes on enduring significance and becomes a matter of urgency. It is this sense of urgency that reshapes our attitude, increases our commitment, and inspires our continuous service to God in readiness for the return of Christ.

6. Eschatological expectations reshape the believer's life. This is so to the extent that such expectations compellingly lead to the reordering of our thinking. This reordering of our thinking influences our behavior and Christian lifestyle. The Christian lifestyle is an eschatological lifestyle because it is lived in anticipation of Christ returning. It is a lifestyle that propels our pursuit of holiness. It moves us to active worship and service. It inspires our prayers and faith. It invokes our obedience and love. It transforms and inspires us to become active and passionate witnesses for Christ as we anticipate His return and the reunion of our souls with God.

ESCHATOLOGY AS A COMPONENT OF SPIRITUAL FORMATION AND TRANSFORMATION (SECTION TWO)

1. Eschatology as an important component of spiritual transformation engages the Father, Son, and Holy Spirit in the formation or reshaping of the Christian's life. As God the Father reaches out to humanity through the life, ministry, death, resurrection, ascension, and intercession of Christ the Son, He also gathers humanity to Himself by the

life transforming power of the Holy Spirit. The coming together of the creative, redemptive, and sanctifying work of the Father, Son, and Holy Spirit means that the Christian is never left alone to fend for himself/herself. Our beginning and our continuation, as opposed to our ending, are together caught up in the divine life of our timeless and eternal God. Our renewed life in God the Father is facilitated by Jesus the Son, and sustained and given power to live the Christian life, by the exuberant and life transforming power of the Holy Spirit. As the Father, the Son, and the Holy Spirit dwell in communion through time and eternity, so too, God communes with us from creation to our final consummation in Him.[344] This means that the God we serve always finishes what He starts.[345]

2. If indeed, eschatology is a theology of hope, this theology of hope is a theology of transformation. Eschatology as a component of spiritual formation and transformation invokes in us a hope that is daily thrived for in our readiness for Christ's promised return in glory. God has indeed infused this hope in our minds and daily beckons us into that hope (Eph 4:4). That hope does not disappoint (Rom 5:5). Whereas hopelessness paralyzes human imagination, we are convinced that the Christian theology of hope ignites and sets the human imagination in forward and upward motions. Such imagination invokes holy actions thus providing the impetus for our spiritual formation. Eschatologically, the human imagination that is inspired by hope and directed toward God is indicative of spiritual re-education that has taken on increased anticipation regarding that which is hoped for, the return of Christ.

3. As we submit to the sanctifying power of the Holy Spirit, then, our re-education and or the reorientation of our minds toward God that began to germinate in worship, developed in mission, now reaches its final trimester of expectancy. As the reorientation of our minds toward God gets to its extravagant level of expectation regarding the return of Christ, His appearing is set in motion, holy actions are urgently pursued, and growth in love blooms in abundance. The implication of this is that the Christian believer having been regenerated and set on the path of holiness in Christ, comes into spiritual

---

[344] Gen 28:15; Ex 33:14; Lev 26:12; Mt 28:20; Jn 12:26, 14:3, 18; Rev 21:3-4
[345] Phil 1:6; Gen 28:15

maturity with increased anticipation of the realization of the eternal hope of glory. Eschatology, as hope in the return of Christ, continues to impact our spiritual formation while giving vigor to our striving to become more Christ-like. This is particularly so because we believe, and are confident, that God who has begun a good work in us will continue the task of perfecting that work until He brings us to full perfection or spiritual maturity on the day of Jesus Christ.[346] Our confident hope also persists because Christians do not believe in a dim, unpredictable unknown, but in the surety of Christ, who was dead and now lives and who has given the promise! He has promised to come again; and we believe Him! **Hallelujah!**

4. Not only that, He who has ascended to the right hand of God the Father, continues to be our advocate before God, while making intercessions for us.[347] The purpose of this advocacy and intercession is to persistently renew us, safeguard our souls, to keep us from falling from grace, as well as to vouchsafe or secure our pardon so that He, Christ, might present us faultless before the presence of His glory with exceeding joy.[348] That means that God is still working on us to make us what He wants us to be in preparation for eternity. Because of the eternal value God has placed on us, even now, Christ is working to safeguard our souls and keep what we have committed to Him until that Day.[349] Eschatological promises bring about change and renewal because the realization that God intends for us to be like Jesus has become a lively change agent that results in our dedication to the pursuit of holiness. The Holy Spirit is presently working in us for the achievement of holiness and in order that we might behold our glorious Christ.

5. The ultimate revelation of the glory of Christ and our transformation into that glory is attested to by the First Epistle of John. In this epistle, it is asserted that while it does not yet appear what we shall be, we know that when He, Christ, returns, we shall be like Him.[350] On the basis of that assurance

---

[346] See Phil 1:6
[347] Mk 16:19; Lk 22:69; Phil 2:9; Heb 10:12; Rev 1:18
[348] Jude 24
[349] 2 Tim 1:12; Heb 7:25-28
[350] 1 Jn 3:2

the writer further insists that, "everyone who has this hope [in Christ] purifies himself/herself."[351] This should not be taken to mean that we can purify or make ourselves spiritually pure. The text may therefore be appropriately rendered: Anyone who has hope in the glorious return of Christ should refrain from disobedience and, by all means, avoid the gravity of sin. We do not have the wherewithal to purify ourselves. It is in fact the Holy Spirit through consecration and sanctification that purifies us. Christian salvation, devotion, and sanctification are never the results of our own works, abilities, or anything that we have earned or merited. That is achieved only when we, in faith and obedience, submit to the wonder working power of the Holy Spirit.

6. Eschatology is spiritually transforming because the promise that eschatology proclaims, and the expectations that it instills in us, change the way we think and act. It is that promised return of Christ that continues to reorder our thinking and filter our human will so that our will may surrender to the will of God. That is the mark of spiritual maturity. As we surrender to the indwelling Holy Spirit who knows and executes the will of God in and through us, He changes us into new persons. By faith in the Lord Jesus and as a consequence of the Holy Spirit engrafting us in Christ, we are new persons. Old things have passed away, and all things have become new.[352] The Holy Spirit working in us, changes our words so that we can "talk right." He changes our feet so that we can "walk right." He changes our minds so that we can "think right." He changes our hearts so that we can "act right." We are changed to become new persons when by faith we respond to the Holy Spirit's impressions on us to believe and accept Christ as Lord and Savior. As a result, the life we live in response to God's eschatological nearness in Christ, and in response to God's offer of grace and mercy, is a transformed life orchestrated by the Holy Spirit who renews and directs our minds to God, His Christ, and His eternal kingdom.

7. We are transformed by the renewing of our minds to prove or live according to the acceptable and perfect will of God.[353] The implication of this is

---

[351] 1 Jn 3:3

[352] 2 Cor 5:17

[353] Rom 12:2

that along with our faithful expectation, in the process of waiting, we should not conform to the prevailing influences and standards of a secular world system. Rather, we should be transformed by the renewed knowledge we have of Christ and become committed to the ideals of the kingdom of God. The term "prove," as used in Romans 12:2, suggests proof or demonstration of who we are in Christ, based on a Christian lifestyle that is devoted to God, oriented toward eternity, but is also grounded in the present and manifested through love and justice, mercy, forgiveness, reconciliation, atonement, and regard for our neighbor. As we anticipate the return of Christ, the proof of our commitment to God is therefore manifested through our continuous demonstration of faith, obedience, humility, love, and our active participation in the outreaching life and ministry of Christ to the world. This is what it means to live eschatologically.

4. Eschatological Living: Making Ourselves Accessible Through Active Witnessing

1. While there may not be much talk about eschatology as a serious strand of theology in contemporary churches and theological discussions, though perhaps somewhat dormant, there is within the Church and society a sort of renewed interest in the return of Christ. Along with that interest is the subtle or covert emergence of a sort of escapist mindset that envisions being privately or secretly raptured to heaven. This escapist mindset may be motivated by the statements of Matthew 24: 39-41 regarding what is generally considered to be the rapture of one and the leaving behind of the other. This escapist tendency may also be the human individual desire to avoid the responsibility and radical adjustments that our relationship with God demands as we wait for the return of Christ. The desire to avoid responsibility, or even to cheat suffering and persecution, rather than endure the process of faith and character building that comes from perseverance and victory through hope in the eternal promise

of God, may be responsible for this passive and escapist approach to living. This escapist tendency may potentially make us inaccessible to God who is seeking to make use of us in a world standing in need of a word of hope and living examples of Christ.

2. As God made Himself accessible to us through Christ and daily available to us through the presence of the Holy Spirit, we are called to make ourselves accessible to those to whom we are called to witness. How can we make disciples for Christ when we withdraw ourselves form the world in search of personal holiness? When Jesus says, "I will make you fishers of men" and "Go therefore and make disciples of all the nations, baptizing them…and teaching them to observe all things that I have commanded you…,"[354] He was saying make yourselves accessible. From the highest mountain to the deepest valley; in joy and in sorrow, in comfort and in pain, in life and in death, Christ has need of us in the world. As we wait expectantly for His return, it is imperative that we make ourselves available for God's use of us. If indeed, our hope is grounded in God, and assuredly it is, then that hope must be expressive of God's accessible and descending love and grace to us through the Lord Jesus. God's accessible and descending love cannot find expression in isolation. The God that we serve is a communal God who makes Himself available to us through Christ and the manifested power of the Holy Spirit. God changes us; not that we might become content with where we are in our faith or become secluded with our new discovery of holiness. God changes us so that He might send us out as living and active witnesses to the wonder-working power of His transforming grace. God changes and sends us out so that we may become available to a people longing for direction and examples of faith that lead to a life of hope.

3. As we wait expectantly for Christ, eschatological hope is therefore grounded in the accessible grace of God that reaches out. This accessible grace that reaches out also touches the human life, leads people to Jesus, offers forgiveness and atonement, and empowers the redeemed of God to live the Christian life. As grace is the means of our continuous empowerment

---

[354] Mt 4:19, 28:19-20

in our worship, in mission, and our daily living out of Christ, who makes Himself accessible to us, we also need to make ourselves accessible to a world that hungers for righteousness so that they too may benefit from the richness of God's outpouring grace. As we wait for the final consummation of the cosmos and the manifestation of the greater glory by the realization of God's eternity, and as we are caught up in the paradox of the now and the not yet, time and eternity, we should not be complacent nor should our position be one of a passive escapist search for individual salvation and the pursuit of personal holiness.

4. Full salvation is not a static experience gained in isolation. Salvation is an active experience that is grounded in faith in the accessible life, ministry, and finished work of Christ. Christians are not called to be passive and isolated storehouses of divine truths. We are carriers and depositors of the Good News not storehouses for it. God has renovated us and reorganized our lives and priorities so that we may do His work in the context of community alongside the saints of God who are also caught up in the task of elevating and safeguarding the human soul and worth. As we do so, our challenge is to break down the walls that divide us, create opportunities for fellowship, and build bridges for uniting us, as together we go forth to proclaim the glory of God in the world.

5. Eschatology does not call us to live passive lifestyles locked away as it were, in our individual cocoons. Eschatology is an alarm that alerts us to the need to rise up, get out, and actively embrace both the Object hoped for, and the hope inspired by that Object. The Object embraced and hoped for is Jesus Christ, who proclaimed the kingdom of God to have come.[355] Eschatology does not call us to retreat in isolated surrender in search of personal piety. Eschatology calls us as persons and as the Community of Faith, the Church, to confront and embrace the world with the message of the Gospel as we actively participate in the redemptive work of God in the hope of reaching all people for Christ. If indeed eschatology is hope in a future that is promised, we should be actively engaged in Christian service because hope is always the basis for action.

---

[355] Mk 1:15; Mt 4:17, 10:7-8

6. The notion of active engagement in Christian service as opposed to a passive escapist mindset resonates well with the message of Christ who tells us to work while it is day for the night comes when we cannot see to work. As we have opportunity then, we should do good to all those who are of the household of faith and to those who are outside of our fellowship but are also in need of mercy and grace.[356] One of the most fundamental contributions the Church can make to the expansion of God's kingdom is to actively participate in the evangelization of the world so that all people may come to know the love of God and live in His fellowship, communion, and holiness. If one indication of holiness is taken to be our faithful demonstration of love for God and neighbor, then eschatology and all that it implies, should inspire us to diligently please God by our intentional ministry with Christ in the world. Actively pleasing God means that we should give Him of our time, our resources, and our lives, in service and active witness in the world. Eschatology as hope in the return of Christ should therefore be our impetus for continuous participation in the life and ministry of Christ. Getting caught up in the life of Christ is a source of renewal and motivation to rise above our personal desires and needs so that we may be free and available enough for God to make use of us in His continuous ministry of reconciliation and the dispersing of hope.

7. To that extent, eschatology forces us out of our everyday fixation on ourselves and renders unacceptable, any desire to withdraw into isolation in search of personal religiosity. Eschatology compels us to intentionally contemplate the nearness and activities of God in the world so that we may actively participate in what God is doing to change the world. Eschatology is therefore a message of urgency. It announces the nearness of God who has invaded the human community in the person of Christ in order to save and reconcile humanity to Him. That nearness of God also warrants all of us to respond to God's activity with active service and expectant faith.

8. The nearness of God, then, is salvation for those who not only take notice but also act upon that awareness with faith and proceed to participate

---

[356] Jn 9:4 and Gal 6:10

in His work of calling the world to Him. The nearness of God necessarily invokes the human decision and response to active faith and service, as opposed to passive waiting in our individual cocoons for an undetermined outcome. This taking notice and acting toward God is what shifts our focus from ourselves, and directs our vision towards God's present activity while keeping in view His promise of eternity. Those who have caught hold of this vision, and developed faith in the Lord Jesus, have already received salvation and eternal life.[357] The nearness of God and the eschatological promise of eternity are the blessings of God already made available to those who have taken notice of that nearness and, through Christ, have accepted God's offer of accessible grace through repentance and true faith. The nearness of God invokes and inspires our urgent responses and active faith based on what we have already experienced or realized in Christ while filling us with hope concerning what is still eschatologically expected.

5. Eschatology Realized, Eschatology Expected (The Paradox of Time and Eternity) (Section One)

1. According to Konig, "Eschatology is not restricted to a future expectation. Its focus can be about that which is ultimate in significance rather than [in] time. It begins with the incarnation and includes Christ's earthly activity, death, resurrection and ascension as well as His present work through the Holy Spirit."[358] In a real sense then, what is expected is being realized through Christ who brought God to us and by the Holy Spirit who continues to work in our lives to keep us living in the promise while preparing us to inherit it. Ah....the paradox of time and eternity!

---

[357] Jn 3:16, 5:24; 6:40; Gal 6:8
[358] A. Konig, The Eclipse of Christ in Eschatology, (Grand Rapids, MI: Erdmans, 1989), 15

2. The notion of realized eschatology finds reasonable support in the New Testament, the Gospel of John in particular. Here, the Christian believer already "has eternal life and shall not come into judgment but has passed from death into life."[359] We also see that "now is the judgment of this world..."[360] Indeed, the promised Comforter has already come to abide with the believer forever.[361]

3. This undoubtedly speaks of God's gift of eschatological salvation. Eschatological salvation has a three dimensional thrust. In the first dimension, it is salvation that is already realized by the coming of Christ who ushered in the kingdom reign of God and by His atoning and finished work on the cross. In the second dimension, it is salvation that brings us joy right now by virtue of our living out the Christian life through Christ who lives in us. The present operation of the Holy Spirit also makes Christ present and reminds us that Christ has sealed and secured our salvation for a future manifestation and life in His eternal glory. In the third dimension, eschatological salvation is grounded in a future hope. This will be for us our ultimate salvation and greater glory. By faith, those who accept Christ who came with the message of the invading kingdom of God[362] are saved,[363] have eternal life,[364] and shall appear with Him in glory.[365] Eschatological salvation is therefore interwoven in the proclamation of Christ concerning the nearness of God and the promise of eternity in His eternal kingdom. This proclamation announces the salvific benefits to those who through faith have taken notice of the present dispensation of grace. Those who have taken notice and believed in God's Christ are already saved by that proclamation and dispensation of redeeming grace. They are also being preserved and positioned for the manifestation of the glory that is yet to be revealed.

---

[359] Jn 5:24
[360] Jn 12:31
[361] Jn 14:16
[362] Mk 1:15
[363] Rom 8:24, 10:9
[364] Jn 3:17-18, 5:24
[365] Col 3:4

4. Eschatology as a lifestyle is therefore a present living experience of Christ, as well as our living in a hope that transcends time and space whereby the Christ we experience now, is the Christ we yet hope for. To restrict eschatological expectations to an undetermined future would be to neutralize the very purpose of eschatology, which is the radical transformation of human attitudes and behavior by the Holy Spirit, in the present paradox of time and eternity. Most assuredly, the creative, redemptive, sanctifying, and consummative acts of God are not necessarily distinct, but are of the one great action of a holy God who transcends time and space and who is at one and the same time both dynamic and stable, invisible yet manifested, anticipated yet already realized. Certainly, we live in the presence of eternity and to that extent, eschatology as a promise and a hope is not restricted to an undetermined future. Indeed, for the reason that the Holy Spirit has been given to us and is present and operating in our lives, the Spirit of the future has already been given to us in the here and now. Bultmann believes that "for the believer who is already in Christ, the decisive event has already happened."[366] The future glory is not entirely futuristic at all if it is lived for in the present due to Christ who now lives and reigns in and through us. After all, it is the present that makes the future possible. Eschatological outcomes are therefore not separate and apart from our present experience with Christ, but are necessarily linked to the present condition of our lives that are being lived in Christ.

Eschatology Realized, Eschatology Expected (The Paradox of Time and Eternity) (Section Two)

1. Realistically, the promise is being experienced now. Through the Holy Spirit, the God and the Christ of the promise are with us. Our experience of God gained in this present life has become for us a sort

---

[366] R. Bultmann, <u>The Presence of Eternity,</u> (NY: Harper & Bros., 1957), 43

of anticipatory and at the same time a priori knowledge[367] concerning a future, which, in a spiritual sense, is being lived. By reason of the knowledge of God imparted to us through the Lord Jesus who ushered in the kingdom and reign of God amongst us, and by the absolute merit of the present operations of the Holy Spirit who makes the Christ of the promise present with us, realistically, we are already living the promise. Our hope is still in the ultimate realization of it; but the Christ who has promised it is with us and we are indeed living in Him and through Him in the here and now. Indeed, whatever is designed for the future must be lived for and aspired toward in the here and now. An eschatological lifestyle keeps our faith grounded in the present, but we are being continuously stirred up with hope so that we may begin to live the promise as we develop deeper anticipation of the greater glory that is yet to be realized.

2. It is certainly conceivable that in order to realize God's glorious future, it must be recognized and lived in the present so that it may be diligently and faithfully pursued and attained to as grace moves us from glory to glory.[368] This means that the believer is already caught up in a progressive experience of transformation beginning with the present, yet hoping for final consummation in Christ Jesus. This final consummation in Christ Jesus is the ultimate salvation of which I speak. God's future, indeed, God's reign that cuts through time and space, seeks and meets us where we are, so that we, through divine grace, may live and work for Christ in the present, and yet continue to anticipate that future hope in God's eternity.

3. Having already received the gift of salvation in the present, we have a constant yearning for a future glory and communion with God. That yearning empowers us to pursue things eternal in response to the eternity implanted in all of us.[369] As redeemed persons in Christ, we live in God's salvation in the here and now, while we yet long for a life with Christ in the New Jerusalem.[370]

---

[367] A priori knowledge is knowledge gained independently of experience
[368] See chapter two, section F "Moving From Glory To Glory"
[369] Ecc 3:11
[370] Is 65:17; Rev 3:12, 21:1-2, 5; 2 Pet 3:13

4. Such is the paradox of Christian life and living. Wainwright speaks of this paradox as the tension between the already and the not-yet of Christian existence. Fascinated by the present in which we joyfully live, and intrigued by the future for which we yearn, it is as though we are being treated to a sort of unfolding of the potentialities already manifested through Christ. This is God's way of giving His redeemed people a foretaste of divine glory. Wainwright supports this view when he says: "Our expectation is increased precisely because we already have the promise, the pledge, the earnest, the taste. We have started to enjoy God."[371] **Hallelujah!** Fanny J. Crosby, reflecting on the Christian life and Christ's promise of eternal glory, lends testimony to this affirmation of divine foretaste when she penned her hymn "Blessed Assurance" that has for many generations brought joy to those who sang and continue to sing it with faith and hope:

"Blessed assurance, Jesus is mine!
O what a foretaste of glory divine!
Heir of salvation, purchase of God,
Born of His Spirit, washed in His blood.

Perfect submission, perfect delight,
Visions of rapture now burst on my sight;
Angels descending bring from above,
Echoes of mercy, whispers of love.

Perfect submission, all is at rest;
I in my Savior am happy and blest,
Watching and waiting, looking above,
Filled with His goodness, lost in His love.
This my story, this is my song,
Praising my Savior all the day long."[372]

---

[371] Wainwright, _Doxology_, 41
[372] Words by Fanny J. Crosby (1820-1915)

5. As surely as Christ came and called our attention to the kingdom of God which is at hand, or, indeed, already here, the eschatological reign of Christ has already begun in the reign and dispensation of grace. God's reign through Christ has already begun. God's sovereign past, and God's active and present dispensation of grace are not discontinuous from God's future kingdom of glory. That which is past with God is that which is both present and future. God does not make it up along the way. God established His plan from before time and eternity.[373] All that we are and hope to be in Christ Jesus is grounded in God's foreknowledge and eternal purpose. Our salvation begins with God's thought and love for us. It continues in the present with His forgiveness, justification and sanctification of us through Christ; and it will be consummated when God raises us up into the reaches of His eternity and future glory.

6. Consequently, the power to live in Christ and the manifestations of the fruits of the kingdom are available now because our past, present, and future, are inextricably wrapped up in God who is the same yesterday, today, and forever. God is immutable, faithful, has been, now is, is to come, and can be trusted to always keep His promise.[374] Because of the surety of God's word and promise, and because the One that promises is with us, we are already living in and enjoying that which He has promised.

7. Assuredly, the promises of God are as sure as the realization of the promises. I do not believe that we can appropriately distinguish between God promising it and doing it. As far as God is concerned, when He promises it, it is already done. In one sense then, we are realizing the eschatological promises given by God and His Christ while at the same time expecting the fulfilment of them in the culmination of the greater glory. Eschatology expected is eschatology realized! As we continue to live in the glorious life and presence of the risen and exalted Christ through the power of the Holy Spirit, we are at the same time living in the expectation of the greater glory. A life lived in the knowledge and nearness of God's Word, and manifested through love for

---

[373] Rom 8:29-30; Eph 1:4-5, 11
[374] Ps 33:11, 102:27; Mal 3:10; Heb 1:12; Jas 1:17; Eph 1:6; Rev 1:8

God and neighbor in the here and now therefore renders the believer "not far from the kingdom of God." [375]

8. Indeed, the kingdom and reign of God has come in the person of Christ, is dwelling among us, and has already taken authority of believers' lives and hearts. For indeed, all who have surrendered to Christ and accepted Him as Savior and Lord have made their hearts the domain of God. Kingdom means the king's domain (king-dom). If God lives and reigns in our hearts, it means that we are already His daughters and sons and therefore heirs of His kingdom. God's kingdom has already come and He is reigning and taking authority over us right now. Right now, we know that God lives and reigns in us, and through us, and around us. Nonetheless, that sense of eternity implanted in our hearts, which is that desire of our hearts for God and the pursuit of heaven, is still directing our focus to a future that is more glorious. God designs it to be so because God has more for us than the foretaste He has already given to us. That something more which God has for us is eternity, our ultimate sharing in the eternal likeness and glory of Christ.[376] Job had this hope when he tabled this declaration: "For I know that my Redeemer lives and He shall stand at last on the earth. And though after my skin is destroyed, this I know, in my flesh I shall see God, whom I shall see for myself, and my eyes shall behold and not another. My heart yearns within me!"[377] The Psalmist David supported that declaration saying: "As for me, I will see Your face in righteousness; I shall be satisfied when I awake in Your likeness."[378] The beloved Disciple, John, echoes both sentiments when he resoundingly declares: "Beloved, now we are children of God; and it has not yet been revealed what we shall be, but we know that when He is revealed, we shall be like Him, for we shall see Him as He is..."[379] **Hallelujah!**

---

[375] Mk 12:34

[376] 1 Jn 3:2; 2 Cor. 3:18; Phil 3:21; Col 2:10; Heb 2: 10; 2 Pet 1:4

[377] Job 19:25-27

[378] Ps 17:15

[379] 1 Jn 3:2

DR. WALKER WALKER

Eschatology Realized, Eschatology Expected (The Paradox of Time and Eternity) (Section Three)

1. Living the life of eternity or living eschatologically must therefore be taken to mean living joyfully in the present, as we are inspired by a promised future that is guaranteed. That joyful living in the now is fundamentally based on the blessings and grace of what is already experienced in Christ. That joy also comes from our sense of God making use of us as we faithfully serve God in the present, filled with a deep anticipation of the glorious not yet. We are also joyful now because the One who promises is the keeper of His word. By virtue of the pervasiveness of God's reign and grace, and given the all-encompassing power and reign of the risen and exalted Christ mediated to us in and through the Holy Spirit, there is a definite sense that "the eschaton has been realized in a person and a life."[380] That Person is Jesus Christ, the carrier and agent of God's manifestation and kingdom. Because we are in Christ, we are already living in joy and expecting a greater joy when we shall have come into His eternal glory.

2. When we speak then, of the dawning of the kingdom of God as Jesus announced at the beginning of His ministry, we can conclude that God's present reign implies a realized eschatology. Indeed, the glory and reign of God reside in the hearts of those who recognize His nearness and accept His Christ as Savior and Lord. In John Wesley's theological paradigm for example, the kingdom of God and the kingdom of heaven are one and the same. This means that we are not only promised a guaranteed future state of happiness; we are also already called into an abundant state of enjoyment on earth.[381] This is so because the kingdom of God has already invaded the hearts and lives of those who have taken notice and have believed His Christ. Given that understanding, it is critical to maintain a balance between the believer's present experience and future hope. The notion of a present foretaste of glory should not however,

---

[380] C. Sullivan, <u>Rethinking Realized Eschatology</u>, (Mercy University Press, 1988), 103
[381] Jn 10:10

diminish the Christian's anticipation of a future eschatological event; neither should it cause us to become complacent in our pursuit of holiness.

3. The Christian life is indeed "a process toward an eschatological goal attainable in its fullness in the world to come, but attainable in part within time and history."[382] The Christian is therefore one, who, though being in Christ and living for Him in the here and now, is yet going on from glory to glory in the might of the Lord. The very notion of going on from glory to glory is suggestive of a progressive activity orchestrated by God. This is an activity of grace whereby God is continuously acting toward us to pull us into His divine life while at the same time sustaining us and keeping us on the path of holiness by His prevenient grace.

4. Salvation is indeed a continuous process. As we wait in anticipation of the manifestation of the greater glory, caught up as it were between the already and the not-yet of time and eternity, our salvation continues to be an active faith response to the continuous outpouring of God's grace. This continuous and active faith response of which I speak is our service to God and the basis of Christian participation in the redeeming mission of Christ to the world.

6. Eschatology and the Christian Community: Our Continuous Working for Christ in the World

1. Eschatology as hope is a source of inspiration for the Christian's continuous work and participation in the ministry of Christ. Motivated by the hope of a new heaven and a new earth, the believing community is called to work, through proclamation and service, which are our performances of justice and love, and the exercise of mercy toward our neighbor, as we seek to extend the reign of God in the world. Again, eschatology does not call us to sit in isolation and passively wait for Christ

---

[382] Clarence L. Bence, "Processive Eschatology: A Wesleyan Alternative," Wesleyan Theological Journal 14-15, (1979), (45-59), 54

to return. The very notion that we are waiting for the return of Christ, ought to engage us in continuous prayer and worship, as well as through mission, the making of disciples for Christ.

2. We are called, changed, and inspired to do the work of Christ in the world. It is by doing the work of Christ through demonstrative faith accompanied by good works that the Christian grows into spiritual maturity. Demonstrative faith and good works are our holy strivings and the manifestations of our saving faith. Let me emphasize again that our works cannot save us. However, while the good works apart from faith through grace cannot save us, we perform these good works because we have already been saved and justified by faith through grace to perform them.[383] As such, grace that saves is also grace that informs and inspires the fruit of justifying faith, which is our good works. Justifying faith is faith that works to perform good deeds to God and for God's eternal pleasure. Change in our lives therefore comes when the issue is about God and His righteousness. When the issue is God's worship and God's mission and God's righteousness and the anticipation of God's eschatological action, God shows up and transforms us into vessels of righteousness that not only believe now, but also work now, as we faithfully anticipate the return of Christ.

3. Certainly, righteousness is not grounded in works; but good works are the manifestations of our having been made righteous. Calvin and the more theologically and doctrinally mature post-Aldersgate Wesley, would both agree that righteousness is not grounded in works, but in grace through faith. Calvin believes for example, that boasting about the merits of work destroys our praise of God for having bestowed righteousness as well as the assurance of our salvation.[384] Calvin does not, however, undervalue the merits of good works. For Calvin, the value of good works comes from God's grace. This grace is manifested in the context of community where we worship, serve, and anticipate good things from God. In answering the question: "If it be God that works in us both to will and to do, what need is there for our working?" John Wesley has always insisted that holiness is salvation contin-

---

[383] Eph 2:8-10; Tit 2:11-14

[384] See for example Calvin's <u>Institutes</u>, VXX, 788; see also Eph 2:9

ued, faith working by love, and if God works, therefore we ought to work.[385] Our working is the practical manifestation of our faith.

4. In James 2:26 for example, the author indicates that "faith without works is dead." For James, works show the genuineness of the faith we profess. Such faith is made perfect by our works. Based on the biblical principles of James 2:22, "Works do not give life to faith, but faith invokes good works and then is perfected by them...Faith [has] not its being from works (for it is before them), but its perfection."[386] Certainly, we are not justified as a result of any duty we perform. Rather, it is by our faithful response to duty already performed by Jesus Christ, a duty of love and grace demonstrated through His finished work on the cross. Our salvation is not the result of our works. Our salvation is the result of the work of Christ. Our works are, however, the outworking or the putting into action the faith that we have confessed in Christ so that it might find work to do in bringing glory to God in the world.

5. To effectively serve God and witness to the saving power of Jesus in the world, individual pursuits must give way to the uplifting of community. Whether within the Community of Faith, the Church, or the secular (wider) community we seek to reach out to and embrace, as we witness to God's saving grace, working in the community not only implies, but also demands the denial of self. In order for us to be effective servants in the kingdom of God it is necessary for us to go beyond our individual existence to embrace community. The Church represents Christ vicariously by virtue of being the ambassador for Christ in the world. To that extent, we urgently need to continue the proclamation of His message in His name and to do His work through His power in the context of community. That way, we may become useful in the kingdom by our gathering up of the unchurched and our nurturing of the churched. Eschatologically, since faithful participation in the life and ministry of Christ does not remove us from the present realities and existential concerns of those around us, there is no better place to exercise active witnessing than within the human community.

---

[385] See for example 1 Cor 12:6; Phil 2:13; Col 1:29

[386] Leon O. Hynson, "Christian Love: The Key to Wesley's Ethics," in <u>Methodist History</u>, (Vol. 14, 1975-1976), 50.

6. Active witnessing implies the proclamation of the love of God and the Good News of salvation in Christ. Our witnessing should not only be to the community, but also with the community. As the Father, Son and Holy Spirit are communally drawing us into the divine life so that we may become sons and daughters of righteousness, we need to go beyond ourselves and become actively engaged in God's redemptive work so that by the grace of God, the world may be transformed into an altar of salvation. Though we wait in anticipation of the return of Christ, the Christian mission remains an ongoing process in the here and now that needs to be fulfilled by us, working in and with the community.

7. Hope that is not proclaimed in the community, but is reserved for selfish, passive, individual pursuits and denominational monopoly, does not spring from Christian eschatology. Such hope is merely cheap optimism grounded in individual ambitions without spiritual and lasting value. Christian hope is grounded in the promise of final victory by Christ for all people, and springs forth in active proclamation and service alongside those who live with the conviction that Jesus is coming again to gather up the community of the faithful. Our missional engagement in community, where we seek to offer hope and affirm our faith in the eschatological promises of Christ, may potentially deconstruct the uncertainty embedded in human communities along with the hopelessness that has been mistakenly engraved in a secular worldview. The task of deconstructing human uncertainty and elevating human hope is, indeed, the eschatological task of the Church.

7. Eschatological Hope As An Alternative to a Secular Worldview and Faulty Human Optimism The Eschatological Task of the Church (Section One)

1. Eschatology is where the road forks. As it relates to the direction and eternity of humanity in general, and people of faith in particular, eschatology is decision time and is therefore where the road forks. It is

there that we choose whether to tell the unsaved people of the world how much better they can do with God than they have been doing without Him. It is there that we choose whether to ignore the mandate of the Gospel, sit back in our individual cocoons and allow this unredeemed world to follow the human pathway and self-help bridges that lead to nowhere, except to despair and hopelessness, or rise up and actively make disciples for Christ. Eschatology is where the road forks and we have to decide whether to point people in the direction of the Way that leads them back to God and His glorious eternity with endless hope, or allow them to go after fleeting human bridges and optimisms that only lead to a hopeless end.

2. As we are caught up, as it were, between time and eternity, the task of the Church is to shift the world's view from physical, temporary optimism, human systems and day-to-day pursuits of mundane, hopeless, and purposeless things, to matters of hope and eternal value. Eschatology is a worthwhile alternative to human optimism for the following reason. Whereas human optimism hinges on relatively baseless projections of probable causes, changes, and outcomes for human conditions that never seem to change for the better, eschatological hope is based on faith in the historical Christ who was dead and is now alive, risen and exalted, and who promised to come again to receive in glory those who believe in Him. With eschatology as an alternative to human optimism, the human understanding of life's outcomes may begin to make sense when lived in faith, and understood in time with eternity always in view.

3. Eternity helps us make sense of time. Eternity helps us to make sense of time because eternity tells us that human life and existence have value beyond the here and now. As people become locked into what seems like an irreversible stranglehold of time and history, which for many may be moving hopelessly and painfully slow, the believing community is mandated to offer hope in Jesus Christ in contrast to fleeting human optimism. In Ephesians 4:17-18 for example, the Apostle Paul talks about the futility or the emptiness and purposelessness of the unsaved world based on their darkened understanding, and challenges us to not walk as the rest of the world walks.

4. Not walking as the rest of the world walks should not be taken as judgmental or separatist in its emphasis. The truth is that we were once in that darkness[387] and are familiar with its bondage and struggles. However, because of our own surrender to Christ, He has delivered us from the power of darkness and has conveyed us into His kingdom of light.[388] Since we have been delivered from such darkness and brought into the marvelous light, which is freedom from the power of sin and a new life in Christ, and since we know the redeeming benefits of walking in the light of Christ, our task is to proclaim that good news. This way, others may come to understand, experience, and benefit from the same awareness and freedom we have found in Christ. Our task is therefore to go where people are hurting and hopeless and without regard to their stations in life, offer them Christ, their hope of glory.

5. Whoever you are and wherever you are, in Sunday school, Bible study or small group study, alone at home, in the park or in prison, you are not reading or studying this book and this section of it by chance. It was purposed for you to know and believe in your heart that Jesus is the Savior for your soul, the answer to your every problem, and the solution to all of your confusion. Know therefore, that if Jesus can save your soul, He can change every oppressive behavior and deliver you from anything. If you are hooked on drugs, Jesus can deliver you. If you are an alcoholic, Jesus can deliver you. If you are a child molester, repent of it and confess before the Lord Jesus; and He will deliver you from the bondage of it. In His mercy, He will deliver and rid your soul of the guilt of such monstrosity. If you are a thief, Jesus can deliver you. If you are held bondage by the spirit of sexual perversion and pornography and desire to be set free, Jesus can deliver you. If you are an abusive person, Jesus can deliver you from every abusive spirit. If you are bound by the spirit of sadness, Jesus can deliver you. Whatever the sin and the condition, if you repent of it and confess it before God in the redeeming name of Jesus, He is merciful, willing and able to pardon, forgive, and change the direction of

---

[387] Eph 5:8

[388] Col 1:13; 1Pet 2:9

your life. If you are lost and cannot find your way, I have good news for you—Jesus is the way, the truth, and the life.[389]

6. All you need to do, in response to what Christ has already done, is truly confess Him as the Son of the living God; truly believe that He died to offer you pardon for your sins; sincerely surrender to Him and accept Him as your Lord and Savior, and you shall be saved to the glory of God.[390] When you accept Jesus Christ into your heart and life, He will not only save you, He will provide an entrance to the kingdom of God for you.[391] That is Bible truth. It is that truth that sets all of humanity free:[392] Free to understand and respond to God in faith; free to worship and serve the Lord; free to laugh and experience the joy of Christ; free to love and be loved; free to live a life that pleases God; and free to claim by faith through grace, your right as heirs to the eternal kingdom of God. Those whom the Son sets free are free indeed.[393] The Christ of the eschaton, indeed the Christ who came and is coming again, is truly the best alternative to human optimism, failed systems, and fleeting self-help programs. Choose Christ and find hope in this life and a guarantee of eternity with God!

Eschatological Hope As An Alternative to a Secular Worldview and Faulty Human Optimism
The Eschatological Task of the Church (Section Two)

1. By secular world standards, human knowledge, philosophical systems, and self-help programs and seminars seem capable of offering at least some semblance of optimism though transitory in nature. However, self-help programs and systems cannot rid the human spirit of the bondage

---

[389] Jn 14:6
[390] Jn 5:24; Rom 10:9; 1 Jn 1:9
[391] 2 Pet 1:11
[392] Jn 8:32,36; Rom 6:22, 8:2-6
[393] Jn. 8:36

that has crushed it and stolen its joy. Because of the bondage of sin and the human propensity to sin, and since the human's sins, shortcomings, and hopelessness are not so easily overcome, Christ is the only and appropriate answer because He has overcome them.[394] It is in Jesus Christ that the grace of God is invested and He can give you the grace to overcome. Christian witnessing, in light of eschatological hope, needs to be based on this fundamental truth of the Bible. Jesus Christ is the foundation of real and lasting hope that can neither be found in human philosophy and systems nor human institutions and theoretical paradigms. We may still have struggles to overcome, sin to contend with, and persecutions to endure, but Jesus has already accomplished the ultimate victory. Therefore, our belief in Him fills us with the expectation of victory. This issue should not be seriously in doubt when one considers that Jesus, by the resurrection, has overcome and destroyed the last bastion of human fear and hopelessness— death. His overcoming is our persistent overcoming and His victory is ours to claim. **Hallelujah!**

2. Lasting hope can only be found in God's activity and presence in the world.[395] When secular world systems and philosophies have faded with their fleeting optimism, God will always be there, forever in control, navigating us to our eternal destiny in Him. It is important to know, believe, accept, and live this truth because only truth is permanent. God is truth and therefore the only permanence. When everything else around us changes, for better or for worse, God remains the same, loving, merciful, gracious, compassionate and kind God! Everything else will change or fade away, but God, the embodiment of truth and permanence, will always be there as our constant way-maker.

3. Hope is only found in God and will only be truly realized in Him and His eschatological Christ. Outside of God there is only unbearable and endless despair with no enduring expectation for favorable outcomes. Life outside of God only succeeds in keeping us in survival mode. That life is daily haunted by futility, human inhumanity to each other, suffering, failures,

---

[394] Jn 16:33
[395] Ps 146:3-7; Is. 30:1, 31:3; Jer. 17:5-8

death, and hopelessness.[396] In God, and through His Christ, even when we are haunted by said sufferings and hardships, we have the hope of change and abundant life.[397] Assuredly, as in God we live, move, and have our being,[398] it is also in God and His Christ alone, that human activity finds meaning and completion beyond the futility and quickly passing whim of the world.

4. As believing servants of God, having known the severity, oppressive, and destructive nature of sin, our task is to be witness bearers of God's forgiveness in the world. It is our task to spread the good news that God loves the world.[399] It is our task to proclaim to the world that God offers pardon instead of condemnation because His goal has always been to save us. As God came to us in Christ, our task is to go into the world as living witnesses to the love and transforming power and grace of God. As God did not leave us to our own mangled mess, we cannot leave the world to its own damaged existence. Nor can we leave the world to be suffocated under the blanket of hopelessness and despair, lost in the misguided maze of human opinions, and persistently disappointed by fleeting optimism. We have been called, mandated, and divinely anointed to impress upon the world, the Good News that God has a place for each and every person who believes in the Lord Jesus Christ as Savior and Lord. We have been entrusted with the Gospel of Christ to change lives and bring others into the restorative knowledge of God's love.

5. Our eschatological task is to take the Gospel message of salvation to the world. Somebody once said "that the Gospel came to the Romans and the Romans turned it into a system. The Gospel came to the Greeks and the Greeks turned it into a philosophy. The Gospel came to the British and the British turned it into a culture. The Gospel came to America and the Americans turned it into a business."[400] A system, a philosophy, a culture, or a business cannot and will not save humanity. The Gospel is not a tool or

---

[396] Eph 2:12; 1 Thess 4:13

[397] Jn 10:10

[398] Acts 17:28

[399] Jn 3:16; Rom 5:8

[400] From Ed Stetzer, "The Problem With Pastor As Rock Star," Tim Challies' blog, www.Challies.com July 13, 2010

mere means to an end. The Gospel of Christ is the Good News that Christ died to save us and was resurrected to give us the victory over death and life's nuances, and the assurance of a glorified continuity beyond the limited prospects of time.

6. I give you not a philosophy. I offer you not a culture and certainly not a business. All I offer you is Jesus Christ, the way the truth, and the life. While there are many faith positions in the world today, all of these positions cannot be true. Now, you may ask me: "You believe that Christ and Christianity embody that truth, right?" And my answer will be "Yes! I do believe that Jesus Christ is the truth!" Christ, the Son of God, is also God's bearer of the truth in the world. It is only that truth that can set us free.[401] By the standards of Jesus Christ, the line is drawn and the road is forked, thus establishing the demarcation between truth and falsehood. A choice therefore needs to be made! Make Jesus your choice! With the lines drawn and the road forked, the "grey area" is no longer a viable option. Jesus is the world's most viable option! While the world thrives on the existence of the "grey area," there are such things as right and wrong and absolutes. People subscribe to the existence of the so called "grey area" probably to make themselves feel less accountable for their actions. The "grey area" is often imagined because it gives people a false sense of freedom from the moral expectations of God. Probably with a self-imposed (perceived) sense of freedom from God, they can claim freedom to do whatever makes them feel good: the freedom to be selfish; the freedom to commit grievous atrocities against each other without a second thought; and the freedom to deny the truth. I believe God to be the embodiment of truth and that Jesus Christ is the representation of that truth to humanity.

7. You may say that I am arrogant to affirm this conviction and for projecting Jesus as the correct way to God when there are so many religions and faith positions in the world. Let me illustrate this conviction. I once watched a short film, "The Stranger" with a subtitle "Salt." The plot as it unfolded went this way: "Two men were sitting on an airplane while it was being boarded. After a few moments, they struck up a conversation. One man was from New

---

[401] Jn 8:32, 36, 14:6; Rom 8:2; Gal 5:10

York and he was talking about how anxious he was to see his family again. The other man was talking about how excited he was to be visiting Denver for the first time. The only problem was that the plane was not going to Denver. It was going to New York. Only the New York man realized that his friend had somehow got on the wrong plane and was not headed to his intended destination. So, tell me, would it have been arrogance for the New York man to tell his friend the truth while there was still time for him to get on the right plane? Or, do you think the best thing he could do is sit silently so as not to offend or embarrass the man, and let him think that he was right and going in the right direction even though he was not?"

8. Now then, let me ask you, if you saw a valued friend in error, would you just sit there and say nothing because you do not want to offend or embarrass your friend? I do not believe that it is OK to sit idly by and watch someone in error going in the wrong direction, thinking that all is well, when I know the truth about whether or not that person is on the "wrong plane" or going in the wrong direction. As human beings, our task is to help one another along the way just to make life a little bit easier. A multitude of faith positions do not absolve us from helping others navigate through life nor do they restrain us from proclaiming the truth about what we know and have experienced with Jesus Christ.

9. The world, often through the guise of other faith positions, has become good at imitating the light,[402] but the world does not have the power to be that Light or the capacity to duplicate that Light. Jesus Christ is the Light of God in the world and without Him all of us will stumble and fall in darkness.[403] In Him and through Him, the glory of God shines in every dark crevice of human existence. It was Christ that said in John 9: 5 "While I am in the world, I am the Light of the world." As the redeemed of God, it is our task to offer Jesus to the world as the alternative to the world's overwhelming darkness and fleeting optimism. While the world is always seeking to be politically correct, its goal should be to become biblically correct. The world is filled with religions, philosophies, political predictions, and opinions about

---

[402] 2 Cor 11:14-15

[403] Jn 8:12

everything. However, religions, philosophies, political predictions and associations cannot save anyone from the oppressive grip of sin. Knowing the truth, believing that truth, and having a relationship with the truth, Jesus Christ, is the only way by which we can be saved from sin and all of the debilitating conditions of the present life. Getting on board the Lord Jesus is the "correct flight" to get on because this plane, bound for glory, will take you safely to an eternally desirable destination. That desired destination which the human heart longs for is not New York or Denver. That destination is eternity with God and the Lord Jesus. Jesus is stronger than death. Greater is He that is in us, than he who is in the world. Jesus Christ is our hope of glory! Jesus is the answer for our questions and the solution to the human condition. He is the only Savior of the human soul and the way to your eternal destiny.[404]

10. For me, at a personal level, believing in and experiencing Jesus Christ in my life has been the source of my greatest assurance and comfort. Honestly, if I were to wake up and find that experience gone, I would do everything with every fiber of my being to get it back. Through faith in God, life has meaning for me. I believe that it can be the same for all who place their faith squarely on Jesus. If you have never tried Him, give Him a try. I guarantee you that you will like Him as much as He likes you. He has already loved you enough to die for you. Try Him and I guarantee you that He will give you additional reasons for believing, loving, and hoping in Him. Let me offer you some rationales for placing your hope in Christ as the alternative for the hopelessness and uncertainty in the world.

8. Rationales for Projecting Christ as the Only Alternative and Hope (An Overview)

Hope in Christ is God's divine alternative for a world lost in hopelessness and despair. God has equipped the Christian community with the necessary means to offer Christ as an alternative to human despair and hopelessness on several

---
[404] Jn 3:16-17, Jn 14:6

grounds. These are: (i) The evidence of creation, faith, and the activities of God in the world; (ii) The resurrection of Jesus; (iii) The promised return of Jesus Christ; (iv) God cannot lie (The Immutability of God); and (v) History is not accidental (God Controls Time and History). Let us take a moment to examine these reasons for our projection of Christ in our witness to the world.

(i) The Evidence of Creation, Faith, and the Activities of God in the World

1. Our first alternative and response to a secular worldview is the pervasiveness of God's grace, presence, and activity in the world. We believe that God is indeed responsible for creating, sustaining, and directing this world through time, beyond death, and toward His glorious eternity. Because God is eternal and therefore transcends time and space, we believe that He is the Master of time and eternity. The world, without faith in God and the Lord Jesus, sees time and space and life as having no purposeful continuation beyond death and the grave. This view of life, as a journey towards a meaningless and unfulfilled end that comes with death, is largely responsible for much of the hopelessness and despair that is gripping the unredeemed human spirit like a vice.

2. If it is indeed in God that we live, move, and have our being, and if knowledge of Him and faith in His Christ is eternal life,[405] it follows that God's overarching providence guides human affairs and the entire cosmos, to their completion in Him. Since God created time and space, and all that dwell therein,[406] and since God exercises sovereignty over all things, peoples and nations, without faith in God, the world is walking blindly into its own self-imposed uncertainty. However, when faith is placed firmly on God, eternity comes into focus and suddenly life is opened to a whole new world of possibilities. When faith is invested in God, impossibilities are transformed into possibilities, hopelessness into hopefulness, uncertainty into blessed assurance, insults into invitations, injury into pardon, self-indulgence into faith-filled and Spirit driven lives, and the temporary and fleeting into the eternal and everlasting.

---

[405] Jn 17:3
[406] See Gen. 14: 19; Ex 19: 5; Ps 24:1, 89:11; Jer 27:5; Acts 17:25

3. Faith in God makes the difference between our grasping for the straws of human optimism with the intention of not drowning in the miseries of life, and our holding firmly and staying grounded on faith in the assurance of God's promise. When we believe and hope in God even when there is no human evidence or basis for doing so, we are honoring God with our faith and it is that faith that God honors in return. As we grow into our knowledge and experiences of God, faith provides its own evidence.[407] To someone who has never experienced God or exercised faith in God, our belief in God is sometimes mistakenly considered blind faith.

4. Blind faith is the human term for human pursuits that are not based on any prior examination and knowledge of what we are getting ourselves into or without knowing what the outcomes are likely to be. Blind faith is the human way of saying you are working without supporting evidence and expectation of intended outcome. But that is precisely the faith that God honors. God honors faith that goes beyond human's natural sight and scientific probabilities to become squarely invested in Him. Those who are not of our faith persuasion may say our faith is blind, only because they are not able to see and hear the things believing sons and daughters of God are empowered to see and hear when they begin to trust God.[408] Romans 2:9-16 speaks for example, of a vision concerning things that are only manifested or revealed by God, to those who have invested their faith in Him, to those who have moral affinity to Him, and to those who have experienced Christ and have a personal relationship with Him.

5. The Apostle Paul speaks of the things we are gifted to see as "a mystery, the hidden wisdom"[409] that is concealed from the world, but made known to those who have taken notice of God's nearness, and believe in His Christ. Mystery here does not mean that which is impossible or difficult to understand. Rather, it is suggestive of a truth that is hidden and is only revealed by the Holy Spirit to whom God may elect to reveal it.[410] The Holy Spirit can

---

[407] Heb 11:1

[408] 2 Kings 6:8-17; 1 Cor 2:9-14

[409] 1 Cor 2:7

[410] Jn 16:13

reveal the hidden things, even the content of the mind of God because the Holy Spirit knows the mind of God.[411] For that reason, the Holy Spirit who helps us in our weakness also enters our hearts when we pray, teaches us concerning what we should pray for, and makes intercessions for us to the Father, because He knows the will and purposes of God for us.[412] Given the prior knowledge of the will and purposes of God that the Holy Spirit possesses, it is the prerogative of the Holy Spirit to reveal the hidden things of God to people of faith. The manifestation of things hidden or in the supernatural realm, revealed to us in the natural, gives us reasons to look beyond the limitations of the tangible realm of human existence so that we may see divine possibilities. God fits us with the eyes of faith to behold such things because they open us to a realm of endless eschatological hope and possibilities beyond the realm of the natural world.

6. This eschatological and rather spiritual grasp of a reality beyond the tangible world, is intended to equip us to live in hope while confidently offering the world this hope in God. God, by His sovereign power and wisdom, makes known His hidden plan to people of faith. Surely, we walk by faith, not by sight.[413] Faith in God is not blind faith. Despite the uncertainties around us and notwithstanding the existence of prevailing reasons for despair and hopelessness in the world, based on what we have seen and heard and believed about God, faith in God gives us hopeful resolve and settled expectations hinged on the possibilities already seen in God's activity in creation and grounded in the resurrection of Jesus Christ.

7. Christian faith is not without basis or evidence or substance. Our faith in God is indeed based on the substance of things hoped for[414] and is motivated by the evidence of things already accomplished and established by God in human history. The established work of God in time and history becomes for us the guarantee of our hope in the not-yet seen. Faith in God is also grounded in what God has already shown us and what He has done

---

[411] 1 Cor 2:10-11
[412] Rom 8:26-27
[413] 2 Cor 5:7
[414] Heb 11:1

in our lives. To believe in things that are not seen is to believe in outcomes that are not yet realized. Assuredly, as evidenced by creation, we believe in God who is able to call forth things that are not, as if they were[415] so that they may manifest in time and history for the benefit of our faith and expressly for His glory and praise. For a more detailed look at the evidence of creation, please see chapter two section 3, Six Steps for Understanding Spiritual Transformation, Step One: Recognizing and Knowing God, subsection (i) Knowing God by His Divine Qualities and Works through Creation, Redemption, and Incarnation.

8. The evidence of creation and the evidence of the resurrection of Jesus are supporting pillars of our faith. We look to the God of creation, and to Jesus Christ who defeated death by His resurrection, for enduring value in the life we live now and for our hope of eternity. Misguided human ideologies and systems encourage us to look to ourselves. They are in direct opposition to faith and are contrary to the principles of faith simply because of humans' attempts to remove God from the equation in order that they might insert themselves. Lost humanity cannot find its way without God's help.

9. I submit that the human opposition to the principles and Object of faith, God, is one of convenience and a cop-out for easing the human conscience. With God removed from the equation, our sense of right and wrong becomes so warped, that we feel less accountable for what we do, no matter how atrocious in nature the action is. The human opposition to a faith position may also be motivated by the natural human desire to have the freedom to carve out our own destinies, and even the freedom to deny any possibility of divine existence and truth. That way, we can live our lives doing what we want to, when we want to, and with whomever we want to; without any sense of responsibility or guilt.

10. While human ideologies and systems may offer some degree of optimism, that optimism at best, is rather fleeting and therefore unfulfilling. Human existence is incomplete and unfulfilled when we are disconnected from our life Source, Creator God! Outside of God's reign, outside of God's

---

[415] Rom 4:17

activity in time and space, human activity cannot find fulfillment and lasting purpose and satisfaction. The satisfaction of the human heart and our search for contentment and inner peace are the work of grace which is God's to give and is indeed given to all who believe in His redeeming Christ, and are walking by faith in Him.

11. The human heart is persistently searching for fulfillment and satisfaction because human systems, philosophies, and scientific discoveries still leave a void in us that only our encounter with God can fill. When we human beings continue to look for fulfillment in ourselves, we will only succeed in becoming more confused, more frustrated, more depressed, more anxious, and therefore emptier, unfulfilled, and left without purpose. When by faith we look to God, God becomes the source of the freedom, contentment, and purpose that our hearts are seeking after. Faith in God is the empowerment we need to live above the frustration and despair that so often accompany our human failures and the inability to deliver ourselves from the hopelessness that is closing in on us.

12. Contrary to popular secular opinions, faith in God is not the Christian's safety net. Faith is not wishful thinking concerning the invisible world or an uncertain future. Faith is not will power or the human ability to manipulate outcomes and circumstances. Faith is not a belief in what we have determined to be probable. Faith is an assured confidence in God who is able to do exceedingly great and wonderful things. Faith is the Christian's assurance in the promises of God based on the evidence of who He is and what He has already done. Faith in God is what transforms us from children of misery and despair, to children of hope and glory. Faith in God elevates us from death to life and from hell to heaven. For, the same power that raised up Jesus Christ is still able to cover you with divine love that stretches to the end of the universe. That same power is still able to comfort you in sorrow by surrounding and indwelling you with the pervasive presence of God. Place your trust in God and submit your future to the resurrected Christ and watch Him change your life situation in time, fill your life with hope, and position you for eternity.

(ii) The Resurrection of Jesus
(Section One)

1. Our second alternative to the prevailing secular worldview on the matter of life, death, and the meaning of life beyond the grave, is the Christian claim and evidence of the resurrection of Christ. On that first Easter morning, in the midst of death, God spoke life through the walls of the tomb where the crucified Christ was laid. An empty tomb is there to prove that Jesus lives! **Hallelujah!** Through that empty tomb God announced His divine power over death and hell, unveiled His intention to vindicate the righteous, establish justice, and once and for all crush the fear of death that has haunted humanity for millennia. From that empty tomb the voice of God still echoes through the annals of time because He, who was dead, has been raised up, vindicated, and now lives forever.[416]

2. The resurrection of Jesus is a good indication that when you live your life believing God and trusting His providence, when you are abused and mistreated, even unto death, He will vindicate you and take your life to greater levels. If the resurrection did not happen Jesus would still be in the grave. If the resurrection did not happen, evil, death, injustice, abuse, bigotry, and human inhumanity, would have the final word. But Jesus got up. He got up to give us the assurance of hope. In the midst of despair and hopelessness, the results of failed investments in human systems, the world needs to know that God is their hope. He is the lifter of the human spirit and hope for all who are cast down in sorrow with little or no expectation for brighter tomorrow. In a world where the lack of conscience causes some to be mistreated, the world needs to know that God is the vindicator for all those who have been mistreated. In a world where people are dying without hope, we need to proclaim the saving power of the resurrected Christ; our resurrection and life.[417] The power of life and death is under God's control. People in the world who have not yet come into the saving knowledge of Jesus, need to understand that past

---

[416] Rev 1:8, 18; 22:13
[417] Jn 11:25

sins can be forgiven and new life received through faith in Christ Jesus who died to redeem them and rose to give them the assurance of victory.

3. When you know, despite the negativity, the defeats, and the hopelessness around you, that you can have victory in the present time and hope for a better future, life and eternity become something to care about. In Rome, it is said that a tombstone was discovered with the inscription: "I was not, I was, I am no longer…I don't care." These uncertain and hopeless words echo the prevailing sentiments and unbelief of a world that lacks purpose beyond the here and now. The conviction of the world is this: "You are born, you live for a short time, you die; that is that and no one cares!" Interestingly, even with this warped view of life and the end of it, the notion of an afterlife remains a topic of conversation even among skeptics. The Sadducees denied the resurrection but even in their denial, they were still overwhelmed with lingering uncertainty and questions about it.[418]

4. If the resurrection is true, and we believe that it is, in a world filled with skeptics, many need to rethink their positions, reorder their lives, and make the changes that faith demands so that they too can become children of the resurrection. For that matter, we believe in the God who is God of the living and not of the dead.[419] Moses and Elijah for example, who had long been dead, are reported to have appeared with Jesus as witnessed by three disciples on the Mount of Transfiguration.[420] This is a strong affirmation that the God in whom we believe gives life and keeps alive for eternity those who invested their faith and time in Him. This God, the Creator of the universe, the Author and Giver of life, raised up Jesus Christ from the grave and has effectively shattered the crippling and debilitating hopelessness that once held the world in a vice grip of uncertainty and despair. It is in this God that we believe and in whom our hope of eternity is invested.

5. The New Testament has nowhere described the actual raising of Jesus from the grave. However, the empty tomb and subsequent appearances of Jesus became the basis for the unshakable conviction of the Early Church that

---

[418] Lk 20:27-33

[419] Lk 20:36-38

[420] Mt 17:3-4

God raised Jesus from the grave. While there are some that have debated whether the resurrection is history's most influential error or history's most tremendous fact, it is our belief and forgone conclusion that the resurrection is history's most tremendous fact.

6. In retrospect, Jesus did predict victory beyond the grave for Himself and His divine purpose. He had for example, spoken of the Son of Man becoming a sign like Jonah emerging from the belly of a whale, thus signifying His resurrection[421] In Luke 9:22 and 18:33, He says, [The Son of Man] will be scourged and killed and on the third day He will rise again. Jesus' prediction was designed, even at that point in His ministry, to give lively hope to those who followed Him. They did not however, realize the significance of His words until after the resurrection. Clearly, Jesus, knowing Himself to be the servant Messiah, expected God, the Father, to vindicate Him by raising Him up.

The Resurrection of Jesus
(Section Two)

1. Do you still have doubts about the resurrection of Christ? Come with me for a moment and consider this. When Jesus was crucified, His disciples hid themselves because of dismay, disappointment, and fear for their own lives. How then, did a group of frightened followers of a brutally crucified Master become the very center of a militant Church that has endured for over two thousand years? The Church has stood for all these years because the faith on which it is founded is grounded on the resurrected Christ who became the Rock upon which the Church is built.

2. Using five other supporting sources of evidence, let us further examine the resurrection of Jesus.

First, the tomb that contained the body of Jesus was found empty. The Gospels reported it; the Epistles not only implied it, but were also inspired by that fact.

---

[421] Mt 12:39-42

Second, some argue that the body of Christ was stolen. However, the silence of the Jews and the Romans strongly indicates that is not the case. The disciples were too scared to even venture near the tomb that was heavily guarded. It is also clear that the disciples did not take Jesus' body. If they did, they would not have been willing to give their own lives for a lie. The resurrection is an eternal truth from which the disciples did not deviate, a truth, which many of them sealed with their own deaths. Furthermore, if either the Jews or the Romans had removed the body, they would have produced it in order to discredit the Christians' claim and in order to silence the Church. They could not produce the body because they did not remove it.

Third, during the forty days between His resurrection and ascension, the Gospels testify to several of Jesus' appearances— to the women, to Peter, then to the twelve, to 500 people, to James, to all the apostles, and then later to Paul.[422]

Fourth, a man named Flavius Josephus, a Jewish historian and a Roman citizen, in 93 AD, published his work on the <u>Antiquities of the Jews</u>. This historical work included accounts of the works, death, and yes, the resurrection of Jesus.

Fifth, the birth, life, ministry, death, and resurrection of Jesus are fundamentally based on facts. While questions of authenticity will continue to arise particularly from skeptics and from interfaith discussions, one thing is sure; He who was dead is alive to the glory of God! Based on the historical evidence of the resurrection of Jesus, our faith is not based on fables or selective ghostly illusions. Our faith is based on substance and fact-based historical evidences, including the birth, life, ministry, death, and resurrection of Jesus Christ. As Hebrews 11:1 classically defines faith, faith is the substance of things hope for and the evidence of things not seen. Faith is based on substance and can therefore be substantiated. It is based on evidence and can therefore be supported. The "Substance" in this sense is God, that ultimate Reality that underlies all outward manifestations that give meaning to life. This Reality we call God, is the Substance in whom our faith is grounded. Evidences are a series of

---

[422] Without special emphasis on sequences, see for example Mt 28:9, 16-17; Mk 16:9; Lk 24:15-31; Jn 20:19, 24, 26-28, 21:1-24; Acts 1:2-6, 9:1-5; 1 Cor 15:5, 6-8

systematically outlined facts to support a case or a cause. The evidence of God's creation and the evidence of His involvement in our human situations are outlined in the Bible and grounded in the human existential condition and life experiences. Our own life experiences are testimonies to what God has done and what we have seen and heard and therefore believe. If evidences are a series of systematically outlined facts used to support a case or a position, here are some supporting facts concerning Jesus.

Fact: Christ was born in Bethlehem.

Fact: Christ was crucified and buried. The Gospels affirmed it, and Josephus wrote his historical witness to it.

Fact: The body of Jesus was laid in a tomb.

Fact: Measures were taken by both Jewish religious leaders and Roman authorities to keep the body of Jesus in the tomb. Those who conspired to crucify Jesus were insecure, paranoid, and fearful. So, a watch was ordered to be kept at the tomb for fear that the body would be stolen[423]

Fact: After His death and resurrection, Jesus showed Himself by many infallible proofs. His disciples touched Him, ate and drank with Him, and many others saw Him ascending to Heaven.[424]

3. Calvary seemed to have been an irreversible disaster and a hopeless ending. Christ who had been born in a borrowed manger, and rode to Jerusalem on a borrowed donkey, was finally crucified and buried in a borrowed tomb and it seemed like the end. But the stone was rolled away, and out of that empty tomb came the glorious song that still rings from here to eternity: "He is risen, Jesus Christ is risen today. **Hallelujah!**" During the crucifixion and subsequent death of Jesus, the disciples were bound by fear and transfixed by disappointment. But thank God, the news that Christ is risen and alive released that stranglehold of fear. With that release, came the freedom and the boldness to proclaim the Good News of the risen Lord and Savior. The resurrection of Jesus took the fear out of both life and death because Jesus is no longer a memory. By the power and present operation of the

---

[423] Mt 27:63-66
[424] Acts 1:9-11

Holy Spirit, Jesus is a living presence and our guarantee of life eternal.[425] Just when Good Friday seemed to have closed a door on life, just when the darkness of Calvary caused hope to no longer see a star, there came the voice of Jesus: "Be not afraid because I am alive; I am the resurrection and the life." Through the resurrection, the disciples were given the evidence,[426] a message to preach, and a second chance at hope to become "fishers of men" to the glory of God.

4. The resurrection, a fable, an illusion? I do not think so! So the question you may be asking at this juncture is: "If it was by His death that we are redeemed, why was it necessary for Jesus to be resurrected and appear to the disciples and others after His resurrection?" Without the resurrection, questions about death and the afterlife would still be unanswerable. The resurrection of Jesus answers those questions. It tells us "yes, God has authority over life and death." Without the resurrection, Christianity would be a sad and mournful religion. Because Jesus got up, Christianity is a celebratory relationship and a celebration of life and hope in an eternity that has been promised.

5. Also, by the resurrection of Christ and His subsequent appearances to the disciples, their fears were removed, their faith received assurance, and their ministry received power. The resurrection of Jesus was the resurrection of your hope and mine. Jesus died to save us and was raised to supply your life and mine with hope and purpose. Christianity provides a message of salvation deeply rooted in the conviction of a Savior who died and now lives. To assure the disciples that they were not having some sort of ghostly illusion and that what they were seeing was real, Jesus gave them a familiar greeting, "Peace be unto you" and asked for something to eat.[427] Ghosts do not eat. To further assure them that He was the real deal and not an illusion, He allowed them to touch Him and see the nail prints in His hands and feet. Jesus lives. I know that my Redeemer lives. He lives! I spoke with Him today! He lives! He hears me when I pray. He lives! He soothes me when I hurt and mends me when I am broken. Jesus lives! **Hallelujah!**

---

[425] 2 Cor 1:20-22; 5:5; Eph 1:9-14

[426] See for example Lk 24:37-43; Jn 11:25, 20: 27

[427] Lk 24:36, 41

6. The resurrection demonstrates once and for all, that it is God, not any human that is in control of life, time, and eternity. By His providential control of space and time, God continues to involve Himself in human history by the life and redeeming work of the resurrected Christ, and through the transforming presence and power of the Holy Spirit. Based on the promises of the One who died and is alive again, the world's notion of life, time, and human destiny as having no meaningful outcome beyond death, has been put to rest. Based on the historical evidences of the resurrection of Jesus Christ recorded not only by the four Gospels, the epistles as in the case of 1 Corinthians 15:6, but also recorded by the Roman historian Josephus, we need to proclaim to the world that human life and destiny do not revolve around humans' limited view of life and time, but around God who is the Master of time and eternity. It is only when our lives are lived for God and invested in Christ, that we can have real purpose in this life and enduring hope beyond the grave.

7. The dignity of God implanted in us is of eternal value my friend. The resurrection of Jesus affirmed that value. Christ died to redeem our eternal value and rose from the dead to seal that purchase and elevate our worth. In light of the resurrection of Jesus Christ, we do not believe that the final events of death will mean the end of our biographies. For, as the life of Christ began anew at the empty grave, so will the life and destiny of all who believe in Him, even those who have already died.[428] Considering the life-giving love of God, and based on the resurrection of Jesus Christ, we recognize that adverse circumstances, even death, are not periods or dead ends in the Christian's faith journey.

8. The resurrection affirms that death is not the end or the master of the believer's destiny. Through the overarching providence and life-giving love of God, adverse circumstances, even death, become allies of the human soul rather than enemies of it. The resurrection of Jesus Christ resoundingly announces that death is not the master and end-all for human existence. Death is only the porter at the King's lodge, appointed not to close, but rather, to open the gate and let the King's guests into the realm of eternal glory. God is KING and we are His guests; even better, we are God's sons and daughters,

---

[428] Mt 24:31; Jn 5:24; 1 Cor 15:52

heirs of His kingdom; made for eternity! Because death is not the end, we live today with the wonderful prospect of an eternal tomorrow. Indeed, the words of eternal life are entrusted to the eschatological Community of Faith, the Church. We need to urgently give the world these words of assurance and hope so that they, like us, may hear, believe, and find hope and life in Christ Jesus.

9. By the resurrection of Christ, a believing humanity is given a vision of life that does not end at death, but begins anew in a more glorious form of existence. Assuredly, through Christ, humans have hope, and with our response of faith to the presence and eternal reign and grace of God, we are no longer held hostage by the perceived rule of the kingdom of death.

10. In God, humanity has a future that goes beyond the fatalistic and meaningless ethos of the world. God, through the resurrection of Jesus Christ, has set us free from the limitations of the world's systems and false sense of completion. Contrary to the world's perception of a fatal and meaningless end, the resurrection of Jesus has shown once and for all that death is not the end; it is only a new beginning for those who believe in the Lord Jesus. The evidence of Christ who died and now lives, and our belief in that resurrected life are the foundations upon which our Christian faith and hope for eternity are built.

11. An empty tomb without the living Christ would have left the matter still open to debate and uncertainty. Even though the disciples and others went in and found the empty tomb where the body of Jesus was placed, it was not the empty tomb alone that gave credibility to their testimony. The empty tomb set their convictions in motion but the thing that gave power and credibility to the testimony of the disciples was their personal encounters with the resurrected Christ. As you search for Christ, you cannot truly experience the joy of the resurrection until you have had your personal encounter with the risen Lord. You are assured that Jesus was raised, not only by the historical evidence we are presented with, but also by your personal encounter with Him. You too can have assurance with your acceptance of Him as the Son of God who died to redeem your soul and who rose from the dead to give your life victory and hope. As the disciples ran in search of the risen Christ, found

Him, and surrendered to Him, I pray that all of us, yes, you too my dear reader, may be empowered by the Holy Spirit to run to Jesus, encounter Him in a personal way, and surrender to Him today in faith and obedience.

12. Based on the resurrection of Jesus, Christian eschatology, through the active witness of the Christian Community, needs to be an ongoing challenge to the dominant ethos of the secular world where hopelessness, despair, and death have been projected to have the last laugh. If indeed we are living and serving God in the present and seeking to faithfully participate in the life and ministry of Christ through service in the world, by the Holy Spirit working in us, we need to be actively engaged in reaching the world with the Good News that human existence surrendered to the Christ of the promise, has a "deathless and joyous meaning."[429] By our faithful affirmation that Christ died and now lives and shall come again, the world might be led by the Holy Spirit to believe that life does not end in hopeless darkness, but in the light of eternal hope for those who believe in the Lord Jesus. The final victory, therefore, belongs to God as we see in 1 Corinthians 15 where death is swallowed up in victory. By the resurrection of Jesus, death has been defanged and its power nullified.[430] That power, the kingdom, and the glory, belong to God and God alone![431] Death is dead and our hope is alive in the resurrected Christ who promised to come again!

(iii) The Promised Return of Jesus

1. The third reason for our continuous witness to the world and our projection of Jesus as hope for the human despair is based fundamentally on our convictions regarding the promised return of Jesus, as attested to by Scripture.[432] As believing Christians, rejuvenated by the assured promises of the Lord, our mission is to faithfully seek to direct people's attention from the cynical, the hopeless, and the disillusioned, to Jesus

---

[429] R. E. Coleman, Songs of Heaven (Fleming Revell, Co., 1980), 18
[430] 1 Cor 15:54-58
[431] Mt 6:13
[432] Ps 98:9; Mt 26:64; Mk 14:62; Lk 21:27-28; Acts 1:11; Heb 9:28; 2 Pet 3:10,13

Christ the hope of glory. Given the operation of the Holy Spirit upon our witness and given His application of divine constraints and influence on the human mind and heart, those to whom we witness may be empowered by grace to look with eyes of faith to see beyond the obvious and tangible so that they may embrace the Christ of the eschaton and lay claim to the intangible possibilities of eternity.

2. Based on the promised return of Jesus, as an eschatological community waiting for His return, we need to be diligent about the proclamation of that promise. As we wait we cannot afford to become complacent in our worship. We cannot relent in our witness to the world. Let us not lapse in our faith, faint in our mission, nor become derelict in our continuous service to a world that stands in need of an encounter with Christ. On our journey of faith, let us continue to be committed in our active demonstrations of saving faith in the resurrected Christ. Based on the promise of Christ to come again, let us by the power of the Holy Spirit working in us, become the Church triumphant, burning with flames of love, rekindled by the torches of peace and joy, set alight with the blazing inferno of justice, and glaring with holiness and righteousness, so that we may passionately proclaim with bold faith, the life transforming power of the resurrected Christ until His coming again.

3. Because of the promise and because of the integrity of the One who promised, the risen and exalted Christ, this eschatological expectation warrants us to active proclamation of the promise even at the expense of our own comfort and convenience. That promise challenges us to not retreat for our own self-preservation or in search of our personal piety or holiness. The promised return of Jesus commissions and engages us into Christ's continuous ministry of healing, atonement, and reconciliation in the world. As we continue to witness to the world and share the hope that we have in Christ, and as we faithfully continue to direct others to the kingdom of God, we may have to suffer ridicule and persecution. Like others before us, driven by the reality of the life, death, and resurrection of Jesus and inspired by His promise to come again, "we who live [for Jesus] are always delivered to death for Jesus' sake."[433] To us, God's servants and witnesses in the world, "it has

---

[433] 2 Cor 4:11

been granted...not only to believe in Him [Christ], but also to suffer for His sake."[434] But committed we must remain because the same One that promises to come again has also promised to be with us. We have the assurance that even though we walk through the valley of the shadow of death, we will fear no evil because the Lord is with us; His rod and His staff will bring us deliverance and comfort.[435] In Psalm 27:13 the Psalmist declares: "I would have despaired unless I had believed that I would see the goodness of the Lord In the land of the living." The promised return of Jesus is for us that radical stimulus for our ceaseless proclamation; the proclamation of His power to save and His obligation to come again to receive the faithful into His eternity.

4. Having sensed the calling of God on your life for active and participative witness in the world, are you willing to suffer inconveniences so that Christ may be preached and so that people may come to know the power of God? Are you willing to endure ridicule for the cause of the kingdom of God if necessary? If we can suffer long and not lose our focus of the goal before us, if we can suffer long and not lose our joy, suffer long and not lose our peace, and suffer long and not lose our praise, the grace and power of God in us will be our strength. Furthermore, because of the promise, notwithstanding the changes and inconveniences that we might experience in our proclamation of Christ, our destiny with Christ is eternally the same. In our witness to the world, we are confident that no matter what the obstacle, the hardship, or the challenge, God will preserve us. We were created with the fortitude of endurance, and we shall continue to be "strengthened with all might, according to His glorious power, for all patience and longsuffering with joy" until "He who has delivered us from darkness [conveys] us into the kingdom of the Son of love."[436] That is the hope of all believers.

5. Because of the promised return of Christ, we are persuaded that in Christ, the regenerated life has become a life of glorious hope. We have a glorious and living hope because God who is abundant in "mercy has begotten us again to a living hope through the resurrection of Jesus Christ from the

---

[434] Phil 1:29

[435] Ps 23

[436] Col 1:11-13; Rom 4:20

dead."[437] We are filled with hope because the Spirit of Him, who raised Jesus from the dead, lives in us and will also raise us up to eternal life, which is the fulfillment of eschatological promise. Because of God's precious Spirit in us, which is His seal of the promise, we have hope of the resurrection, hope of joint sonship and daughtership with Christ, and hope of final and ultimate redemption. It is this hope that enables us to face the future with complete confidence in Christ. We can face the future with confidence because the One in whom we believe is the One to whom we have entrusted our souls for safekeeping until that Great Day of His glorious return! Based on this promise, we are confident that God is leading us into triumph.[438] When that Day comes, we who have overcome shall march in a victory parade that begins to glorify God here and into the reaches of eternity. We believe the promises are true because He who has proclaimed the promise cannot lie. **Hallelujah!**

(iv) God Cannot Lie
(The Immutability of God)

1. The fourth basis on which to build our witness to the world is our conviction that God cannot lie. The basis for our affirmation concerning the promises of God is our conviction that the word of God is truth and that God cannot and will not lie. Listen to some of the evidences of scripture: "He is the Rock, His works are perfect, and all His ways are just. A faithful God who does no wrong, upright and just is He."[439] "O Sovereign LORD, you are God! Your words are trustworthy, and You have promised these good things to Your servant."[440] "Once I have sworn by My [name] holiness, says the Lord, I will not lie..."[441] Psalm 146:6 says that the Lord who made the heavens and the seas keeps truth forever.

---

[437] 1 Pet 1:3
[438] 2 Cor 2:14
[439] Deut 32:4
[440] 2 Sam 7:28
[441] Ps 89:35

2. We have hope of eternal life because God who cannot lie has promised it. His word is life. It is a sure thing. It is a guarantee. Because God cannot lie, we have strong consolation to lay hold of the hope that is set before us. This hope that we have has become an anchor for our souls because it is established by God who cannot lie. Because God does not change, His Promises stay the same. As 2 Peter 3:9 affirms, "...The Lord is not slack concerning His promise, as some count slackness, but is longsuffering toward us, not willing that any should perish, but that all should come to repentance." Because He is immutable, His love stays the same. Based on that truth, we have hope of entering His presence behind the veil[442] so that through Christ we may enter into the supernatural and the eternal. Eternity with God is a guaranteed investment that we can place our future in because the God who controls time and eternity has promised it.

3. God cannot lie; and by virtue of His immutability, He will not change His mind or go back on His word. His position never changes. "I Am the Lord,' says God, 'I do not change.'"[443] Because He is immutable, that is, unchanging, His word is forever true. God is immutable. We change but God never changes. Our circumstances change, but God remains the same. Change happens because time and history are always in motion. Seasons and circumstances change and humans struggle in their attempts to adjust and find meaning through their changing life situations. God does not change because perfection does not need to be adjusted or altered or reconstructed. God is perfection. God is immutable!

4. If God changes, He would not qualify to deal with the changes we go through and have to deal with in time and history. God qualifies to deal with and handle and guide us through the changes we are compelled to go through because of His immutability. Because He is immutable, when everything around us changes, it is good to have the only true God that remains eternally the same. No matter what our past looks like, no matter what the present brings, and no matter what the future holds, God is still God; His status never changes and His Word is forever true. What God says and promises to do, He

---

[442] Heb 6:19
[443] Mal 3:6

does. We are assured of this promise because we have considered the source. The Lord God Himself is the source and God cannot lie![444] All of the promises of God in Christ are "yes" and "amen" to the glory of God.[445] Because God cannot lie and because God is immutable, He is most qualified to direct the annals of time and history.

(v) History Is Not Accidental
(God Controls Time and History)

1. The fifth premise upon which our proclamation of a hopeful outcome for humanity is built is the premise that history is not accidental. History is not based on accidental outcomes but has always been part of God's grand scheme of things. Eschatologically, human existence and activity were always intended to be exercised and pursued in time and ultimately find their purpose in the triumph of good over evil. We are confident that God's kingdom will, in the final analysis, triumph purely by the sovereign power of God. Even though we live in time, we are not invested with the privilege to manipulate time and so determine the outcomes of history for ourselves. Such activity and prerogative belong to God because it is only in God that time, space, and eternity are ultimately consummated. I submit that when we act outside of God's time and purpose for our lives, we are operating in futility. God has purposed us for eternity. We must therefore allow Him to guide us through time and history into eternity.

2. Human history, time and space, as we know them, find their completion in God because He is the Author and Finisher of time and space. According to the promise given us before time, and sustained in us in time by the coming of Christ, we look with earnest expectation to that promise of a future glory, a new heaven and new earth.[446] Human existence, past, present, and future, are the results of divine purpose and the plan of God from before

---

[444] Num 23:19; Tit 1:2; Heb 6:18
[445] 2 Cor 1:20
[446] 2 Pet 3:13

the foundations of the world. Before the foundations of the world, God had His design on us for hope and completion in Him. Listen to the words of Ephesians 1: 11-14:

> "In Him we were also chosen, having been predestined according to the purpose of Him who works out all things according to the counsel of His will, in order that we, who were the first to put our hope in Christ, might be for the praise of His glory. And you also were included in Christ when you heard the message of truth, the gospel of your salvation. When you believed, you were marked in Him with a seal, the promised Holy Spirit, who is a deposit guaranteeing our inheritance until the redemption of those who are God's possession, to the praise of His glory."

This implies that when we are faced with the reality of our own weakness and hopelessness, we have assurance that God has a wonderful design for our glorious outcome by the counsel of His own will. Attention must be paid to the term counsel because it embodies deliberation on the part of God. Despite the human ills and evidences of evil, hopelessness, and despair in the world, by the counsel of His own will God is not planning, but has already planned, arranged, and established the purposeful outcomes of His will. God plans so that He might work. He is working so that He might bring us into the realization of hope in Christ Jesus. Here is the assurance: NOTHING in heaven or on earth can prevent the fulfillment of God's ultimate purpose in history. That is the source of our confident faith and hope in Christ in whom all things are made much clearer.

3. Because of the variableness or changing nature of time and history, without a constant and sovereign power to guide it, total and reckless abandon would ensue. God is in control of time and history because He was, before there was time. He created it for us to live in and is therefore the Master of it. However, though we live in time and are restricted by it, eternity is implanted in us[447] so that we can aspire for the glory that transcends time. God

---

[447] Ecc 3:11

is in control of time and eternity because there was never a time when He was not God. He did not become God. He is God. He was not appointed God. He is God. He was not elected God. He is God. No one else has to approve His plan. No one else has to be advised before He implements His will. No one else has to give permission because God is the Authority. He requires no other master's approval because He is the Master. The God that we glorify does not need permission to execute His divine will and purpose because He acts and works all things according to the counsel of His own will.[448] If He puts in place, or takes away, who can say to Him, "What are You doing?"[449]

4. The God that we glorify is of infinite duration who sits enthroned as sovereign King forever.[450] That means that God is in total control without limits and without boundaries. A finite or limited duration and power is therefore inconsistent with our understanding of God. The creature is finite and limited by history, time, and space. But the Creator, the God who alone is worthy of worship, is infinite and therefore endless in duration and unlimited in power. The God that we glorify has no beginning and therefore has no ending. From everlasting to everlasting, He is God. In the beginning, God, as presented in Genesis, could therefore be rendered, "God, in the beginning, made heaven and earth."[451] The implication here is that before there was a beginning, there was already God. There was when everything we now see was not.[452] But there was never a time when God did not exist. He is the Alpha and the Omega, the beginning and the ending. Not that He has beginning or ending in Himself, but that all things have their beginning and their ending in Him. When therefore we say that God is the beginning and the ending, we are simply saying that God is the beginning and the ending of all things. He is forever God Almighty to whom we ascribe worship, glory, and praise. **Hallelujah!**

---

[448] Eph 1:11; Heb 2:4, 6:17-18

[449] Job 9:12

[450] Ps 29:10

[451] Gen 1:1

[452] Since everything exists in time and not before, except in the mind of God, we cannot say there was a time when it did not exist.

5. Everything has its beginning and ending in God. Because everything has its beginning and ending in God, we find confidence in the knowledge that in time and history, even though in this life circumstances may create feelings of despair and hopelessness, inconveniences, sorrow, and pain, God is working out everything for our good. In God, who is eternal, and by virtue of the knowledge that He made us with eternal duration, we find meaning and value that endure in this life and extend to eternity. I submit that the true meaning of life is found in and determined only by the Power that rules and directs the outcomes of life— God!

6. Some may say that God does not control history because history is something that has already happened. However, before history happens, God was, is, and always will be existing and working! Because He is before events unfold in time and history, He sees and knows their outcomes. If, before time God exists, then it follows that when events happen in time God already has prior knowledge. God controls human history because He knows the outcomes of nations and kingdoms. The prophetic statements of scripture are testimonies that God knows everything from beginning to end. The accuracy of Bible prophecy is an astounding testimony of that realization. There is no other religious book that contains the exactness and accuracy of historical statements and predictions and therefore God's foreknowledge and control of their outcomes. The revelations of scripture concerning God's knowledge of outcomes which are often spoken through prophesy is God's way of letting us know that He is sovereign. It is also God's way of announcing to us that His perfect purpose will be accomplished despite the obstacles that arise before those to whom He has given the promise. Because God is in control, adverse circumstances cannot undermine His eternal purpose. That is a good reason to invest our hope in God.

7. As the providential and sovereign God, nothing escapes the Great CEO of heaven and earth. The word *sovereign* implies "super." It embodies the notion of superior and supreme, primary and paramount, unequaled and unexcelled. The God of the Bible is eternal and self-existent and therefore sovereign. He is supreme in excellence and perfect in all of His ways. He is the one and only Autonomist, self-contained and self-controlled, with the right

and power of self-government and adjudication. God is infinite in His imperial independence. His capacities and capabilities far surpass the scope of human reason, time, and history. Who then, is better qualified to see about us in the changing of time and history than God? There is none better! That is precisely why we have entrusted our souls to Him for safekeeping (2 Tim 1:12).

8. And so you may ask, "How do we reconcile God's existence and sovereignty with human suffering in time and history?" "How does someone reconcile God's sovereignty with human suffering and affliction?" "How does a Christian subscribe to the sovereignty of a loving, kind and compassionate God when someone she/he knows and loves is burdened by the circumstances of life and lays helpless and suffering before her/him?" Multitudes have suffered and died, and multitudes continue to suffer, without knowing the reason why. I think the more appropriate question would be: "If we remove God from the equation would there still be evil and suffering in the world?" Assuredly, there would still be evil and suffering. Therefore the existence of evil and suffering does not mean there is no God or that God is not good. The very notion that you question the existence of God based on the existence of evil, suggests that you believe in the existence of God and His goodness. After all, your thoughts, which seem to conflict with the existence of evil are reflective of a deeper moral guide for that goodness, which in you, is opposed to evil.

9. I am sure you believe in the existence of attributes such as courage, generosity, beneficence, justice, forgiveness, mercy, even truth. So, then, I ask you, "If there were no suffering or evil in the unfolding of human history, would we have instances or need for courage, generosity, beneficence, justice, forgiveness, mercy, and even truth?" I think not! Ultimately then, good exists, therefore God exists. The existence of evil presents you and me and certainly God, the opportunity to act with goodness, love, courage, generosity, beneficence, justice, mercy, forgiveness, grace, and compassion. Our disgust with evil and suffering is our longing for these virtues that emanate from God. Our longing for these virtues is essentially our longing for God. Evil compels us then to look to the goodness of God so that we may find reason, answers, and perspective from this moral compass, God! He is the Author

and Executer of human excellence and moral compass. Furthermore, while God may not prevent all of human distresses, He gives us grace to endure and ultimately rise above them.

10. In the midst of evil and human suffering, I do know that God gives grace for those times when our spirit is hurting and we are driven to the breaking point. The Lord gives strength to his people and blesses His people with peace that surpasses understanding.[453] The Bible says, "There is no temptation that comes to us, that is not common to every human. But our assurance is that despite the temptation and sufferings, God is faithful, and will not cause us to suffer or [be] tempted above what we are able to bear. But with the temptation and the suffering, He will also make a way of escape that we might be able to bear it" (1 Corinthians 10:13). This is God's promise that He will place a limit upon the severity of the trial and that He will give us sufficient strength to bear up under it. When life seems to be too much for you to bear, cast you cares upon God. He is your burden bearer.

11. When evil overwhelms us and when trials come, it helps to see them in relation to God's will. It is not God's will that you should suffer evil of any kind. It is God's will to deliver you from evil.[454] It is not God's will for you to have problems and burdens. When they do arise, it is God's will to help you solve and bear them.[455] It is not God's will for you to have tribulations in whatever forms they may come. It is God's will to deliver you in the midst of your tribulation.[456] Because it is God's will to turn your bad situations into good outcomes, when problems and trials and tribulations come into your life, never perceive them to be God's fault. Know instead, that God is already in your life and even though trouble may come to you, sooner rather than later the problems and the trials and tribulations will end. Trouble often comes to us but because of the grace and mercy of God in and around us, we have discovered that trouble does not last forever.

---

[453] Ps 29:11; Phil 4:7

[454] Lk 11:4

[455] Ps 55:22; Mt 11:29-30; Heb 4:15-16; 1 Pet 5:7

[456] Ps 34:18-20

12. When I am in hardship and when I experience suffering, and the occasions have been many, they have never been occasions or opportunities for me to turn away from God. Rather, they have become opportunities for me to seek after God. I seek after God despite the troubles in my life because I know that no matter what, God loves me. The Bible says you should draw near to God and He will draw near to you (James 4:8). I do not believe that God ceases to be God just because the circumstances in our lives have changed and are challenging us. I believe that He is still God, that He will give us the grace to manage, and ultimately empower us to overcome and rise above the circumstances, trials, and suffering in our lives. Though we are vulnerable and daily exposed to evil and suffering, God in time and history gives us a vision of our destiny in Him so that we have something to strive after and hope for when life with its worries and sufferings seems to be weighing us down. When we have a vision of the outcome and believe in it, the process of getting there, though sometimes slow, painful, and filled with despair, becomes more tolerable. The apostle Paul puts it this way:

> "I consider that the sufferings of this present time are not worthy to be compared with the glory which shall be revealed in us. For the earnest expectation of the creation eagerly waits for the revealing of the children of God...For we were saved in this hope, but hope that is seen is not hope; for why does one hope for what is already seen? But if we hope for what we do not see, we eagerly wait for it with perseverance."[457]

We believe, according to Scripture, that even though we might experience suffering, "the God of all grace, who called us to His eternal glory by Christ Jesus, after [we] have suffered a while, [will] perfect, establish, strengthen, and settle [us]' (1 Peter 5:10). Because of the hope we have in the promised return of Christ and a glorious future with Him, "we also glory

---

[457] Rom 8:18-19, 24-25

in tribulations, because tribulation produces perseverance and perseverance produces character, and character hope. And, thank God, hope does not disappoint."[458]

13. Our confidence as an eschatological community soars because the Holy Spirit has lavished our hearts and minds and faith with the truth of God's word and evidence of God's love for all of us through Christ. There is no fear in love.[459] Despite the obstacles and the distractions that we may encounter in time and history, as we continue to worship God and witness to the saving power of Christ on this side of time, we forge ahead because the present calamities are not to be compared to the glory that shall be revealed to us in eternity.[460] This does not by any means underscore the intense hardships and sicknesses to which we may become vulnerable. Despite that reality, we are the more convinced that nothing shall separate us from the love of God in Christ Jesus.[461] With the anticipation of God's new and glorious future, our souls are given unshakable assurance because Christ has placed us in the secure hand of God and has already given us the guarantee of eternity.[462]

14. By virtue of the present operation of the Holy Spirit in our lives and community, we are equipped to remain firm in our purpose and diligent in our witness to the world despite the changing circumstances around us. We are further confident in the knowledge that we have God as our rearguard and vanguard. He is acquainted with our past; He is involved with our present; and He has already established our guaranteed future. Though we are daily tempted and often distracted from the goal before us, because of the Holy Spirit indwelling us, we remain firm in our convictions and resolute in our witness to the world. Let us with determination stay the course because the Gospel of Christ, the mission, and the kingdom of God are altogether bigger than the misfortunes and the sufferings and the

---

[458] Rom 5:1-5

[459] Jn 3:16, 14:23; Rom 5:5; 1 Jn 4:18-19

[460] Rom 8:18-19

[461] Rom 8:35, 37-39

[462] Jn 10:28-29

obstacles we may encounter in this life. Because God is with us on our faith journey, and because we have a glimpse of glory by the operations and manifestations of the Holy Spirit, we get up when circumstances knock us down. Sure, we may look like fools getting up every time circumstances knock us down, but we would much rather be considered fools for Christ now[463] and receive eternity with Him, than to settle for the fleeting wisdom and follies of the world.

15. As we continue to witness to the power of God in the world, notwithstanding the opposition we may face, and despite our human sufferings and frailties, we should not fear what mankind can do.[464] We are confident that God is able to undo the suffering inflicted on us and do us one better, by raising us up and setting us on our way upward and into His eternal glory. **Hallelujah!** As we continue to witness for Christ and demonstrate the goodness of God in the world, let us do so unwaveringly. Let us be vigilant because we have the expressed backing of the sovereign God, the mediation of Christ, and the ever-present operation of the Holy Spirit who are actively engaged with us on every step of our faith journey. Since we have the backing of the Father, Son, and Holy Spirit, we are further convinced that if God is for us, no one and nothing can successfully rise against us.[465]

16. The one power, the one presence, the one constant, the one great order of the universe, is God. Eschatology as the theology of hope in a purposeful and eternal future that transcends time and history is echoed in the words of Coleman who asserts:

> "[Our] paeans of praise provide a celestial background to history that amid the dissolution of human institutions, abides the unchanging reality of an eternal world in which God's purpose is unfailing and in which His Christ is victorious."[466]

---

[463] 1 Cor 4:10
[464] Heb 13:6; Ps 27, 46: 2, 49:5, 91:5, 118:6; Lk 1:74; 2 Tim 1:7; 1 Jn 4:18
[465] Rom 8:31
[466] Coleman, *Songs of,* 17

Therefore, as we wait for the return of Christ, and "since we have confidence to enter the Most Holy Place by the blood of Jesus, by a new and living way opened to us...let us hold unswervingly to the hope that we profess, for He who has promised it is faithful."[467]

9. What Do We Do While We Wait?

1. As we wait for the return of Christ, it is imperative that we continue to worship and practice discipleship. Our anticipation of the return of Christ should renew our desire for worship as well as instill within us the urgency to actively witness to the world. Inasmuch as the life and ministry, death and resurrection, ascension and promised return of Christ have impacted our entire life and faith by the hope that they instill, we need to continue worshipping and serving God in the world with a deep sense of commitment and urgency. The task of spreading hope is ours to do because we have experienced the glorious benefits of it. Even though we are filled with hope, and even though we are guaranteed eternity with God, we cannot be passive observers of the events of time. As we wait for eternity, in time, we must continue to be active witnesses for Christ in the world.

2. The very belief in Christ's returning necessitates us working to sustain the change in the new order that He has already established. Our faith concerning Christ places us under a new order that has cancelled the old. In the old order, self-importance, human systems, opinions, philosophies, theoretical probabilities, presumed power to influence outcomes based on intellectual and technological prowess, social status, economic and political power, tended or pretended to be capable of defining human values, relationships, and outcomes. In the new order, Christ, not a system, Christ, not a philosophy, reigns. In the new order, service, humility, love for God and neighbor, and holy dependence on God define the redeemed people of God. Our task as the redeemed of God is to continue the proclamation of Christ to

---
[467] Heb 10:19, 20, 23

the world so that those who have not heard may hear, and in faith and humility come to the Lord Jesus so that He may elevate all of us above the limitations of time and history.[468]

3. If indeed we believe that something is wrong with the world around us, as the redeemed of God, we should also believe that we have been mandated to fix it. The task is ours to transform the world by the power of the Holy Spirit in us by intentionally making disciples for Christ and, on the authority of the word of God, proceed to preach and live with conviction and decency in the world. As the redeemed people of God, we are called and sent to be faithful participants with Christ in His mission to bring all persons into a believing community of love. If we believe that something is wrong with the world, as God's change agents, our mission should be taking place in the world and not within the restricted and secure walls of our sanctuaries.

4. It was in the world that God sent His only begotten Son to redeem it.[469] It was in the world that Christ sent His disciples to transform it.[470] It is in the world that intentional ministry and mission ought to take place. We believe that where sin abounds, grace much more abounds. We also believe that God's love, in the final analysis, will triumph over hate, His justice over injustice, and His freedom over bondage. If, then, we so believe, we ought to take our message to the world so that we might fulfill our responsibility of pointing the world to Christ. If we believe that there is something wrong with the world, and there is, then we do not have the luxury, the right, or the privilege to lock ourselves away in our private and secure holy cocoons as we passively wait for the divine drama to play itself out without us getting involved.

5. Our redemption comes with the responsibility of seeking out others as we engage ourselves in Christ's ongoing ministry of reconciliation. God has called and anointed us to participate in His divine drama of bringing about change in the world by preaching and living scriptural holiness,

---

[468] Jas 4:10
[469] Jn 3:16
[470] Mk 16:15; Jn 15:16; Acts 1:8; Col 1:6

changing social structures, influencing the human heart by the way we conduct ourselves in the world, and elevating the human condition by exercising justice, demonstrating mercy, and exemplifying humility. As a transformed people, living, as it were, in an eschatological community, the very essence of eschatology ought to ignite in us the desire to reach out in love, service, and witness to others. That way, the "whosoever will" for whom Christ also died, may be transformed and repositioned for eternity.

    6. If our purpose in the world is to make Christ known, then the methodology for doing so needs to be our outreaching love and service. Because of the complexity of the human condition, and because there are no aspects of humanity to which God does not speak with infinite wisdom and redeeming grace and power, our continued witness demands all the natural and spiritual means available to us. As a measure of our commitment to make Christ known in the world, the questions that each of us needs to ask are: "To what extent am I living for, thinking of, speaking about, and giving of my resources, gifts and graces to the cause of the kingdom of God? Am I living in and doing the will of God? AM I daily seeking to carry out His purpose, and praying for others so that Christ may be seen and heard and believed and known in the world?" To what extent have I exercised justice, show mercy, and extended kindness and compassion to others? It is only when we reach out to the world with love and compassion and all the spiritual and natural means available to us that we truly bear witness to our faith and the social principles of the Gospel.[471]

    7. As we prayerfully wait for the return of Christ, let us dedicate ourselves to living out the meaning of hope through active service and witness in the world. Let us remember that by the grace of God, we are liberated to praise God through service to our sisters and brothers, the churched and the unchurched, so that all peoples and nations, by the grace of God and faith in the Lord Jesus, may be redeemed. I think Migliore says it best when he writes:

---

[471] Mt 25:31-46 and Mt 28:19-20

"Christians learn the meaning of hope in the grace of God only in the practice of discipleship. That practice includes proclaiming the gospel and sharing with others the forgiveness, peace reconciliation, liberation, and hope that are the gifts of God.... As the church waits and prays, it also acts. Christian hope does not immobilize people but makes them eager to get to work. It is not escapist hope but creative hope. It encourages anticipatory realizations of God's new world of justice and peace."[472]

Rise up, then; rise up you redeemed and mighty sons and daughters of God and witness to the love of God in the world!

---

[472] Daniel L. Migliore, Faith Seeking Understanding: An Introduction to Christian Theology. (Grand Rapids, MI: William B. Eerdmans Publishing Company, 1991), 249

Chapter Eight

Motivated And Transformed By Love

Prayer:
Dearest and most loving God, we give You thanks for the great love that You have given us through our Lord Jesus. We confess that we have not loved You with our whole heart. We have failed to love our neighbors and we have been slow in responding to the cry of the needy. Forgive us we pray and renew in us Your Spirit of love so that by Your indwelling Spirit, we may be moved to respond to You and others with love. Move us to joyful obedience we pray. As we set out to serve others today, inspire us by Your Holy Spirit to do so with an attitude of love. This we pray in the wonderful name of Jesus, Amen!

Suggested Hymns:
"Come, Thou Fount Of Every Blessing"
"I Love To Tell The Story"
"Love Lifted Me"
"Love So Amazing"
"Love Divine All Love Excelling"
"My God, I Love Thee"

"Take My Life And Let It Be"
"O How I Love Jesus"
"And Can It Be That I Should Gain?"
"Jesus Loves Me"

Scriptures: Lev 19:18; Ps 91:14; Mt 5:44-46; Prov 10:12; Mic 6:8; 1 Cor 13; Rom 12:9, 13:8; 1 Tim 4:12; Heb 13:1; 1 Jn 4:7-21

1. Love As The Divine Economy of God

1. Love is the divine economy of God that permeates everything that God does for us. Generally speaking, an economy is a plan put in place to carry out a certain distribution and management of a specific purpose. Divine economy has to do with God's plan, handling, management, and dispensation of His gifts and graces (Ephesians 3: 2). The divine economy of God should therefore be understood as God's management or method used for governing the world and His arrangement for rescuing or redeeming and sustaining fallen humanity. God's arrangement to rescue fallen humanity is also well known as God's plan of salvation carried out by His only begotten Son Jesus, by His sacrificial offering of Himself on the cross at Calvary.

2. Love as a divine economy or method is the impetus that God uses to manage and disperse His favor toward us. In human terms, God is like an immensely wealthy King who desires to dispense His unsearchable riches (Ephesians 3:8) to the citizens of His kingdom. To accomplish this enormous task, the King, God, must put in place a plan, an arrangement— an economy. So, then, God's plan for salvation and redemption through the Lord Jesus is part of God's divine economy. God's sustaining of us through the presence and sanctifying work of the Holy Spirit is part of God's economy. God working in and through us to transform us and ready us for eternity is part of God's divine economy. God loving us, blessing and prospering us and distributing His grace to us is part of God's economy. All that God does is motivated by love. Love is therefore the divine economy of God.

3. God's sustained presence and self-revelation through His creative, redemptive, and sanctifying work are the results of God's overflowing love for us. What God does for us is the result of His love directed toward us. The mercy, the grace and favor, the forgiveness, the regeneration, the sanctification, God's justification and blessing of us are all born out of God's love for us. Love motivates everything that God is and does. Love balances the wrath of God against sin and makes Him a merciful, just, loving and forgiving God

toward the sinner. God is love! That means that God does not love us any less than He loves His beloved Son Jesus Christ; nor does He love Him more than He loves us. John 3:16 states, "For God so loved the world that He gave His only begotten Son so that whoever believes in Him should not perish but have everlasting life." God's persistent love and grace toward us in worship, in mission, and during our period of eschatological preparation and waiting, is the result of God's outpouring love.

4. In creation, God began His mission of love toward us. It was through creation that God's grace and loving outpouring of Himself to us began. God's act of grace, which we have affirmed to have begun in creation, is at the same time an overflow of His love being extended toward us. God's integrity and dignity were imparted to us when He formed us into His own likeness and image. God must have loved us in order to be motivated to form us into His own image. Since God is love, God creating us through love and by love, also implies that God conferred Himself on us and therefore furnished us with the capacity to give of ourselves to others in love as He has given of Himself to us. The grace and love of God, reaching out from creation, began with the purpose of redemption and sanctification and will ultimately lead to our final consummation in His eternity

5. Love is therefore the telos, the goal, the end result, the completion, and the fulfillment of all that God is and all that He does to us and for us. In time, God's love is the sole end of every dispensation of God towards humanity. In eternity, it is the ultimate outpouring of the glory of heaven on His redeemed and sanctified people. Love therefore creates and will ultimately consummate or bring the entire cosmos back into union with its Creator, God. Love creates the universe; love redeems it, and love, God's love, will ultimately gather redeemed humanity around God's throne. So that, whereas hope, faith, and love abide, the greatest gift of all is love.[473] Love is the greatest gift of all because love is God's gift of Himself to us.

---

[473] 1 Cor 13:13

2. Our Response to the Love of God

1. Our response to God should always be one of love. It is God who first loved us. Love did not originate with humans. Love has always been from God first. We love and know how to love God and neighbor because we learned from God who first loved us.[474] The first activity of love has always been a Godward-humanward activity. Our humanward-Godward act of love is and will always be a response to a Godward movement that began with God who lovingly poured out and gave of Himself to us in creation and by the sacrificial atonement of Christ. We worship God because He is God and we love Him. We witness to His power in the world because we have been transformed to love Him and share His love with the world that He loves, and for whom He has already provided the means of salvation through the self-giving sacrifice of Jesus on the cross. We wait for the fulfillment of His eternal promise because we desire to be eternally in the presence of the One who loves us.

2. As we continue to worship God, our worship response should always be one of self-giving love. From a humanward to a Godward direction, our worship in response to God is only true or sincere if it is offered up by our self-giving love that mirrors the self-giving love which God has already extended to us through His gift of Jesus Christ. Any encounter with God, whether in worship, mission, or through our eschatological living, needs to be translated and understood in terms of our faithful response to the love of God. Our faithful participation in the means of faith, worship, mission, and eschatology, is the result of God's love bearing fruit in and through us. When our participation in the means of faith is a response of our love to God's love, Christian worship and mission are safeguarded from degenerating into what Shafer calls some "kind of ecclesiastical etiquette" or mere "forms and formality."[475] It is never enough to just go through the formalities of worship. God wants us to invest our quality time, our hearts, our minds, and spirits

---

[474] 1 Jn 4:19
[475] Shafer, 1

into loving and worshipping Him. After all, God invested all of Himself to us in the person of Jesus.

3. Our loving response to the love that God has already given to us should never be based on our desire to get more from God. It is not a reward for which we strive in worship, mission, or our eschatological lifestyle. Reward is the compensation for work done. Eternal life is not a reward of works, but an inherited promise given by God because He loves us. So, then, while eschatologically, we anticipate "God [changing] into greater good all the evil things [we] have suffered"[476] we serve Him because love constrains us to give of ourselves to the One who gave Himself to us. It was love that sent Christ and it will be love that compels God to "receive His own people from toil into repose, from affliction into a prosperous and desirable state, from sorrow into joy, from poverty into affluence, from disgrace into glory."[477]

4. Everything that we are and hope to become is based on the knowledge that God loves us. We are assured that the Lord will deliver us from every evil work and preserve us for His heavenly kingdom because He loves us.[478] Furthermore, we know the One in whom we believe and based on His promises, and His love demonstrated toward us through Christ Jesus, even though we suffer great things in this life, we are confident that His love for us will cause Him to keep what we have entrusted to Him.[479]

5. The centrality of love in the Christian's scheme of things is critical for our understanding of all that we do in response to God. Our worship, participation in mission, our transformed life, and our eschatological expectations, are indicative of God's love for us and the results of our responsive love for God. Our love for God, demonstrated through devotion and sincere commitment to worship and mission, and for our neighbor through love and mercy, is the foundation upon which the Christian's lofty ideal is built. This lofty ideal is a biblical formulation that becomes evident by the transformed life that is dedicated to loving God and neighbor. Because of the transforming power

---

[476] Calvin, Institutes, v. xx, 825
[477] Calvin, Institutes, v. xx, 825
[478] 2 Tim 4:18; 2 Tim 2:1-13
[479] 2 Tim 1:12

and value of love, Jesus has challenged us to love God and neighbor to the fullest extent of love, with all of our heart, mind, spirit, soul, and strength.[480] As Christians, we worship, serve, and act toward God and neighbor in the spirit of reverence and respect because we love God. From a biblical perspective, then, the ethical ideal that guides the Christian's motive in life and service is our active engagement in love for God and neighbor.

3. Practicing Love for God and Neighbor

1. Love for God and neighbor is a gift of grace. The Holy Spirit, having transformed us, also brings about adjustments in our attitude and behavior so that we may develop the propensity or tap into our predisposition to respond to God with love. If loving God and our neighbor means having the mind of Christ who, because of His love for the Father, obeyed Him even to death, and through love for us, gave His life, we cannot say we love God and continue to disregard and hate our neighbors, our brothers and sisters in Christ whom God loves.

2. To love God and not love our neighbor makes us half a Christian. As partial obedience is total disobedience, partial love is equally unacceptable. Loving God requires us to love our neighbor and faithfully give of ourselves— body, heart, mind, and spirit— to God, not in part but completely. We cannot affirm our vertical relationship with God while disavowing our horizontal relationships with our neighbor. We cannot claim to have been reborn and spiritually transformed if we do not demonstrate the fruits or evidences of our transformation— love, peace, mercy, patience, empathy, compassion, forgiveness, and common human decency— in our dealings with our neighbor. In order for us to both embrace and manifest a totally transformed life in Christ, we need to love both God and neighbor.[481] God redeems and sets us free from the constraints of self so that we

---

[480] Lev 19:18; Deu 6:5; Mt 22:37-40

[481] 1 Jn 4:20-21

may be free enough to embrace community and so love and serve Him as well as our neighbors. The perfect love of God operating in us is therefore the love that casts out fear,[482] sweeps away our tendency toward selfishness, and subdues the human inclination toward hatefulness, revenge, and resentment. We cannot effectively and faithfully function in the kingdom of God without love for God and neighbor. In order to fulfil our responsibility to love God and neighbor, such love needs to be grounded in the unconditional love of God.

3. Love fulfills three functions in the Christian's life. The first function that love accomplishes in us is to invoke and stir up actions that become visible manifestations of the presence of God in us.[483] This means that our demonstration of love toward others becomes the means by which the invisible God is seen in us and through us. Though God is invisible,[484] we reflect His loving nature in the world by the Christian lifestyle that we live in the world. The degree of the human affinity towards God is profoundly dependent on the extent of our love and devotion for God. How we respond to God and neighbor is therefore dependent on how we feel about God. How we feel about God also influences the way we feel about our neighbor. We cannot feel good about God and not feel good about our neighbor whom God loves.

The second function that love brings to completion in the Christian's life is to perfect or develop our affinity toward God. When we learn to love God and neighbor we are demonstrating our advancement in grace, which is God's love being perfected in us. The more we practice love towards others, the more the love of God grows and is therefore perfected or come to maturity in us. The more God's love comes to maturity in us, the more we become like God. Our becoming more and more like God means that the love of God is being ripened or made mature, or perfected in us. It is that love of God in us that empowers us to grow in Christ. Love then, shows that God is in us and that we are coming into maturity in Christ.

---

[482] 1 Jn 4:18
[483] 1 Jn 4:7-11
[484] Rom 1:20; Col 1:15; 1 Tim 1:17; Heb 11:27

The third function that love fulfills in us is to inspire us to become witnesses to the redeeming power of Christ in the world. As it was love that sent Christ, and as it was love that took Him to the cross, love ought rightly to move us to embrace God, believe in His Christ, and become lively witnesses to the loving-kindness of God in the world. Love for God obligates us to reach out to others so that they too can come into the knowledge and love of God in Christ Jesus.

4. As beneficiaries of divine grace, administered to us through the love of God in Christ Jesus, we do have a moral and ethical obligation to God and to each other. This moral obligation is first our spontaneous love response to the love of God. Second, it is the working out of our faith through love. And third, it is the evidence that we are morally aligned with the Object of our faith and the holy standard of our morality, God. Altogether, love for God and neighbor indicates that we have been changed, and are growing in grace.

4. Love as the Evidence that We Have Been Changed

1. When the life that we live becomes a manifestation of love in the world, it also becomes demonstrative evidence that we have been changed. This change or transformation that has come over us is the result of our encounter with God and the transforming work of the Holy Spirit who engrafts us in Christ. As 1 John 4:12 indicates, the evidence that we have been changed to be like Christ, and that we are in union with God, is love.[485] To love is Christian, and the Christian's life is a transformed life that has been changed to reach up to God and reach out to the world with love.

2. The love of God in us must therefore be manifested in deeds of kindness wrapped up in a life-style that reflects the abiding presence and perfect love of God. That way, as we wait in anticipation of the return of Christ Jesus, when we give to others of our worldly goods and show compassion

---

[485] Jn 17:21-24; 1 Jn 4:13; Col 3:14

to those in need, we are not just speaking of love; in practical terms, we are demonstrating the love of God in us. Because of the persistent presence of God in the Christian's life, love impacts and permeates our will, affections, and intellect. Love influences our behavior, shapes our lives and relationship with God, while all the time shaping us into kingdom citizens and positioning us to eternally live in the kingdom of God. We were made for eternity!

Chapter Nine

One Final Question: Do You Know Jesus?

Prayer:
GOD OF WISDOM and power, You gave us Your Son Jesus Christ because of Your great love for us. Open our eyes to the reality of Christ so that we may come to know, confess, and by faith in Your amazing grace, accept Him as Lord and Savior to the glory of Your name. We pray that You grant us a deeper knowledge of Jesus and fill our hearts with love that we may obtain the freedom and the joy to proclaim Christ in the world so that others can come to know Him and be saved. This we pray in the redeeming name of Jesus, Amen!

Selected Scriptures: Jn 8:19; Phil 3:10; 2 Tim 1:12, 2:25; 1 John 2:3-4

Hymns:
    "Jesus, Savior, Pilot Me"
    "Jesus Is All The World To Me"
    "I Know Whom I Have Believed"
    "Rejoice, The Lord Is King"
    "To God Be The Glory"

"**Hallelujah**! What A Savior"
"At The Name Of Jesus"
"His Name Is Wonderful"
"Hope Of The World"
"Who Is He In Yonder Stall"

1. ON KNOWING JESUS (SECTION ONE)

1. At a critical point in the life and ministry of Jesus, He was moved by the need to examine His disciples concerning their knowledge and understanding of Him. According to scripture, Jesus and His disciples stopped in a garden near Caesarea Philippi, so that they might relax and rest for a while (Mathew 16: 13-15). As they were relaxing, Jesus proceeded to ask His disciples a very important question: "Who do men (people) say that I, the Son of Man, am?" The disciples replied, "Some say John the Baptist. Some say Elijah. And others say Jeremiah or one of the other prophets." Their replies indicated that Jesus attracted multiple descriptions and comparisons to well know personalities. Popular opinions of the day sought to identify Him with one of the national heroes of the past, Elijah. Faced with the acclamation of public opinion, Jesus changed His question from "Who do men (people) say that I am" to "But who do *you* say that I am?" With the first question, Jesus asked what the secular world thought of Him. With the second, He asked the disciples what they thought of Him. Every now and then it is important to know what the people you associate with think of you. Every now and then, you need to know what those who sit and eat and drink with you, actually think of you. Jesus needed to know what His close friends and traveling companions thought of Him because it was necessary for their faith and salvation.

2. What we have here is a very important juncture in the teaching ministry of Jesus and a turning point in the life and faith development of the disciples. All of the prior teachings and mighty works of Jesus were designed as a build up to this inevitable moment in His ministry as well as in the life, faith, and training of the disciples. The disciples had been sitting in class, so to speak, observing all that Jesus said and did in the world for almost three years. For those three years, Jesus carefully taught, affirmed, reaffirmed, and demonstrated through one miracle after another, who He was, and still is. Now, after three years of full-time lessons based on prayer, teachings about God, love for God and humanity, and after practical involvement through social

action and service, withdrawals for spiritual retreats, and round table tutorials with Jesus, the disciples were faced with a final one question examination: "Who do you say that I am?" Jesus was not looking to extract their opinions. Jesus wanted to know what they believed about Him. Peter, as a result of his keen observation and the divine inspiration of God the Father, aced the test with his answer which, essentially, is a confession that echoed from heaven into the reaches of eternity: "You are the Christ, the Son of the living God."[486]

3. Jesus affirmed the absolute spiritual correctness of Peter's confession when He said in Matthew 16:17: "Blessed are you Simon Bar-Jonah, for flesh and blood has not revealed that to you, but My Father who is in heaven." Peter, having been persuaded by the modeled life and ministry that Jesus exemplified, and by the miracles performed by Jesus, now under divine inspiration and compulsion, voluntarily confessed Jesus to be the Son of the Living God. Upon the confession of Peter concerning the nature and person of Christ, everything changed. On the basis of that confession, Peter and the rest of the disciples were truly drawn into a saving knowledge and relationship with Christ. At that moment in time, Jesus was no longer just their hangout buddy and instructor in the ways of God. Jesus became their Savior, Master, and Lord.

4. "Who do people say that I am?" There were and still are many popular opinions about the person of Christ. Popular opinion declared Jesus to be John the Baptist come back to life. Others saw him as Elijah whom God was to send again before the terrible day of the Lord. Some saw Him as Jeremiah or one of the prophets. Perhaps they saw in Jesus something of the character and zeal in the message of John the Baptist. Perhaps they saw in Jesus the fire and intensity of Elijah, or perhaps they saw in Jesus the tears and grief of Jeremiah who cried over the sins of his people. Regardless, their personal assessment, adulation, admiration, and proclamation concerning the person of Christ still fell short. They fell short because they did not recognize and confess Him as the Son of God, the Lamb of God that takes away the sins of the world. They could not deny His supernatural power, but they failed to confess and through faith accept Him as their Savior and Lord. The world

---

[486] Mt 16:16

will not go to hell because it does not have a Savior, but because it refuses to accept and believe the Savior, Jesus Christ.

5. Many religious groups have different views as they relate to the person and nature of Christ. Christian Scientists conclude that Jesus was an outstanding man and a great teacher but was not the Son of God. Jehovah's Witnesses resolve that Jesus was not the Son of God but a created being that returned to earth invisibly in some point in time and now rules earth from heaven. Islam is content with believing that Jesus Christ was an ordinary man but a good prophet. Judaism concurs that Jesus was a great teacher/Rabbi but He was not the Messiah. The Buddhist believes that Jesus was a great teacher but not as great as Buddha. Hindus claim that Jesus was no more divine than any other man and that He did not die for the sins of the world.

6. Jesus is more than the sum adulation of these religions' points of view. He is Lord and Savior. It is He that was dead and is now alive to the glory of God. I submit to you, that if you examine the tomb of Mohammed, you will find his skeletal remains there. If you exhume the coffin of Buddha you will find his skeletal remains there. If you unearth Krishna's coffin you will find physical evidence of his remains there. But if you comb through the place where they laid Jesus, the crucified Son of God, you will find that the grave is empty."[487]

7. The grave is empty because Jesus got up. Mohammed did not get up! Confucius did not get up! Buddha did not get up! Joseph Smith is still dead. Jim Jones is still dead. David Koresh is still dead. But Jesus got up and He is alive today! Do you know Jesus?

8. As Jesus examined His disciples with that one-question final examination, He also examines each of us today— "Who do you say that I am?" Having seen water turned into wine, the dead raised and the lame walk; "Who do you say that I am?" Having seen the hungry fed, and the blind receive sight; having heard the dumb speak, and having seen the leper cleansed, "Who do you say that I am?" Jesus asked the disciples then because they were being prepared to be His witnesses in the world. We, who claim to believe, are being asked now because we cannot present a Savior for the world to

---

[487] Mt 28:6; Mk 16:6; Lk 24:3, 5; Jn 20:6, 11-18

believe in for salvation, if we do not know who He really is and what He has accomplished on the cross for our salvation. "Do you know Jesus?"

9. Do you know Jesus whom heaven and earth adore? Do you know Jesus before whom angels in heaven bow? Do you know Jesus, conceived by the Holy Spirit, begotten of God the Father? Do you know this Jesus who defied nature and was born of the Virgin Mary? Do you know Jesus, the mention of whose name causes demons to tremble? Do you know Jesus who healed the sick, raised the dead, and caused the blind to see? Do you know Jesus who walked on water and whose words calmed raging seas? Do you know Jesus who at Calvary paid the price for your soul, a price that you could not pay, by dying on the cross for the remission of sins? Do you know Jesus, the Son of God, who, though we were suited for condemnation to death and hell, took the stand on Calvary's mountain, adjudicated our case before God the Father, and dropped the charges against you and me?[488] Do you know Jesus? Do you know Jesus by whom and through whom the forgiveness of God flows to us so that we might be set free from the debilitating effects of sin? Do you know Jesus whom they crucified and buried on Friday and who, on that first Easter morning, got up from the dead, walked out of the tomb, took the sting out of death, and snatched victory out of the jaws of hell? Do you know this Jesus? Do you know this Jesus who ascended into heaven, sits at the right hand of God, and continues to make intercessions for your soul and mine? Do you know Jesus who promised to come again to take the redeemed of God into eternity?

ON KNOWING JESUS (SECTION TWO)

1. Do you know who Jesus is? You know and delight in learning about botany, the study of plants and plant life, but do you know The Lily of the Valley? You know about geology, the study of rocks and rock formations, but do you know the Rock Of All Ages and the Rock of our salvation? You know about astronomy, the study of stars, but do you

---

[488] Rom 5:9, 10; Tit 2:14

know the Bright and Morning Star? Do you know Jesus? Everybody has to know who Jesus is. He is the Son of the Living God. He is the Ancient of Days. He is the Alpha and the Omega. He is the Emmanuel, the One in whom God was wrapped so that He could dwell amongst us. Jesus is the eternal hope for every believer's soul.

2. Do you know Him as Savior and Lord or do you just think highly of Him? No matter how highly you think of Jesus, your thoughts are inadequate until you personally accept and confess Him as the Son of God, Lord, Savior, and Master of your soul. No matter how great your impressions are of His glory and power, that impression is not enough. Until you recognize and believe Him to be the Son of God and the One that died for the forgiveness of your sins, you will only continue to deny yourself the salvation that He died to offer you. No one's soul is lost because of sin but because of that person's refusal of the Savior who died to save him or her from the destructive and debilitating nature of sin. Jesus is the remitter of sins, yours and mine. When we demonstrate faith in Him and believe Him for salvation; by the grace of God, our sins are remitted and we are saved. **Hallelujah!**

3. Do you know Jesus, the Shepherd of your soul? The story is told of a famous actor and an old preacher. The actor was the guest of honor at a social event where he was requested by other guests to recite favorite excerpts from a number of literary works. An old preacher, who happened to be there, asked the actor to recite the Twenty-Third Psalm. The actor agreed to do so if the old preacher also recited the Psalm. The actor's rendition of the Psalm was presented with polished oratory and great dramatic emphasis for which he received a standing ovation. To honor his agreement, the old preacher stepped up to recite the Psalm. As the old preacher recited the Psalm, it became obvious that his voice was rough and broken, perhaps from many years of preaching. His diction was anything but polished. But when he was finished reciting the Psalm, there was not a dry eye to be found in the auditorium. When some of the people gathered there asked the actor what made the difference between his rendition of the Psalm and that of the preacher's, he replied, "I know the Psalm, but that old preacher knows the Shepherd." Do you know Jesus?

4. Knowing Jesus is indicative of our pursuit of God's moral standards. Knowledge of Jesus must necessarily lead to our pursuit of the ways of God. To know Jesus means that our lives are influenced by His life and ministry. Knowing Jesus dictates that your life is a life that is committed to doing justice, helping the poor,[489] and acting toward others with love, compassion, and mercy. Knowing Jesus comes with the responsibility of faithfully doing what He has commanded us to do.[490] Our response of obedience is one indicator that we know Jesus. Ultimately, our appropriate response to knowing Christ is to believe in and trust Him as Savior and Lord. Having believed in Christ, we should proceed with the help of the Holy Spirit, to do good works that elevate humanity and bring glory to God. While you may never grasp the whole spectrum of knowledge concerning God and His Christ, your faith response to Him will wonderfully impact your life so that you can develop deeper knowledge of Him. As your knowledge of Him grows, so does your relationship and friendship with Him.

5. There is a difference between merely hearing about Jesus, reading about Jesus, reciting written works about Jesus, talking about Jesus, knowing of Jesus, and having a personal relationship with Jesus. While hearing, reading, talking, and having intellectual knowledge of Jesus are critical interplays in the process of knowing Him, it is by confessing and experiencing Jesus as Lord and Savior that our knowledge of Him is complete.

2. Our Necessary Confession of Jesus

1. Your salvation from sin requires that you confess and believe in Jesus Christ. Without your faith's confession of Christ as the Son of God, the One that died to save your soul and the One whom God raised from the dead,[491] salvation is not received. Even though you may have lovely thoughts and profound admiration for Jesus, if they do not lead you to

---

[489] Jer 22:15-16
[490] Jn 2:3-7, 15:14
[491] Rom 10:9

confess your faith in Jesus, your lovely thoughts and admiration are hardly of any consequence for the salvation of your soul. Knowledge of creeds and books about Jesus are inadequate without your confession. Knowing Christ Jesus has to do with experiencing Him as Savior for your soul, Lord of your life, healer and provider, the lifter of your heart and spirit, and the mender of your brokenness. To know Jesus is to have knowledge of who He is. That knowledge through the inspiration of the Holy Spirit is what leads all of us to know Him as the Son of the living God in whom God's gift of Salvation was wrapped. By faith in His redeeming grace we are drawn into a saving relationship with Him. We are drawn into a saving relationship with Jesus Christ when by faith we voluntarily confess Him as Lord and Savior.

2. Our confession of Christ does two things at two distinct levels, at a personal level and at a relational level.

At a personal level, to confess Christ is to disclose our faith in Him and all that He is. At the same time our confession of Christ the Son of God, Lord and Savior, is also a disclosure of our faults and sins and therefore of our need for a Savior. To know Jesus is to have a personal relationship with Him. Having a personal relationship with Jesus is the direct result of having confessed and believed Him for salvation. You receive salvation when you confess or speak or declare your faith in Jesus Christ, accept Him as the Son of God, believe that He died for your sins, and that God raised Him from the dead.[492] By your faith in Him and the grace that He gives to help you in your faith, you are drawn into a personal and saving relationship with Him. Salvation does not come from merely reading about or hearing about Jesus. Salvation comes upon your personal confession of faith in the blessed Son of God. Upon our confession and disclosure of our sins through repentance, God responds to us with the gift of forgiveness and grace. That is what we mean when we say we are saved by grace through faith on the Lord Jesus. My dear friend, it is only when you get to the point where you personally acknowledge, confess, and believe Jesus for salvation that you are saved unto eternal life. Jesus, in John 5:24 stresses that salvation is based on the foundation of faith's confes-

---

[492] Rom 10:9

sion when He says: "Most assuredly, I say to you, he who hears My Word and believes in Him who sent Me, has everlasting life, and shall not come into judgment but has passed from death into life." The Bible says in Romans 10:9-10 "that if you confess with your mouth the Lord Jesus and believe in your heart that God has raised Him from the dead, you will be saved. For with the heart one believes unto righteousness, and with the mouth confession is made unto salvation."

At a relational level, to confess Christ is to declare or make known our faith in Christ based on who we acknowledge Him to be— Son of God, Savior, Lord, and a sinner's best friend. Our confession of Christ draws us into a saving relationship with Christ and with others who believe and share our convictions concerning Christ. Also, when in our witness to the world, we publicly confess Christ, verbalize and actively demonstrate our faith in Him, we are encouraging other people's awareness of Christ so that they too may believe and become engaged in a saving relationship with Him. As we relate others to Christ through our confessions of Him and as we witness to His grace and love, as a result of our experience of Christ and saving relationship with Him, we are effectively making disciples for Christ.

3. Our confession of Christ, whether done privately or publicly, is essential for the foundation and development of the Christian's faith, Church, and Christian lifestyle. After all, the founding of the Church was based on Peter's confession of faith in the person of Christ. The existence of the Church has been sustained by believers' continuous confession of the Lordship of Jesus. The eternity of the Church, indeed, the eternity of your soul and mine, will be dependent on our confession of our faith in the Lordship and eternal reign of Christ. "Who do you say that I am?" This is the ultimate question that all of us must face and answer: Who is Jesus Christ? Our response to this critical question is important because the eternity of our souls is dependent on our answer and faith response to the Son of God. This question is inevitable. It is a question that we cannot negotiate and dance around. It is a question that we cannot rationalize away. It is a question that the agnostic, the philosopher, the naturalist, the atheist, the empiricist, the humanist, and the skeptic cannot intellectualize away. For, in the final analysis, "at the name of Jesus every

knee shall bow and every tongue shall confess that Jesus Christ is Lord, to the glory of God the Father."⁴⁹³

4. Knowing Jesus is God's gift of salvation to us. To receive this gift of salvation is to confess and believe in the bearer of that gift, Jesus Christ. If you do not know Jesus as Lord and Savior, you need to know Him. If you have not been saved by faith in the Lord Jesus, all you need to do is respond with faith to the prompting of the Holy Spirit of God upon your heart. You can know that the Holy Spirit is tugging at your heart when you begin to seriously think about Jesus, become aware of how far you are from Him, and when you begin to have a desire to know Jesus better. That tugging is God's way of lovingly encouraging you to turn away from sin; and, through repentance, turn to God through faith in the Lord Jesus. As you turn to God, tell Him you are sorry for staying away so long. Tell Him you are sorry for all the wrong things you have done. Tell Him that you are tired of running. Tell Him that you are ready to surrender and receive Jesus as Savior and Lord. That is your repentance. Speak your faith in Jesus who was crucified for your redemption and raised by God to give you victory and eternal life. Invite Jesus into your heart and accept Him for salvation because only He can save you. You do not have to use fancy words for God to hear you or for Jesus to come into your heart. All you have to say is:

> **"Dear God, I confess my sins before You. Forgive me for my sins. I believe that Jesus Christ, Your blessed Son died for me. Come into my heart and change me. I accept Your will for my life. I surrender all that I am to You, and pray that You change me so that I may become all that You intend for me to be. Let Your Hoy Spirit take control of my life and my soul and lead me into the path of righteousness. I pray in the name of Jesus, Amen."**

If you have said that prayer and you are sincere about it, you are saved to the praise and glory of God. **Hallelujah!**

---

[493] Rom 14:11; Phil 2:10

5. Now that you have confessed and accepted Jesus Christ as your Lord and Savior, trust in Him and let Him lead you in order that you may discover the ways of God and begin to live a life that is pleasing to God. To live a life that is pleasing to God means that you trust God and are willingly walking before God in faith and obedience; exercising justice and showing mercy, and walking humbly before God.[494] Trusting God means that you rely on Him for direction and strength rather than depending on your own understanding. The Bible says, "Trust in the Lord with all of your heart and lean not on your own understanding; in all your ways acknowledge Him, and He shall direct your paths."[495] When you receive Jesus Christ into your heart, you will be given the power to overcome your past, live joyfully in the present, and with the glorious hope of eternity as heir to the kingdom of God always in your heart. It is indeed by receiving Christ that we become sons and daughters of God;[496] and if sons and daughters, we are heirs to His eternal kingdom.

6. Having confessed Jesus Christ, and as you give your life and soul to Him, you can begin to live a life of victory. You may still have to overcome some setbacks. You may still have some rivers to cross. You may still have some mountains to climb, some personal demons to rebuke and overcome, and some battles to fight. But remember the battle is not yours; the battle is the Lord's. The good news today is that God has never lost a fight. Because of the victory that Jesus brings into your life, your question signs will be turned into exclamations of praise. As you grow into a deeper knowledge of Jesus Christ and as you come to know God more and experience His transforming power in your life, your questions will be answered and you will receive the power of the Holy Spirit to help you live the Christian life. In a sense, to have the Holy Spirit is to have Jesus in your corner.

7. To have Jesus in your corner means that you have a lasting and eternal friend. In this life, when you know Jesus as Lord, as Shepherd, as Savior, as Friend, you know that when your peers forsake you, He will welcome and

---

[494] Micah 6:8
[495] Prov 3:5-6
[496] Jn 1:12

embrace you with His love.[497] When you know Jesus and have developed a personal relationship with Him, He will become for you: a bridge over your troubled waters; hope when you are in despair; healer when sickness invades your body; peace when your life is filled with turmoil; sanity when life is driving you crazy; and comfort when sorrow overwhelms you. When you know Him as the resurrection and the life, in trouble you can find deliverance; in death you can receive life eternal. **Hallelujah!** I thank God that you have come to know Jesus.

8. Every soul shall be pinned against the wall of eternity and be required to answer this one question, "Who do you say that I am?" A savior by any other name is not the redeemer of the human soul. Jesus is the name above all other names. There is no other name given among mankind whereby we must be saved. There is salvation in no other. Anything or anyone else is a cheap and inadequate substitute. Only Jesus, the begotten Son of God, Jesus, the crucified, resurrected, and ascended Christ, Jesus, the giver of true and lasting peace, can save and deliver to the uttermost.[498] He is the Way, the Truth, and the Life.

3. Jesus, the Only Way

1. In the Gospel of John, Jesus declares Himself to be "the Way, the Truth, and the Life."[499] Religions and religious leaders in the world today offer many paths to God— the path of philosophy, the path of human psychology, the path of scientology, the path of legalism, the path of self-help and self-determination, the paths of human knowledge, systems, cultures, social, and economic practices. Such paths are often human constructs and designs that emerge from the human pursuit of truth and understanding. They also emerge from the human innate desire to believe in something or to find purpose and value in the tangible things and processes of life. Jesus does not offer us a method, a system, a culture,

---

[497] Ps 27
[498] Heb 7:25
[499] Jn 14:6

or a philosophical pathway to God. He offers us Himself. Jesus is the way to God because He comes from God, begotten of the Father. He is the way to God because historically, He is God's divine and empirical or existential model of morality and holiness in the world. Spiritually, Jesus is the way to God's divine purpose in our lives because He proceeds from God and therefore knows the mind, will and purposes of God. He is the way of righteousness and truth. He is the way to humility and obedience. He is the way to faith. He is the way to love and mercy, justice and grace.

2. The Paths carved out by human constructs, customs, and traditions that are not expressly inspired and facilitated by the Spirit of God, are essentially carved out by human efforts and designs. As such they are intended for self-fulfillment and momentary sentimental self-gratification. The way to God is the way of grace that leads to eternal fulfilment that begins in the present and culminates in eternity. Jesus is the bearer of that grace. Human paths and efforts and striving will never get us to God. Jesus has all the qualifications to lead us to God because He proceeds from and knows God the Father.[500] Because of Jesus' intimate knowledge and exclusive relationship with the Father, He has exclusive access to Him. As such, Jesus can accurately reveal the Father, and lead us to Him so that we may have an inclusive faith-filled and purposeful relationship with God. It is only through Jesus that we can come to know the truth about God and experience the real purpose and meaning of life. It is only through Jesus, the Son of the living God that we can find and experience peace for our souls. After all, it He that the God of peace[501] sent into the world with the gifts of peace and good will.[502] As the Way, Jesus brings us into union with God the Father. As the way, Christ, who died to save us, also reconciled us to God in order to restore our relationship with Him. Christ who died to save us also rose to give us the assurance of victory. Christ who rose from the grave is also He who ascended, and is seated at the right hand of God interceding and mediating our cause before God. Even in His ascension, Jesus leads and represents us to God.

---

[500] Mt 11:27; Jn 8:42
[501] Rom 15:33; Heb 13:20
[502] Lk 2:14

4. THE SIGNIFICANCE OF THE ASCENSION OF JESUS

1. By His ascension, Jesus lives to represent us in heaven. What this means is that we have direct representative access to heaven. The ascension of Jesus is therefore not removed from the salvific work of Jesus, His life, death, and resurrection. As such, the ascension is a critical source for our eternal hope and salvation that has been given far too little attention in theological discourses and talks about salvation. For, whereas Jesus died to save us and was raised to give us hope and victory, through the ascension, in our existential condition, Jesus has given us a direct line and access to heaven. While in His earthly ministry Jesus was our High Priest in worship and life, representing us before the Father, by His ascension, Jesus has effectively become our heavenly High Priest representing us on the very throne of God in the presence of the eternal Father.

2. The ascension of Jesus is not a metaphor used merely to describe Jesus' elevation to another level of existence. It was a public event witnessed also by His disciples and two others believed to be angels.[503] This makes this event another important historical fact of Christ as well as a foundational basis upon which the church's faith and life are built. The doors of the Christian faith and Church therefore swing or turn on five historic hinges: The birth of Jesus, the life and ministry of Jesus, the crucifixion of Jesus, the resurrection of Jesus, and the ascension of Jesus. And, glory be unto God, those doors are now anchored to the promised return of Jesus, which essentially, is our hope and final opening of those doors leading into eternal glory with Him.

3. The ascension makes everything about Jesus a present reality and experience for the Christian believer. For those who have confessed Him to be the Lord, and for all who shall confess Him as the name above all other names by which all people must be saved, the risen and ascended Christ is forever present and working in us to renew and represent our existing conditions before God the Father. Without the resurrection and subsequent ascension of Jesus, our hope would have been buried in the past and left in the events of

---

[503] Acts 1:9-11

Calvary. However, because Jesus got up, lives, and now sits at the right hand of God the Father, we have a present hope that keeps us steadfast, sure, and filled with the expectation of a glorious future. The ascension of Jesus not only opens us to a future that is bright and glorious, the ascension of Jesus is loaded with benefits for our present Christian experiences.

4. What then, are the benefits of the ascension of Christ to us? The benefits of the ascension of Jesus to us may be seen at five levels. Let us examine them:

- **Level one**: At the first level, the ascension means that our redeemed human nature has been reunited with the divine nature of God. He who descended has also ascended, signifying the coming together and reconciliation of divinity and humanity. By coming where we are, in His divinity, Jesus brought God to us. Having ascended, in His humanity, He has carried our humanity before God. By His ascension, Jesus also carried our cares and prayer requests to the Father at whose right hand He is seated in glory praying (making intercessions) on your behalf and mine before God.[504] The Bible story of the ascension tells us that Jesus was taken up in the glory of His resurrected body.[505] This means that in His humanity, Jesus ascended to represent our humanity to God. Because Christ the Son shared in our humanity through His union with us, and because of His ascension to the Father with whom He shares divinity and eternal union, we are carried into, and remain in union with God the Father.
- **Level two**: At the second level, the ascension of Jesus means that we have access to heaven. We have been crucified with Christ by reason of our death to sin, and the surrendering of our will (the old self) to the purposes of God for our lives. Since we have died to sin, we believe that we also live with Christ who has been raised from the dead.[506] Having ascended and now living eternally with God the

---

[504] Acts 7:55; Rom 8:34; Heb 10:12
[505] Acts 1:11
[506] Rom 6:5-11

Father,[507] we have also been raised with Him to live a life that is eternally saved and dedicated to God. In His death and resurrection, Jesus essentially shuts the gates of hell to keep believers out, thus relieving all believers once and for all from the prison and fear of death, which was the devil's stranglehold on us. If in His death and resurrection Jesus essentially puts the devil in his place and shuts the gates of hell, in His ascension, He has essentially opened the gates of heaven to all believers. Since Jesus by the incarnation brings God to us in His divinity, and since in His ascension, Christ takes our humanity to God wrapped up in His own humanity, while all the time possessing divinity, He has effectually reconciled us with the Father, thus granting us access to heaven where the divine and the human natures are again in eternal fellowship and communion.

- **Level three:** At the third level, the ascension implies that Jesus stands before God the Father as our advocate. That makes Jesus our go-between us and God. As the propitiation for our sins on the cross, He is also now our appointed advocate.[508] In a real sense, as Jesus on the cross shed His blood to redeem and reconcile us to God, in His ascension, He remains the link between God and us. Seated at the right hand of God, that link is sustained by His perpetual intercession to God on our behalf. When Jesus was crucified, He became sin for us by taking our sins upon Himself.[509] Our sins were therefore nailed to the cross.[510] Consequently, when God looked at the cross and turned away, which was the moment Jesus felt forsaken,[511] it was not Christ from whom God turned. It was our sins that God turned away from because God cannot look upon sin.[512] Now, Jesus having died for our sins, and having resurrected and ascended, has become

---

[507] Rom 6:10
[508] Rom 3:25; Heb 2:17; 1 Jn 2:2; 1 Jn 4:10, 1 Jn 1:1-2
[509] 1 Pet 2:24; Rom 5:8
[510] 2 Cor 5:21; Col 2:14; 1Jn 3:5
[511] Mt 27:46
[512] Hab 1:13; Lk 16:15

our go-between us and God. Therefore, when God looks upon us now, it is not our sins that God sees. When God looks upon us, He sees the righteousness of His beloved Son Jesus, who, as our Advocate and heavenly High Priest, covers us with His righteousness as He stands between God and us. As our advocate, Jesus takes all of us before the love and care of the Father in heaven so that we may receive covering and forgiveness from our sins, and so that the Father's love given to Him, may also become ours.

- **Level four:** At the fourth level, the ascension means that our prayers have a direct line to God. Jesus, as our Advocate, is the direct representation of our voices and concerns to God. As our Advocate, and since it is Christ that prays, our prayers are answered when in faith we pray to the Father, by the power and sincerity of the Spirit and in the effectual name of Jesus.[513] The prayers of the righteous and faithful are answered[514] because Jesus lives to represent us and lift our prayers before the Father. Since Jesus lives eternally, He eternally intercedes on our behalf. When therefore, we are through praying on earth, and when we do not know what to pray for, through the power of the Holy Spirit, Jesus is continuously interceding for us and making requests of the Father on our behalf.[515] Our prayers on earth are therefore not disconnected from the intercessions of the ascended Christ on our behalf before the Father in heaven. We celebrate Jesus today because in His worthiness, He stands up for us before the Father so that our unworthiness will not be held against us.
- **Level five:** At the fifth level, the ascension of Christ empowers us to live in hope. In view of the knowledge that Jesus has gone up, and since Jesus sits at the right hand of God making intercessions for us, and because we live in the presence of His Spirit, even though we experience hardships in this life, we have hope in the victory of good over evil. Because Christ returned to heaven and promised to come

---

[513] Mt 21:22; Mk 11:24; Jn 14:13-14, 15:7; Rom 8:26-27
[514] Ja 5:16
[515] Rom 8:26-27

again to receive us unto Himself,[516] we are empowered to live in hope as we continue to pray, lift up fallen humanity, and bring glory to God on the earth. Indeed, inasmuch as we may suffer with and for Christ, we shall also be glorified with Him.[517] Jesus tells us in John 16:33 that though in the world we have tribulations, we should be of good cheer, because He has overcome the world. Our hope is invested in the knowledge that Jesus who suffered and died for our sins, has risen and ascended with authority and power, and has become our strength, our joy and peace on earth now, and our guarantee for future victory.

5. When we look at the ascension of Jesus from the perspectives of these levels of benefits to us based on the faith we have developed in Him, we are empowered by this added assurance to live out the Christian life and faith on earth. This assurance enables us to live our lives in this world knowing that our eternal interest is being represented by Jesus and already sealed and guaranteed by the Holy Spirit.[518] Also, our hope is at its apex because our eternal promise is secured by Jesus who lives to represent us before the Father.[519] We experience Christ and live in hope even in the midst of despair, because in Christ, our hope is already laid up for us in heaven.[520] In our weakness, then, we find strength in the promises of Jesus as we behold the mystery and power of heaven working in us and for us and through us. In this present life then, our hope in Christ causes us to experience exchanges of our ashes for beauty, our mourning for gladness, and our despair for strength.[521] Because of the promises of the crucified, risen, and ascended Christ who promised to come again, even though in this life, the devil still haunts us with diverse temptations, we are not driven to despair because the power and authority

---

[516] Jn 14:2-3
[517] Rom 8:17
[518] 2 Cor 1:22, 5:5; Eph 1:14
[519] Eph 1:3-14
[520] Col 1:5, 27; 1 Pet 1:4
[521] Is 61:3

given Jesus over heaven and earth[522] will keep the devil in check and preserve us for eternity with God.

6. The good news today is that because Jesus lives, if you are seeking strength to live day-by-day, you can find strength in His dominion, power, and authority. If you are seeking redemption, you can find it in His passion. If you are seeking sanctification, you can find it in His sacrifice. If you are seeking to be purified, you can find it in the cleansing power of His precious blood. Because He who was dead is alive, and lives to represent us in heaven, if you are seeking hope and newness of life you can find it in His resurrection.

7. Because of the life, death, resurrection, ascension, and promised return of Jesus, you can have holy confidence in approaching the throne of grace. Because every rich and overflowing goodness comes from Jesus Christ, you can approach the throne of God with confidence, kneel at the altar of mercy, and feast at the Lord's Table, knowing that your eternal salvation comes from no other than Jesus who died and is risen, has ascended, and will come again to receive you into God's eternity. This completes the reconciling work of Jesus! **Hallelujah!**

8. Now tell me, what do you have to lose by believing in the Lord Jesus? I believe that He is the Son of God who died for your sins and mine. I believe that He is alive forevermore. By placing your faith in Christ you have nothing to lose and everything to gain. Personally, I would rather live believing that there is a God, that Christ died to save me from my sins, that there is heaven and a hell, and find out in death that there is no God and no heaven and no hell, for then, I would have lost nothing. I would rather live believing that, than to live believing that there is no God, no Christ, no heaven and no hell, and find out in death that there is indeed a God, there is a place called heaven, and there is hell, for then I would have everything to lose.

9. You have absolutely nothing to lose by believing in God and accepting Jesus Christ as Savior and Lord. But you do have salvation and eternal life to gain when you do. What are you going to do about it? Believe on the Lord Jesus and be saved today! Please pray this prayer with me:

---

[522] Mt 28:18

Dear God, I believe that You created me. I believe that You sent Your Son Jesus into the world to die for me. I repent of all my sins. Forgive me of all my sins and by Your Holy Spirit, change me and give me a brand new start. By faith I claim Jesus as my Savior and Lord right now. Come into my heart Lord Jesus; come in today; come in to stay. I pray this prayer in the name of Jesus. Amen!

I thank God for you my dear reader and friend. Now walk and live in the authority of Christ because you were made for eternity. **Hallelujah!**

Chapter Ten

Reflections, Implications, And Potential Contributions

In order to change the prevailing dynamics and correct the deficiencies that have held the church and worship experience hostage, renewal needs to come through a mutually transforming information model. Worship programs and/or workshops designed to educate and inform pastoral and lay leadership on issues relating to knowledge of God, worship, mission, and the importance of Christian eschatological hope for our spiritual formation, need to become a priority in local churches. Understanding the God-humanward movement and the human-Godward movement of grace in worship, is essential for our understanding and meaningful participation in worship and therefore needs to be taught. I believe that this book is a reasonable representation of that model.

One of the goals of this Information Model was to develop a teaching tool that is aimed at creating a paradigm shift in people's awareness of worship and what the worship experience entails. I think it is reasonably safe to conclude that intentional cognitive learning is an essential tool for elevating worshippers' awareness of some critical components of Christian worship. Intentional cognitive learning, when participated in by clergy and laity/worshippers, can potentially lead to the reorganization of worshippers' understanding. This reorganization of worshippers' understanding may potentially lead to the reshaping of their perspectives and worship experiences. When the Christian experience is informed and affirmed by knowledge, leading to a proper Christian understanding of worship, change for the better in some worshippers' prior perceptions, attitudes, values, and beliefs may become possible.

Cognitive learning based on an informative and experiential paradigm such as this book, along with explanatory clues or directions in worship and worship bulletins, personal reflections, and ultimately, divine inspiration, are wonderful approaches for developing intentional awareness and participation in worship. Since true worship comes about as a result of our knowledge and understanding of God, it is imperative for pastors and worship (liturgical) leaders to prayerfully lead worshippers through the processes of worship. It is also important for theological and liturgical clarity to be interwoven into the doctrinal components associated with denominational or congregational worship practices. That way, worshippers and worship leaders, lay and clergy alike, may develop mutual theological comprehensibility of the liturgical and doctrinal processes of worship.

Such leadership should not be limited to setting worship goals and determining liturgical components and affirmations for inclusion in the order of worship. During the worship service, liturgical leadership should also be extended to the provision of explanatory notes either directly from the pastor/worship leader or by inclusion in worship bulletins. These explanatory notes may be presented in Bible study and Sunday school classes, in the form of bulletin inserts, footnotes, and verbal preludes to the various liturgical components of worship. Doing this may potentially create a sense of understanding and clarity for worshippers. This may be particularly useful for guests and new members who might not be familiar with the worship customs and liturgical content of the congregation they are visiting and potentially seeking to make their church home. With such clarity, the greater potential for intentional participation and therefore passionate worship may be encouraged.

It is critical to enhance the mutual elevation of lay and pastoral leadership in our attempts to make sense of what we are called and empowered to do together for the glory of God. Since cognitive learning is only a small piece of the knowledge that renews, pastoral and lay leadership must go beyond what may be taught and learned. They should therefore be intentional about embracing prayer and encouraging trust in God's grace to manifest, while leaving room for the Holy Spirit of wisdom to direct and facilitate worship. That way, lay and pastoral leadership may be spiritually elevated to a level of passionate worship that human understanding alone cannot take us. That kind of elevation is only reached when human knowledge and preparation meet with the Spirit of wisdom that inspires and lifts our feeble praise. Until we get to that place, that secret place of the heart where worship, communion, and fellowship through the operation of the Holy Spirit take place, regardless of what we may have learned cognitively, passion for worship will continue to elude us.

Passion for worship comes from the heart. While we should by all means bring our expertise to the worship experience as it relates to knowledge, leadership, and technological applications, real worship only happens when we surrender our own expertise and know-how and subscribe to the Holy Spirit who works in us to make our worship one that is in Spirit and in truth. The thing to remember is that the methods, the instruments, and different applications that we use in worship, are not actually worshipping God. We are. The methodologies, instruments, and applications are used to enhance worship but ultimately, we are the ones that are worshipping God. We are the ones with whom God is seeking fellowship and communion. Since we are the worshippers, we need to apply our understanding and thoughtfulness to the worship encounter, while all the time staying open and receptive to the flow and inspiration of the Holy Spirit. In so doing, the Holy Spirit can and will make use of us as we seek to give glory and praise to God.

Even though our commitment to worship may be enhanced by our knowledge of God, our understanding of the worship processes, and the application of worship tools, our worship experience without the inspiration of the Holy Spirit will only be a sort of spiritual anticlimax. Anticlimax, because worship without the influence of the Holy Spirit, leaves us spiritually half-full. Without the Holy Spirit, and without the application of our hearts to worship, despite our expertise, theatrics, technological capabilities, and our ability to lead worship, the worship encounter will remain a noisy gong and a clanging cymbal.[523] Such attempts at worship would only be sequences of religious rituals.

God is not interested in religious rituals. The rituals help us; but our faith, hearts, and sincerity of spirit are what magnify and please God in worship. We should therefore leave room for the Holy Spirit to stir us up, surprise us, and manifest the glory of God in our lives and worship. In order to do so, we need to be humble enough to seek the help of the Holy Spirit knowing that by our own knowledge and efforts, we would fail to worship God in spirit and in truth. If worshippers know what they are doing and why they are doing it, as we trust the Holy Spirit to lead us into the worship experience and to please God, our worship encounters may leave us transformed and spiritually fulfilled.

As a reminder, while perfect knowledge is not a requirement for worshipping God, our desire must always be to grow in the grace and knowledge of God. The importance of knowledge cannot however, be overstated. As Jesus indicates, knowledge goes beyond true and meaningful worship to encompass eternal life.[524] Our acknowledgement of God and subsequent worship of God mark the beginning of a remarkable journey with God that leads to eternity with Him. Without enlightenment then, can we truly participate in the divine life? Knowledge of God does indeed lead to worship that is true. As White asserts, "knowledge does not save, that is the error of Gnosticism; but true worship is unattainable without knowledge."[525]

Knowledge of God also implies worshipping God as He exists and works to accomplish His divine purpose. Christian worship is founded on Christian truth and acknowledgement of the God who comes to us as Creator, Redeemer, and Sanctifier. By extension, this acknowledged truth is grounded in the understanding and reality of God who is revealed through the Son in the power of the Holy Spirit. As such, God in worship needs to be understood in terms

---

[523] Amos 5:23-24; 1 Cor 13:1
[524] Jn 17:3
[525] White, 195

of the unity of the Father, Son, and Holy Spirit. Understanding God's descent and ascent, presence, and continuous work among us in worship and daily life through Christ in the power of the Holy Spirit, is fundamental to our understanding of God. Since knowledge is the bedrock of understanding and the basis of making sense of life experiences, including worship, having proper knowledge of God may result in worship that is purposeful and therefore removed from the shallow repetitive patterns of self-centeredness, and the purely mysterious and meaningless episodic routines. If therefore, we develop practices based on wrong information, leading to defective knowledge, our worship experience may become lessened due in part to lack of proper information.

The interpretation of rituals, religious symbols, liturgical practices, doctrinal creeds, the Scripture, and the human experiences in worship, is the task of pastoral leadership. Given the symbolic nature of worship and liturgical practices, pastoral leadership, as it relates to the worship process, needs to be urgently redefined. This redefinition needs to put the pastor and worship leaders not so much in a controlling and directorial role, but in an explanatory, informative, and nurturing role. That way, understanding of liturgical practices in worship may be established and mutually understood. For the purpose of clarity and understanding in worship, pastoral leadership also needs to become a symbolic activity that makes church life and worship both understood and meaningful.

While proper information regarding who God is may lead to proper worship of God, I do not believe we need to create a new liturgy. What we need to do is bring new meaning and renewed attention to the stirring up of an old tradition that is still good for you and me and for the glory of God. That way, as we are inspired by the Holy Spirit, we may appropriately participate in worship that is alive and passionate and meaningful.

If worship is to be elevated through understanding, transformational pastoral leadership is necessary. A transformational approach is essential because transformational leadership is indicative of mutual elevation. If the pastor or worship leader is the only person that understands the worship process and the liturgical content and practices in a given worship setting, neither transformational leadership nor communal worship for that matter, has taken place. This mutual elevation of pastor and laity is essential for moving individuals from the level of individuality and the quest for personal quiet time in public worship, to the level of interactive praise, relational, and communal responses to God. Transformational leadership is therefore indicative of mutual understanding at a relational level in the course of active and passionate participation in worship.

Attempts at mutual elevation in our understanding of worship may also help worshippers to see each other as fellow Christians in a worshipping relationship rather than mere individuals having casual weekly encounters in search of personal piety and emotional satisfaction. Informing, nurturing, and encouraging the laity may mutually elevate us to see worship as a gift of participation. That realization may also help worshippers to appreciate the value that God places on them. This too may inspire passionate worship.

In addition, if meaning is to be attained in worship and in mission, there is a definite need for us to appreciate the relations between worship practices and our missional goals. Worship should not be seen as a disconnected part of our lives that we engage in on Sundays and then put in some private compartment for the rest of the week. For the Christian person to be a complete participant in the means of faith, worship and Christian mission need to be seen as a dialogue that is sustained after the formal worship service comes to its formal liturgical conclusion. I intentionally employ the term formal liturgical conclusion to emphasize that worship in its purest form is never ended. The formality of public worship may come to its formal conclusion but it should always spill over into the practical liturgy, which is the outpouring of worship through Christian mission and service in the world.

When we fail to sustain the continuity of worship and its practical transition to service, we run the risk of falling into a sort of cavalier mindset. That mindset can be avoided if our celebration of the formal liturgy is translated into the liturgy of service or mission or witness or Christian discipleship. When Jesus says, "Follow Me," for example, He certainly means that in order to be His disciples we need to do the works that He did. Following Jesus therefore implies that our lives and Christian practices mirror His. The

Gospels bear witness to the fact that Jesus was equally engaged in worship to the Father as He was engaged in the mission of the Father in the lifting up of humanity. As Jesus worked to redeem humanity, we need to live and serve God in the world where the pervasive grace of God is already working to transform the human heart and restore broken humanity.

Consequently, the love of God that we encounter through Christ in worship needs to spill over in our daily living out of Christ in the world. The whole person, the person who believes and worships God, the person who lives and works in the world, and the person who, from an eschatological point of view, hopes in Christ, is summoned by God, and quickened by the Holy Spirit, to both worship God and witness to His Christ in the world. That way, instead of being limited to our Sunday only formal ingathering, God's will, mission, and purpose are always being faithfully and responsibly lived and carried out.

Whereas the formal liturgy is an opportunity for the Father, Son, and Holy Spirit to lovingly draw us into divine union, mission is an opportunity for the Father, Son, and Holy Spirit to work through us, our voices, and our actions, to bring others into the loving communion of faith in the Lord Jesus Christ. As in worship we respond to God, in mission we impart and reflect God— His forgiveness, His grace, His mercy, His love, His justice, His joy, and His peace— in the world. The purpose is to shine our light in the world so that others may see and come to faith in Christ, and respond to God through worship, service, and with a life of faith and obedience. When we become true and anointed reflections of God in the world, we make God visible to those who otherwise may not see the wonders of His love. Indeed, as we wait eschatologically for the return of Christ, it is in the world that we, God's salt and light, are summoned by Christ to lend godly flavor and let our light shine.[526]

Given the diverse environments in which we worship, understanding the different cultural forces and expectations that are brought to bear on the worship encounter will also be beneficial for pastoral leadership. Worship services with contents that include the diversity represented in worship will

---

[526] Mt 5:13-16

enhance relevance in its presentation and clarity and ownership in its participation. People must be led to feel that they belong. In order for worship to move from the casual gathering of people to an encounter and experience of God, it must be understood and made sense of. We are more inclined to make sense of activities and rituals that we participate in when they speak to our diverse experiences and understanding.

Diversity is also critical to the pastoral care process because it makes us deeply aware that the spiritual, physical, emotional, mental, and medical conditions that so often impact human beings are not limited to any one gender, race, culture, or ethnicity. As we reach out to God's diverse peoples, the Christ in us demands that we are always mindful that regardless of the person's race, age, gender, religion, or political orientation, the compassion of God does not know any boundary. God's diverse activities and manifestations of grace require that we adapt relevant methodologies for addressing and caring for diverse persons. If we fail to adapt, without compromising our faith and loyalty first to God, we run the risk of rendering ourselves culturally irrelevant. Since God has created humanity with such rich diversity, which is a reflection of His own nature and richness, we need to adapt and develop diverse methods or approaches for doing ministry and caring for God's broken and hurting people.

Eschatology also has serious practical implications for pastoral ministry and Christian living. Eschatology demands the shifting of the Christian's focus from self-preservation to the giving of ourselves to the community, and for the elevation of it. In our attempts to pursue personal piety, we run the risk of losing focus of the true meaning of mission and spreading of the Gospel of Christ. The true meaning of mission and the spreading of the Gospel of Christ is making Christ known in the world by reaching people (making disciples) for Christ and caring for those around us. As an eschatological community, living and worshipping, we also need to be intentional about proclaiming Christ and serving God in the world.

As we live eschatologically, the true meaning of worship and mission continues to entail reaching others as Christ reached us. After all, genuine salvation and faith are not gained in our individual search for piety. Faith and salvation are largely grounded and invested in community where faith finds opportunities to practice and develop the spiritual muscle to serve and endure while waiting for the promise of eternity, the ultimate goal of our salvation. As God works in community with the Son and Holy Spirit to redeem and sanctify us, we are also called in community to reach the world for Christ.

By virtue of the concerns for others that eschatology ought rightly to invoke in us, eschatological living is not separated from community. The Christian community needs to be engaged in a mission to the world where holiness, demonstrated through love, finds its true home. Consequently, eschatology does not call the Christian to be separated from the world in the quest for personal holiness. That would be a perversion of God's will and a contradiction to the Gospel imperative of Christ who sends us to preach His Gospel throughout the world.

We may have encountered Christ in our private moments; but developing holiness in Him, takes place in a public world. Holiness is developed in the world because it is there that it receives practice and is therefore perfected. It was not a mistake that Jesus sent the disciples and us into the world. He sent us out to practice what we have both learned and preached. It is in the world that intentional discipleship takes place. Inasmuch as worship informs and empowers our faith at the altar, our growing in faith takes place on a global platform (in the field, in community, or in mission) where our service to God, our character, and our preparation for eternity are developed and perfected. In the world, the arena of public observation and scrutiny, character is built because it is there that we become vulnerable. This is the place where we give of ourselves to others, and become neighbors to the marginalized and excluded of society. It is in the world that we follow the model of the Samaria bound Jesus in order to cross cultural boundaries. It is in the world that we demonstrate solidarity with those who suffer wrong, are alienated and discriminated against, and are waiting with a deep need for a friend and a Savior. It is in this arena where we get knocked down but are always picked up by the grace of God.[527] We obtain strength when we truly learn to lean on the Jesus whom we meet at the altar and feast upon at The Lord's Table. Having

---

[527] Prov 24:16

leaned on Jesus, He renews us and sends us out to bring flavor and light to an otherwise insipid and darkened world. Even as we wait and continue to serve God in community, and as we risk ourselves for the kingdom and glory of God, which is our mirroring of the self-giving sacrifice of our blessed Lord, the Holy Spirit forms and develops holiness in us.

This work of developing holiness in us by the Holy Spirit is our preparation for eternity. I insist that holiness happens in the world. Even if we conclude that the holiness of God is dispersed to us through faith and our encounter with Christ, we cannot deny that the social principles and mandate of the Gospel and the divine photos of the Christian nature and characteristics can only be truly developed and reflected in the dark contexts of the world. It is in the world that the rubber hits the road as we truly offer up ourselves and our service to God. It is in the world that faith finds traction and where character and spiritual fortitude are developed. It is there when trials and tribulations come that we push against the impossible, declare the devil a liar, and claim possibilities in the eternal purpose and promises of God with whom all things are possible.[528]

Eschatology or eschatological living does not call us to retreat from the present realities into which we human beings are physically embedded because of our heavenly view and hope. Eschatology on the contrary, is a reminder for us to remain active participants in God's work of continuous reconciliation in the world until Christ comes to complete us and all things in Himself. Eschatology is a reminder for us to act with love toward God and our neighbors. Christians were never intended to be passive observers but active participants in God's redemptive work in Christ Jesus. By grace, as we continue to live eschatologically with our vision set on heaven, we need to remember that we have been liberated by the finished work of Christ to serve Him in time.

Eschatological hope is really the transforming and embracing of the world and faith community to which we belong so that together they might be caught up.[529] Social isolation does not bring people to God. Neither is so-

---

[528] Mt 19:26
[529] 1Thess 4:17

cial isolation of any value to the formation and nurturing of our human spirit. The spiritually transforming value of eschatology may therefore be seen in the power of eschatological expectation to elevate us above individualism so that we may embrace community. If indeed, our hope is grounded in God, our eschatological hope can only be affirmed and manifested when, in community, we do the work of God who also works. Eschatological hope is therefore active hope displayed through service in community where hope is both affirmed and nurtured.

So then, in worship, through mission, and by our eschatological living, the Holy Spirit continues to direct our attention to Christ, so that we may look inward, outward, and upward with expectation. We look inward not merely for self-gratification, but especially for personal inventory of our attitudes and behaviors displayed toward God and neighbor. In worship we look inward to see ourselves in communion with the Father and the Son and the Holy Spirit. We also look inward to see ourselves in worshipping relationships with our sisters and brothers. Through grace, we look outward to see God through Christ, in the power of the Holy Spirit, working through us in mission to manifest His power, disturb the status quo, and bring down the strongholds of the kingdoms of the world. We look outward to see opportunities to witness to others and to see the change that comes over human lives and situations, as the kingdom of God is established in the hearts and lives of people. We look outward to see God's glory shining and dispelling darkness throughout the world. As we live eschatologically, filled with hope in the triumphant return of Christ, we look upward to behold our resurrected and ascended Savior, seated at the right hand of God and bidding us through grace to come into the blessed kingdom that has been prepared for us before the foundations of the world.[530]

As we continue to live and worship, engaging ourselves in mission with Christ, with the expectation of the eschaton, we are daily being motivated and transformed by love. Love, the divine economy and nurturing energy of God, is what moves God to mercy and transforming grace. Love moves God to offer us forgiveness as He changes our lives for the better. Love, the divine

---

[530] Acts 7:55-56; Jn 14:2-3; Rom 8:29-30

economy of God, is God beginning a good work in us, orchestrating His plan, and sustaining that work until He accomplishes His restoration of us.[531] Love is therefore the dispensation of divine grace and the sole end of every dispensation of God in the world.

It is God's outreaching love that changes us and draws us into His holiness. We are changed by God's love so that we may learn from God what love is and how to love. Our response of love is therefore a response of gratitude for the love that God first gave us. Love did not originate with us. Love has always been first a God-humanward force before it became a human to human and a human-Godward movement. The first activity of love has always been a God activity. Our human act of love is only in response to an already Godward movement of grace toward us.

The centrality of love in the Christian's scheme of things is therefore critical for our understanding of all that we do for and with God in worship and mission. It calls us to love our neighbors and give of ourselves, our goods, and resources to others for the glory of God. Because we were created in the image of God's love, it follows that everyone who loves is born of God.[532] Consequently, the life that has been renewed and spiritually transformed is a life that is reflective of the moral image imprinted within us by Creator God. This moral imprint that God has placed in us has also wired us with the capacity to know, follow after God, and perfectly seek to love God and neighbor.

Love for God demonstrated through devotion and sincere commitment to worship and mission, and for our neighbor through love and mercy, is the purest indicator of our spiritual transformation. Love changes us to act toward God as well as to act like God in the world. The gift of God's love dispensed to us through Christ is that gift of grace by which the Holy Spirit transforms the Christian's attitude and behavior and lovingly brings the Christian into conformity with Christ. If loving God and our neighbor implies having the mind of Christ, we definitely cannot say we love God and not love our neighbors also. The love that we demonstrate in the world is a manifestation of our transformation and our making visible the presence and work of God in us.

---

[531] Phil 1:6; Heb 13:20-21

[532] I Jn 4:7

To love is Christian, and the Christian's life is a transformed life that has been changed to reach the world in love.

We are changed by the love of God to go out and change the world by the power of love that God has invested in us. Our encounter with, and response to God, whether in worship, mission, or by our eschatological living, should therefore be translated and understood in terms of our faithful response to the love of God. Apart from the framework of love that reaches out, holiness has no contextual environment within which to grow. Holiness develops in us through the practicing of love. For that reason, Christ sends us out in order that we might have ample room and time to practice and develop our love and faith beyond the safe confines of our sanctuaries. Since holiness is understood as the love of God that is being perfected in us, if we fail to give love to the world, we are also failing to reflect and extend the holiness of God. The faith that we confess should therefore be displayed through love. That way, our faith finds opportunities to act and therefore grow. I again emphasize that we are not made holy by what we do. What we do is however, a reflection of our having already been made holy by God's grace that makes it possible for us to perform works or deeds of love.

Finally, knowing Christ is essential for our Christian witness in the world because we cannot effectively speak of Him whom we do not know; nor can we give to the world what we do not have ourselves. So, the question, "Do you know Jesus?" is critical for our own conviction as well as the conviction of the world. Everybody has to know who Jesus is. Knowledge of Jesus, though it might have initially developed in the human intellect, must be translated into a saving knowledge of the One that died to redeem us. Intellectual or cognitive assent or awareness of Christ, though illuminating, is not sufficient for salvation. While hearing, reading, talking, and having intellectual knowledge of Jesus are critical contributors in the process of knowing Him, it is only by believing in and confessing Christ as the Son of God, and Savior and Lord, that we are saved. Our intellectual knowledge of Jesus is of no consequence for the salvation of our souls without faith's confession.

To know Jesus is to have a personal relationship with Him. Having confessed Him to be the Son of God who died for our sins on the cross, and as we proceed to accept Him as our Savior and Lord, salvation is gifted to us. As we recall, Jesus established the foundation of the Church on Peter's confession of faith regarding who Jesus is. The very existence of the Church is sustained by the continuous confession of Christ by every generation of believers. The eternity of the Church, indeed, the eternity of our souls and those of every generation, will be dependent on our ceaseless confessions of the Lordship and eternal reign of Christ to the glory of God.

As we continue to worship and witness to all that we know and believe about Jesus, let us not forget that as Jesus examined His disciples with that one-question final examination, "Who do you say that I am?" He is examining each of us today. All of us will be pinned against the walls of eternity as we give account of our time and faith here on earth and must answer this question. Unless ours has been the faithful confession of "You are the Christ, the Son of the Living God," we will have fallen short. Let us not wait until the final day to figure out what we think of and believe about the Son of God. Let us affirm our faith now in a true confession of Him as Savior and Lord because it is He who died that we might live the abundant life on earth; and, it is He who is coming again that we might live eternally with Him. The key to eternal life is our knowledge of God and our confession of faith in His Christ. There is no other name given among mankind whereby we must be saved. That name is Jesus.

Regarding the potential utility and contributions of this book, by reason of the informative framework within which the content of this book is grounded, this material may add another dimension to the list of studies seeking to explain the process of the Christian's spiritual formation, growth, and faith journey. I propose that our spiritual formation, growth, and faith journey are the results of our encounter with God, an encounter that becomes the source of our transformation, our motivation to worship, our zeal for mission, and the basis of our eschatological hope.

While there are large numbers of writings on worship, on mission, and also on eschatology, this book has made a systematic link between these three spiritual components of faith in order to show how God uses our faithful participation in these means of faith to bring about our spiritual transformation.

By virtue of our faith response to the operations of God in worship, mission, and a mindset that is developed out of our eschatological anticipation of the return of Christ, this systematic analysis of these three spiritual components of faith and God's use of them for our spiritual formation, provide a reasonable paradigm for understanding God's impartation of Himself to us throughout our faith journey. This way, we are better able to understand how we are never left on our own at any stage of our journey toward eternity, but are constantly being formed into Christ by the Holy Spirit. Since worship, missions, and eschatology are the three components of faith that most occupy the Christian's thought and time, this book is an attempt to contribute to contemporary theological discussions within the existential framework of pastoral education and practice as well as to increase the laity's theological understandings of these processes.

The content of this book is also of value to the extent that it offers a refreshing and practical model for making real what we believe and do for and with God in the process of becoming Christ-like. The focus and content of this book embody cognitive, experiential, and practical strands that may be utilized for bridging the gap between congregational theological understanding, pastoral practices, liturgical formulations, and lay awareness of these processes within the local church setting.

The information and theological thrust of this book are a purposeful attempt to engage worshippers into thinking about what we are participating in so that we can find meaning through a shared informative paradigm that is aimed at the mutual transformation of pastor, laity, and potential seekers of faith in the risen Christ. Also, because this book emerged out of the need to promote an engaged understanding in the local context within which it is grounded, its content may also be useful in similar congregational settings for the transformation of worshippers' attitudes and the elevation of their commitment, participation in worship, and the making of disciples for Jesus.

Of significance, is the intentional attempt of this book to concretize our theological understanding by the development of a systematic synthesis of the three components of the Christian faith— worship, mission, and eschatology— by grounding them in the human experience. As such, the empirical thrust, conversational, and experiential designs of this book are intended to help in removing the myth, the mystical and the abstract, and in bringing the process of our faith response to God closer to our human understanding. This experiential approach also helps to bring our faithful participation in these processes, and the operations of the Holy Spirit into the existential (the empirical realm of human existence and activity) so that we can see and experience how God through Christ is actually transforming our lives. That way, the Holy Spirit is not viewed as an abstract entity, but as a real and transforming power that is present and actively engaged in our faith, worship, lives, and work, as well as in our vertical and horizontal relationships with God and neighbor. By bringing clarity to our participation in these means of faith, we are also empowered to see how God, in the presence and power of the Holy Spirit, accompanies Christian believers in all areas of their lives in order that He might accumulatively nurture and refashion them into His own likeness. If these pursuits and sense making are important to you and your pursuit of clarity and understanding, and I sense that they are, this book was designed for you.

Owing to the mutually transforming design and the informative paradigm within which this book is embedded, its content has the potential to enhance the cognitive awareness of worship leaders and worshippers alike. Also, due to the potential for replicating the data gathering methodologies, and their interpretations and applications, this book represents an acceptable and significant breakthrough for accessing worshippers' perceptions and theological understandings. The experiential thrust, and intentional attempt to correct misconceptions, affirm, nurture, and develop proper understandings about worship, mission, and the implications of an eschatological lifestyle, may also help worshippers concretize and therefore make sense of their experience and faithful participation in these means of faith.

As we are anointed and empowered in this life by the Holy Spirit to worship and praise God, let us proceed to bring glory to Christ as we continue His mission of service and love in the lifting up of humanity. As we eagerly await the return of Christ and the fulfillment of His promise, let us go forth for Christ, nurturing the churched and reaching the unchurched, so that when our work here on earth is done, all of God's redeemed people may be gathered up in that one unprecedented scoop of God's embrace and be transitioned into eternity.

Through faith in His Son, Jesus Christ, and by the presence and power of the Holy Spirit, God has accompanied us on every step of our faith journey so that we may grow into the fullness of His divine life and purpose. Blessed be the Lord our God who invades our lives through worship, sustains us with His presence through mission, and keeps us steadfast by our eschatological hope that is grounded in His eternal promises. To the only wise God our Father, Jesus Christ His only begotten Son, to the Holy Spirit our Comforter and Guarantor of eternity, be glory, honor, dominion, and praise, now and forever.

In the name of Jesus who died, lives, and promises to come again, I declare on the authority of His promise and under the aunction of the Holy Spirit that "You were made for eternity!" **Hallelujah! Amen!**

APPENDICES

Appendix 1

Methodologies: Development and Implementation of the Study

The study was developed out of the desire to ascertain worshippers'/parishioners' understanding of God, the practical and spiritual implications of worship, mission, and an eschatological lifestyle. In order to develop a worthwhile curriculum to inform, and correct any deficiencies, it became necessary to obtain parishioners' predisposed and existing perceptions and understanding of these components and practices of Christianity. If strategies are to be developed for informing and transforming people's thoughts, attitudes, and behaviors, then it becomes necessary to determine what those predisposed and existing perceptions are that may be impacting those persons' ideas, attitudes, and behaviors.

The first step for ascertaining perceptions, and in order to develop strategies for addressing those perceptions was the establishment of a Focus Group. A Focus Group consisting of eleven members from the local church was selected. This Focus Group was the data-gathering source needed to measure perceptions and to determine, if needed, the content of the curriculum (Informative Teaching Tool). The members were purposefully selected and were regular adult attendees of Sunday school and Bible study. Purposeful sampling seeks information-rich cases for in-depth study.[533] The selection process, while being purposeful, was also designed to meet the criteria of gender representation. Different educational levels, though not a criterion, were fairly well represented. While the Focus Group was the primary source for data gathering and specific information sharing, the content of the study was also incorporated into worship services by way of the liturgical and sermon contents for the benefit of the congregation as a whole.

The second step of the implementation process was the development of a Worship, Mission, and Eschatology Questionnaire (WMEQ).[534] The WMEQ was developed as the data-gathering instrument. The purpose was to determine whether or not there was a real need to develop an Informative Teaching Tool, the curriculum. In the event that this became necessary, the data gathered from the Focus Group responses would determine the extent and content of the curriculum. Deficiencies were found[535] and necessitated the development of the Informative Teaching Tool (curriculum). Because of the complexity of the subject areas being studied, triangulation (multiple data- gathering instruments) was used. These multiple data-gathering instruments included the WMEQ, observation, weekly evaluations of Focus Group members, interviews, and final evaluations. The interviews and final evaluations were implemented to help guarantee the trustworthiness and usefulness of the data. The interviews and evaluations were used to navigate through and affirm the interpretations of the data from the WMEQ, as well as to safeguard the integrity and final outcome of the study.

While a pretest/posttest design would have been useful for this type of analysis, I feared that Focus Group members would be influenced in their posttest to offer responses that they might think seemed right to me in the short term. Because I presumed this could contaminate the data gathered from the questionnaire and the final outcome of the study, in order to

---

[533] M. Q Panton, <u>Qualitative Evaluation and Research Methods</u> (Newsbury Park, CA: Sage).

[534] Appendix 2

[535] Please refer to Introduction, section 2, "The Problem and Basis for the Development of this Resource."

safeguard the integrity of the study, I elected to follow a single distribution and response design to the WMEQ.

The WMEQ consisting of open-ended questions was distributed with the stated purpose and overall objective(s). Members of the Focus Group were instructed not to share their responses with each other nor aid their responses with research. The goal was to minimize the potential for artificial responses to the WMEQ. The Focus Group was given a week to reflect on, and state their understandings of worship, mission, and eschatology at that point in their Christian experiences and awareness.

The third step was the collection of the data. The data was then coded to identify any thematic reference to the Father, Son, and Holy Spirit in the responses either in isolation or in combination. The objective was to determine the extent to which the unity of the Father, Son, and Holy Spirit occupied participants' understanding in the worship processes. I also wanted to determine whether or not participants had any clear understanding or hints regarding the channel of communication in worship as it relates to the God-humanward and human-Godward movements of grace and faith in worship as well as in the daily life of the believer. My objective was also to see if there was any understanding of the initiative and responsive processes in worship.

The data was also coded to ascertain participants' awareness of the connection between worship and Christian mission, and how worship might be related to Christian mission. This approach was also designed to test for any understanding of eschatology and how such understanding might impact the believer's attitude and Christian behavior, thus potentially leading to spiritual formation and transformation.

The fourth step was the development of the Informative Teaching Tool (curriculum). Based on the data gathered and the extent of deficiencies identified, the curriculum was developed to address those deficiencies and correct misconceptions. The curriculum was built around a series of presentations on worship, mission, and eschatology that were shared weekly with the Focus Group in single ninety minute sessions. The (original) curriculum was covered over a period of six months. (The content has since been vastly extended within the context of this book with a curriculum resource that extends beyond a calendar year, perhaps two).

The objective of the curriculum was to bring about awareness through instructions and discussions about worship, the continuous interrelatedness of worship and mission, as well as the significance of eschatology for the Christian's spiritual formation. The goal was to highlight the impact of our participation in these means of faith and the extent to which they may lead to the spiritual formation and transformation of the believer.

The fifth step was to observe for the duration of the study, the Focus Group's participatory responses in particular and that of the congregation in general. The goal was to gauge levels of awareness, identify any transformation that may have become apparent, and to assess how that transformation may have changed worshippers'/participants' attitudes and levels of participation. Panton makes the point that "the purpose of observational data is to describe the setting that was observed, the activities that took place in that setting, the people who participated in those activities, and the meanings of what was observed from the perspective of those observed [and that of the observer]."[536]

Admittedly, the development of worship patterns as well as adjusting worshippers' attitude and understanding of worship is a lifelong commitment. This would make this six month period of study an unrealistic one for bringing about significantly immediate change. The objective was not, however, to bring about significantly immediate change. Instead, the objective was to encourage awareness through an informative paradigm that may potentially lead to long-term transformation in worshippers' attitudes toward worship.[537]

The sixth step in the implementation process was to engage the Focus Group in weekly written evaluation, critiques, and assessment (appraisal) of each segment of the curriculum. This was done in order to validate parishioners' responses as well as to apply reasonable interpretations of their responses

---

[536] Panton, 202

[537] It should also be noted that the observational aspect of the study goes back to 2001-2002 when the first level of the Curriculum on Worship, was first presented. That process of observation continued for the duration of the study which concluded in 2004.

to the WMEQ. This process also helped in testing for the emergence of any new understanding of the areas covered in the curriculum.

At the conclusion of the curriculum, participants were asked to evaluate the overall content and value of the study. Though the final evaluation was intended to take just two weeks, with two ninety minute sessions, because of the interests and enthusiasm engendered by the study and the Focus Group members, the final evaluation took four useful and revealing weeks. Though participants were allowed to ask questions for their own personal clarity, the final evaluation process was guided by a combination of standardized open- and closed-ended question formats.[538]

The seventh and final step in the data-gathering process was the interview segment. The interviews were useful for determining the practical value of the study as well as for revealing how Focus Group members may or may not have benefited from the study. The purpose here was to determine from participants whether new information, intentional cognitive learning, purposeful observation, or experience through conscious participation in worship led to any new awareness and attitude changes toward worship and their understanding of Christian mission and eschatology. During the interview process, predetermined questions were followed up with probes that asked for specific examples and explanations. Panton explains that "the purpose of interviewing is to find out what is in, and on, someone else's mind."[539] Bogdan and Biklen agree that interviewing is "a purposeful conversation…in order to get information."[540] Verbatim notes were taken from the interviews for inclusion in the final discussion of the study's outcome.

My intention for the final evaluation and interviews was to determine how well the participants understood and applied the material content of the curriculum. I was also seeking to ascertain how the study might have produced any implicit change in theological understanding, Christian values, beliefs, and assumptions that may be used by Focus Group members as

---

[538] Appendix 4

[539] Panton, 278

[540] R. C. Bogdan, S. K. Biklen, <u>Qualitative Research for Education: An Introduction to Theory and Methods</u> (Boston: Allyn & Bacon), (1982), 35

guideposts for their day-to-day Christian living. How parishioners benefited from their understanding and how that understanding may or may not have changed their attitude and priorities for worship and daily Christian living formed an essential part of the evaluation. The discussions and outcomes of the study were presented to Focus Group members for their assessment, approval, and confirmation before the final study was compiled and submitted.

An entirely qualitative and analytical approach was taken with the data.

The study was further guided by the following research questions:

1. What is worship and how do we encounter God in worship?
2. Does proper knowledge and understanding of God lead to proper worship?
3. To what extent is worship transforming?
4. What is Christian mission, and what are the relations between worship and Christian mission?
5. What is eschatology and to what extent is eschatological hope a source of spiritual transformation?

Appendix 2

Worship, Mission, and Eschatology Questionnaire (WMEQ)

Purpose:

The purpose of this open-ended questionnaire is to gather information for testing a hypothesis regarding congregational understanding of God, worship, liturgical practices, Christian mission, and eschatology.

Instructions:

Please do not write more than half a page for each question (typewritten single-space preferred).

If this project is to be helpful, it is important that you answer each question as frankly and honestly as possible. <u>Your answer should be based on your own knowledge and experience at this moment in time.</u> This is not a test. There are no wrong or right answers. <u>Please do not do any research on these questions</u>. It is important for this study to get <u>your opinion</u>.

The WMEQ consists of three sections. Each section has five questions.

Section 1: Worship
Questions:

1. What is your understanding of God?
2. What is worship?
3. Who do you think is responsible for initiating, facilitating, and sustaining worship?
4. What is the liturgy and what purpose do you think the liturgy of worship serves?
5. How does worship impact your life?

Section 2: Mission
Questions:

1. What is Christian mission?
2. What connections do you think there are between worship and mission?
3. How do you think we are equipped for Christian mission?
4. In what ways do you think our service to the world through Christian mission brings glory to God?
5. How do you think Christian mission spiritually impacts your life?

Section 3: Eschatology
Questions:

1. What is eschatology?
2. What do you think is the importance of eschatology for Christian living today?
3. How do you think belief in the return of Christ impacts your attitude and behavior?
4. What do you think is expected of you while you wait for the return of Christ?
5. What do you understand by the phrase "moving from glory to glory?"

Thanks for your cooperation with this worthwhile exercise.

Appendix 3

Sample Questions for the Interview/Discussion Segment of the Study

Instructions/Purpose:

The main purpose for this session is to follow up on your responses to the Worship, Mission, and Eschatology Questionnaire (WMEQ). It is hoped that your responses to these questions will bring more clarity to the responses you gave to the questionnaire so that I can better understand your perspectives. I also need to determine, from you, where you are at this stage, in your understanding about God, worship, and eschatology. For the purpose of clarity, I may ask you probing questions in order to obtain specific examples from you. I will be taking notes of our conversation and we should be finished in about 25-30 minutes. Are you willing to participate in this interview? Thanks for taking the time.

Questions:

1. How do you compare your understanding of the topics we covered, before we began this process to the present time?
2. To what do you attribute that new awareness or understanding?

3. Based on your observations, have you been able to identify any change in the overall attitudes of the church towards worship?
4. Based on your observations, have you seen any improvement in the level of participation in the worship service?
5. What is your understanding of God?
6. How does that understanding affect the way you feel about worship?
7. Do you think you are more enthusiastic about Christian mission now than when we first began?
8. Can you please share with me your thoughts on eschatology?
9. Would you recommend this study approach to anyone or Bible study groups?

Thank you for your participation and contributions to the development of this study.

APPENDIX 4

FINAL EVALUATION

Directions:

A COMBINED OPEN-ENDED AND **close-ended** set of questions form the basis of this evaluation. Both types of questions, the open-ended questions in particular, are intended to facilitate group discussions. This final evaluation seeks to gather information at several levels: (1) Application, (2) Participation, (3) Renewal, (4) Revitalization, and (5) General. Your evaluation— comments, criticism, appraisal, and suggestions— of the study will give the feedback needed to determine the value of this study to this Focus Group and for possible future application in the church as a whole. Please take your time and give some thought to your responses.

APPLICATION:

1. What is your understanding of Worship, Mission, and Eschatology at this moment in your life?
2. How would you apply the lesson on worship, mission, and eschatology, to your daily life?

PARTICIPATION:

3. The lessons have encouraged me to become more actively engaged in the life of the church.
    1. **Agree**   2. **Disagree**

4. My interest in worship and Christian mission has increased as a result of the study.
    1. **Agree**   2. **Disagree**

5. The lessons on mission and eschatology have helped me to become more engaged in community witnessing/making disciples for Christ.
    1. **Agree**   2. **Disagree**

RENEWAL:

6. I am better able to understand how the Holy Spirit changes my life through Worship, Mission, and Eschatology.
    1. **Agree**   2. **Disagree**

7. My understanding of worship and the liturgy is much clearer from the lessons.
    1. **Agree**   2. **Disagree**:

REVITALIZATION:

8. Based on your observation, have you seen any difference in the responsive behavior of participants in worship?
9. Since we began this learning process, there has been a sense of spiritual renewal/awakening in worship
    1. **Agree**   2. **Disagree**

10. I have been personally changed by these lessons to faithfully worship and serve God.

      1. **Agree**   2. **Disagree**

11. How have these lessons helped you to see yourself as continuously worshipping God beyond the Sunday morning worship service?

GENERAL:

12. What other questions would you have asked in this evaluation, and what would be your answers/responses to those question?
13. What criticisms/appraisals do you have of these lessons?
14. I would recommend these lessons to others.

      1. **Agree**   2. **Disagree**

15. What recommendations do you have for improvement?

Appendix 5

Samples of Calls to Worship

Sample 1:

Leader: Who is it that you seek?
People: We seek the Lord our God.
Leader: The Lord our God is right here with us.
People: We rejoice in the presence and power of the Lord our God!
Leader: Come then, let us sing unto the Lord; come let us heartily rejoice in the strength of our salvation.
People: We rejoice in the Lord and have come before His presence with praise and thanksgiving.
Leader: Let us glorify the Lord, Father, Son, And Holy Spirit!
All together: Glory be to the Father and to the Son and to the Holy Spirit; as it was in the beginning, is now, and ever shall be, world without end. Hallelujah, hallelujah, hallelujah, Amen!

Sample 2:

Leader: The earth is the Lord's and the fullness thereof;
People: The world and those who dwell in it belong to the Lord our God!

Leader:	For God has founded it upon the seas,
People:	**And established it upon the rivers.**
Leader:	Who shall ascend to the hills and stand in God's holy place?
People:	**Those who have clean hands and pure hearts and do not lift up their souls to what is false nor swear deceitfully.**
Leader:	Yes, they will receive blessings from the Lord and vindication from the God of their salvation. Holy is the Lord our God!
People:	**Holy, holy, holy is the Lord our God. Angels and archangels glorify His holy name; Hallelujah! Amen!**

Sample 3:

Leader:	Hosanna to the King!
People:	**Blessed is He comes in the name of the Lord.**
Leader:	Glorify the Lord with me!
People:	**We glorify the name of the Lord who brings peace from heaven and won us the victory.**
Leader:	Praise the Lord Church!
People:	**Hallelujah!**
Leader:	Praise Him again!
People:	**Hallelujah!**
Leader:	Praise the Lord, Father, Son, and Holy Spirit!
People:	**With joyful hearts we praise His holy name; Hallelujah! Amen!**

Sample 4:

Leader:	I was glad when they said to me, "Let us go into the house of the Lord!"
People:	**Our feet have been standing within Your gates, O Jerusalem.**

Leader:	A day in the courts of the Lord is better than a thousand elsewhere;
People:	**We would rather be doorkeepers in the house of our God than to dwell in the tents of the wicked.**
Leader:	Blessed are those who dwell in the house of the Lord. They shall flourish in the presence of our God.
People:	**O Lord, we love Your habitation, the place where Your honor dwells.**
Leader:	Come, then, let us sing to the Lord a song of praise!
People:	**We will sing to the Lord. We will sing of His glory and eternal praise. Hallelujah! Amen!**

Sample 5:

Leader:	O come, let us sing to the Lord;
People:	**We have to make a joyful noise to the Rock of our salvation!**
Leader:	Let us come into His presences with praise and thanksgiving;
People:	**We give thanks to the Lord and bless His holy name!**
Leader:	For the Lord is a great God and Ruler above all gods;
People:	**We give thanks to the one true and living God; Hallelujah! Amen!**

Sample 6:

Leader:	The Lord's name be praised.
People:	**We laud and magnify His holy name.**
Leader:	Let us praise the Lord, Father, Son and Holy Spirit.
People:	**Hallelujah, hallelujah, hallelujah, Amen!**

Sample 7:

Leader:	The Lord be with you!
People:	**And also with you!**

Leader:	Lift up your hearts.
People:	**We lift them up to the Lord!**
Leader:	Let us give thanks to the Lord.
People:	**It is right to give thanks to His holy name.**
Leader:	Let us praise Father, Son, and Holy Spirit.
People:	**The Lord is worthy of our praise, Hallelujah, Amen!**

<u>**Sample 8:**</u>

Leader:	O Lord, shower us with Your mercy;
People:	**And grant us Your salvation.**
Leader:	O God, make clean our hearts within us,
People:	**And take not Your Holy Spirit from us;**
Leader:	O Lamb of God that takes away the sins of the world,
People:	**Grant us Your peace.**
Leader:	O Lord, open our lips
People:	**And our mouths shall show forth Your praise.**
Leader:	Let us praise the Lord, Father, Son, and Holy Spirit
People:	**Praise be to the God and Father of our Lord Jesus, Hallelujah, Amen!**

Appendix 6

Vision and Mission Statements

A vision statement describes what we desire to become and defines what we will look like in the future

Who Are We?

We are a diverse congregation that believes in the celebration of human differences. We believe in the existence of God as Creator, Redeemer through Jesus Christ, and the Source of our Sanctification through the continuously transforming work of the Holy Spirit who executes His work of grace to and through all who believe. We believe that Jesus Christ is the Son of God and our only means to salvation. We believe that inasmuch as God radically loves all people, we, as a church, should be intentional about reaching out in love to all of humanity with the message of redeeming grace. Our congregation is one in which differences are respected, celebrated, and honored and where human dignity and worth are mutually elevated above human prejudices. As a diverse community of believers created by God, we are driven by the common goals and values of faith, love, respect, humility, justice/fairness, mercy, compassion, devotion to God, and service to our fellow humans.

Our Vision Is:

- To become a center for revitalized worship and biblical clarity where God is glorified through passionate worship and Christ is preached as we witness the ministry of the Holy Spirit in our lives and church
- To become a spiritually aware and healthy faith community
- To become a culturally relevant and diverse church that embraces all people without compromising our Christian convictions
- To become a church that thinks and acts externally

The Scope of Our Vision Is:

- To become equipped and empowered by the Holy Spirit to effectively and faithfully participate in Spirit-filled worship and through mission in God's redemptive and liberating acts in the world
- To become a culturally relevant Church where we actively seek to promote the glory of God and His Christ in a changing world
- To love our neighbors, honor, respect, and protect the value and dignity of each person/member
- To become a missional church

Mission Statement

A mission statement guides our actions in our pursuit of our vision. It also defines our purpose and values, and what we intend to do in order to realize our goals.

The specific mission of a congregation is its answer to the question, "Who are we and whose lives are we called and empowered to change and in what way?" A congregation that limits its vision and mission to personal preferences and pleasing its members more than it does the kingdom principles of God, may fall short of its true purpose which is to honor God through worship, make disciples for Christ, and intentionally elevate the dignity and worth of its members through a transformed and Christian lifestyle. While membership growth, expanding budgets, building programs, and such trappings of success really do matter, they should not supersede positive spiritual transformation. Instead, they should be reflections of the already transformed lives of people who are called, anointed, and appointed to pursue the work of the kingdom within the context of the church and wider community.

Our Mission Is:

- To make disciples for Christ
- To cultivate a healthy worship environment
- To be a prophetic voice that draws people's attention to the presence and glory of God
- To help people know Jesus Christ as Lord and Savior by the examples of our own Christian living
- To help people discover their purpose in living out the divine life
- To advance the cause of righteousness in the world beginning with our community, by displaying a Christian lifestyle, spreading scriptural holiness, healing relationships, feeding the hungry and transforming social structures and by helping people turn problems into possibilities
- To develop and nurture our commitment to connectional awareness

Scope of Our Mission Is:

- To develop a closer relationship with the Father, Son, and Holy Spirit
- To have a global impact as we minister to the spiritual, social, and emotional needs of people beginning with those in our community
- To train and develop an informed laity for Christian leadership
- To raise our level of spiritual awareness, commitment, service, and Christian stewardship
- To rebuild our faith, increase and sustain our membership by calling the churched and the unchurched into an awareness of the

transforming power of God's love, and by nurturing God's gathered people through sincere and committed Christian love and discipleship without regard for race, nationality, or social standings in society

VISION/MISSION STATEMENTS FOR CHILDREN'S MINISTRY

- To create and develop a safe and healthy learning environment where God rules and our children rock
- To offer our children Christian choices
- To connect our children with God, with Christ, and with the working power of the Holy Spirit
- To partner with parents in building godly families and discipline for their children
- To help our children reach broken, forgotten, neglected, and abused children in our community
- To teach our children the value of love and respect for others

REFERENCES

Bence, Clarence L. "Processive Eschatology: A Wesleyan Alternative," Wesleyan Theological Journal 14-15, (1979), 45-59.

Bogdan, Robert C., and Sari K. Biklen. Qualitative Research for Education: An Introduction to Theory and Methods. Boston: Allyn & Bacon, 1982.

Brown, Edgar S. "The Worship of the Church and the Modern Man," Liturgical Renewal in the Christian Churches (ed. Michael J. Taylor), (1967)197-221. Baltimore/Dublin: Helicon.

Brueggemann, Walter. The Prophetic Imagination (Second ed.). Minneapolis: Fortress Press, 2001.

Bultmann, Rudolf. The Presence of Eternity. NY: Harper & Bros., 1957.

Calvin: Institutes of the Christian Religion, Ed., John T. McNeill, v xx, Library of Christian Classics, (Philadelphia: The Westminster Press).

Charry, Ellen T. By the Renewing of Your Minds: The Pastoral Function of the Christian Doctrine. New York: Oxford University Press, 1997.

Coleman, Robert E. Songs of Heaven. Fleming Revell, Co: 1980.

Hynson, Leon O. "Christian Love: The Key to Wesley's Ethics," Methodist History, 14, (1975-1976): 44-55.

Knight III, Henry. H. The Presence of God in the Christian Life: John Wesley and the Means of Grace. Lanham, MD & London: The Scarecrow Press, Inc., 1992.

Konig, Adrio. *The Eclipse of Christ in Eschatology.* Grand Rapids, MI: Erdmans, 1989.

Layton, John T. "We'll Praise The Lord," in *African Methodist Episcopal Church Hymnal*, 1984, # 60.

Lindsley, D. H., D. J. Brass, and J. T. Thomas. "Efficacy-Performance Spirals: A Multilevel Analysis," *Academy of Management Review*, 20, (1995): 645-678.

Macquarrie, John. *Principles of Christian Theology.* New York: Charles Scribner's Sons, 1966.

Migliore, Daniel L. *Faith Seeking Understanding: An Introduction to Christian Theology.* Grand Rapids, MI: William B. Eerdmans Publishing Company, 1991.

O'Connor, Elizabeth. Journey Inward, Journey Outward. New York: Harper & Row Publishers, 1968.

Panton, Michael Q. *Qualitative Evaluation and Research Methods*. Newbury Park, CA: Sage, 1990.

Shafer, Floyd D. *Liturgy: Worship and Work.* (Board of Christian Education of the United Presbyterian Church USA, 1952).

Songs of Zion "*Woke Up Dis Mornin'*: Abingdon Press, 1981, No. 146

Sullivan, Clayton. *Rethinking Realized Eschatology.* Macon, GA. Mercer University Press, 1988.

Talbot, Bishop Frederic Hilborn. *African American Worship: New Eyes for Seeing*. Little Rock, Ark: Fairway Press, 1998.

The Forgotten Trinity, The Report of the British Council of Churches, (London: Inter-Church House, 1989).

Thompson, John. Modern Trinitarian Perspectives. New York: Oxford University Press, 1994.

Torrance, James B. Worship, Community and the Triune God of Grace. Downers Grove: InterVarsity Press, 1996.

Torrance, Thomas F. "Come Creator Spirit for the Renewal of the Worship and Witness," in Liturgical Renewal in the Christian Churches, (ed. Michael J. Taylor), Baltimore and Dublin: Helicon, (1967): 127-143.

Torrance, Thomas F. Scottish Theology. Edinburg: T. & T. Clark, 1996.

Volf, Miroslav. After our Likeness: The Church as the Image of the Trinity. Grand Rapids, MI/Cambridge, UK: William B. Eerdmans Publishing Co., 1998: 101.

Wainwright, Gregory. Doxology: The Praise of God in Worship, Doctrine, and Life. NY: Oxford University Press, 1980.

Webster, Douglas. "The Mission of the People of God," Liturgical Renewal in the Christian Church, (ed. Michael J. Taylor), Baltimore and Dublin: Helicon, (1967): 180-196.

White, James R. The Forgotten Trinity: Recovering the Heart of Christian Belief. Minneapolis, MN: Bethany House Publishers, 1998.

Willimon, William H. The Service of God: How Worship and Ethics Are Related. (Nashville, TN: Abingdon Press), 1983.

BIBLIOGRAPHY

Bernadot, Marie Vincent. <u>The Eucharist and the Trinity</u>. Wilmington, DE: Michael Glazier, 1977.

Bobrinskoy, Boris. "The Indwelling of the Spirit in Christ," <u>St. Vladimir's Theological Quarterly</u>, 38 (1994): 49-65.

Collins, Kenneth J. <u>The Scripture Way of Salvation: The Heart of John Wesley's Theology.</u> Nashville, TN: Abingdon Press, 1997.

Erickson, Craig D. <u>Participating in Worship: History, Theory, and Practice.</u> Louisville: Westminster/John Knox Press, 1989.

Gardner, D. G. and J. L. Pierce. "Self-esteem and Self-efficacy Within the Organizational Context: An Empirical Examination," <u>Group & Organization Management,</u> Vol. 23 (1), May, 1998: 48- 70.

Gist, M. E. & T. R. Michell. "Self-efficacy: A Theoretical Analysis of its Determinants and Malleability,"<u>Academy of Management Review,</u> 17, (1992): 183-211.

Jarvis, Peter. <u>Paradoxes of Learning: On Becoming an Individual in Society</u>. San Francisco: Jossey-Bass Inc., 1992.

Mercer, Jerry L. "The Destiny of Man in John Wesley's Eschatology," <u>Wesleyan Theological Journal</u>, Vol. 2 No. 1, Spring 1967: 56-65.

Outler, Albert C. and Richard P. Heitzenrater. <u>John Wesley's Sermons: An Anthology.</u> Nashville, TN: Abingdon Pres, 1991.

Runyon, Theodore. <u>The New Creation: John Wesley's Theology Today</u>. Nashville, TN: Abingdon Press, 1998.

Zernov, Nicholas. "The Meaning of Holy Communion," <u>Liturgical Renewal in the Christian Churches,</u> (ed. Michael J. Taylor), Baltimore and Dublin: Helicon, 1967